THE

GEOGRAPHY

A TOUR OF THE

OF HOPE

WORLD WE NEED

CHRIS TURNER

VINTAGE CANADA

VINTAGE CANADA EDITION, 2008

Published in Canada by Vintage Canada, a division of Random House of Canada Limited, Toronto, in 2008. Originally published in hardcover in Canada by Random House Canada, a division of Random House of Canada Limited, Toronto, in 2007. Distributed by Random House of Canada Limited, Toronto.

Vintage Canada and colophon are registered trademarks of Random House of Canada Limited.

www.randomhouse.ca

Library and Archives Canada Cataloguing in Publication

Turner, Chris, 1973–

    The geography of hope : a tour of the world we need / Chris Turner.
Includes bibliographical references and index.

ISBN 978-0-679-31466-0

1. Environmentalism. 2. Sustainable development. 3. Sustainable development—Case studies. 4. Environmental protection. 5. Community life–Environmental aspects. 6. Turner, Chris, 1973– —Travel. I. Title.

GE105.T87 2008   333.72   C2008-900314-4

The author gratefully acknowledges the financial support of the Alberta Foundation for the Arts and the Canada Council for the Arts.

Every effort has been made to contact copyright holders; in the event of an omission or error, please notify the publisher.

Lyrics to "Twilight Campfighter" by Guided By Voices used by permission of the songwriter, Robert Pollard.

Lines from The Lorax by Dr Seuss, copyright ® and copyright © by Dr Seuss enterprises, L.P. 1971, renewed 1999. Used by permission of Random House Children's Books, a division of Random House Inc.

This book is printed on paper that is ancient-forest friendly (100% post-consumer recycled) and chlorine-free.

Design by Kelly Hill

Printed and bound in the United States of America

10 9 8 7 6 5 4 3 2 1

FOR SLOANE

Only where there is disillusionment and depression and sorrow does happiness arise; without the despair of loss, there is no hope.

HARUKI MURAKAMI,
Hard-boiled Wonderland and the End of the World

You want us to feel better
On these darker trails
With light revealing holy grails
To hike through dangerous weather
You need twilight eyes

GUIDED BY VOICES, "Twilight Campfighter"

"But *now*," says the Once-ler,
"Now that *you're* here,
the word of the Lorax seems perfectly clear.
UNLESS someone like you
cares a whole awful lot,
nothing is going to get better.
It's not."

DR. SEUSS, *The Lorax*

CONTENTS

PROLOGUE

TWO HORIZONS

I don't have to go very far to find a certain kind of reassurance that I live in a golden age. Out my back door and down the back alley to a steep-sloped residential street, and then it's just a two-minute upward scramble to the crest of a ridge known as Scotsman's Hill, which affords one of the city's best views. Here is Calgary, Alberta— Canada's fourth-largest and fastest-growing metropolis. Here is a panorama Fritz Lang could only dream of, a marvel of engineering genius and financial might that even today equates in the minds of most of the world's people with progress, prosperity, hope and ambition, *the future:* a glittering skyline.

In the middle distance, the downtown core stabs at the wide prairie sky with a hundred sleek fingers. At one end are the twin knife-blade towers of the Petro-Canada Centre, on the other a pair of older, squatter office blocks topped with the sled-dog logo of Husky Energy, and in between are anonymous skyscrapers housing the local offices of Chevron and Shell and Halliburton and dozens more companies with less famous names, all of them dedicated to the lucrative business of extracting fossil fuels from the earth. The whole scene is punctuated by the exclamation point of the Calgary Tower, a torch-shaped needle that belches a natural-gas flame from its crown on special occasions.

Farther south is the white dome roof of the cavernous fitness centre where my wife and I sometimes go to swim and play badminton— the Talisman Centre, named for the last Canadian company to divest itself of oil investments in Sudan. The foreground is dominated by the city's temple of hockey, the Pengrowth Saddledome, its last name referring to its whimsically bow-shaped roof and its first name to a lucrative fossil fuel investment trust.

This is the vista that's sometimes used to illustrate the copious news stories that have appeared in recent years to document Calgary's increasing prominence in the life of the nation and the energy economy of the world. These stories, too, offer a kind of reassurance. The headlines yelp excitedly about the "unprecedented boom," about an "economic juggernaut," about "streets paved with black gold" as "the good times roll." The reports underneath detail the runaway growth of a city lucky to be situated in the middle of a wide prairie pocketed with vast pools of natural gas and blessed to be christened the corporate hub of a colossal mining operation far to the north. This, they say, is a city coming into its own, making its mark. A city entering its golden age.

Maybe those stories make passing mention of the catalyst for that mining boom—the skyrocketing price of a dwindling resource in relentlessly increasing demand, a global thirst for oil so inexhaustible that even the marginal, low-quality fossil fuel deposits buried in the "tar sands" of remote northern Alberta must be put to use, even if the operation required to mine and refine the stuff requires feats of engineering on a scale that would've given pause to a Kremlin apparatchik. *Maybe* this is mentioned; rarely is it suggested that it could be anything other than admirable and beneficial and *essential;* certainly it's never even hinted that it might be a symptom of a particularly advanced strain of mass insanity.

And who could be so impertinent, so misguided—so *deluded*— that they saw such things from this perspective? Look again from atop Scotsman's Hill, peer beyond the office towers to the great blooming city stretching off in all directions. See the wide avenues, the meandering suburban boulevards, the eight-lane freeways as broad as the Champs-Elysées. Look at the big houses—mansions, really, in any other age but this—stuffed full of the latest in digital gadgetry; the elegant shops and cavernous warehouse stores overflowing with anything else the heart might desire. Look to the horizon, to the jagged line of peaks—the Rocky Mountains, where championship golf courses and world-class ski resorts await anyone who wants to top up the hundred-litre tank in the ole Cadillac Escalade and rev up that growling 6.2-litre V8 and roar right on out into Paradise.

Look further still, use the mind's eye, extend your vision to Houston and Caracas and Dubai, to cities where the fossil fuel wealth is perhaps less overt but no less ubiquitous, to New York and London and Tokyo and even—especially—delirious Shanghai. Isn't all this as impressive a facsimile of perfection as humanity has yet devised? It can be hard to argue otherwise: the fossil-fuelled, hyper-consumerist capitalism that has spread around the globe since the Second World War is quite possibly the most successful social experiment the world has ever seen, and it has birthed by far the wealthiest and healthiest societies in human history. A chicken in every pot and a car in every driveway. The Good Life: democratized, trademarked, mass-produced, shipped worldwide.

What a time to be alive, what good fortune, and what a joy it must be to be a Calgarian right about now. To live in one of those blessed cities on a hill at the end of history. "Put your hands on the wheel / Let the golden age begin." That's a Beck lyric, sung in a thin whisper over a country waltz as cold and cutting as a winter prairie wind, as sharp and precise as a glass office tower. A biting breeze of a tune, the vocal almost blown away completely, as if to suggest what the breathless news stories never do: that golden ages aren't often found where they claim to be.

· At night, the farmers' fields north of Calgary look like a candle-light vigil on an Olympian scale: vast, empty prairie dotted at wide intervals with narrow multistorey scaffolds, blazing fires atop each one. These are the flares that arise from burning off the "sour gas"—hydrogen sulphide—in the natural-gas wells. Ranchers have long suspected the flares to be the cause of stillbirths and other health problems in downwind livestock; the sour gas itself is potentially fatal to humans at concentrations of more than 500 parts per million. That's 500 ppm—in a curious coincidence, a figure that's also the most liberal estimate of the maximum permissible level of carbon dioxide concentrations in the earth's atmosphere before a process often called "catastrophic climate change" (sometimes known, in more anxious circles, simply as *apocalypse*) will likely become inevitable. Prior to the onset of the fossil-fuelled industrial age, the concentration was 280 ppm; right now, it's about 380 ppm. If the status quo that's propelling Calgary's giddy boom continues unchecked, it's a scientific certainty that 560 ppm—sufficient, by most estimates, to trigger catastrophic climate change—will be reached by mid-century.

You can't see those sour-gas flares from Scotsman's Hill, not even on the clearest night. You can see only the sparkling city, a gilt cubist sculpture of triumph against a blackening sky. This is the blaze of colour on one horizon, and maybe it's up to the beholder whether that brilliant light portends dusk or dawn. I can see only sunset myself.

My daughter—two months old as I stand on Scotsman's Hill on a warm spring day in May 2005, wondering at the darkening horizon— will be fifty-one years old in 2056, at which point our current trajectory would reach 560 ppm with a bullet. And who knows whether by then she'll have a house worth keeping here, a life worth living, a world here or anywhere else sturdy enough to sustain her? I can't say for certain, and it makes me positively *ache* in places I didn't know I had until she was born that I can't make her any promises.

And so I don't take her to Scotsman's Hill to see the Petro-Canada towers or the Talisman Centre's rippled roof or the Calgary Tower's natural-gas blowtorch. Instead, on a holiday Monday later that May—Victoria Day, Canada's vestigial tribute to the world's first fossil fuel empire, the one built on coal that led to my country's founding—my wife and I take her on a field trip south to another ridge, another horizon, a place that to me represents the dawn of a new hope.

Traffic on Highway 2 is thin on this holiday Monday, and before too long, Calgary's lolling southern suburbs give grudging way to empty prairie, and we are on our way. To our right, the jagged peaks of the eastern wall of the Rockies are our constant companions, ancient and certain and still dappled with last winter's snow. We zoom south through rolling ranchland, past barns clad in chipped red paint, through quiet towns where the local tack shop is the main merchant. We stop at a gas station where a handmade poster outside the bathroom advertises a year-old gelding for sale, "keep the coyotes out of your correl"—and, whaddaya know, there's a coyote loping casually along in the roadside ditch a few kilometres further on.

Fifteen klicks north of Fort Macleod, an unforgiving crosswind sets our small car to weaving, and a bit beyond that there appears on the horizon a long, low ridge crowned with a row of thin sticks, like a faint pencil sketch of some grandiose reimagining of Stonehenge. This is our destination: the McBride Lake Wind Farm, at this moment the largest single wind-power generating facility in Canada.

As we draw closer, turning onto a narrow secondary highway pointed straight at the ridge, the gyrating blades of the turbines become visible, chasing each other in not-quite-perfect lockstep, a race of giant prehistoric storks marching across the ridgeline. We crest the ridge and are soon surrounded by dozens of enormous wind turbines—a forest of 50-metre towers, each crowned in a three-bladed pinwheel with arms 23 metres long. There are 114 turbines in all, arrayed in tidy rows that stretch to the horizon, the white machines gleaming against the dun and straw hues of the farmers' fields they stand in, their oscillations looking from one vantage like geese in flight, then like palm fronds in a stiff breeze, a moment later like a kaleidoscopic screensaver on the largest LCD screen in all Creation.

We turn off the highway onto a gravel access road, driving slowly now, the turbines just a couple dozen metres away on either side of us. We stop at a little observation nook the wind farm's owners have built, and still there is no sense of being in the presence of industrial-scale power. The noise of the spinning blades—what little can be heard amid the constant howl of the wind across this bald ridge—sounds a bit like a sheet-metal utility shed being rattled in a gale. There is no roar of engines, no black smoke, no mammoth cooling tower, no warning signs save the one asking visitors to respect the privacy of the local residents and stop only at the designated observation area.

I take my daughter out of her car seat so she can feel the driving wind against her cheeks, and then we return to the car to wait while my wife takes pictures. It is evening, and the shadows thrown by the great blades have grown long against the field. The shadows spin like the hands of clocks moving forward at varying speeds. It's an odd effect, hypnotic, and my daughter watches it with the observant contentment of one who has only recently awakened to the shape of the world. This is new for her, and delightful, but so is everything else. As far as she knows, the unique oscillating effect created by the spinning blades of an industrial wind turbine at sunset is as commonplace as the sound of spring rain against a car's windshield and the rich aroma of a gas station. Soon—too soon— she'll learn otherwise.

The 114 Vestas V47 wind turbines that make up the McBride Lake Wind Farm each have a generating capacity of 660 kilowatts; the farm as a whole has a capacity of a little more than 75 megawatts. The Sundance coal plant in northern Alberta—western Canada's largest coal-fired power plant—has a capacity of 2,020 megawatts all by itself. Wind power accounts for less than 1 percent of total energy production in the province of Alberta, and even if every wind turbine in Canada were operating at maximum capacity twenty-four hours a day, wind would still produce less than 1 percent of the nation's total energy. And just the projected *increase* in global energy demand far outstrips the world's current or near-future wind-power production capacity. But this is the wrong way to count. This is like showing up at Thomas Edison's workshop with ledgers detailing whale-oil sales or lamplighter employment figures, or like stopping by the Xerox Palo Alto Research Center in 1974 and asking why you can't watch live video on this fancy new computer network.

There are much better ways to quantify what's happening on this windswept ridge in southern Alberta. Canada's wind-power production grew by more than 30 percent every year from 1998 to 2002, and McBride Lake added another 19 percent all by itself when it came online in 2003, and wind power remains Canada's fastestgrowing energy source today (In 2006, installed capacity grew by 113 percent). If the 75 megawatts of energy being generated at McBride Lake was produced instead by burning coal, 195,000 more tonnes of carbon dioxide would be released into the earth's atmosphere; the 8,000 megawatts of wind power added to global capacity in 2004 means 20.8 million fewer tonnes of CO_2 emitted. The power from McBride Lake's turbines enters the larger electrical grid operated by TransAlta for its customers across western Canada, so there's no way to separate it from the juice coming from Sundance's coal furnace, but nevertheless that 75 megawatts represents about 32,500 homes powered by nothing more noxious than a stiff spring breeze. And even if these are tiny drops in a mammoth bucket, the game being played is one of absolutes, and so they irreducibly count. We have but one earth, blessed with finite amounts of coal and light sweet crude, nurtured by a closed loop of a climate with only one external input: the energy of the sun.

So I sit with my daughter, watching their blades spin, and I begin to understand what *sustainability* truly means. Removed from the spin cycle of corporate public relations, a flat buzzword reinflated to its full weight, *sustainability* again becomes epochal, a wellspring of social change, a revolutionary concept as powerfully, progressively disruptive as *democracy* once was.

The idea of sustainability began as the central concept in the landmark report *Our Common Future*—the 1987 document that defined "sustainable development" and precipitated the 1992 United Nations Earth Summit in Rio. What sustainability describes, at its core, is this: My daughter and I can sit here, in the shadow of these blades, as long as we'd like, and no matter how long they turn, no matter how many megawatts of power they generate, they'll do us no harm. This is what fundamentally distinguishes these turbines from coal plants and natural gas wells, from Alberta's bitumen sands and the reservoirs of crude oil beneath the desert of Arabia and the Niger Delta and the Gulf of Mexico: there will be no toxic emissions, no hidden bills that come due two or three generations from now, no invasions necessary to procure further supply. As long as there's a sun in the sky to heat this world unevenly, there will be breezes to spin these turbines. Sit still underneath one for long enough, and the simplicity of it becomes quietly, transcendently awesome.

I want to know more—for my daughter's sake, I *need* to. I peer through the oscillating blades, out across a wide plain rutted with deep ravines, beyond that to the mountain peaks on the horizon, fading now to purple and grey in the approaching dark. I gaze into the distance, and I know I have to find dawn.

I try to imagine a sustainable society radiating out from the feet of these turbines, a whole civilization. I imagine gathering bits of it like cloth swatches and discarded rags, carpeting the prairie with them, covering the whole world in a single sustainable patchwork quilt. What sort of houses would be there? What kind of cars? No cars at all? Would there be only farmers' fields and thatch huts, or could there be skyscrapers and office parks as well? Who would live there, and what would they do for a living? How would they make light and heat, grow and cook their food? Would they need more of these turbines?

Fewer? Who would be their heroes? What gods would they pray to? Is there room here on this empty prairie—and know-how, and will, and time—to build the new capital of a sustainable world?

My wife returns to the car long before I can speculate on the answers to any of these questions, and we pack up and leave. Our daughter falls fast asleep on the dark drive home. I don't completely realize it yet, but I've started on a journey to fill in that space between the alloyed reality of the turbines and the promise of dawn on the horizon.

Life is not an either/or proposition, and it's always a bit melodramatic to reduce it to any single choice. Still, this is as close to a fundamental crossroads as humanity's ever come, and the implications of our choice of path are global in scale and monumental in impact.

So then: Two ridges, not so very far apart, and two directions for civilization. Each as real as the long shadows thrown across a farmer's field or the electric glow of an office tower's fluorescent lights.

From Scotsman's Hill, the route to the horizon is the path of least resistance. The vehicle's been built, it's in motion, and a leaden foot is already pushing hard on the accelerator. Ahead lies a good smooth stretch of contentment and prosperity, of steady annual growth— perhaps, globally, the 3 to 5 percent so treasured by economists and investors, certainly much more than that for the captains of industry in Calgary's office towers. And beyond that, even more certainly, an abyss, a fall of some indeterminate distance, enough to blow out a tire or two or mangle an axle or maybe total the vehicle. And who, gazing at the wreckage, would be proud to say they'd been an integral part of the Era of 3 to 5 Percent GDP Growth?

From the ridge at McBride Lake, there is no road, only transport and provisions of uncommon and sometimes unproven character, and a trail to be blazed over forbidding terrain. A trickier mission, worth doing only if you accept a few very compelling points. First among these is that the destination at the end of it is a world worth building, a future worth dreaming of, a place of hope. Its bottom line—clean air and water, limitless pollution-free energy, good nutritious food, liveable communities worth investing in, a deliberate and fulfilling life—beats any bottom line I've ever heard of. The second—probably the more important—point is that we don't actually have a choice, unless you consider rendering the planet unfit for human life a viable option.

But finally—and here's the real crux of it, the thing that puts the bounce in the step of the ones already on this path—there is the chance to be part of possibly the greatest project in the history of civilization, to be at the forefront of the generation that confronted the worst conflagration the world had ever seen—and sorted it out. *Scientific American* calls climate change "arguably the most imposing scientific and technical challenge that humanity has ever faced"; a veteran British politician warns of "an ecological time bomb ticking away"; and the former chief economist of the World Bank predicts "major disruptions on a scale similar to those associated with the great wars and the economic depression of the first half of the twentieth century." To look back, perhaps half a century from now, to say to our children—to our grandchildren—that we took all this on, fought and thought, worked our asses off, tried and failed and tried again, and finally got this wondrous new contraption moving down a clear path toward that sustainable city on a hill—what could be better, more worthwhile, more flat-out balls-to-the-wall *exhilarating*, than to be part of that?

What else are you working on right now? What great project that would rest upon your soul like the many bars of ribbon on a war hero's chest? What that you would point to, and look your grandkids in the eye, and say, "Now *that* was worth the fight"? I know how I'd answer this one: There's nothing else.

Only this:

To be part of the generation that beat climate change.

"Anything that exists is possible."

That's Kenneth Boulding, an economist sounding like a poet, and when I first heard the line, it was all I knew of him. Turns out Boulding was an eminent economist indeed, author of a major textbook on the subject in 1941. But Boulding was also an "impure" economist, self-confessed. He felt compelled to look beyond classical economics to truly understand economic reality or any other kind of reality. Three to five percent GDP growth is a statistic, an abstraction. To find what exists, what is worth keeping and propagating, to explore the bounds of what is possible—this requires a search beyond the scope of the usual metrics.

What follows is not a how-to guide or a technical manual or a set of policy recommendations to achieve that goal. It's a scrapbook of a year spent living optimistically. And if it is anything beyond that, it's an incantation. An incantation: an attempt, by my words, to make of these scattered specifics a singular universal entity, a place in the mind worth fighting to build. To turn a sketchy prospector's map of the world we need into something more complete: a geography of hope.

The front pages of the newspaper might look like bad news, an ominous and intractable mess—storm clouds on the horizon, the four horsemen at the gate—but the back pages and the margins are filled with solutions. Tools and technologies, organizations and ideas—everything we need to avoid catastrophe. And they lead to a better way of life. That's maybe the most surprising, electrifying thing about this geography of hope: it beats what we have now, even if our climate wasn't compelling us to change.

The world we need: it all exists. It took only a year to find. And anything that exists is possible.

To be part of the generation that beat climate change: *this* is possible.

THE GEOGRAPHY OF HOPE

ONE

THE REBIRTH OF HOPE

[sustainable vision]

THE FIRST-BORN CHILDREN OF RACHEL CARSON

I have no discrete memory of how or when or where environmentalism became a fixed part of my consciousness. Like learning to walk or coming to know the music of the Beatles, it seemed like an inevitable part of growing up in the last decades of the twentieth century. It was a twilight time, an age at the end of something important, miraculous and grand, something just recently doomed. Perhaps environmentalism was the only fitting soundtrack.

Or maybe it happened while I was watching one of those *National Geographic* documentaries as a grade-schooler, following its roller-coaster trajectory from nature's majestic beauty to the wise and complex logic of its design to the inevitable, gut-churning, final-act lamentation for its imminent demise. They all went like this: here is a whale, a Bengal tiger, a stand of pristine redwood; now the elaborate ecosystem that supports it, interacts with it, makes it whole and magnificent; and finally the encroachment of one virulent strain or another of human folly—the runoff of petro-chemical pesticides, the poacher's blaring rifle, the chorus of chainsaws—working overtime, with cold industrial efficiency, to seal its sad fate.

Or it could've been the World Wildlife Fund calendars my aunt used to send me for Christmas: each year another dozen stunning portraits of magnificent animals in elegant repose, twelve more flawless natural masterpieces soon to vanish, a childhood thus enumerated by extinctions.

Later, in an adolescence set against the decadent, careless 1980s, I absorbed a deeper ecological consciousness incidentally and intermittently, through some sort of mass-media osmosis. I had a subscription to *Rolling Stone,* which tucked essays and investigative reports from the frontlines of the environmental crisis amid the popstar profiles and record reviews. I became a religious reader of the searing satirical comic strip *Bloom County,* whose lovable penguin protagonist composed laments for a despoiled planet. I caught newscasts and headlines from time to time. And as I swam through this information soup, a portentous new vocabulary seeped in: *endangered species* and *deforestation, smog* and *effluent, toxic waste* and *acid rain.*

It could have been any of these, or all of the above, but in any case I reached adulthood with a clear sense that modern human activity was often poisonous to the health of the planet—more often than not, it appeared—and growing more toxic with each passing year. This seemed a truism of life on earth as inescapable as natural selection and as certain as gravity's guarantee that shit would flow downhill. The planet was sick, maybe even dying, its illness traced throughout my childhood in an escalating series of catastrophes. First there were whales and great apes in declining numbers, then rainforests and coral reefs in crisis. Finally, the entire planet in peril: acidic lakes filled with dying fish scattered poxlike across its habitable surface; air and water gone noxious from a sort of biospheric kidney failure; a hole in the ozone layer expanding like a festering sore. And dark portents, as I reached adulthood in the early 1990s, of an even graver prognosis: a dangerous excess of *greenhouse gases* in the atmosphere causing *global warming.* More newfangled terminology to describe looming cataclysm. To become an environmentalist against this grim backdrop was simply to accept the harsh reality of the ailing world into which I'd been born.

In a sense, then, I was among the first-born children of Rachel Carson, a member of the first generation to grow up with the echoes of her *Silent Spring* clanging constantly in our ears. Carson warned of a deadly poison—the pesticide dichloro-diphenyl-trichloroethane, or DDT—and feared with all her being for a world without songbirds. The problem, awful as its consequences were, was discrete and quantifiable, a single chemical of human manufacture. You could carry it off in a pail, store it away on a shelf, never hear from it again. Carson's book inspired a movement, and the movement knew what it needed to do. And progress, it seemed, marched on.

But the ominous reverberations that came in the wake of her warning grew only more inchoate and less easily contained with each passing year. The alarms grew so frequent and so awesome in scope as to defy the boundaries even of our nightmares. Though few yet knew it for sure, we were coming of age in a kind of mental environment not seen since the Enlightenment's clear, rational, scientific light dispelled the dark shadows of Biblical apocalypse and banished invincible demons and dragons to the wastes of superstition. We lived basically from birth, that is, with the omnipresent possibility—the *scientific* possibility—that even if we didn't blow ourselves up with atomic bombs, human life might not be perpetual. That the gods, though their will was now quantified in field-surveyed population studies and parts per million of carbon dioxide, were growing so angry with our meddling in their domain that they were preparing to banish humanity to the wastes of an ecological hell. Bob Dylan had warned of a hard rain coming, but he was singing about a figurative storm, a sort of fever dream of the world's sociopolitical unravelling that found its symbolic apotheosis in nuclear fallout. A generation later, the hard rain was literal, and our shelters and everything else we'd erected against nature's ferocious will had birthed the storm clouds themselves. The rain was a-fallin' already, harder than in Dylan's worst nightmare, fallin' everywhere. *What'll you do now, my darlin' young one?* Nobody had a ready answer to that question anymore.

The world of discrete environmental crises sketched out in the documentaries and on the wildlife calendars of my youth—here an endangered species, there a threatened forest—gave way to a larger and much more amorphous problem. The entire planet's climate was changing—at a rate, we'd eventually learn, more rapid than anything seen in millennia, brought on by perilously swelled atmospheric concentrations of carbon dioxide and other greenhouse gases. The sky, weighted with the emissions from the relentless burning of countless tons of coal and oil, was in effect falling, and the ocean rising to meet it. This wasn't just a new and more virulent strain of anxiety but a fundamentally different and much more precarious kind of world.

I was born, as it turned out, into the Anthropocene Era. *Anthropos,* from the Greek, meaning "human": an age whose defining features—its climate, its atmosphere, its ecology—are manmade. And a name, finally, to acknowledge the size of the shift, which has been occurring on the scale not of calendar years and human lives but of geological progression—from Jurassic to Cretaceous, from Pleistocene to Holocene, and now to Anthropocene.

The term was coined only in 2000 by the Nobel-winning atmospheric chemist Paul Crutzen and the ecologist Eugene F. Stoermer, but the Anthropocene Era is a good deal older; it began with the first rumblings of the Industrial Revolution in the late eighteenth century. (To give it a precise date, Crutzen and Stoermer have suggested 1784, the year the steam engine was invented.) The atmospheric warming effect of carbon dioxide emissions was established by the late 1800s, but only in the past couple of decades have we begun to calculate the full consequences of our two-hundred-year bonfire.

There's no need to rehash here the fractious arguments that have dominated the topic of anthropogenic (i.e., manmade) climate change in recent years. The data grows only more damning, the repercussions more catastrophic in potential impact. Among climate scientists, the only serious questions that remained by the dawn of this new millennium concerned how fast the change was occurring, the magnitude of the transformation, and how much damage it would cause.

In a valiant attempt to bring the misinformed public "debate" about the issue to a close, the Royal Society (Britain's national science academy, founded in 1660 and presided over by Isaac Newton for a quarter-century) published a concise report in early 2005 entitled "A guide to facts and fictions about climate change." The document methodically refuted the twelve most pervasive falsehoods on the subject, the ones that had nurtured the lingering doubt in the public mind. And as the year wore on, one scientific study after another emerged to confirm some of the climatologists' darkest fears: atmospheric CO_2 levels at a 650,000-year high, arctic ice melting at the fastest rate ever seen, sea levels rising at twice their nineteenth-century rates. A British government report asserted that the melting of the vast ice sheet covering Greenland—*in its entirety*—was a very real possibility, with consequences of proportions suitable for a dystopian sci-fi flick. The permafrost covering much of Siberia has already begun to melt, creating a "positive feedback loop" in which the vast amounts of methane locked beneath the ice are released, causing further warming and melting. The glaciers that gave Glacier National Park in Montana its name will be gone before mid-century, and green meadows are emerging from the formerly frozen wastes in Antarctica.

"The earth's climate is nearing, but has not passed, a tipping point, beyond which it will be impossible to avoid climate change with far-reaching undesirable consequences"—this was James Hansen of NASA, against a kaleidoscopic backdrop of slides packed dense with surface-temperature maps and satellite data, speaking to an audience at Columbia University's Earth Institute in New York in the last weeks of 2005. Less cautiously, James Lovelock—the scientist who invented the tool that confirmed the prevalence of DDT in the 1960s and the depletion of the ozone layer in the 1980s, as well as the author of the "Gaia hypothesis," a revolutionary ecological theory that conceives of the earth as a single interdependent organism—began, in early 2006, to speak with certainty of something verging on apocalypse. "Before this century is over," he wrote, "billions of us will die and the few breeding pairs of people that survive will be in the Arctic where the climate remains tolerable." Looming catastrophe or catastrophe already unfolding—whatever "debate" remains over climate change will occur within these parameters.

"A Threat Graver Than Terrorism" warned the cover of *Vanity Fair*'s first-ever "Green Issue" in April 2006. If anything, this is an understatement. "The moral equivalent of war" was how the American philosopher William James envisioned the struggle for social justice in 1906, and his phrase comes closer to articulating the proportions of the climate change challenge. What James meant was that a lasting peace could be created only if it harnessed the same unrelenting, all-encompassing energy that war did. "It is only a question," he wrote, "of blowing on the spark until the whole population gets incandescent, and on the ruins of the old morals of military honor, a stable system of morals of civic honor builds itself up. What the whole community comes to believe in grasps the individual as in a vise." Nearly a century later, U.S. president Jimmy Carter transformed James's entreaty into a call to arms against the energy crisis of the 1970s, couching it in terms of choosing a warm cardigan over a cranked thermostat on a cold night. Carter didn't know the half of it. Today, as the scope of the Anthropocene Era's climate crisis becomes daily more apparent, the phrase could only refer to the duty we all have—to ourselves, to our children, to the human species as a whole—to contain its impact. Not just ways of life and livelihoods but millions of human lives are at stake. This is not just an ecological problem but a social and political and economic one, and it is deeply personal, as only a basic question of survival can be.

Climate change is at its most disturbing on this personal level. I have a daughter, as I said, and she has her whole life ahead of her. I know enough of the world's imperfect ways to understand that she'll inevitably know hardship and disappointment and pain, that there will always be conflict and injustice. I think I could teach her to face war, poverty, famine—human problems with practicable solutions, however complex. I could explain to her that life, as wonderful as it can be, is sometimes far from carefree. But I can't even tell her with any confidence that there is a future with sufficient durability to serve as a drawing board for her lifelong dreams. There's a legitimate possibility that she'll face calamity on a scale I can't imagine, on a scale beyond anything humanity's ever seen. This is a prospect that makes it hard to think, makes my vision blur with angry, impotent tears. It *terrifies* me.

Environmentalism has long spoken directly to this feeling. This isn't exactly praise: the movement has nurtured such fear, fed on it, instilled it with a kind of virtue. Rachel Carson's litany against the silence of poisoned birds has grown into a chorus of voices crying out against a vast and perpetually expanding list of violations, despoilments, crises and catastrophes. Apocalypse, Armageddon, Holocaust. Environmentalism has become a sort of mythology of death—passionate, lyrical, righteous and hopeless—with a seemingly inexhaustible store of awful endings and not nearly enough to say about new beginnings.

If ecological crisis isn't the Great Cause of Our Time—yet—then it is in no small part because environmentalism has proven so completely inadequate as a myth of renewal. Like many great social movements, it has done amazing, life-sustaining work both at the broad level of public awareness and at the grassroots level of local action. There aren't many places left in the world where the degradation of the natural environment is not recognized as a problem, and almost as few where you don't find at least a handful of enlightened souls working to fix it. But environmentalism has failed as a common language of hope or a ritual of rebirth. It has failed as myth.

Myth, Joseph Campbell wrote, is "the living inspiration" for all human endeavour, a way to transcend the present, to see beyond what he called "the colorful, fluid, infinitely various and bewildering phenomenal spectacle" of everyday reality. To imagine something greater than *this*—this body, this life, this world—and thus to bring a fundamentally changed world into the realm of the possible. To create hope.

Consider the role played by ritual, song and incantation—mythology, that is—in what was quite possibly the twentieth century's most successful social movement: the global spread of democratic civil rights. Think of the marches through Alabama and of Mahatma Gandhi's fasts. Think of Martin Luther King Jr. declaring that he had a dream and of Pete Seeger singing "We Shall Overcome." It may have been legal arguments or legislative acts or the exigencies of fading empire that sealed these victories, but they were won in the songs, symbols and speeches that united people behind the causes and supplied a language with which to describe a better world worth fighting for. The momentum, the unyielding energy—the moral equivalent of war—came from the movement's myths. Even its failures and setbacks had enduring symbolic power: think of the iconic visage of Nelson Mandela shadowed by a prison's iron bars, the stirring silhouette of a lone Chinese protester unmoved by a tank's looming treads.

Environmentalism, in its early days, had some of the same hopeful energy and symbolic weight (and even some of the same songs). There were inspiring images of small bands of warriors in old fishing boats and rubber dinghies blocking the paths of mighty naval frigates and whaling vessels, not to mention the majestic beauty of the whales and towering trees the warriors were fighting to protect. But later there came figures standing theatrical sentry in neon-yellow contamination suits, tight-focus photos of the bloodied pelts of angelic seals and the menacing mouths of steel traps, the yawning maws of industrial chimneys belching choking smoke—as if the best way to imagine a better world was to first memorize every detail of its present ruin. By the mid-1980s, the bards could offer only a desperate plea for mercy—"and ask the sky and ask the sky / Don't fall on me," as REM phrased the entreaty.

I can't think of a single redemptive anthem for the youthful idealism of Rachel Carson's firstborn children. Even U2's "Pride (In the Name of Love)" was a nostalgic song about Dr. King's assassination, a requiem for a certain kind of innocence. Instead, the culture's most gifted pop prophets retreated into irony, satire and nihilism. Detailed, nuanced, stinging critiques of the status quo became the stuff of nightly network TV—*The Simpsons,* for example, annihilating the global-scale pieties of the overconsumptive new world order, *Seinfeld* meticulously cataloguing the amoral self-absorption of small-scale contemporary life—but the powers that be merely lumbered on in their fossil-fuelled way. Ferocious proselytizers like Nirvana, Public Enemy and Rage Against the Machine brought apocalyptic agitprop and bilious contempt for authority to Top 40 radio, but still the times they weren't a-changin'. Sustainability—climate change's counterpoint, the base measure by which a thing could be determined to be part of the solution—should have become the rallying cry of the age, the point of unity for everyone from anti-globalization street protesters to the savers of whales, the means by which we would overcome. It became, instead, a corporate buzzword.

Environmentalism's rhetoric proved incapable of recalibrating itself to address the harrowing scope of anthropogenic climate change, to provide a story or slogan or metaphor equal to the monumental task of ecological salvation that was emerging. *Think globally?* Sure thing: the planet was a mess wherever you turned. If you think L.A.'s polluted, you should see Mexico City or Manila. But *act locally?* Like the weather cared about your diligent use of phosphate-free detergent, as if the neat stack of newspapers in your back hallway would be carted off in the recycling truck to lower atmospheric CO_2 concentrations all by itself. Environmentalism had become little more than another of those self-contained advocacy pods, endemic to Western society in recent decades, that the media theorist Thomas de Zengotita has dubbed "niche commitments." What's more, as de Zengotita explained in his

2005 treatise *Mediated,* the Anthropocene's activists advanced their causes within a "blob" of a mediascape in which the only real goal was *advocacy itself*—"the production of representations" in lieu of political action. "The producers of these images," de Zengotita wrote, "compete with each other to arouse as much horror and outrage and pity as possible, hoping that *this* encounter with a person dying of AIDS or *that* documentary about sweatshop labor or *these* photographs of recently skinned baby seals will mobilize commitment." But the grim environmentalist niche was of course no match for the sexy hip-hop niche and the melodramatic reality-TV niche. There were more channels than you could count. And if this one was too ugly, too depressing, too complex and tangled? Whatever—what's on Fox tonight?

"Fuck it, Dude, let's go bowling"—this is Walter Sobchak's advice to the hero of the Coen brothers' 1998 film *The Big Lebowski,* upon surveying the intractable mess they've gotten themselves into. The narrator tells us this Dude is "the man for his time and place," and his story is a majestic fable of bumblingly impotent action and shrugging retreat, set against news footage of the first American war on the oil fields of Iraq. There was a certain comfort to be taken in dismissing these calamitous times as absurd spectacle, a certain backhanded nobility to withdrawing in disgust (which, as REM told us elsewhere, wasn't the same thing as apathy). *The Big Lebowski,* as one of the most welcomingly whimsical pop-cultural sanctuaries, would in time spawn a quasi-religious cult. I would eventually count myself a proud member.

But before all that, there was my own limp stab at action. In the summer after my first year of university, I decided to join the environmental movement's front ranks—just in time, it turned out, to see the beginning of its death throes.

THE DEATH OF ENVIRONMENTALISM

In the summer of 1993, I took a job with Greenpeace Canada. At the time, I didn't know much about Greenpeace beyond a strong sense that it stood at the vanguard of an environmental movement that surely had to be growing larger with each passing year, a famous name brand that unfailingly appeared on unfurled banners and protest signs as counterpoint to the latest ecological injustice. Whale hunts, nuclear tests, clearcut-logging operations—all the worst troubles in the world—these were inevitably opposed by a small but tenacious band of dissenters flying the Greenpeace colours. If the struggle to save the planet *was* the moral equivalent of war—and I'd been certain of that much since the first of those long-ago *National Geographic* documentaries—then Greenpeace, so it seemed, was the ragtag rebel army fighting back against ecological injustice, defending a liveable earth against the imperial conquest of careless, power-mad humanity. It was Luke and Leia and Han standing up to the Death Star's vast array of planet-destroying weapons, outgunned and struggling against impossible odds, but sure to win because it had the invincible forces of truth and justice on its side. Greenpeace, I reckoned, was on the side of the heroes.

I was the most insignificant of rearguard foot soldiers in the Greenpeace brigade that summer: a door-to-door canvasser. This was in Kingston, Ontario, a pretty little city on the northeast shore of Lake Ontario, midway between Toronto and Montreal. The Kingston I knew was a bucolic college burg boasting one of Canada's most grandly colonial downtowns, but it was home as well to an army base and military college, several prisons, a chemical plant and an aluminum factory. We also canvassed a number of smaller towns nearby—everything from hard-edged pulp-and-paper towns to postcard-pretty tourist enclaves. The job, it turned out, involved much more than convincing my green-minded fellow students to cough up a bit of their beer money for a good cause.

Five nights a week, I trudged through residential neighbourhoods, showing people photos of doomed rainforests and contaminated rivers, quoting spine-chilling statistics about leukemia and asthma rates, talking of decline and destruction and extinction. Residents of the poorer neighbourhoods were more likely to be welcoming and keen to chat, sometimes seeing me off with a snack and gushing thanks for coming by to inform them of these terrible problems. In the upscale enclaves, I was more often treated as an unwelcome dinnertime intruder, though the best-informed people who cut the fattest cheques were sometimes found in these neighbourhoods as well. In the aggregate, though, the people I canvassed that summer met talk of the environment with weary indifference. It was an abstract problem, far from their daily lives, or else they'd heard too much about it already. Or both. Some would point to their recycling bins, note that they were doing their part. The concerned minority—confirmed environmentalists in the main, some already sporting Greenpeace memberships in need of renewal—were usually possessed by a fear that had no apparent outlet. One couple—greying hippyish in appearance, with a composter next to the garage—brought their seven-year-old daughter out onto the porch to listen to my pitch. She was so consumed with worry over the planet's health, they told me, that sometimes it made her stomach ache too much to eat. She watched me deliver my news from the ecological frontlines with eyes wide and searching, filled with horror and betrayal, desperate for reassurance. I'm sure I gave her nothing more than a few new scenarios for her nightmares.

I would return each night to Greenpeace's temporary Kingston office—a sublet student house not far from the university campus—and there would be a bland vegetarian meal, cheap beer, abundant hash and more talk of impending doom amid the occasional leavening round of Hacky Sack. It was the most demoralizing summer job I'd ever had. There I was, showing up on the doorsteps of strangers, in essence to persuade them of the superiority of my worldview, and yet even I found my rhetoric deflating, uninspired, fundamentally unconvincing. This was a movement of despair, a politics of decay. I finished out the summer with Greenpeace, and I was happy to be done with it.

In the years that followed, as the ecological news grew more urgent and troubling, I saw little to draw me or anyone else back to the environmentalist fold. Most governments, their time horizons foreshortened to the next election, faced electorates only casually interested in environmental issues, which were too intractable to fit on such short-term agendas anyway. In the name of economic necessity or pragmatic self-interest, a great many public officials decided to leave that mess for another regime (or another generation) to deal with. The business world, its sightlines even more delimited by quarterly financial reporting and beholden to shareholders interested only in profit and growth, was often outright hostile to matters of ecology. Most tragically, the environmental movement itself appeared rudderless, spinning in circles, unable to generate momentum in its cause at its most crucial hour.

This wasn't entirely its own fault, of course. As Ross Gelbspan exhaustively documented in his 1997 book *The Heat Is On,* the deep-pocketed fossil fuel companies (particularly American ones) that were making the most money from the unsustainable status quo waged a skilful and ruthless campaign to muddy the issues and confuse the public as to their import and scientific validity, which in turn gave elected officials an excuse for their inaction. But environmentalism's paralysis was not wholly—maybe not even primarily—due to external causes. Throughout the 1990s, anthropogenic climate change loomed ever larger in the public consciousness, despite the fossil fuel industry's relentless efforts to marginalize it, and still the environmental movement barely budged. Though it became abundantly clear that climate change was *the* ecological threat, rendering all but redundant issues of regional conservation or local pollution, the movement found no unity. Even as the dire consequences of the greenhouse effect hammered home for good the notion that environmentalism was not about personal virtue or political point-scoring but about humanity's very survival, still environmental organizations clung to their shopworn tactics of political confrontation and myopic lifestyle advocacy. They most visibly dedicated themselves to shaming intractable governments at high-profile meetings and guilting consumers into a distaste for meat and fur and lab-engineered crops. No great leader along the lines of an MLK or a Gandhi emerged to unite this putative movement and carry it to its necessary next stage; there was no regrouping, no reconsideration of strategy, no discernable effort at reorganization. The fate of the world was at stake in the halls of power, and the movement was content to hang its protest banners outside. Even when the issue of climate change finally began to take centre stage, the movement remained on the fringe, marginalized and increasingly irrelevant.

This is what I think Adam Werbach was on about when he stood in front of an audience of concerned citizens at the Commonwealth Club in San Francisco in December 2004 and announced that environmentalism was dead. "The challenges we face are too serious," he explained, "the opportunities too great to miss. I am done calling myself an environmentalist."

Here was Werbach, the American environmental movement's very own wunderkind, formerly the youngest president in the history of the Sierra Club (he took the job in 1996 at the age of twenty-three), performing a public autopsy on the body he'd been ordained to lead. Werbach had been working of late with Michael Shellenberger and Ted Nordhaus, and so was intimately familiar with their recent essay "The Death of Environmentalism," which had sent waves of shock and recrimination through the movement. But Werbach himself was unable to dispute its central claim: that a fatal inertia had taken hold of environmentalism, a narrowness of focus and a calcification of tactics that had induced the political equivalent of heart failure. At the very moment that the delicate ecology it claimed to defend was under the most ferocious attack ever, the movement offered only horror, outrage, alarm—fear and more fear. And fear, for the most part, inspires conservative reactions. A recent study of the public mood toward environmental issues, Werbach noted, "found that the more you scared people about global warming, the more they want to buy SUVs to protect themselves. Miniature Arks." To raise awareness of imminent catastrophe—long the preferred tactic of the movement—was, paradoxically, to hasten its arrival. This was no way to change people's minds about what kind of car to drive, let alone change the world.

"I don't want to have to talk about death anymore," was how Werbach concluded his speech. "I want to build a better world."

A GEOGRAPHY OF HOPE

Here's how I first stumbled upon Adam Werbach's speech: seated in a rocking chair in my darkened living room well after midnight on a cold April night, surfing the internet on a laptop perched awkwardly on a side table next to me. My daughter, barely a month old, was nestled in my arms and just drifting off to sleep. I was coaxing her back to bed after a night feeding. My online reading habits tend toward the manner in which we do so many things nowadays—fast and perfunctory, skipping ahead and anxious to be done—but my daughter, her eyes still fluttering, forced me to stay put for a more deliberate read. Every few paragraphs, I'd cautiously slide an arm from under her little legs to reach over and scroll down. A snippet of a song—Dylan again—popped into my head, looped, ran over and over as a soundtrack: "So let us not talk falsely now, the hour is getting late."

For some years previous, I'd been trying to find an excuse to visit the island nation of Tuvalu, a tiny archipelago of eleven thousand souls in the middle of the Pacific Ocean. If some of the most credible climate change scenarios for the next few decades are correct, Tuvalu will likely vanish into the rising Pacific within my lifetime. Its leaders have been busy in recent years begging the United Nations for dramatic action on climate change and petitioning the government of New Zealand to give its residents a place to live once their country is gone. I wanted to see Tuvalu before it ceased to be; I'd come to think of it as the canary in the global coal mine, the planet's most profound symbol of the cataclysm that awaited us all. An entire nation, a place with its own language and customs and culture—*gone.* I imagined that if somehow Tuvalu's fate could become as universally known and fretted over as that of, say, oil-rich Iraq—well, maybe then we'd find the will to slow this process, to start building a future worth passing on to my girl. It even occurred to me to bring her with me to Tuvalu, to let her stand on infant legs upon an island that her adult feet would never touch. In the dark of my living room, her deepening breaths providing a quiet cadence for my reading, it struck me that there was nothing more resolutely hopeless I could do for her.

So I decided not to take my daughter to Tuvalu, and I may never see it myself. Instead, I embarked on a journey to map a new world: one that could replace Tuvalu and everything else we'll lose if we continue on our current course; one that might save it. The world she needs, the world we all need—desperately, urgently, *now.*

The criteria for inclusion on my map would be as straightforward as possible, with the baseline being this: sustainability. Now, *sustainability* has been applied widely and carelessly enough that it verges sometimes on meaninglessness. But I adopted this simple litmus test: Would *this*—this place, this machine, this social system or way of life—be capable of continuing on its present course for the foreseeable future without exhausting the planet's ability to sustain human life at something like the current population and quality of life? I would look beyond energy technologies and overtly green-minded ideas to encompass as close to the whole range of human life as possible, from how we feed and shelter ourselves to the governments that represent us and the institutions that fulfill our social lives to the ways and means of the soul that make our lives worth living. And I would search not for theories or prototypes or extrapolations from lab results but for actual stuff actually being used today.

Remember Boulding: "Anything that exists is possible." This became my mantra. I would find a sustainable version of reality, jump-cut and episodic, strewn in pieces around the globe. It would consist of true things, real life—stuff that existed, that was therefore manifestly possible—but it would be as much myth as documentary. *Myth* the way Joseph Campbell meant it: a vision quest that expands the realm of the possible.

I began with a wind farm not far from home. Strangely beautiful, inspiring in its way, but in the end just a small auxiliary power plant woven into a grid of much larger, completely unsustainable ones, on the edge of a prairie being mined for every last non-renewable drop of fossil fuel it had to give. It was a start, but for all I knew a false one. My goal was not merely to find a duplicate version of our current social order, minus the greenhouse gas emissions, but to find the right fragments to assemble into a whole new way of life. Surely there were places of greater ambition and better execution. I wanted to see the best, the state of the art, to discover microcosmic isles of sustainability to fill my map with enough detail to chart a course in a new direction, away from the hopeless waters dead ahead and toward more sustainable shores.

My first destination, fittingly enough, was an island in rough seas, where the Anthropocene's defining problem—the production of energy—has been all but completely solved.

BUMPER CROP

The relentless Baltic waves notwithstanding, the tiny island of Samsø is a tranquil, unhurried place. Though it sits at pretty much the dead centre of the Kattegat, the narrow channel that separates the two most populous regions of Denmark—the Danish mainland and the large island of Zealand, upon which Copenhagen and Roskilde and Hamlet's fabled castle at Elsinore lie—Samsø has never been any-where near the heart of Danish life. It's just a bump in the channel, a mere 114 square kilometres of rolling pasture, small farms and tidy, picturesque villages, with a population of about 4,400. Along narrow, gently winding roads, Shetland ponies watch passersby from pad-docks, and every so often there's a flock of sheep or small herd of cat-tle grazing in a pasture. At the roadside, Samsø's citizens place goods for sale in trim wooden hutches: fruit and vegetables most often, but also antiquey knick-knacks and handicrafts, used crockery and appliances. In each hutch, there's a small cashbox with a slit in its lid; it's taken for granted that the buyer will deposit the posted price within.

Inside Denmark, Samsø is known primarily as the proud producer of the country's finest potatoes, the namesake of a cheese that's no longer made there, and a serene spot for a weekend getaway; outside Denmark, Samsø is so little known that it doesn't even warrant passing mention in travel guides. Denmark's dominion encompasses seventy-eight inhabited islands, and Samsø is but one in this rank.

But Samsø is, for all of this, revolutionary: the site of quite possibly the most ambitious experiment in renewable energy the world has yet seen.

There are many elements to a comprehensive geography of hope—homes and businesses, economic and social systems, philosophical constructs and political arguments—but the most critical questions come down to energy. The CO_2 emissions that threaten to make the earth inhospitable to abundant human life come from many sources (from the methane produced by flatulent cattle and respiring trees and melting permafrost, for example), but the bulk of it, more than 75 percent in the industrialized West, is the result of burning coal, oil and natural gas to fuel our insatiable thirst for energy. If there's a thread that tethers together the sporadic pockets of sustainability that make up the world we need, it is how the people living in these places think about, obtain and use their power. And it was on a small island in Denmark that I found the most comprehensive response to this conundrum, a place where the realm of the mythically possible has been made manifest, an island where fossil fuels have been rendered all but extinct.

I came to Samsø by ferry, as virtually everyone does, on an early-morning launch out of the grimy Zealand port of Kalundborg. The boat steamed past a hulking power plant in the harbour; a mammoth freighter was in dock at its base, unloading coal to fuel the plant's boiler. Then on into the open waters of the Kattegat, and for an hour there was only the sea. Toward the end of the journey, around the time you might expect to see shorebirds, we came upon a mirage in the watery desert—a collection of shadowy lines on the horizon, grey-black against the white morning haze. As the ferry chugged closer, they resolved into a row of towers that seemed to hover just above the water: Samsø's offshore wind farm. I ran to the window with my camera as the other passengers continued with their morning papers and gossip. As I'd soon learn, one of the most remarkable things about Samsø's revolution was how commonplace it already seemed, how much a fixed part of a social order continuing on its tidy way.

On arrival, I made my way to the Brundby Rock Hotel, a venerable old inn in a postcard village given a funky new life by the inn's matronly Norwegian owner, a lifelong lover of loud live rock & roll. It now doubled as both a cozy hotel and the island's premier concert venue. At the top of the stairs, a golden Buddha and a half-dozen photos of Jimi Hendrix (whose Danish former girlfriend lives just up the lane) kept groovy watch. I settled into my room and threw open the curtains to find a singular tableau that seemed oddly timeless: a trim yellow farmhouse, a small paddock populated by a handful of miniature ponies, and a row of wind turbines turning steadily on the horizon. Dali's take on a Constable scene, except that the ponies and the turbines seemed to be as easy neighbours as Jimi and the Buddha were.

While most of the world has been spinning in stagnant circles of recrimination and debate on the subject of climate change, paralyzed by visions of apocalypse both natural (if nothing of our way of life changes) and economic (if too much does), Denmark has simply marched off with steadfast resolve into the sustainable future, reaching the zenith of its pioneering trek on the island of Samsø. And so if there's an encircled star on this patchwork map indicating hope's modest capital, then it should be properly placed on this island. Perhaps, for the sake of precision, at the geographic centre of a dairy farm just outside the village of Brundby.

There are, I'm sure, any number of images called to mind by talk of ecological revolution and renewable energy and sustainable living, but I'm pretty certain they don't generally include a hearty fiftysomething Dane in rubber boots spotted with mud and cow shit. Which is why Samsø's transformation is not just revolutionary but inspiring, not just a huge change but a tantalizingly attainable one. And it's a change that seemed at its most workaday—near effortless, no more remarkable than the cool October wind gusting across the island— down on Jørgen Tranberg's farm.

Here, at the revolution's vanguard, came the man himself, Jørgen. Tranberg—tall and sturdy, straw-coloured hair at odds with his fifty-odd years, his boots caked in crud—striding across the dirt courtyard of his half-timbered farmhouse to greet me. He offered a Danish howdy that was all gruff good nature, contemptuous of small talk, his English thickly accented and punctuated by stern rhetorical bursts of "Yes? *Yes?*" As in: "We go have coffee, yes? *Yes?*" So we did.

He ushered me out of the biting wind into a comfortable kitchen that was homespun in every way except for its battalion of sleek German-engineered stainless steel appliances, hinting at the exceedingly good times being had these days on Tranberg's farm. We sat down at the small, plain kitchen table, Tranberg settling into his seat heavily, with that slight restlessness you often find in people accustomed to physical work. Over coffee, he ran me quickly through a traditional life lived unconventionally.

Tranberg grew up in Jutland, the Danish mainland. Like many of his generation, he came of age in the early 1970s overflowing with idealism and deeply committed to the social-democratic ideals that governed postwar Denmark. Barely in his twenties, he joined with four other high-minded Danes to acquire a piece of land and start a collective farm. For the usual reasons—personality conflicts, uneven reactions to the sweaty hands-on work that turns lofty ideals into tilled-soil reality—the collective lasted only a couple of years. Tranberg, undeterred, set out for Samsø, where he'd heard that good land was available on the cheap. He found 100 hectares on the south side of the island, just outside a pretty village of thatched roofs and cobbled laneways. He married, raised two daughters, kept dairy cattle and grew a few crops. Like most small farmers, he had good years and bad, but enough good ones that he reached his fifties with the possibility of retirement not so far off. And then, in the late 1990s, things went from good to much better. Tranberg now talked about retirement as a fixed landmark fast approaching on his horizon.

Our coffee done, Tranberg jumped up, keen to be moving again. We crossed the courtyard and entered a large aluminum-sided barn filled with a range of hulking machines for industrial milk production, where a tall, sturdy slab of a Ukrainian farmhand, a recent hire, was hard at work with a hose. Behind the machinery lay a wide, low, open-sided area strewn with hay. Tranberg gestured at it—"Here is for sleeping, yes? *Yes?*"—and then noted casually that the waste heat from his milk-cooling machine was repurposed for heating his house; his fireplace saw use only in the dead of winter.

I followed Tranberg across a clearing behind the barn. Dairy cattle—a few dozen of his 130 head, which produce milk that's wholesaled to a farmers' co-operative in Jutland for bottling and export—were grazing in the wide pasture to our left. To our right was a patch of ripe pumpkins, splashes of brilliant orange against the dun of the field and the grey slate of the sky. We climbed into his tractor, a late-model Massey Ferguson, and chugged along a muddy path, past a large field of organic onions (sold to an enterprising exporter up the road in Brundby), bound for a pasture in the distance.

We stopped at the base of a slim, sleek white tower 50 metres tall, crowned with a three-bladed rotor that whirred in the stiff breeze—the combination scythe and silo with which Tranberg harvests his newest cash crop. A wind turbine, that is—one of the neat line I'd seen from my hotel window. We hopped out of the tractor, and Tranberg tramped ahead of me toward a door in the turbine's base. He ducked inside, removed a control panel the size of a hand-held videogame system from a transformer box mounted there and hit a button. Twenty seconds later, the turbine's giant blades came to a stop. "Now we go up. *Yes?*" he said. He tucked the control panel in his overalls and started up a series of offset ladders inside the narrowing tower with the easy, youthful vigour of a man twenty years his junior. Which is to say, I could barely keep up.

I rejoined Tranberg in the cramped, bullet-shaped nook that crowns the turbine and houses its gearbox and generator—the *nacelle,* in wind-industry argot—where he was reconnecting the control panel to another electronic panel. It was a plug-and-play affair, no more difficult than connecting a joystick to a gaming console. At the press of another button or two, the nacelle's roof opened like a blooming two-petalled flower to reveal a vertiginous view of Samsø and the sea beyond.

Tranberg stood, the howling wind rippling his blond hair, and surveyed the landscape. To the northwest, seven other turbines stood in a neat line on neighbouring farms, their blades oscillating industriously in the breeze. To the southeast, three and a half kilometres offshore and just out of sight on this overcast day, was the sentry detail of offshore turbines I'd seen from the ferry. Much further north, almost at the northern tip of the island, another trio of turbines stood, far beyond our sight, spinning in the same gale. All of them, like the one we were perched atop, were owned locally, either by farmers or by co-operatives of local shareholders. Tranberg had bought his turbine six years before with a US$800,000 loan, and the investment had paid off sufficiently that he had capital to reinvest in a half-ownership of one of those new offshore windmills—the state-of-the-art, 2.3-megawatt turbines that together produce an amount of green power roughly equal to the amount of gasoline-generated power used by the islanders' vehicles (which was the goal of their construction). Twenty-one turbines island-wide, then, that transform Samsø—in effect, if not quite in literal truth—into the modern world's first island to be powered entirely by renewable energy.*

A CONGRESS, NOT A KING

Truth be told, it's not wind turbines alone that have ushered Samsø into the Age of Sustainability. And it's central to Samsø's importance that this is the case—because, for starters, very few of us live on windswept isles. Like the vast majority of Denmark's windmills, the ones on Samsø connect to a national grid still powered primarily by fossil fuels, guaranteeing uninterrupted electricity even on calm days. And for energy needs other than electricity, there are other kinds of systems scattered across the island. Wind power, by itself, cannot supplant fossil fuels even in one isolated patch of Danish countryside.

"It's time to step up the search for the next great fuel for the hungry engine of mankind," *National Geographic* declared in an August 2005 cover story on "future power." "Is there such a fuel? The short

---

* Let's split this hair only once and be done with it: the processes used to manufacture modern renewable energy technologies are not themselves intrinsically sustainable. They need energy—in some cases lots of it—and in a world powered by fossil fuels, there has been, for example, no great compulsion to begin forging the steel for wind turbines from heat produced by solar panels (whose own manufacture is a highly energy-intensive process). At least one prominent climate change activist—Thom Hartmann, author of *The Last Hours of Ancient Sunlight*—has suggested using what oil remains exclusively for the production of green-tech devices ("an investment rather than an expenditure"), but in the absence of a much more tangible crisis, an industrial redirection on this scale is unlikely. In the meantime, burning coal to make turbines beats burning it to provide electricity to a million flat-screen TVs in standby mode. The perfect is *not* the enemy of the good.

answer is no." At which point hope seems to grind to a halt with the same push-of-a-button abruptness as when Jørgen Tranberg stops the blades on his turbine. Here, usually, comes talk of hard sacrifices and reduced expectations, of a future-tense world that seems so radically transformed, so riven by economic chaos and environmental collapse, that it is all but post-apocalyptic. And here, in brightening contrast to such gloom, comes *National Geographic*'s aphoristic reply: "The successor will have to be a congress, not a king." The myth's hero, if you will, might be not an individual but a collective.

Samsø's revolution has certainly been nothing if not collective: born of a Danish government initiative; assembled village by village by local officials with the assistance of citizens' work groups and business organizations; implemented with tools ranging from towering wind turbines and solar panels to free beer and an industrial fruit press. I'll come back to the critical role played by those last two in a moment. First, though, some backstory, because the process that would lead, in time, to the revolutionary restructuring of Samsø's energy regime began decades earlier, in the wake of the OPEC energy crisis of the early 1970s.

The OPEC crisis, of course, sent shockwaves around the world, producing mile-long gas lineups and precipitating recession throughout the quaking West, but few nations were rocked as hard as Denmark, which at the time depended on oil imports for 94 percent of its energy consumption. The Danish government's response to those OPEC shocks was similarly singular in its intensity: a resolute commitment to pursuing energy self-sufficiency that continues to this day. Denmark has no significant local energy resources—its flat, pastoral landscape contains not even a single river that flows fast enough for industrial-scale hydroelectric power—and the Danish public soundly rejected nuclear power as an option, so the Danes built their energy self-reliance instead on a motley assortment of new approaches. First among these (and still the chief source of the country's energy today) was a wholesale move from OPEC-controlled crude to more stable fossil fuel sources: coal replaced oil as the primary fuel for electricity and heating, and the Danish government started pumping natural gas from its piece of the North Sea. Most significant, though, was Denmark's early recognition that renewables could play a key role in its quest for self-reliance.

Throughout the 1980s and into the 1990s, while much of the West celebrated the return of cheap oil with a twenty-year orgy of consumption—indeed, even as fossil fuel streamed steadily ashore from the bottom of the North Sea—Denmark made a top priority of exploring the potential of such fuel sources as the howling winds that blew across the sea's choppy surface. Through an innovative package of emissions and consumption taxes and seed grants for wind-power companies, the Danes transformed their country into a world leader in energy efficiency and renewable-energy production. Denmark is now the highest per capita producer of wind energy on the planet, with stiff breezes nationwide providing fully 20 percent of its domestic electricity needs. It's also home to the world's largest wind-energy industry, manufacturing more than 40 percent of the world's wind turbines.

By 1997, sure of its standing in the front ranks of the renewable-energy field, the Danish government invited its dozens of small islands to participate in a contest. The goal was to create an island fuelled entirely by renewable energy as a kind of microcosmic show-case of the country's global leadership in green power. The winner would get pride of place and some government money to help make the shift.

Samsø, circa 1997, was slightly down-at-heel by Danish stan-dards, cursed like many islands with steep energy and transport costs that made it hard to attract new business. With a bid put together by an ad hoc committee that included the head of the local trade board, the mayor of the Samsø municipality (which governs the entire island), and an enterprising engineer from a mainland energy consulting firm, Samsø entered the contest, hoping to give the local economy a kickstart. It was named Denmark's "Renewable Energy Island" over four other competitors in November 1997, and in short order a local business (Samsø Energiselskab, the Samsø Energy Company) and a local governing body (Samsø Energi- og Miljøkontor, the Samsø Energy and Environment Office) were estab-lished to make its winning plan a reality.

In 1997, Samsø was getting 92 percent of its electricity and 85 per-cent of its heat from fossil fuels. There had been windmills on the island since the seventeenth century, and it got its first modern turbine back in 1979, but for the most part Samsø started its transformation mired in the same kind of oil/gas/coal dependency that defines most of the world's energy production. The project of turning Samsø into the world's first fossil-fuelless island was scheduled to take ten years. By the time I surveyed it from the crown of Tranberg's turbine in the fall of 2005, Samsø was getting all of its heat and *more* than 100 percent of its electricity from renewables, and CO_2 emissions were down 140 percent once you factored in the work Samsø's wind turbines were doing on behalf of Danish electricity users further afield.

Tranberg's turbine and its neighbours had gone up in 2000. The offshore wind farm came online in 2003. Halfway between Tranberg's farm and the village of Brundby stands a nondescript warehouse clad in red siding, which houses a new district heating plant, straw-fired and hyper-efficient, from which the Brundby Rock Hotel and virtually every other building in the village get their heat. The plant also supplies the heat for the harbour village of Ballen to the east. To the north of Tranberg's farm, over a rolling hill or two, lies another straw-fired plant, which generates heat for Tranebjerg, Samsø's administrative hub. The straw comes from 15 hectares of elephant grass raised by local farmers expressly to feed the furnaces. And at the northern tip of the island, outside the village of Nordby, there's a district heating plant completed in 2002 that generates heat using a 2,500-square-metre array of solar panels and a wood-chip backup stove. Seventy percent of Samsø's residents obtain their heat by these means; the remaining households—250 or so, all told—are warmed either by single-home solar arrays or by in-home stoves burning straw or wood. The usual suspects—natural gas, coal and oil—have been turfed onto the smoggy funeral pyre of history, and home-heating costs are *down* 20 percent island-wide.

And on it went: old farmhouses got energy-efficiency retrofits (with 50 percent of the costs to pensioners reimbursed by the Danish state). One elderly lady from Ballen got to talking to the Samsø Energy and Environment Office about what it would cost to convert her tidy little home completely to solar power, and it turned out the price tag was about the same as her life savings. She reckoned that the 2.5 percent annual "return" on her investment in the form of no more electricity bills was a full point better than what she was getting on her savings account, so she covered her sloping roof in 60,000 Danish kroner worth of photovoltaic (PV) cells. Samsø's revolutionaries even looked into converting every car on the island to biodiesel, but that would have required practically every farmer on the island to switch over to growing rapeseed, so instead they built the offshore wind farm to offset their automotive emissions.

Meanwhile, so many curious energy bureaucrats had started showing up to take a gander—an estimated one thousand trade visitors a year, mandarins from Beijing and Native chiefs from the United States, representatives of energy-starved islands from Greece to Micronesia—that ground had been broken on the Samsø Energy Academy, so as to provide more comprehensive and systematic replies to the inquiries. (The Academy—itself a marvel of energy efficiency, boasting everything from rainwater toilets to solar heating—opened its doors in May 2007.) There were plans for a biogas production plant to make productive use of the island's waste and the methane excreted by local cows. And still chins were being scratched on Samsø about how to harness the excess heat that the ferries carry with them when they come steaming into port every day. The price tag to date: 420 million Danish kroner (about US$76 million).*

The wind and the sun, straw and wood, plus longer-term plans involving biogas and the excess heat from ferries—here, in miniature, was a congress to replace a fossil king.

But what was truly surprising about Samsø was how little the landscape had changed. Cattle still lowed in the fields, the boats still bobbed in the waves of Ballen Harbour, locals still navigated the narrow roads on bikes and in cars to run errands in Tranebjerg. The houses of thatch and timber still begged to be photographed and slapped on postcards, the tiny, tender potatoes of local fame still melted in your mouth. Not only had there been no economic

---

* It's customary in journalistic circles to diligently attach dollar figures to building and infrastructure projects whenever possible. I've obliged in the case of this Renewable Energy Island project and will do so hereafter when it seems especially relevant, but in general I reject the notion that such random, decontextualized statistics are of any particular significance. By way of elaboration on that point, I'll simply note this: the cost of Samsø's transformation to near-total sustainability amounted to a little more than half as much as the estimated $125 million production budget for the climate change catastrophe movie *The Day After Tomorrow.* Which, to my mind, says pretty much all that needs to be said about the arbitrary economic priorities of the modern West.

hardship—let alone a meltdown—but Samsø's conversion to renewables had created a few dozen jobs and revitalized a stagnant economy. Local electricians had been trained to do routine maintenance on the offshore wind farm. Guf, the Brundby Rock Hotel's affable proprietor, pointed out that her formerly seasonal business had been given a huge year-round boost by all the visiting VIPs. Not to mention that fully four-fifths of the money invested in the turbines and everything else had come from private local investors—including average Samsø residents by the hundreds, each with their own small share in the island's turbines, which had already begun to produce dividends.

This all hints at the truly innovative thing about Samsø's energy revolution. Not only had it reconfigured the archetypal image of a post-carbon future from looming apocalypse to regional renaissance, it'd done so with readily available tools and the skills and enthusiasms of conservative people living in villages that were all but antiquated. There's not one radically new technology installed on Samsø, not a single untested experiment. Samsø's real revolution was *social,* and it provides a compelling model of how to implement radical change without freaking out the regular folks whose lives are disrupted by it. To work, these new techniques had to find an agreeable spot in Jørgen Tranberg's muddy pasture, the proper tone for an island populated by tradition-minded, budget-conscious Danes, the right fit in a functioning community. Which is to say that Samsø's revolution, if it was to succeed, had to be much more than a simple, surgical swap of carbon-burning energy sources for renewable ones. And it found the appropriate, Samsø-sized scale by starting with much less: a few bottles of cold beer, a fruit press, and a friendly discussion or two.

THE FREE TUBORG REVOLUTION

The revolutionary movement in Samsø began with what has to be the most innocuous manifesto in the annals of radical social transformation. The document appeared in the local newspaper in March 1998, announcing a civic meeting in the village of Nordby to discuss two unrelated matters of local import: applications for new liquor licences and the Renewable Energy Island project. Samsø had been declared the winner of the Danish Energy Agency's contest just a few months before; the Energy and Environment Office had just opened, and a local man had been newly hired as "energy adviser," charged with overseeing the implementation of the non-technical aspects of the plan. That man was Søren Hermansen, and the meeting in Nordby was his idea, the cornerstone of his radically homespun strategy.

Søren Hermansen is, if anything, an even less likely revolutionary than your friendly neighbourhood dairy-and-wind farmer. Middle-aged and slightly balding, bespectacled and tidily dressed, Hermansen comes across as the prototypical Scandinavian mid-level bureaucrat, a guy who looks like he'd be completely comfortable at an EU plenary session. Beneath this façade, though, lurks a lively and calculating mind finely tuned to the exigencies and eccentricities of civic life on Samsø.

Hermansen grew up on a farm on the south side of the island. He left Samsø for school, returned with a "green certificate" in agriculture, took over the family farm. After five years, he was off again, this time in pursuit of a degree in environmental planning. He came back to teach at a boarding school, leaving the island every so often to teach (and soak up the latest progressive ideas) at one of Denmark's *folkehøjskoler*—the "folk" high schools for adult education that have been a fixture of Danish life since the nineteenth century. He co-owned a small wind turbine, and because it stood right next to his farm, he also maintained it. He came to the energy-adviser gig, then, with a strong knowledge of renewable energy and an intimate understanding of traditional ways of life and entrenched patterns of thought on Samsø. He was perfectly suited to his new job, and that first meeting in Nordby, the largest village on Samsø's northern cape, was incontrovertible proof of it.

Samsø, tiny as it is, has its regional biases, and one of these says that the north end of the island is just a little more set in its ways, a bit further out of the modern loop. It's connected to the rest of the island only by a sliver-thin isthmus, which is bisected by an ancient canal the Vikings once used as a shortcut between the mainland and Zealand—a symbolic division, if little more than a ditch nowadays. It's the poor rural cousin to the cosmopolitan south, the least obvious place to commence a campaign for big, bold, future-is-now change. So naturally it was one of the first places Søren Hermansen went calling.

The meeting took place in the banquet hall of the Hotel Nordby Krø, a cozy brick inn with a steep-pitched, dormer-studded roof, a venerable institution so utterly old school it shows up on postcards. A crowd of about seventy-five showed up, drawn mostly by the talk of new liquor licences—a vital issue in a tourist town such as Nordby. In solidarity with the liquor-licence applicants, Hermansen and his colleagues brought a few cases of beer—Carlsberg and Tuborg, the alpha and omega of Danish lager, free to all comers. They introduced themselves by wishing the applicants luck with their admirable and reasonable and sure-to-be-successful attempts to obtain licences, and mentioned that they'd be talking a bit about renewable energy and such afterwards. Have a Tuborg on us, they said, and we'll get to our stuff once this serious business of liquor licensing is finished.

The renewable-energy revolutionaries sat unobtrusively through talk of which cafés wanted to serve booze and why, and then Hermansen got up and gave his soft-pedal project-overview spiel. After which he mentioned how *little* this concerned the good people of Nordby. "Well, you're so far away from the central administration of the project, which is in Tranebjerg," Hermansen explained, invoking the name of Samsø's administrative hub the way an Alberta populist might bring up Ottawa, "we think this is going to be the *last* place we're going to make any kind of development. You are a little bit old-fashioned out here, and we don't expect you to make the move on this project for years." Now the obligatory pirouette: "But if, of course—*if* you come up with some activity, we will support you. But we don't really expect you to do anything." In passing—all but on his way out the door—Hermansen mentioned that projects would go forward only if 70 percent of local households would sign a petition stating their intent to participate. *Thanks for listening, and we'll be on our way. Enjoy your free beer.*

A month later, the good people of Nordby came to the Energy and Environment Office with a district heating agreement boasting signatures from more than 80 percent of village residents. In the spring of 2002, Samsø's first solar-powered district heating plant came online on the outskirts of the village.

This outcome was far from inevitable. A less nuanced, less *local* approach could easily have led to the kind of digging in of heels and knee-jerk, not-in-my-backyard resistance that has often plagued top-down renewable-energy developments. When an English consortium introduced a proposal in 2006 for industrial-scale wind farms on a handful of islands in the Scottish Hebrides, for example, it prompted more than ten thousand complaints out of a voting population of barely twice that. One local crofter—a pretty much precise Scottish analogue to the small farmers of Samsø—told a reporter, "There has been little attempt to sell the idea to the local people." On Nantucket Island in Massachusetts, meanwhile, a Boston developer's proposed offshore wind farm has led to a bitter feud with wealthy residents that's been running for four years now.

Renewable energy might have had a more familiar ring to it in windmill-studded Denmark, but the prospect of a dramatic campaign to eliminate fossil fuels entirely was still no easy sell on Samsø. Prior to their victory in the contest, Hermansen and his colleagues had worked essentially in private. They'd assembled a proposal and consulted a few local officials, but the announcement of Samsø's selection was likely the first most residents had heard of the Renewable Energy Island plan, and from a less familiar angle it could've resembled some reckless imposition from distant Copenhagen.

Hermansen: "You had to make a local context so people could make a comparison to other projects they knew already. Just to demonstrate that it wasn't that complicated, it's just another household thing to discuss, not to be too sophisticated. Because I've seen many places that they carry on trying to make renewable-energy development political, and make a political statement out of it, saying it's because of saying no to nuclear power, it's because of climate change problems in the world, it's because of too much CO_2 in the atmosphere. Where we didn't talk about that at all in the beginning of the meetings. That would be a positive side effect of the project development. But we talked about the advantages for the village, that they could get together in a community build-up process, where a lot of people could be involved and they could get something new and useful."

This was to be the guiding principle of Hermansen's backhanded, unassuming, folksy-as-hell revolution. Village to village and inn to inn; a second meeting, a third, whatever it took. The details were tailored to each place, but the approach remained the same: a meeting at a well-known local establishment, a place where civic affairs had always been chewed over. No fancy PowerPoint show, no bold pronouncements. Ideally, as in Nordby, the meeting wouldn't even be primarily about renewable energy. Hermansen and his team caught their flies instead with honey—or nectar, actually. And not just the malted kind: the Energy and Environment Office also bought itself a fruit press, a big old hand-operated monster that took two men to work it. They went to a village called Østerby around harvest time, and they set up their fruit press on the grounds of the local *pension*. The locals showed up toting crates and pushing wheelbarrows full of apples, and afterwards everyone went inside to have apple pie and coffee and talk about renewable energy. "A lot of people came only to have their apples pressed," Hermansen recalls. "And they stayed along because they thought, well, that was impolite, just to leave the meeting after the pressing. So they stayed, and they had coffee, and we had a very good meeting—a very interesting talk about village development." The fruit press would be later trucked out for meetings in other villages. If it wasn't a beer bash, it was a juicing bee. Anything to avoid looking at all like a top-down development scheme dreamed up in Copenhagen or—worse—a political rally.

Either at these public assemblies or through one-on-one meetings, Hermansen specifically targeted local bigwigs: school headmasters, the owners of small companies, prominent farmers. People well-known locally, the ones everybody trusted. "People saw that these important guys, they want to enlist, then they changed their attitude a little bit, saying, 'Okay, if this guy, he is participating, and this one over there, he is participating, I might as well just join in.'" Efforts were also made to keep the project *out* of the hands of its most obvious champions: the hardcore environmentalists, the ones with long-established reputations as impractical local radicals—the ones who, as Hermansen puts it, "are eager to make the whole world change." Following the lead of the local potentates, the villagers formed working groups, went door to door to explain the project to their neighbours, came back with signatures and suggestions. They got *invested* in being citizens of a Renewable Energy Island; they took ownership of it.

It's worth noting here that, apparently unconsciously, Hermansen launched a flat-out classic of a viral marketing campaign. It was *The Tipping Point* in traditional Danish translation. I mean, what were these local opinion leaders if not Samsø's version of Malcolm Gladwell's "connectors," the hubs of the social network? Who took those ideas to the rest of the village if not the "salesmen" in those workgroups? And most of all, what was Søren Hermansen if not a Gladwellian tour de force, "maven" and connector at once, the guy not just hip to the new idea but shrewd enough to package and deliver it in a way that would transform it into a social epidemic?

An epidemic, then, but an ambling one: the architect of the Free Tuborg Revolution worked slowly, methodically. Hermansen spent two years hopscotching the island until every village was involved, until the farmers' association and the trade board were satisfied. His engineer doppelgänger at the Samsø Energy Company—one Aage Johnsen, a frequent presence at the village meetings—may have been busy drawing up technical plans, but as far as most residents were concerned, this was *their* thing. By the time construction of turbines and heating plants began in 2000 and 2001, the Renewable Energy Island project was no more disruptive to Samsø's cozy society than the opening of a new Netto grocery store in Tranebjerg. If anything, less so—a multinational grocer like Netto surely didn't go village to village before it opened to explain why it was pricing the little family-owned stores out of the Samsø market.

By the time I made it to Samsø in the fall of 2005, it was as if the island had been a global pioneer in renewable energy for about as long as it'd been a good place to farm potatoes. I could've walked down the bustling main street in Tranebjerg a dozen times, and if I'd noticed the Energy and Environment Office at all, it would've hit me with all the incongruity of a tourist bureau. I showed up one morning ready to talk about the revolutionary transformation going on, and Søren Hermansen just grinned and ushered me out to a waiting car, where one of his colleagues was heading out with a couple of slick, suited gents from the mainland who'd come to talk about what their fuel-cell systems might be able to do for petroleum-free transportation on Samsø. We drove out to Nordby and oohed and aahed dutifully at the solar panels, and then headed down to Brundby to gawk at the straw-fired furnace. Every now and then there'd be a wind turbine, and every now and then there'd be a square-steepled Viking-era church or a herd of grazing miniature ponies. Here was a roof half-tiled in photovoltaic cells, and there was one covered in thatch. Once, on a subsequent tour with Hermansen behind the wheel, I spied a unique windmill next to a long farmhouse—the shaft built of metal scaffolding instead of sleek white steel, the rotor blades smaller and flatter. Oh *that,* Hermansen replied. It was from a previous generation of technology, had fallen into disuse. But the farmhouse owner was converting the place into a youth hostel, so they were in the process of refurbishing the windmill to deal with the anticipated increase in power load. This was just how it was on Samsø. Just another few thousand kilowatt hours of green energy, where it was needed, provided by the best and most readily available tools.

I feel compelled to reiterate the basic facts, like maybe this all seems *too* commonplace. So listen: there's an island in Denmark where they've reduced CO_2 emissions effectively to less than zero. Built a sustainable society in microcosm—a model for the coming transformation and a beacon of hope. In less than ten years. And they're *thriving.* The changes have all been for the better and life carries on much as it always has. Maybe that's the point: on one island in Denmark, virtually overnight, *sustainability has become commonplace.* It's as much a part of the fabric of everyday life on Samsø as a cold bottle of Tuborg at the village inn. The catalyst for Samsø's transformation may have been a much larger thing, much further off—an oil cartel's manoeuvring thirty years earlier in the Arab desert, a policymaker's decision twenty years after that in the faraway capital—but it was on the human scale of free lager at the village meeting hall that the island's revolutionaries figured out what sort of engine would best turn that spark into a sustainable power source.

This too is worth underscoring: the free beer, the fruit press, the village-level organizing strategy—these are not incidental details. These are the *only* essential elements of Samsø's revolution, the fundamental tools it now offers to a world that needs to create two, three, many Samsøs (to paraphrase Che Guevara). The most important lesson of the Free Tuborg Revolution, in other words, is the Tuborg part. The world, as vast and populous as it is, can be divided into millions of little islands—towns and villages, neighbourhoods and subdivisions, enclaves and prefectures—and each little island can determine its own climatic conditions, calculate its own energy demands, figure out what suite of sustainable technologies will do the job, and decide whether to serve cold beer or press fresh apples at the local meeting hall when everyone gathers to work out the details.

This was a revelation no less startling because it crept up so gently and spoke so softly. An end to dependence on fossil fuel wasn't just within the realm of possibility; it was *all there*. It took eight years or so of work—hard work, sure, but also fun and fulfilling. It was a question, mainly, of the right people and the right kind of tools.

MEANWHILE, BACK ON THE FARM

Meanwhile, back on the farm, Jørgen Tranberg, small farmer and quiet revolutionary, led me down from the summit of his wind turbine and back across the muck to his farmhouse. He wanted to show me the last of his crops, the one we couldn't see from atop the tower. We went into a small room off his kitchen and he booted up the computer on the table. A few clicks later, we were viewing real-time data from a turbine three and a half kilometres offshore in the Kattegat—a power plant of which he's part-owner. Work overalls and big calloused hands aside, Tranberg looked at ease at the computer as he surveyed his farm's yield. He clicked through to check this or that stat on current or daily or monthly output with the same matter-of-fact directness he brought to reaching underneath to test the fullness of a cow's udder. The integration was seamless: both cows and turbines were important producers on his prosperous farm, so he'd come to know both intimately.

I left just before dusk and pedalled my rented bicycle to Ballen, the little seaside village up the road from Tranberg's farm. I bought a Tuborg, found a seat at a picnic table by the harbour, and drank my beer watching the light fade over the Kattegat.

There are any number of comfortable places to see a sunset in this world, but the harbour at Ballen on a cold October evening was one of the most unexpected. The wind blew a frigid, stinging drizzle against my face. The grey sky faded fast into black. In fits and starts, the lights of the village came on, gold and orange and the strobing blue of a TV or two against the encroaching dark. I felt ecstatic in the warm embrace of it all.

There's an especially alluring quality to a brightly lit house on a cold night, a radiating glow of comfort, heavy with the promise of fires in stone hearths and soft, thick blankets; as a Canadian, I've been seduced by more than my share. But the lights of Ballen through the rain of an autumn night exuded a warmth all their own, something wholly new: the heat of inspiration, a perfect contentment that came from the knowledge that they could burn this way as long as there was wind to blow across this green island. For somewhere not too far off in the grey-black gloom of the Kattegat, I knew—Jørgen Tranberg had just shown me—blades were spinning. Generating the energy that lit Ballen's cozy homes, and harming nothing in return. Sowing the seeds of a quiet revolution. Marking the first indelible X on the map of a geography of hope.

TWO

THE RENEWABLE ENERGY ARCHIPELAGO

[sustainable power]

WORLD ENOUGH & TIME

On January 31, 2002, an enormous sheet of thick Antarctic ice called
the Larsen B ice shelf, riven with meltwater cracks caused by years of
abnormally warm weather, began to collapse. For thirty-five days it
crumbled into the ocean in great chunks. The scale of it was almost
unimaginable. By the time it was over, a vast field of polar ice measuring 3,250 square kilometres in area was gone. Before its collapse,
this piece of the Larsen B ice shelf could've carried twenty-eight
islands the size of Samsø on its back with room to spare.

There is a kind of vertigo, endemic to the Anthropocene Era, that
results from events of this scale. In a few traumatic hours, Hurricane
Katrina created a homeless population in southern Louisiana that
eclipsed the population of Samsø by a factor far greater than the
Larsen B dwarfed its size. Every six months or so, China brings as
many new coal-fired 1,000-megawatt power plants online as there are
wind turbines on and around Samsø. The fossil fuel boom in my
hometown of Calgary draws five or six Samsøs' worth of new residents each year. I could assemble phantasmagorically disproportion-
ate comparisons like this a thousand times over, and in each case it'd
point to the same question: What the hell difference does it make to

the price of tea in coal-clouded China that some little sandbar in Denmark doesn't use oil and gas to heat and light itself anymore?

We can allow the hope embodied by Samsø's transformation to founder against these craggy truths, or we can steer nimbly around them and soldier on. Even if it's not the first step in the thousand-mile journey prophesied by old Confucius, it could be instead the first of a thousand journeys. There is nothing unique about what's happened on Samsø except in the will to make it happen—in the concentration of effort and the assembly of tools, and in the steadfast, systemic approach to putting them to sustainable use. There are as many Samsøs as there are communities willing to build them.

"Humanity already possesses the fundamental scientific, technical, and industrial know-how to solve the carbon and climate problem for the next half-century. A portfolio of technologies now exists to meet the world's energy needs over the next 50 years and limit atmospheric CO_2 to a trajectory that avoids a doubling of the preindustrial concentration." This is from a study in the August 13, 2004, issue of the journal *Science* by Stephen Pacala and Robert Socolow, co-directors of Princeton University's Carbon Mitigation Initiative, and it bears repeating: *Humanity already possesses the know-how to solve the carbon and climate problem.* We have the tools. The sociopolitical paralysis that has characterized most of the world's response to climate change was not born of a paucity of options but of a tragic failure of will. Solutions exist, not just for a few blessed enclaves but for the entire planet.

Against the seeming insignificance of a single island in the Danish sea, Pacala and Socolow introduce fifteen "stabilization wedges." Fifteen tricks and tools—two million more wind turbines, enough photovoltaic (PV) panels to carpet the entire Hawaiian archipelago and all of French Polynesia to boot, a doubling in the fuel efficiency of two billion of the world's automobiles, and a dozen other measures—each of which would avoid the emission of a billion tonnes of CO_2 by 2054. The implementation of any seven of these, give or take, would likely stabilize the level of CO_2 in the earth's atmosphere at around 500 ppm—"a concentration," Pacala and Socolow explain, "that would prevent most damaging climate change."

The scale of such a project might seem almost impossibly daunting. How to build a PV array the size of Hawaii? And where? Who would agree to host such a monstrosity? Who would construct it? Who would maintain it? Who would *fund* it? Who could even conceive of such a thing? Break each of these stabilization wedges down into a few thousand parts, though—each the size, let's say, of a farmer's field in Samsø—and the problem begins to take on a human scale. We don't need to actually pave over the Hawaiian islands with PV panels, we just need enough rooftops and empty fields covered in them to equal about 134 one-millionths of the earth's dry surface: 0.0134 percent. It's estimated that paved roads and parking lots cover about 1.6 percent of the United States—more than a hundred times the proportion that would need to be solar panelled to make up America's part of the wedge. Pacala and Socolow's solutions, then, are well within the range of conceivable human endeavour.

In fact, they're no more daunting in scale than some of the monuments we've built for no good reason other than human conceit. There are two eighty-eight-storey towers standing side by side in downtown Kuala Lumpur, Malaysia, simply because we're capable of building such wonders. (They take their name, Petronas, from the state oil company.) There's a 39,000-tonne mass of steel 600 metres tall standing in the middle of the Gulf of Mexico, 210 kilometres southeast of New Orleans, mainly because we like to drive cars. (It's called Petronius, after the field of oil and natural gas beneath the seabed it's moored in.) And when it comes to stabilization wedges, there's an enormous added incentive: we're talking about constructing colossal monuments not because we can but *because we have no other choice.*

Well, one other choice.

"Is humanity suicidal?" asked the renowned biologist E.O. Wilson in his 1993 essay of that title. "Is the drive to environmental conquest and self-propagation embedded so deeply in our genes as to be unstoppable?" Wilson's short answer was no. "We are smart enough and have time enough to avoid an environmental catastrophe of civilization-threatening dimensions. But the technical problems are sufficiently formidable to require a redirection of much of science and technology, and the ethical issues are so basic as to force a reconsideration of our self-image as a species." Assessing the same question a decade later, the Canadian historian Ronald Wright concurred. "The most compelling reason for reforming our system is that the system is in no one's interest," Wright wrote in *A Short History of Progress.* "It is a suicide machine." Comparing us to Easter Islanders sizing up the last stand of trees on the island, he saw an urgency that had grown significantly more intense since Wilson's prognosis. "Now," Wright concluded, "is our last chance to get the future right."

It's long past time, in other words, to get on with building PV arrays—enough to carpet Hawaii. And to get on with much else besides. Fortunately, we're not starting from scratch.

THE RENEWABLE ENERGY ARCHIPELAGO

The Hawaiian island chain formed over a volcanic hot spot far beneath the earth's surface. At irregular intervals over the past forty-four million years, the hot spot has thrown up volcanoes in great tectonic belches, forming an archipelago of 132 islands, which are merely the highest peaks of a vast undersea mountain range. The origins of the Renewable Energy Archipelago are less fixed. The sun, of course, has been providing life on earth with energy—*all* its energy—for as long as there's been an earth, and people have basked in the benefits of biomass and geothermal energy since our ancestors first lit fires and waded into hot springs, and there have been windmills for well over a thousand years and sailboats for much longer than that. The archipelago, however, consists primarily of places where this energy is converted into power—heat and light, BTUs and alternating current by the kilowatt hour—and it's both plausible and symbolically tidy to trace its origins to Denmark. Specifically to the *folkehøjskole* in the town of Askov, where in 1891 a meteorologist and teacher named Poul la Cour pioneered the use of windmills for electricity generation. He used the juice for electrolysis to produce hydrogen gas, which he burned to keep the school's lamps alight. La Cour went on to found the Society of Wind Electricians and the *Journal of Wind Electricity,* and by 1918 there were 120 local utility companies in Denmark using wind turbines to generate electricity.

For much of the twentieth century, however, renewable energy remained an eccentric footnote to the golden age of oil (and, later, split atoms). Then came the energy crises of the 1970s—the first serious sign of vulnerability in the majestic reign of fossil fuels. OPEC's dramatic displays of its stranglehold on global oil supplies sent prices skyrocketing, induced record-setting inflation rates, and set governments and research labs throughout the industrial West on a half-cocked scramble for "alternative" energy sources. Think of this as the first great eruption from the hot spot that would in time produce the Renewable Energy Archipelago. But once the crisis had passed and the price of oil had dropped back to less than ten bucks a barrel by the mid-1980s, the alternatives receded again into the sea. I suspect I was like many North American children of the eighties in that I saw my first modern wind turbines as atmospheric set dressing in Hollywood movies. As far as I knew, those vast fields of rotating blades in the desert—some of the world's first wind farms—were, like sushi lunch boxes and Valley Girls, strictly a California thing.

In time, renewable energy would prove to be more than a fad. In fits and starts, the technological advances kickstarted by OPEC's threats found enduring, escalating momentum. Costs plummeted and fringe businesses bloomed into mainstream ones.* A scattered assortment of pilot projects and R&D experiments and cottage industries became something more, a permanent feature of the landscape. One now substantial enough, it turns out, to facilitate island hopping on a global scale.

ISLAND HOPPING (I): AMONG THE PIONEERS

In a remote village in northwestern Thailand, I found hut-scale solar arrays mounted on poles in unconscious imitation of the bamboo stilts upon which the huts stood, and I found as well a small run-of-river hydroelectric project, a marvellously simple system that feeds off the local stream's flow instead of damming it behind concrete. I arrived in the south of India in the midst of a boom in solar water heaters. I wasn't in Taos, New Mexico, for the sun, but while I was there, I listened to a radio station whose transmitter got its juice from a 2,500-square-foot bank of solar panels. I saw wind turbines in farmers' fields north of Hamburg, Germany, on the coast of Scotland, overlooking an achingly pretty harbour on the Thai isle of Phuket. I stayed

---

* To quantify that: the cost of a kilowatt hour of wind energy today is one-tenth what it was in 1980, the cost of a kilowatt hour from a PV cell is about one-fifth its eighties-era price, and both industries have been seeing annual growth rates of 20 percent plus for years now. This during a period when what we regarded as a *cheap* price for oil has at least doubled in dollar value.

in rooms lit by the wind, took showers in water heated by the sun, visited offices cooled by the rain. I came to many of these islets and atolls for reasons that had little to do with power generation, but at each stop I'd find signs that I'd arrived in another place born of the same volcanic eruption that had produced sustainable Samsø.

The fall of 2006 was a time of particularly robust growth for this archipelago, with record-setting agglomerations of renewable energy coming together amid the cutting of ceremonial ribbon seemingly every other week, even as new announcements from other corners of the globe promised to eclipse them the following year or the one after that. In September, the world's largest PV array—1,400 auto-tilting, auto-rotating, maximum-efficiency modules with an output of 12 megawatts, enough power for about 3,500 average German homes—went into operation amid functioning farmers' fields in Bavaria. This stole the biggest-in-the-world crown from a 10-megawatt solar plant in another Bavarian clearing, which had been up and running only since April, when it had usurped the throne from a 5-megawatt array in the north of Germany. This last, installed near Leipzig in the former East Germany, maintains the distinction of having been built on 20 hectares of rehabilitated land that had been contaminated by a Soviet-era lignite mine—quite literally on the ruins of the fossil fuel economy. October saw the inauguration of the final phase of the Horse Hollow Wind Energy Center, making it the largest wind farm on the planet: 421 turbines in all, spread out over 47,000 acres (19,000 hectares) of central Texas plain and cranking out 735 megawatts of electricity. The biggest offshore wind farm, meanwhile, is the 160-megawatt Horns Rev facility off the west coast of Denmark, which has been up and running since 2002.

Of course, we've come to expect green-energy leadership from the Continent, and the boast has always been that everything's bigger in Texas; the Renewable Energy Archipelago can offer up some far more unexpected sights. There are, for example, at least 150,000 households in Kenya powered by small-scale PV systems—products of a nationwide rural electrification program dating to the early 1970s, which, starting in the mid-1990s, moved to solar energy after years of sluggish progress by grid-based, carbon-burning means. The same number—150,000 households—is the target of a more recent solar-energy push in rural Morocco. (The tally of solar-powered

Moroccan homes as of 2006 was about 120,000.) Morocco plans to draw 10 percent of its power from renewable sources by 2010, with wind turbines as the largest contributor. Already there are ninety turbines producing energy in the Rif highlands, a region heretofore best known as one of the global powerhouses of hashish production.

So far, so good, but analysis of global energy issues invariably devolves to talk of China and India—the global village's toxic twins, a pair of behemoths in the midst of a coal-fired industrial boom. They form two great dark clouds on the horizon, ready to overshadow any real progress on climate change. Here, however, is a far less famous fact about China and India: both are among the world's fastest-growing markets for wind energy. Turbine installations were up 48 percent in India and 65 percent in China in 2005, and a significant portion of those new turbines were put up not by Continental experts toting European gizmos but by an Indian-born company called Suzlon Energy. It was Suzlon, for example, that built the massive 300-turbine Khori wind farm near Mumbai—"a subject of national pride," as the *New York Times* noted. Suzlon, which does the vast majority of its business outside India, overtook mighty Siemens of Germany in 2005 to become the fifth-largest wind turbine manufacturer in the world. (It wasn't even on the Top Ten list three years earlier.) As for China, it recently became one of the fastest-growing renewable energy markets on the planet, with the announcement of its intent to draw 15 percent of its electricity from green sources by 2020.

And there's much more to the archipelago than just PV panels and wind turbines. The frigid depths of Lake Ontario, for example, have been harnessed as one of the more surprising and innovative sustainable energy sources. Three intake pipes, each more than 5 kilometres long, run below the surface of Lake Ontario to its northern shore, carrying drinking water to the city of Toronto. The water, drawn from a depth of 83 metres, arrives extremely cold—about 4°C, far too cold for drinking. So Enwave, a utility company partly owned by the city, built an industrial-scale heat-exchange facility on the edge of downtown Toronto, where the water's chill is transferred to a vast network of cooling pipes, to provide air conditioning to the city's office towers. As of the blistering hot summer of 2006, this elaborate apparatus—the "Deep Lake Water Cooling

System" by official designation—was providing all the air conditioning for forty-six buildings, including numerous bank towers, the head office and flagship store of the storied Hudson's Bay Company, and the Air Canada Centre (home of the beloved Toronto Maple Leafs). Along the way, it was saving the city about 79,000 tonnes of CO_2 emissions per year and saving the Hudson's Bay Company, for instance, about $400,000 per year in energy bills.

The hidden power of large bodies of water plays a central role in another first-of-its-kind system on the Scottish island of Islay, where since 2000 the world's first commercial-scale, grid-connected wave-power plant has been turning the relentless momentum of the ocean's waves into electricity. The Islay plant, a modest 500-kilowatt facility built by a Siemens subsidiary called Wavegen, will soon be dwarfed by a gargantuan tidal-power plant in Ansan City, South Korea, which will turn the rising and falling tides of Sihwa Lake into enough electricity for all of the city's half-million residents once it's up and running in 2009.

The rushing flow of rivers, meanwhile, has been a reliable source of power for centuries, but it's finding a new and less ecologically disruptive life in the form of small-scale run-of-river hydroelectric plants. There are already dozens of these in operation in one of the planet's most bountiful sources of hydro power: the mountainous wilds of British Columbia. B.C.'s existing run-of-river power plants are all less than 50 megawatts in size, and a 2002 study by BC Hydro (the provincial hydroelectric company) estimated that 2,450 megawatts of potential energy—as much as 20 percent of BC Hydro's total current output—could be generated this way.

Et cetera, et cetera, as we move on to *terra firma.* The Philippines is the world's second-largest producer of geothermal energy: 16 percent of the country's total energy production (and 27 percent of its electricity) comes from using the earth's stored subterranean heat to produce steam, which in turn spins power-generating turbines. Brazil, meanwhile, is a global pacesetter in the production and use of ethanol, a motor-vehicle fuel made from its millions of cultivated acres of sugar cane. This is the result of an initiative that surely seemed quixotic (if not flat-out nuts) when it got going during the OPEC panic, but now looks prescient: ethanol has taken over 40 percent of the market formerly monopolized by gasoline. The Brazilian government estimates that its oil economy reached "equilibrium"—its ethanol exports equal to its crude imports—in 2006. What's more, most of Brazil's ethanol production plants are biomass-powered: they use the waste pulp from pressed sugar cane to fuel the refineries themselves.

Add up these widely dispersed pieces—wind turbines popping up like paleolithically proportioned weeds on the Gaspé Peninsula in Quebec and the coast of Japan, the solar-panelled roofs of supermarkets in Bangkok and parking garages in southern Germany, the tidal power of France and the geothermal energy of Iceland—tally it all up, and renewables account for 2.7 percent of global primary energy production. Nothing like a majority, maybe, but with double-digit growth—24 percent for wind, 45 percent for photovoltaics and 20 percent for biofuels in 2005 (while oil consumption, for example, grew by 1.3 percent)—and new investment at a rate of $30 billion per year, it's something like a phenomenon.

Facts and figures, though, tell an antiseptic version of the Renewable Energy Archipelago's creation myth. The fables are far more fascinating—far more enviable, far likelier to entice a world of imitators—from more intimate points of view. Here's one: the view out the twenty-third-floor window of an office tower in an English industrial city that was on the verge of collapse not long ago, where a story of redemption more than 160 years in the making has finally found its triumphant final act.

The office tower is called the CIS Tower, and the view is of its service column, the leg of the T-shaped building that houses elevator shafts and heating ducts. On a cool morning in November 2005, when I got a look at it, the view was more precisely of a tiling project nearing completion: a blue-black reflective skin of photovoltaic panels was crawling up the tower, cladding maybe twenty-one of its twenty-five storeys at that point. A month earlier, Prime Minister Tony Blair had stopped by briefly to switch on the power. The job would be done by May 2006 and the building reborn under a new moniker: the "Solar Tower," a refurbished icon on Manchester's skyline. It was the United Kingdom's largest solar installation, more than seven thousand PV panels specially manufactured by Sharp Electronics and installed by a London company called Solarcentury (founded, not incidentally, by Jeremy Leggett, formerly Greenpeace

UK's chief scientist and one of the country's most prominent climate change activists, now become one of its most tenacious renewable-energy entrepreneurs).

Up and running, the Solar Tower array is simply a 391-kilowatt power plant—enough energy, as the brochure duly notes, for sixty-one three-bedroom English homes or nine million cups of English tea. Stripped to bare numbers like this, though, it sounds almost incidental—surely Mancunians put away that much tea in a week or so—and so I prefer to talk about what Manchester's tallest building looked like on that morning in November. It was all promise on the verge of fulfillment, an impossible dream come to life. Here, after all, was an office tower preparing to harness the *sun* as its power source in a city with weather so dreary the rest of the English feel justified in making fun of it. It was like a postmodern parody of the legendary English ballad "Scarborough Fair": an acre of land between sea and sand, a seamless cambric shirt, and a solar-powered tower in rainy northern England. *Not to worry about the first two, luv, but that dodgy solar scheme's pure bobbins.**

And it was possible, at that moment, to look out on those panelled walls and ponder something more than simply how much electricity they generated. To wonder instead at the twisting tale of *why* they were there, to trace a circuitous but nonetheless fairly explicit path from this improbable Solar Tower all the way back to the work of angry, idealistic craftsmen thrown into upheaval by the first great wave of the Industrial Revolution well over a century before.

The idealists in question were the Rochdale Pioneers, skilled weavers who lived in a town just outside Manchester in the first decades of the nineteenth century. Tossed out of work by the mechanization of the textile industry, the Pioneers looked upon a social order torn to shreds and tried to imagine a better way forward. The borough

---

* The Co-operative Insurance Society's own brochure describes its Solar Tower as "a talisman," and among its mystical charms is the ability to dispel myths—particularly the one about solar panels needing direct sunlight to produce electricity. Because they are fed not by heat but by light, modern PV panels can generate power even in perpetually cloudy locales such as northern England. "Put another way"—here in the words of the Solar Energy Industries Association fact sheet—"if you can find your way around outside, a solar panel could be working."

of Rochdale had been a quiet English burg before the first textile mill opened there in the late 1700s, but the population quickly exploded from 14,000 in 1801 to 68,000 by 1841. More than 90 percent of Rochdale's residents in those years were working class, and the turmoil of the industrial age's birth precipitated an endemic cycle of bread riots, protest marches and vicious recriminations; from 1808 onward, Rochdale was a "barracks town," home to a permanent military garrison charged with quelling the labour unrest. Out of this chaos emerged the Rochdale Pioneers, out-of-work weavers inspired by the rhetoric of a Welsh social reformer by the name of Robert Owen. Outraged by the extortionate prices workers had to pay for inferior goods at company-owned "truck shops," the Pioneers established the town's first co-operative society and opened a co-op store in 1844.

The Rochdale Equitable Pioneers' Society sold its members pure, unadulterated goods—coffee undiluted by mud, cheese free of chalk—at fair prices. It also produced a founding document that codified the core principles of England's nascent co-operative movement: steadfast commitments to democracy, education, fair trade and political and religious neutrality that continue to govern co-operative societies to this day. The goal of the Rochdale Pioneers was radical, but they rejected violent revolution, calling instead for the establishment of "a self-supporting home-colony of united interests," a microcosmic version of Robert Owen's envisioned "Co-operative Commonwealth"—a parallel universe, more or less. The Rochdale home-colony never materialized, but over the next couple of decades, the society did spawn new institutions catering to the broader co-op movement: a "Loan and Deposit Department" to meet the banking needs of its members, and an insurance company to offer fire insurance to co-op societies. The former would eventually become the Co-operative Bank, and the latter became the Co-operative Insurance Society, CIS.

In 1962, CIS moved into a brand-new twenty-five-storey office spire in Manchester, a simple modernist cube built by the English firm Burnett, Tait & Partners. The English architects took a recent visit to an archetypal Skidmore, Owings & Merrill tower in Chicago as their primary inspiration, but they also decided to adorn the windowless service tower of the building in shimmering Mediterranean-style mosaic tiles. Unfortunately, the tiles proved ill-suited to the harsh climate of northern England: they tarnished quickly and started to fall off within a year of completion. As Manchester's industrial economy rotted away in the following years, it had to be hard not to see the tower and its dingy, crumbling façade as a symbol of the decaying city at its feet. In time, though, Manchester found a new life: its derelict canalside warehouses birthed a global renaissance in music and dance that came to be known as rave, one of its football clubs famously became the invincible powerhouse of the new, glammed-up Premiership of the 1990s, and its beleaguered economy found a sturdier post-industrial footing. CIS finally mated with the Co-operative Bank to form a unified front called Co-operative Financial Services (CFS), and one of its first undertakings was to figure out what to do about those damn mosaic tiles peeling off the service tower of its head office.

Which brings us to the first years of the new century and a redemptive view from the twenty-third floor of the flawed tower, where 160 years of history foreshorten to fit the dimensions of an awkward epic ballad. It goes like this: the twice-born CFS, obliged as per ancient Rochdale Pioneer writ to serve the democratic will of its members, sets up one of the world's most progressive sustainability reporting regimes. As part of this commitment, it goes about procuring renewable energy for its offices and branches, but with those utopian weavers peering over its shoulders, it can't abide half-measures. So CFS enters into an exclusive eight-year agreement with a wind-energy company, which encourages that company to build six new wind turbines across the way in Lincolnshire. And as well— verily—the roof of CFS's smaller Manchester office block is encrusted with nineteen micro wind turbines like a parodic jester's crown made of overgrown pinwheels. And then the true crowning glory: CFS scrapes off the last of those graceless mosaic tiles and turns its headquarters into a sun temple. Aye, the Manchester Solar Tower: a redeemer dressed in reflective black PV, born of the social dislocations of the industrial age's founding to point the way to salvation from the ecological turmoil of its twilight.

Are you going to Scarborough Fair / parsley, sage, rosemary and thyme? On an acre of land between the salt water and the sea sand, there stands an office tower clad in solar panels under a grey English sky. On the horizon, another prodigious acre, and another somewhere beyond that. An archipelago. You see?

This archipelago may be, at present, mostly a collection of tiny, sparsely populated islands next to the vast continents of fossil fuel, but these islands are the places where all the serious volcanic activity is occurring. They are growing faster, multiplying far more prolifically, surfacing in preposterous places. The revolutionary momentum is all theirs. They lack only for a sort of realignment of tectonic plates in the global consciousness, a great continent-building force called human exuberance.

RATIONAL EXUBERANCE (I): THE WORLDWIDE DIGITAL-SPEED REVOLUTIONARY MODEL

Alan Greenspan, chairman of the Federal Reserve Board of the United States from 1987 to 2006, is credited with coining the phrase "irrational exuberance." He first employed it in a December 1996 speech to a black-tie Washington crowd in which he voiced his concern over "unduly escalated asset values" on the stock markets of the world. Greenspan meant the term to be a warning, and it was understood as one: within twenty-four hours, markets from Tokyo to New York to London experienced serious declines. These setbacks were not just short-lived but apparently the stock market equivalent of an ironic shrug: within weeks, the global financial sector returned with renewed vigour to the delirious orgy of irrational exuberance that had given Greenspan pause in the first place. This was the one that began in August 1995 with the soon-to-be-legendary Netscape IPO—the initial public offering of shares in the company that developed the internet's first mass-market graphical browser—and continued throughout the 1990s in a giddy haze of skyrocketing stock prices for (and ever more grandiose revolutionary pronouncements from) anything and anyone associated with the business of capitalizing on the internet and the dramatic reconfiguration of global telecommunications it brought about.

"One of the greatest economic miracles in human history"—that's how Michael Lewis described the internet boom in *The New New Thing*, his intimate portrait of Netscape founder Jim Clark and the irrational exuberance his invention inspired. It was a time, Lewis wrote, when "a lot of the old rules of capitalism were suspended," a time when the global corporate media and telecom giants poured billions of dollars into dead-end ventures just to try to keep up with the likes of Jim Clark, and the general public, abandoning decades of conventional stock market wisdom, embarked upon "a flying leap into the future."

None of this was preordained, of course, and it was far from inevitable. "Rapid technological change," Lewis argued, "threatens people who already have power, even when those people are technologists. . . . While promoting change, big established companies also wish for change to occur slowly enough that it does not overwhelm them." This is as true for the energy business as it was for telecommunications, and it's why, if it is to expand to continental size, the Renewable Energy Archipelago needs to harness at least as much propulsive enthusiasm as the internet boom did. Renewable energy may have revolutionary momentum on its side, but there is a formidable counterweight in the leaden inertia of a long-established, ridiculously rich and enormously powerful industrial order. The renewables industry attracted something like $30 billion in investments in 2005, but just a single oil-industry project in my backyard— the development of the oil-rich tar sands of northern Alberta—saw $10 billion in investment the same year. It seems unlikely that scientific data on the potential impacts of climate change will alone topple this order, unlikelier still that any one government's legislative élan can do the job. What's needed, instead, is an exuberance epidemic on a scale the world's never seen.

It's a daunting task, to be sure, but at least sustainability's champions, led by the renewable-energy industries, have a few critical advantages over the digital-communications revolutionaries. For one thing, most of the newfangled, high-tech toys they play with are already up and running and have demonstrated their usefulness, and the technologies they aspire to replace have widely acknowledged, potentially fatal flaws. What's more, people already want sustainability, are in some markets *demanding* it at almost any cost. And then there's the most important advantage: although dotcom-style irrational exuberance is sorely needed to overcome the catastrophic momentum of the current socioeconomic order, the destination is actually a *more* rational place—that less toxic existence crucial to humanity's survival. The irrational exuberance of the dotcom boom was destined to lead to a bust because it fuelled outsized investment in arbitrary things that possessed extremely marginal utility; the sustainability boom represents an epidemic of *rational* exuberance, a critical reinvestment in the basic essentials of life. A stable, healthy climate, in particular, is the foundation on which all other universal needs are built.

By way of instructive contrast, recall the state of telecommunications technology circa 1992. The internet, born of several decades of high-level, government-funded R&D (first at NASA, then at the Pentagon) and further honed by academics and other elite groups, was a dry, static medium for exchanging scientific data and text files, with a smattering of tech-obsessed geeks playing around with it to add a little colour. Cellular phones were strictly for the most frequently flying of business travellers, the ultra-rich, and a separate smattering of tech-obsessed gearheads. Email accounts were the exclusive domain of certain scientific and academic elites, there were no graphical internet browsers, and the World Wide Web was a year away from worldwide availability. Never mind necessity: the baseline *value* of this stuff was still an open question in all but a handful of rarefied circles. And the notion that average folks would use the internet daily, sometimes from the cellphones they carried in their pockets, was flat-out nonsense as far as most people were concerned.

Barely a decade later, the daily users of web browsers and cellphones number in the hundreds of millions, maybe even the billions. I've sent email from the Himalayas, I've surfed the web in a half-dozen airport departure lounges, and I bought my cellphone from a store that sold little else in a stereotypical suburban shopping mall. And already there's nothing all that remarkable about any of this.

The only truly remarkable thing: I couldn't have imagined any of it in 1992. Almost none of us could have, nor did we demand it in any sort of consumer-market sense. The telecommunications revolution occurred only because it inspired the most truly awesome bout of irrational exuberance in recent history. It happened because of the tenaciousness and gall of world-beaters like Clark and his acolytes and imitators at a hundred or a thousand other dotcoms. It happened because there were starry-eyed, delirious evangelists on every other street corner—or at least every other cable-news broadcast— proclaiming the internet the most important technological advance since the capture of fire, and because the mass media gave the voices of those evangelists global reach. It happened because some of the best minds of our time were attracted by those voices, because they worked overtime, round-the-clock, feverishly, on the task of making it happen. And it happened because they were propelled by a revolutionary model, radically decentralized in both its technological and organizational structure, that proved to be faster, easier, flat-out *better* than the lumbering old-guard telecommunications companies at providing useful communications tools.

It happened because a company you may have heard of—Boo.com—was permitted to spend $160 million to keep a website up and running for less than a year and sell almost none of the hip clothing it was supposed to sell, and because a company you probably haven't heard of—Openwave Systems Inc.—has spent more than $2.7 billion in the past five years developing some of the software that allows your cellphone to access the internet. And because neither company stands out particularly amid the profligate spending and incessant business activity that has brought this formerly fringe medium to every shopping mall and airport departure lounge in the free world. In fact, there were so many stories like this during the internet boom that Boo.com's monumental flame-out ranked only sixth on a nostalgic list of the ten biggest flops of the dotcom age on the tech-news site CNET.com, behind such money-hemorrhaging machines as Webvan (groceries *over the internet!*), Pets.com (pet food *over the internet!*) and Kozmo.com (other-stuff-you-currently-buy-at-any-ole-store *over the internet!*). This was the nature of the wave, and though it could look absurd on its dotcom surface, it crashed ashore carrying all manner of magnificent technological pearls: dirt-cheap, instantaneous, wireless communication of near-global reach; the muckraking citizen journalism of the blogosphere; the spread of telecommuting; the flat-out knowledge-dissemination miracle of Google. And it's reasonable to assume that without the big, dumb wave, the useful stuff would have remained at the bottom of the sea.

So then: Stop for a minute. Hit the END button on your cellphone, close the three windows currently open on your web browser, wrap up that Instant Messenger conversation and hold off on that text message you were just about to start typing on your keypad. Stop. Think of your life in 1992. How you found information, who you shared it with, how long it took to do so. Think of hunting for a pay phone, leaving word with the restaurant's hostess to let your friends know you were running late, hoping they got the message. Think of writing a letter, putting it in an envelope, mailing it and waiting for a reply. Think of the library, of card catalogues, of cranking your way through a dozen spools of microfilm looking for that quote, that bit of trivia, that slice of nostalgia. Think of all the stuff—obscure hobbies, half-formed thoughts, weird bits of pop-culture esoterica—that simply vanished, never to be heard from again. Think of all that went into transforming that world into this one.

Now just imagine all that reckless energy pointed in the direction of a real problem.

ISLAND HOPPING (II): AMONG THE DANES

When you travel the byways of the Renewable Energy Archipelago, it sometimes seems like all roads lead to Denmark. In the case of wind power, the appearance approximates reality. Suzlon, the Indian-born wunderkind of the wind-energy industry, moved its headquarters to the Danish city of Århus in 2004. When Siemens, the German industrial giant, decided to get into the wind-power game, it simply bought Denmark's second-largest turbine manufacturer. When you fly into Copenhagen, there's a good chance you'll follow a flight path from the north that takes you over the harbour and the inner city before reaching the airport farther south, and when the weather's clear the first landmark you'll see—before the Danish royal palaces, before the primary-coloured façades of the old port, before Tivoli's grand Ferris wheel—is a broad arc of wind turbines standing in the choppy waters of the Øresund a few kilometres west of the city's waterfront. This is Middelgrunden, one of the world's oldest offshore wind farms, and it's an appropriate gateway for a country in which wind energy is a €3-billion industry employing more than twenty thousand people. Roughly half of the wind turbines in use around the world were manufactured in Denmark, and 492 of the 530 megawatts of current global offshore wind-farming capacity are courtesy of products and projects of Danish origin. Nationwide, there are about 5,500 turbines spinning in the breeze, something like 3,100 megawatts of power-generating capacity, and by these means does Denmark produce one-fifth of its electricity. And provide something like a window on one potential global future: if a renewable-energy boom of similar magnitude to the one that revolutionized telecommunications does occur, the result might be a world that looks a little more like Denmark.

Here is a world of deep but subtle changes, few of them as highly visible as those ubiquitous windmills, but many of them just as significant. Here is a prosperous place, forward-looking but respectful of the value of tradition. Here, moreover, is a place where renewable energy is simply one facet of a broader shift to a more sustainable society, and where that transformation, though revolutionary in impact, has been measured and orderly in implementation. There is some historic precedent for this: the Reformation, for example, wellspring of a century of bloodletting beyond its borders, occurred in Denmark "with a degree of quiet moderation and common sense not experienced anywhere else in Europe," wrote Palle Lauring in *A History of Denmark.* "Revolutions in Denmark have a habit of taking place in their own special way."

So it's gone with the first stages of Denmark's sustainability revolution. Thirty percent of Copenhagen's workforce commutes by bicycle, so there are not just designated bike lanes but also dedicated *traffic signals* for bicycles at major intersections. There are multiple rows of bike racks at subway stations, and at major transit hubs small platoons of free bikes wait for anyone with a 20-kroner coin to pop in the lock as a deposit. You can find automated bottle-return kiosks outside grocery stores in even the smallest and least trafficked villages. I saw my first waterless urinal in the restroom at the Brundby Rock Hotel in Samsø, and I saw a dozen others in the weeks that followed.* Fossil fuels still fire most of Denmark's power plants, but the majority of those, including twelve of the fourteen largest, employ combined heat and power (CHP) schemes, wherein the plant's waste heat is used to heat nearby houses and offices. Fifty-nine percent of Danish homes are warmed by district heating—one big high-efficiency furnace instead of thousands of individual ones—and 82 percent of that heat is waste from electricity production. Which is to say that roughly half of the houses in Denmark are heated by an energy supply that, in the rest of the

---

* The waterless urinal—another talisman of the Sustainable Age—was the one that, maybe more than any other, had me leaning in extra close to examine its miraculous construction. I won't bother with the technical explanation, but the amazing thing is that every drop drains somehow—vanishes—and it *simply doesn't stink.* There isn't even the sickly sweet stench of urinal cake.

world, simply dissipates into the skies in noxious clouds. And then there are all those wind turbines hither and yon—75 percent of them privately owned, with about 100,000 Danes individually or co-operatively invested. A hundred thousand power-plant owners in a nation of 5.4 million.

Here is the nucleus of a radically decentralized energy regime, locally controlled and co-operatively managed. Here's a whole society embracing the challenge of climate change not with fear and acrimony but with resolve and even delight. And if that challenge can be beaten only by an epidemic of rational exuberance, then here, in Denmark, is evidence of that outbreak. Indeed just a few hundred kilometres south of Samsø is another Danish isle rendered so rationally exuberant by its *loss* in the contest Samsø won that it's carrying on as if it had won too.

Aerø, like Samsø, is another island far off the Danish main drag. And Aerø, like Samsø, is a predominantly agricultural island, with a small population of about 7,200 that's been getting smaller for decades. Aside from all the farms, there is Marstal, the largest town and a shipbuilding centre, and Aerøskøbing, the administrative hub of the island—a collection of rambling cobblestone lanes and multi-coloured half-timbered eighteenth-century cottages so ridiculously fairy-tale charming in vibe it could be used to illustrate a Hans Christian Andersen anthology.

Notwithstanding these charms, Aerø's economy was stagnant until renewable energy came ashore. Which landfall occurred in Aerø, it turns out, more than a decade before the Renewable Energy Island contest. Way back in 1984, eleven turbines—Denmark's first modern-era wind farm—went up on a windswept stretch of Aerø's northeastern headland. They were co-operatively owned, born of the pioneering labours of a ragtag local citizens' group. This wasn't quite a world first—California, for example, had built several industrial-sized wind farms in the late 1970s—but because Denmark's commitment to renewables never wavered, and because it can plausibly lay claim to the title of the world's most advanced green-energy regime, it's not overstating the case to say that unknown, unassuming Aerø was the birthplace of the green boom.

"A smith, a farmer, a couple of teachers, a bank manager, and so on"—this is how the instigators of this revolution are described in the backgrounder I was given at VE-Organisation Aerø, the island's renewable-energy office. A vigilante troop of mild-mannered folks— "so-called ordinary people," quoth the backgrounder. "So-called," indeed: I'd barely given the backgrounder a once-over before the director of said renewable-energy office whisked me off to meet one of the most prominent members of that troop, who turned out to be one of the least ordinary people I'd meet in all my travels.

Jørgen Bjørgren lives on a farm on Aerø's northeastern tip, a hilly patch of tall grass and turned earth not far from the site of Denmark's first wind farm. The farmhouse is long and low and L-shaped, with a roof of thatch and whitewashed walls crawling with vines—a typical old-school Danish affair, in marked contrast to its eccentric proprietor. In the fields out back, seeds are indeed sown and crops duly reaped, but to call Bjørgren a farmer doesn't begin to describe his life's work or the singular existence he continues to lead.

At first glance, though, I'll admit there was plenty about Bjørgren that suited his pastoral *mise en scène:* the rubber boots and checked shirt, the trim white beard and elaborately etched complexion of a man who'd reached the far side of middle age after a life lived hard and well. Bjørgren launched into his introductory spiel as we marched out to his vegetable patch. He figured that a good way for me to get a sense of what he was all about, what he was up to on his farm, was to see his cauliflower plants, which he was particularly pleased with. With good cause: they were great mutant giants, sporting hypertrophic leaves like the fronds of rainforest ferns. They were also 100 percent organically grown. Later, he showed me photos of last year's crop: cauliflower heads the size of watermelons, loaded three each in crates built to hold a dozen.

As for the rest of it—the winding amusement-park ride of a life that led Bjørgren to grow gigantic cauliflower—I'll do my best to do it justice, though I found it hard to keep up. Bjørgren had been a pilot in the Danish air force, and then he'd flown helicopters for the oil business in the North Sea and North Africa. Then came an epiphany, a rebirth as an environmental journalist and then a cabinet minister's press agent. And then another reinvention—this time as a sort of green-minded Scandinavian Bob Dylan. A concert tour brought him to Aerø, which he fell head over heels for (and immortalized in "Hymne til Aerø," from the 2003 anthology *Det Graa Guld**). Reinvention again: as a tireless organizer of the grassroots groups that built the island's pioneering wind farm and founded the first Aerø Energy Office.

Tireless doesn't come close to an accurate summary: at one point, for example, Bjørgren mentioned that he'd recently licked throat cancer. Mentioned it in passing, the way most people would say they had a bit of a cold last week. In my disjointed notes, it's immediately after an explanation of how he salvaged one of Denmark's first modern windmills, a 250-kilowatt custom job he'd helped build over in Aerøskøbing back in 1980—"This should be in a museum," I've got him saying—and it's followed by a sentence fragment about how he's trying with "some other clever people" to revolutionize the biodiesel business in northern Europe. You see, I hope, how this Bjørgren gent is the walking, talking, mythmaking embodiment of irrational exuberance.

Bjørgren was, at any rate, a prime mover in the push toward sustainability on Aerø, which was far enough along by the time of the Danish government's Renewable Energy Island contest in the late 1990s that the idea made intuitive sense even to Aerø's conservative, aging population, and indeed seemed like such a natural fit that the island stuck to its plan even after Samsø won the official title. And so, lost contest notwithstanding, Aerø was well on its way to becoming Denmark's *second* Renewable Energy Island by the time I got there. Three brand-new, super-efficient 2-megawatt wind turbines had gone up to replace all but five of the ones that had been erected during the first initiative led by Bjørgren and his colleagues; all told, wind power was supplying about 60 percent of the island's electricity.

The other main thrust of Aerø's Renewable Energy Island scheme was a trio of solar-powered district heating plants, one outside each of Aerø's three largest towns, that had been built with the financial help of the Danish Energy Agency and the European Union over the previous decade and now provide between 85 and 95 percent of the heating needs in those towns. The biggest of these,

---

* That's *The Grey Gold* in English translation, and the album's pretty solid: twangy honky-tonk stuff, more *Blood on the Tracks*–era Dylan than *Freewheelin'*-era Dylan. It is, at any rate, definitely the best folk-rock album I've ever heard by a former Danish military officer.

outside the shipbuilding hub of Marstal, has a couple of particularly notable characteristics: it's Europe's largest solar heating plant, first of all, generating enough heat for nearly all of Marstal's 1,430 households, and—perhaps most significant, at least for our current purposes—it's an object lesson even more distinctive than my encounter with Jørgen Bjørgren in how the rational exuberance inspired by the sustainability boom differs from the irrational kind brought on by the telecom revolution.

The internet economy was driven by the quest for what Michael Lewis called "the new new thing"—a mad dash for the latest and most technically sophisticated, the shiniest and gee-whizziest. It was an inexact science, finding those new new things: after each leap forward, a thousand fancy ideas were pursued and millions of dollars spent in vain before someone found the *next* idea that would push the industry ahead again. In *The New New Thing,* Lewis detailed a particularly dramatic case in point: a massive project undertaken in the early 1990s by Jim Clark's first high-tech company, Silicon Graphics, to develop "the world's first interactive television." After eighteen months of work by some of the best minds in Silicon Valley and the expenditure of $300 million on this, "the most glamorous engineering project in the Valley," the result was a future-tense marvel that did what it was supposed to do—and never made it to the shelves of a single store. Clark himself, meanwhile, went off and started a new company devoted to producing the *actual* new new thing—the graphical internet browser—and ignited the dotcom boom that way.

But the sustainability boom, if its Aerø birthplace is any indication, might have more to do with finding the *rightest* thing: the simplest and most efficient solution, the one best suited to the local climate and culture. There might be more than one answer to any given problem, a number of technically satisfactory *right* ways to do the job, but the *rightest* thing is the one that does it most elegantly— and it might not be the most scientifically advanced. This is where the sustainability boom diverges most sharply from the dotcom approach: it celebrates efficiency, not pure technological achievement. And often as not, this includes at least a partial return to old ways, a resurrection and reworking of abandoned techniques, an embrace of intrinsically more earthbound and rational systems.

Not new gadgets, then, but new strategies. Or, to phrase it more precisely, hungry sheep instead of top-of-the-line lawnmowers.

Let me explain.

I encountered the sheep in question during my tour of Marstal's biggest-on-earth solar heating plant, which had been wowing me up to that point with its engineering prowess. The plant occupies a wide swath of land on a low rise overlooking the town; in aerial photos, it looks like Marstal has built a comically outsized hard-court tennis facility on its fringe. At ground level, that sea of blue-black turns out to be made up of densely arranged rows of solar thermal panels: industrial-sized units the size of garage doors in thirty-six arrow-straight lines a hundred metres long, 18,365 square metres of them in all. Next to the great field of panels lies a small white command centre packed with huge pipes and gaskets and a wall jammed with buttons and dials. It works like this: the sun heats a mix of water and glycol in the tubes beneath the dark surface of the panels, and the mixture is then pumped throughout the town as needed to warm the homes or stored at the site for future use. All very impressive, but aside from some of the materials and regulatory apparatus, the basic technology was over a century old.

The plant had been up and running since the mid-1990s, though it was much expanded and tweaked after the Renewable Energy Island contest amplified local enthusiasm for such projects. One of the only real hitches, it turned out, was what to do about the grass, which eventually grew so tall that it cast shadows on the solar collectors, reducing their efficiency. The obvious solution was to use industrial-sized riding lawnmowers, but they had trouble negotiating the tight alleys between the rows of panels.

The head of Aerø's renewable-energy organization was explaining all this to me as we walked alongside the banks of collectors. Pretty much on cue, the rightest answer came marching toward us in the form of an older man in blue work overalls, who was being followed by a small flock of mewling sheep, several dozen big white woolly animals pushing and nudging to be the first to nuzzle at his legs. He had a big canvas sack stuffed with apples in his arms, and every few steps he dumped another handful of them on the ground. The sheep, thus enticed, had followed him from the clearing above the main heat-storage facility, which doubled as their paddock.

Once the apples were gone, the sheep scattered under and around the panels, munching on grass. I couldn't help but notice that your average Danish sheep was about the same height as the bottom lip of an industrial-grade solar thermal panel. Just the right height—the *rightest* height, if you will—to feed most readily on grass just before it'd grown high enough to block the panels.

It was an almost absurdly elegant solution, and it made me so giddy I had trouble stopping myself from chuckling as my guide recited data and technical specs. The gravest crisis humanity has ever faced, and all it needs is a few solar panels and a flock of sheep. Of course! This was turning out to be one virulent strain of rational exuberance, all right, and I caught it bad from a flock of jostling, bleating sheep at the world's largest solar heating plant.

Marstal's grass-cutting solution also put me in mind of the last place I'd found myself stumbling over free-roaming livestock: in the narrow laneways of a small city in northern India, at the dawn of a previous epidemic.

RATIONAL EXUBERANCE (II): FROM ARCHIPELAGO TO SUBCONTINENT

From the summer of 1999 to the summer of 2000, my wife and I lived in Shimla, a small city in the foothills of the Himalayas in northern India. Shimla first rose to prominence during the long years of British rule—the Raj—in the nineteenth century, when it became a favoured spot for British administrators to build holiday cottages for their families as a refuge from Delhi during the hot season. Before long, the British decided to move the entire capital to Shimla when the brutal pre-monsoon heat of the Ganges plain grew too oppressive. Every April, a procession would climb slowly into the hills, first a parade of elephants and later a narrow-gauge train, weighted down with great stacks of the British Empire's files bundled in red tape (the origin of that universal metaphor for overwrought bureaucracy). After India gained its independence in 1947, this mountainous region eventually became its own state, Himachal Pradesh, and Shimla was named its capital.

When we arrived in 1999, Shimla had far outgrown the thin sliver of land along the top of the ridge that marked the original Raj settlement, spilling chaotically down both sides in a riot of shops, hotels and ramshackle homes, with rhesus monkeys and meandering goats and the occasional sacred cow fighting with the masses for space in the crowded bazaars. My wife and I rented a flat in a rambling complex of apartments owned by an extended Indian family. Thankfully, the place already had telephone service—rumour had it that it could take literally *years* to obtain a new phone line—but at the time Shimla had only two public-access internet sites, both of them laughably inept: there was a single unreliable connection in a small shop set up by the state government to train locals in basic computer skills, and there was another on the ground floor of the Indian Telephone & Telegraph (IT&T) building that was, in our experience, permanently offline. So one day we dutifully marched a couple of floors higher up in that IT&T building—a great brick temple of bureaucracy, one of the city's most prominent landmarks—to turn in our application for a home internet connection. In an office bereft of computers and stacked high with bound files, we were told it would take six weeks to be processed. Two months later, we were issued account information for a hopelessly unreliable and impossibly slow internet connection. (Often, we would input our email login information, click SEND, then go and have a cup of tea while we waited for the new messages to upload. I'm not exaggerating even a little bit.) It soon became apparent that most of the access time we'd bought had been stolen.

In those first chaotic years of the internet's arrival on the subcontinent, India was adapting to the new technology in the way that the received wisdom argued was inevitable for a developing country: by slowly, methodically retracing the steps of the West. The existing state-owned company—IT&T—expanded its monopoly on telecom services in Himachal Pradesh to include internet access. Data flowed up and down between the steep hills and the plain by the same handful of copper wires that provided the piss-poor, hard-to-come-by telephone service. Lousy reception, bureaucratic ineptitude, endemic corruption, even routine theft—all were simply translated from analog to digital. "After some time"—an intentionally imprecise Indian-English phrase beloved by the subcontinent's bureaucrats, meaning anywhere from half an hour to never in a million years—there would presumably be fibre-optic cable, the collapse of the monopoly, a dotcom boom and bust. And each stage would arrive in India in the same order it had played out in the West a few years before, like a series of sporting events on extra-long tape delay.

Discussion of India's role in climate change frequently assumes a similar fate for the development of its energy infrastructure. India—invariably paired with China, the two of them assumed to be the 800-pound-gorilla models for the developing world at large—will burn coal to drive its turbocharged industrial growth. It will damn near destroy its cities with smog, traffic and overcrowding. It will learn the tragic costs of all this in ten years, or in fifty, by which time there won't be much hope for the planet. There's ample data available already to feed this fear: India's CO_2 emissions skyrocketed by 61 percent from 1990 to 2001 (and China's by 111 percent during the same period), and industrially driven wealth creation is clearly a much higher priority than something as insignificant in the short term as emissions in a country with as much abject poverty as India has.

Here's something worth noting, though: India's existing energy infrastructure is, if anything, *worse* than its telecom infrastructure was in 1999. Rolling blackouts are a daily fact of life in many Indian cities, for example, and roughly half of its population is entirely off the grid. And so pay close attention to what happened next in the story of my encounter with India's homegrown internet boom, and understand just how quickly—and how decisively—a wave of human exuberance, if it's strong enough, can shift a society away from its expected course.

Right around the time my wife and I learned that someone was stealing our IT&T access time, our landlord informed us that the local computer repair duo he frequently contracted for such tasks as printing his Word documents for him had started selling a quicker, more reliable internet-access package. We invited them down to our flat post-haste. I don't remember their names, but one did all the talking while the other stood in silence a half-pace behind him wearing a bulky parka, tan in colour and multi-pocketed, which he left on even after he'd been invited inside. Once the Salesman had finished his pitch—they were a sort of two-man local subsidiary of Satyam Online, a new internet service provider (ISP) based in the far south of India, and they could have us up and running that very day—the Quiet One went to work. He dug a CD-ROM loaded with software out of one pocket, a sheet of account IDs out of another, a small electronic gadget out of another. Twenty minutes later, we were online, with far superior internet service at a third of the price. IT&T had the biggest building on The Mall and local staff by the hundreds, and they were being soundly thrashed by an ISP being run out of a parka.

By the time we left India in mid-2000, internet cafés had begun to spring up in major Indian cities and tourist spots, and then to grow like mad to keep up with the demand from travellers and local youth. One hotel in Delhi transformed an entire floor of its rooms into a huge internet café, full to capacity most days with Indian teens and twentysomethings. Even the pathetic little state-run computer-education centre on The Mall in Shimla caught on, reconfiguring a half-dozen of its idle workstations as internet kiosks; on one of our last visits, we watched a deeply unhappy young woman transcribing her own matrimonial classified ad as her father sat next to her in the booth dictating it. Around the same time, India's newsweeklies began to fill with talk of the domestic internet revolution.

I returned to India in January 2006, by which time the low-cost, high-quality work of Indian computer programmers had become worldwide news (not to mention the source of considerable hand-wringing in certain economic circles in the United States). Many of India's ubiquitous STD/ISD/PCO booths—stalls providing metered phone usage for the hundreds of millions of Indians who've never had a home telephone line and never will—had added internet access to their services, and the domestic abundance of skilled coders had made prominent landmarks of first Bangalore ("India's Silicon Valley") and then Hyderabad ("Cyberabad") on the global map of the internet boom.

Much more startling, though, was the proliferation of mobile phones, which had been non-existent on the subcontinent in 2000. These days, there were kiosks selling airtime and SIM cards tucked among the paan stalls and samosa carts on the roadside, the chirrup-ing of ring tones now prominent among the mix of blaring horns and hawkers' calls in the bazaars. On a Bangalore-bound train, I watched a middle-aged woman in a prim salwar kameez tap out text messages as we chugged out of the station. India had, for the most part, skipped the era of land-line telephones entirely. The mobile phone—cheaper, easier to obtain and to use, and so democratic in its distribution that even rickshaw drivers sometimes gave you their mobile number at the end of a ride—had vaulted India right over the twentieth century of telecommunications to hit the ground running in the twenty-first.

Now imagine, just for example, solar panels in place of mobile phones. Hundreds of millions of solar panels. This is an imprecise analogy—power generators aren't likely to be as numerous as communication devices—but consider for a moment the symbolic impact of the parallel. A marginal thing, all but unknown in many corners of the world just ten years ago, suddenly everywhere. A transformation no more difficult to imagine than it was, ten years ago, to imagine that mobile phones would become as commonplace as pen and paper, nearly as cheap and in some cases even more frequently used.

The tools that built the Renewable Energy Archipelago are not quite there yet in cost or simplicity, certainly not in ubiquity, but still . . . imagine solar panels and wind turbines, district heating plants and neighbourhood hydro plants, waterless urinals and traffic lights for bicycles. Imagine all of it as run-of-the-mill as a mobile phone, chosen not to save an ecosystem or save a species, exactly, but simply because it's useful, desirable, *better*.

Finally, imagine this: Bangalore City Railway Station, February 2006. High-tech boom notwithstanding, Bangalore is saddled with a central station no different from the ones in every other Indian metropolis—no less chaotic, no less ramshackle, no more obviously portentous of a better future just around the corner. New arrivals still pour off the concourses in knotted dhotis, families of eight still squat in circles in patches of shade near the front steps to wait for their trains, paan spit still stains the whitewashed cement a deep brown-red colour like dried blood. Cattle still graze on piles of garbage at the parking lot's edge and then, post-prandial, wander nonchalant across eight lanes of traffic. Hand-painted signs by the dozen—some of them for internet companies—adorn side walls and overhangs, even though there's not a public internet connection to be found at the station. And autorickshaws (three-wheeled mini-taxis, urban India's trademark vehicles) still buzz in and out in ceaseless swarms, their ridiculously inefficient two-stroke engines belching thick, black, sickly sweet diesel smoke.

Imagine, amid this run-of-the-mill frenzy, a propagandist's post-card touting the good life on the Renewable Energy Archipelago.

An advertisement, that is. And then another, two more—all of them plastered across the backs of rickshaws where a more tightly regulated and safety-conscious nation might insist on a rear windshield. All of them ads for solar-powered hot water heaters. A couple are for a system from Tata BP, a recent partnership between one of India's largest industrial conglomerates and one of the world's premier energy companies. Another hawks a new "geyser" (the preferred Indian-English term for the device) from an upstart local firm called Global Solar Systems.

Within a kilometre of the Bangalore train station, along the path of a single autorickshaw, I found a half-dozen of these ads. Portentous signs indeed—fleeting, half-obscured by traffic haze, but symbolically potent nonetheless—that even a subcontinent whose growth was being measured in tons of coal could be a landmark in the geography of hope. And evidence, I hoped, that the archipelago's growth had reached digital speed.

THE SUSTAINABILITY BOOM

Here's another scene from the front ranks of a newborn boom.

The setting: Denmark again, this time a charmless, cavernous conference centre in the suburbs of Copenhagen. The date: October 2005. The event: Copenhagen Offshore Wind, a gala confab of the world's leading offshore wind-generating companies. An incongruously airless affair, this conference, the enthusiasm as muted as the hall's acoustics even as the industry's leading lights took the stage, alone or in small groups, to outline the great year they'd had, the explosive growth of the industry, its near-limitless potential.

The opening session in the main auditorium established the dominant mood with a series of dry, leaden presentations. The only leavening moment was a video feed, live via satellite, from the world's largest offshore wind farm. Standing on a control platform a few kilometres off the east coast of Denmark in the North Sea, an engineer from a company called Elsam did his best to remain audible over the screeching gale as he explained that the kinks in the wind farm's initial installation, which had been many and (in offshore-wind-biz circles) notorious, had been straightened out. The churning windmills in the background served as Exhibit A for the defence. Later, a fiery Irishman named Eddie O'Connor, CEO of the ambitious upstart Airtricity, sounded *almost* visionary as he talked about the prospects for the North Sea as the wind-fuelled powerhouse of all of Europe. (The numbers are apparently pretty solid; the North Sea *is* that windy.)

An even more remarkable moment came later in the proceedings, during the roundtable discussion, when the executives from two of the world's leading wind turbine manufacturers—Denmark's Vestas and Germany's Siemens, which had recently purchased Denmark's number-two manufacturer, Bonus, to earn its central role at the conference—took the stage alongside O'Connor. Both offhandedly noted that, although they'd been unable to keep up with orders for the current fiscal year, neither was amping up production. Despite enormous demand, that is, neither saw any reason to go about substantially increasing supply right away. They didn't really say why, and I had to assume it was a matter of simple caution.

The opening session thus concluded, the crown prince of Denmark came into the foyer amid much unfurling of carpet and popping of flashbulb and rushing about of underling to officially open the conference. He said almost nothing, smiled in his boyish way—he's in his early thirties, pint-sized, and bears more than a passing resemblance to Michael J. Fox—and cut the ribbon. In the exhibition hall behind him, booths large and small proffered glossy billboard-sized photos of pristine nature as the background to floor displays of weird oversized gears and motors.

I was a little while into wandering the floor and verging on complete boredom when I was struck by a sharp jolt of déjà vu. Here was a bland corporate setting, a trade fair for the makers of strange instruments comprehensible only to a tiny techie elite. The industry's purported leaders came across as overly modest and sort of dorky (if not flat-out dull). And yet there was multinational electronics giant Siemens with the trade show's largest display, and the most prominent logo on the swanky giveaway tote bag was Shell's. There was even this Eddie O'Connor touching briefly on the notion of revolutionary change—with sober but genuine passion—before conversation swayed back to the more comfortable engineer-geek terrain of installed capacity and grid integration.

It was eerily similar to information technology conferences I'd attended in the mid-1990s. Even the fretting over grids seemed like a kind of energy industry echo of computer-geek worries about bandwidth. O'Connor suggested at one point that if the offshore wind companies started cranking out the power, someone else—national energy monopolies, upstart competitors, *someone*—would figure out a way to distribute it. Which, come to think of it, is pretty much how the world's digital revolutionaries dealt with their bandwidth problem. Once a thing becomes *essential,* the trouble with getting it to eager consumers has a way of evaporating, of seeming less like a problem than an opportunity.

Copenhagen Offshore Wind was a three-day affair, but I didn't return after that first day. I'd seen enough. I'd hoped to find a sort of vanguard, and I had. Most of its members just didn't seem to know it yet.

The early rumblings of the sustainability boom were damn near daily news in the months after Copenhagen Offshore Wind. In November alone, two of the planet's largest and least sustainable corporate behemoths—BP and Wal-Mart—announced significant long-term investments in green enterprises. In December, Whole Foods, the fast-growing North American grocery chain, became North America's largest buyer of wind-energy credits—480,000 megawatt hours' worth, enough to offset the energy footprint of every single store, warehouse and office in its chain. And so on into 2006, the first quarter of which saw $513 million in venture capital funding for new enterprises in the "greentech" industry—this being the term used to describe it in a press release detailing the establishment of a $100-million investment fund by the venture capital firm Kleiner Perkins Caufield & Byers, a name made famous as one of the key financiers of the internet boom. "Greentech could be the largest economic opportunity of the 21st century"—so ran a quote therein from John Doerr, the Kleiner Perkins partner who'd had the foresight to throw the firm's money behind Netscape, the first in a string of his investments in some of the most successful of the digital-tech pioneers. Not only did the sustainability boom radiate the same kind of vibe as its dotcom predecessor, it was now being funded by its profits.

As the dotcom bubble overinflated toward its inevitable pop in the late 1990s, it became fashionable to invoke the memory of "tulipomania," that first and most superficially silly of investment-induced mass insanities, in which a delirious speculative market bubble in tulip bulb futures led to nationwide economic ruin in seventeenth-century Holland. No doubt all this greentech hype has already induced visions of tulip bulbs—not to mention the repossessed foosball tables of failed dotcoms the world over—in some circles. The big difference, again, is that neither tulip bulbs nor petfood websites served fundamental needs, whereas nearly all the change and innovation feeding the green boom does.

Consider Wal-Mart, whose pretensions to greenness met with the most skepticism. What, after all, did the world's mightiest purveyor of cheap plastic, shipped by carbon-fuelled supply chains that circled the globe, care about climate change? From a July 2006 cover story on Wal-Mart's "green machine" in *Fortune* magazine came an unequivocal answer: there was a buck to be made, and another to be saved. Not even a year after the company's CEO, Lee Scott, had declared his green intentions, Wal-Mart had become the planet's largest buyer of organic milk and organic cotton. It had also figured out, for example, that simply reducing the amount of packaging on its private-label toy line could cut shipping costs by US$2.4 million. The markets for milk and textiles were well-established, the uses of reduced costs proven long ago. Sustainability, it turned out, could be plain old profitable.

BP had come to similar conclusions. The energy company formerly known as British Petroleum made headlines back in 1997 when its CEO, Lord John Browne, became the first oil company chief to acknowledge the existence of anthropogenic climate change, and it had been working on rebranding itself as a green company—"Beyond Petroleum"—ever since. Its critics called this "greenwashing," corporate spin-doctoring of the most egregious kind. It still ran mammoth CO_2-belching refineries (its third-largest, located on the Gulf Coast of Texas, killed fifteen and injured more than a hundred when it blew up in early 2005) and crude-filled pipelines (when one sprung a leak on Alaska's North Slope in the spring of 2006, it spewed hundreds of thousands of litres of oil into the Arctic Ocean). And there was no getting around the fact that its investment in its celebrated solar division for 2004, for example, was an amount equal to 0.14 percent of its revenue that year. On the other hand, the formation of BP Alternative Energy in November 2005 included $8 billion in further investment in solar energy over the following decade. And wherever

I went in search of the state of the art in sustainability—from solar water heaters in India to climate change confabs in Germany—I found the BP logo. What was the $1.8 billion BP was promising to spend on solar over the next three years against the $18.5 billion it had spent looking for new fossil fuel deposits in 2004 alone? Well, it was about $1.8 billion more than any oil company spent on renewable energy back in 1997. That BP had wholly self-serving motives—profit in the long term, positive brand-image building in the short term, which is also ultimately about profit—is beside the point. The exuberant billion-dollar spending sprees needed to ignite world-changing industrial revolutions happen *only* for self-serving reasons, and it's to the sustainability boom's credit that a corporation of BP's size, stature and cautious disposition would deem it worthy of its self-serving spending.

Et cetera, et cetera: General Electric (GE), builder of thousand-megawatt coal-and-gas-burning behemoths the world over, debuted its new "Ecomagination" program to much fanfare and similar measures of skepticism in the spring of 2005. Why was GE suddenly so keenly interested in renewable energy and hyper-efficiency? Simple: it wanted to see 60 percent of its revenue growth—the lifeblood of a rapacious corporation—in those industries. What was shameless glory hog Richard Branson doing, claiming he'd be dumping every dime of profit from Virgin's transport divisions over the next ten years—maybe $3 billion, all told—into green energy? Reducing long-term fuel costs, that's what. (Well, that and trying to keep up with all the other billionaire philanthropists at the 2006 Clinton Global Initiative forum, which is where he made his grand gesture.)

And all of this, of course, is simply the response of the old guard to the potential disruptions caused by the problem they've profited so greatly from creating. This is just a lumbering dinosaur of an industry responding with a cantankerous wave of its mighty tail to a shift of potentially world-altering proportions in the technological and social centre of gravity in its business. It's the equivalent of all those billions spent by old-guard telecom and media companies as their monopolies crumbled beneath their feet in the mid-1990s. The first big-time dot-com in Toronto, where I was living at the time, was born of Bell Canada's R&D largesse; AT&T was responsible for the first truly overblown advertising campaign of the era; and, as I mentioned, my first Indian ISP was Indian Telephone & Telegraph. None of these set the pace of the internet boom.

No wonder so many dotcom financiers have moved into this greentech game. Not only does it look like the same crazy (and crazy-lucrative) one they just played and won, but the stakes are so much higher. As *The Economist*'s Vijay V. Vaitheeswaran noted, "energy is the world's biggest industry, by far." The "global energy game," he estimated, was worth about $2 trillion in prizes every year. And so it's not just John Doerr of Kleiner Perkins but also Microsoft's Bill Gates and AOL's Steve Case and Sun Microsystems' Vinod Khosla who are dumping venture funding by the millions into the sustainability boom. And, one imagines, heading out to survey their investments to find a familiar sight: mad geniuses and eccentric scientists holed up in labs and research institutes—maybe even a garage or two—banging together some of the most magnificent toys the world's ever seen.

ISLAND HOPPING (III): AMONG THE FUTURISTS

Freiburg, Germany, bills itself as Europe's "Solar City," and I'd been gawking at its many PV-panelled buildings for a couple of days. I'd seen solar-powered houses that produced more energy than they consumed and parking garages crowned in PV cells. I'd passed by the city's main soccer stadium, which has enough PV tiles on its roof to power the floodlights. I was even staying at a hotel that got most of its electricity and heat from the sun. One afternoon, I made my way to the Solar Info Centre out by the city fairgrounds to see if there was anything I'd missed. Oddly enough, the place was mostly empty the day I stopped by, and I never did find out what solar info it might've had for me.

This, I later learned, was the least of my oversights. A more significant one: pretty much directly behind the Solar Info Centre was a sleek but substantial curvilinear building that housed the Fraunhofer Institute for Solar Energy Systems. The Fraunhofer is possibly Europe's most prestigious solar-energy research laboratory, and somewhere inside were a certain number of prototypes of a thing known as a crystalline silicon thin-film solar cell. That's CSiTF for short, not that *that* makes it any more comprehensible. And not that it necessarily matters, because the current leaders in the quest to bring thin-film solar to market claim that CSiTF has been eclipsed in efficiency and commercial potential by a new generation of technology. The prototypes of this generation have some clunky names as well: cadmium telluride (CdTe) thin-film solar, cadmium-indium-gallium-selenide (CIGS) thin-film solar. And, as with CSiTF, the awkward abbreviations describe an extraordinarily complex technological process in which energy-producing solar cells can be dusted or vacuum-evaporated or printed or in some way or another-anyway *installed* on materials thinner than a credit card and just as flexible. Thin-film solar cells are also much cheaper to manufacture than the PV cells I'd seen all over Freiburg, and they're made from much more easily obtained and considerably less toxic materials.

I don't really begin to understand how thin-film solar works, actually, and like anyone else who isn't a highly specialized chemistry Ph.D. or electrical engineer working on those prototypes, I don't really care and don't really need to. What I *do* care about—what makes me kind of euphoric when I think about thin-film solar, and makes me pissed at myself that I didn't realize I was within a couple hundred metres of sneaking a peak at the stuff, even just the possibly outdated stuff, when I was crossing the parking lot at the Solar Info Centre in Freiburg that day—is that thin-film solar is one of those next-generation technologies that has smart people working overtime and rich people emptying their investment funds to bring it to a building near me as soon as possible.

"A Solar Panel On Every Building"—that's the registered trademark by which a California company called Nanosolar, one of the handful of global leaders in commercial thin-film solar, states its mission. And it claims to be very close to embarking upon it: there's a manufacturing facility in the works that should start producing 430 megawatts of Nanosolar's CIGS thin-film cells per year within the next few years. The cells will come off the production line, they say, in great sheets, flexible and durable and most importantly *cheap* enough—as little as a tenth of the cost of current-model PV cells of similar wattage—that it will soon be feasible to carpet the roof of every office block and condo complex and big-box warehouse on the planet with it.

Nanosolar is far from alone. HelioVolt, based in Austin, Texas, has come up with a manufacturing process for CIGS cells that would allow them to be pre-installed in a new building's construction materials. A company called Konarka of Lowell, Massachusetts, received funding from the same government program as Nanosolar for its thin-film product, which it calls PowerPlastic. But all of them were beaten to market by a household name: Honda intends to open the first fully operational production plant for CIGS cells in Kumamoto, Japan, in the fall of 2007.

So. Thin-film solar: in five years, it could be on my roof, embedded in your new windows, all but fully encasing the buildings where we work and buy groceries. It could render Manchester's astounding Solar Tower as run-of-the-mill as any old mirrored-glass office block. Or it could fail to meet its hype, be overtaken by another generation of solar technology that's more efficient, or cheaper, or simply marketed better. Or none of the above, because there are similar volcanic explosions of innovation elsewhere—whiz-bang high-tech toys, bold pronouncements of intent, clever-as-hell twists on old ideas. A whole new archipelago in the making, if you will, with new islets emerging constantly to fill the empty waters between the older land masses. Some of these, to be sure, will recede into the sea with the first attempt to stand upon them; others, though, might prove to be the beginnings of new renewable-energy continents.

Here's one: the "floating wind generator." Looks like a cross between a kite and a tethered zeppelin, spins in the wind to send power humming down that tether. The Magenn Power Air Rotor System by name, it comes courtesy of Magenn Power of Ottawa, Ontario. The Canadian government threw in some R&D funding in late 2006; manufacturing is set to commence in 2008. Could be gone soon after, or the skies above the cities of the future could look like a *Blade Runner* take on the Macy's Thanksgiving Day parade. Here's another: the PowerBuoy, an open-water wave-power generator developed by a company called Ocean Power Technologies, the first of which was set to begin cranking out electricity in the seas off the coast of Spain by the summer of 2007. If it catches on, the company estimates that a 100-megawatt system could be installed in any given 40 acres of ocean.

There's also a diverse and curious assortment of new ideas— generally more earthy, in some cases plainly so—on the subjects of how to mine more power from the fuel we've already got and how to make less of a mess out of its use. Methane, for example, has been a fuel source for as long as people have been burning dung, but it's now being mined out of landfills and burned as biogas to feed electricity to carpet factories in Georgia and cassava processing plants in rural Thailand, to bring cheap power to a rural Ontario township and cheap cooking fuel to villages in Nepal (and reducing the intensity of the methane's CO_2 emissions in every case). A "thermal conversion plant" has been built next to a massive Butterball turkey processing plant in Carthage, Missouri, to convert the waste turkey guts into fuel oil. And then there's GreenFuel Technologies of Cambridge, Massachusetts, which was founded with $11 million in venture money to commercialize a breakthrough at the nearby Massachusetts Institute of Technology, in which certain carbon-eating strains of algae are given new homes in the smokestacks of power plants, where they soak up as much as 40 percent of the outbound CO_2 and are converted into biodiesel in the process.

Move to a more ethereal plane, and you'll find scores of unverified technological revolutions and as-yet-unproven miracle cures. A news report in the *Guardian* in the fall of 2005, for example, told of a medical doctor based in New Jersey who'd discovered a new energy source called a "hydrino," born of a sort of supercharged electrolysis, fuelled only by water, and capable of producing a thousand times more heat than conventional sources (and disproving certain fundamental principles of quantum mechanics along the way). Somewhat more plausibly, a super-secretive Texas company called EESTor made headlines in the spring of 2006 with its "ceramic ultracapacitor"—a new breed of battery with a storage capacity ten times any seen before, which could dramatically increase the viability of everything from electric cars to wind turbines in places of sporadic wind. Head-spinning breakthroughs of this sort don't often make it out of their laboratory cloisters intact, but they're indicative nonetheless of the excited blue-sky thinking inspired by an exuberant industrial boom, and the enormous potential for radical change it can create.

Consider, for example, another grand pronouncement that made headlines in early 2006: the government of Sweden declared that it would eliminate fossil fuels from within its borders by 2020. A nation of nine million had dedicated itself to the same transformation that had reshaped two tiny Danish isles, amplifying the scope of the procedure 750-fold and recalibrating the global boundaries of the realm of the possible. I mean, if Scandinavia's most populous country could soberly consider the state of the world's climate, its energy resources, the available technologies, and simply *plan* the building of a renewable-energy nation—well, then, what *are* the limits of this boom's potential?

The answer to this kind of open-ended question is the stock-in-trade of that unique hybrid species of planner and prognosticator called the futurist. With one foot planted in the hard-truth world of energy-policy roundtables and prices per kilowatt hour, and the other dangling out in the infinite speculative space of hydrinos and perpetual-motion machines, the renewable-energy futurist aims to describe a future-tense world that's at least plausible, if far from inevitable. This, at least, is how I'd assess the vision I heard described by the prominent futurist Jeremy Rifkin at a climate change symposium in northern Germany in May 2006.

The meeting itself was a close-knit affair called the Ankelohe Conversations, the inaugural of what was to become an annual event in which a small group of journalists would meet to discuss a pressing topic of their particular interest with experts in the field. The theme for the 2006 event was "climate change and the oil endgame"—the potentially catastrophic intersection between a radically reordered climate and the dwindling stock of the world's preferred energy source. The gathering took place on a bucolic estate on the edge of a village called Gut Ankelohe; the host and lord of the manor was Lutz Kleveman, a journalist and author of a book on the oil-fuelled geopolitics of central Asia.

In lectures and panel discussions over three days, a diverse assemblage of reporters, geologists, oil-company executives and environmental activists provided a comprehensive crash course in the related sciences of peak oil and anthropogenic climate change. The scientific foundations and global implications of "Hubbert's Peak"— the increasingly prominent and credible theory, postulated by the American geophysicist Marion King Hubbert as far back as the 1950s and illustrated by a humpbacked bell curve, that the last years of the twentieth century were the beginning of the end of the age of oil— were examined at length by several of the world's most prominent fossil fuel researchers, among them Princeton geologist Kenneth Deffeyes, physicist David Goodstein of the California Institute of Technology, and Colin J. Campbell, who founded the Association for the Study of Peak Oil and Gas after a long career as an exploration geologist and executive for pretty much every oil company you've ever heard of. The subject of oil's putative successor—renewable energy—yielded cautiously optimistic pronouncements from the vice-president of BP Alternative Energy, former Shell chairman Lord Oxburgh (who was particularly excited about recent breakthroughs in battery technology), and British solar-energy entrepreneur Jeremy Leggett. And before and after and in between there were declarations, comments and rants from German newspaper reporters and Swiss documentary filmmakers and British research fellows, muckrakers from England and America, former diplomats and current activists. Throughout, there was an intensity heretofore unknown to any gathering I've ever encountered that called itself a symposium. These were ominous times, and this was heavy talk.

Though the mood was hardly buoyant, there was a kind of quiet exuberance in the air at Ankelohe. Between sessions, at dinner, around a blazing bonfire in a clearing in the woods behind the manor house in the evenings, the excited chatter of a dozen passionate debates carried on undiminished. Maybe it was the setting—the country estate and intermittent rain, the hard-talking days and debauched nights—but Ankelohe felt to me like a sort of Anthropocene Era analogue to those secret conclaves you see in movies about the Second World War. It was some postmodern mix of Casablanca and Yalta, a rollicking protracted negotiation between diplomats and propagandists, frontline soldiers in the resistance, guilt-ridden war profiteers and defectors from the other side. It had grim pronouncements, skeptical rebuttals and black comedy, blunt pragmatism and fervent idealism in roughly equal measure. But it didn't achieve much in the way of naked exuberance until Jeremy Rifkin showed up to deliver the closing address.

Rifkin is a prognosticator of considerable notoriety and influence, the author of a series of bestsellers whose titles alone foretell great change soon to come: *The End of Work, The Biotech Century, The Hydrogen Economy.* Officially, Rifkin is a fellow of the prestigious Wharton School of the University of Pennsylvania, the founder of a Washington think tank called the Foundation on Economic Trends, an adviser to CEOs and heads of state. But in person he is first and foremost an itinerant preacher in the classic American mould. Stout and bald-pated, with a thick but tidy moustache and round owlish glasses, Rifkin paced the floor of the conference room like an evangelist upon a dais. He moved his hands in slow, careful, even strokes to punctuate his key arguments, as if he was plotting graphs or else calling down God's wrath, and he described our sustainable future as if he were just back from a grand vacation there. Which, in a way, he was: Rifkin had recently visited a newly minted clean-tech hub in the Spanish province of Aragón, and he held it aloft for the Ankelohe crowd like the living, breathing embodiment of the hydrogen economy he'd predicted. "I saw the future" was how he put it.

What Rifkin saw in Aragón was Walqa Technology Park, a government-sponsored tech cluster intended to vault Spain to the forefront of the renewable-energy boom. The steep hills of the Pyrenees thereabouts were crowned in wind turbines, Rifkin explained. There was hydro power in them thar hills as well, and solar power in the valley below, and plans afoot to build industrial-scale hydrogen fuel cells to store it all, thus to drive the internet-enabled next-generation business activity in the park itself. Here was the revolutionary union of a new means of energy production and the communications technology to harness its power—which, Rifkin argued, was one of the fundamental engines of human history.

Like any preacher worth his salt, Rifkin traced his vision back to antiquity: to ancient Mesopotamia, where a new food-production technology (agriculture) precipitated the development of the first written language (cuneiform) and led to the birth of civilization as we know it. Since then, there'd been two industrial revolutions: the printing press and the coal-powered steam engine had created the first; the telegraph, the telephone and all those barrels of oil had brought about the second. The third industrial revolution, Rifkin intoned, was just now being born in Aragón by the convergence of digital telecommunications and renewable power stored in hydrogen fuel cells.

Rifkin:

> A fuel cell is analogous to a personal computer. When you get a personal computer, you generate your own information. You become the producer and the distributor, and you can distribute to a billion people if you so choose. With a fuel cell powered by hydrogen, extracted from renewable energies, it's analogous to a personal computer. You become your own

producer of energy; you become your own utility; you become your own power plant. You have to imagine in twenty-five years from now—*not* fifty—millions and millions and millions of fuel cells powered by hydrogen, extracted from renewable energies.

This would be a "big disruptive revolution," Rifkin explained. It would be decentralized and open-source, the wellspring of "real globalization," reaching even the one-third of the world's population without electricity, the half of the world who'd never made a phone call.

In under an hour, Rifkin had stood the whole Ankelohe conversation on its head. As far as he was concerned, the end of abundant oil couldn't come soon enough.

In the energy vacuum left by his dizzying speech, I noticed a generalized sort of distaste among the Ankelohe participants, mostly mild and imprecise, which by the end of that evening's boozy bonfire had turned petty in some quarters. I heard no serious rebuke of the facts of Rifkin's case—it wasn't that this so-called third industrial revolution was impossible but that it was *improbable*. Starry-eyed, overexuberant, crass. A salesman's spiel. Who was this guy in his too-slick gold-checked suit and his mannered preacher's gestures and his gauche Midwestern-used-car-lot moustache to talk about revolution? What was he doing spouting all that evangelical garbage when there were cold-hearted science and hard-nosed politics to be discussed?

I have to admit I found Rifkin a bit hard to swallow myself, though I couldn't really say why either that night. I figured it out on a train to Berlin the next day: I was *afraid* of Rifkin. Afraid of his overheated rhetoric, afraid most of all to let myself believe it might be possible. That we could make his prophesied revolution happen. It wasn't, after all, particularly far-fetched. Indeed, Vijay Vaitheeswaran of the august *Economist*—an Ankelohe participant himself—had distilled his years on the energy beat into essentially the same conclusion as Rifkin's; he'd just delivered it in a more sombre tone. "The emerging Energy Internet," he wrote in *Power to the People,* "will be the happy result of the collision of distributed generation with distributed networking, which has already given the world such anarchic and empowering technologies as cellular phones, personal computers, interactive media, peer-to-peer systems like Napster, and, for that matter, the Internet itself." And hadn't E.F. Schumacher said essentially the same thing—and hadn't it rung just as head-spinningly true—in *Small Is Beautiful* thirty years earlier? "The technology of *production by the masses*," he wrote, "making use of the best of modern knowledge and experience, is conducive to decentralisation, compatible with the laws of ecology, gentle in the use of scarce resources, and designed to serve the human person instead of making him the servant of machines." And wasn't it Gandhi, a generation before, who had articulated the demand for "production by the masses" in the first place? Weren't we simply two generations *closer* to this goal? Gandhi's call was essentially a rhetorical flourish—a slogan—and Schumacher had given it the scaffolding of economic theory, but here was Rifkin offering a solid technical proposal, complete with first-hand reporting on the success of the prototype. We're tantalizingly close to reaching this goal; Rifkin's vision is out of reach only for as long as we refuse to lean in and take hold of it.

The digital boom was improbable, and a great many people doubted its revolutionary promise until they surfed the right sites or started their own blogs or had BlackBerries forced upon them by their employers. Denmark's Renewable Energy Islands sounded like a gimmick until you hiked and biked the back roads of one. This energy internet was certainly no further from our grasp than the defeat of fascism or the fall of the Soviet Union. At Ankelohe, Vijay Vaitheeswaren told me about how he'd come to my hometown to report a story for *The Economist* on Calgary's oil sands boom, and while he was there someone told him, in the midst of a flight of rhetorical fancy, that maybe they could build a nuclear power plant up near Fort McMurray to feed the colossal energy demands of the boom's breakneck expansion. The idea made Vaitheeswaran chuckle, but I found local oil barons discussing it earnestly on the front page of my local paper just a couple of months after I got back from Germany. That was undoubtedly a better home for my fear. The future prophesied by Jeremy Rifkin already existed in at least one fearless corner of Spain, and *anything that exists is possible*. And it's nothing to be afraid of. It is, in fact, good cause for delirious celebration.

I'd been on the trail of this geography of hope for nearly a year at that point, but it was only in the afterglow of Ankelohe that I *embraced* it. Our little conclave had had its esprit de corps, its own quiet excitement, but it'd needed that big, final, Patton-rallies-the-troops push. Contrary as it was to the well-honed and doubtless well-earned cynical instincts of the participants, Ankelohe needed a big gleeful dose of rational exuberance.

RATIONAL EXUBERANCE (III): SEEDS

Which brings us back to Jørgen Bjørgren's farm, the pride and joy of which isn't his mammoth cauliflower or any of the other organic produce he grows. It isn't even intended to be eaten. It is, rather, a patch of bushy plants speckled with delicate purple flowers and garlanded with bean-like pods. This was the first thing Bjørgren brought me to see, even before the Flintstone-sized vegetables. He didn't know the English name, but it was a type of radish grown for its seed pods, which are particularly rich in oil. "Better than rapeseed," Bjørgren noted sagely. He'd found the plant somewhere in southern Europe (France, I think), where he'd been told it didn't stand a chance as far north as Denmark. Bjørgren—former pilot, ex-journalist, sometime troubadour and renewable-energy pioneer—has never had much time for other people's limits on what's possible, so he brought some seeds home anyway. The plants were now in their second year on his farm, and they were clearly thriving.

Later, Bjørgren took me to another part of his field. He'd built a low planting box there and he'd covered it in an old wood-framed, multi-paned window: a makeshift greenhouse. "Step into my laboratory," he said with a grin as he lifted off the lid. In the rich black soil beneath, there were several rows of tiny seedlings—newborn specimens of five oil-rich species he'd collected across Europe. He was planning to plant them the following spring, to see if any of them could top the oilseed radish that was doing so well already. He was looking for fuel—a replacement, one day, for the last remaining tanks of gas on the island.

"I've promised to stay here," he told me, "until Aerø is 100 percent renewable. And every car, every tractor, every truck is on renewable. This is my dream—people say I'm crazy—to get this island on the world chart as a leading place for this." There was not a hint of doubt in his voice, no trace of a man wearied by his burden. There was only excitement and resolve.

As I left his farmhouse a couple of hours later, Bjørgren handed me a baggie full of small orange-brown pellets. For my garden back in Canada, he said. They were seeds from his radish patch.

I didn't get around to planting them, but I hung on to them nevertheless. They sit prominently on a shelf in my back hallway. As a reminder, I guess, that there's nothing to fear. Not out on the Renewable Energy Archipelago, anyway.

THREE

OUT OF GAS

[sustainable transport]

TERRA INCOGNITA

I'll be motoring along shortly to cars and trucks and things that go—as Richard Scarry so memorably summarized the world of transportation—but first I'd like to take a detour back a few hundred years and a few revolutions in consciousness, because I think part of the problem with the Anthropocene Era is its dearth of genuine awe, an atrophy of collective imagination that saps us of the will to kick out at the limits of possibility. This condition seems particularly acute when it comes to the automobile, which despite its abundant inefficiencies, its wanton wastefulness, the ruin it makes of human life and landscape with clockwork frequency, often seems like the most intransigent contributor to anthropogenic climate change, the ever more ubiquitous mode of transport we can't imagine living without. This isn't a testament to the car's advantages—though there are many, and I'll get to those as well—but to our failure of imagination.

"We inhabit, in ordinary daylight, a future that was unimaginably dark a few decades ago," writes the American social-justice activist Rebecca Solnit, "when people found the end of the world easier to envision than the impending changes—in everyday roles, thoughts, practices—that not even the wildest science fiction antici-pated. Perhaps we should not have adjusted to it so easily. It would be better if we were astonished every day."

The dizzying heights of our technological mastery have rendered us paradoxically unable to see very far past the great and wondrous everyday now. The world, even one transmogrifying and discombob-ulating as fast as this one, has become *too* known, and this somehow reduces everything in it—a city of millions in China where ten years ago there was little more than a country village, a cloned sheep by the unassuming name of Dolly, a permanent alteration of the composi-tion of the earth's atmosphere—to just another blip on the informa-tion superhighway. "Once in a lifetime . . . same as it ever was," to borrow David Byrne's prophetic hiccupped phrasing. The instanta-neous global cellphone call? The non-stop flight from New York to Hong Kong? A moment of wide-eyed novelty—a couple of years, at most, in which they remain objects of amazement—and then imme-diately they are swallowed into the yawning norm. The process takes no longer, actually, than it used to take an explorer to travel to *terra incognita* and back again.

It's hard to imagine at this moment, when I'm less than a minute and a couple of mouse clicks away from a detailed satellite photo of the Taj Mahal, the Great Wall of China or my own humble abode on Google Maps, what it must have been like to live in an age when maps were incomplete. What kind of magic aura was there to the words *Terra Incognita* at a map's edge? Uncharted territory, the unknown land. *Here There Be Serpents.* And who can even guess what it was like, for the peoples of those uncharted regions, to awake one day with the world as small and familiar as it had been for a life-time, for a thousand lifetimes, and then to see on the horizon a mast, a great cloth sail, a *ship* of a size and shape beyond what could be seen until that moment even in dreams? How to apprehend this ghost vision? Was it a portent of unknown terror—or of a whole new dimension in hope?

On July 12, 1776—barely a week after the United States issued its Declaration of Independence from Britain, launching into another kind of uncharted territory—a great sailing ship set out from Plymouth, England, on an epic voyage. The vessel was called *Resolution,* and its captain was James Cook. Its mission was to find the Northwest

Passage—that fabled seaway to the north of the American continent, the focus of a sort of exploration-age outbreak of irrational exuberance that dated back to Columbus's fifteenth-century quest to sail across the Atlantic to India. Whoever claimed the Northwest Passage, it was believed, would be buried in a vast and perpetually replenished hoard of Asian treasures and rule global trade.

There were few mariners better qualified for the task of finding the Passage than James Cook. Veteran of the siege of Louisbourg in Nova Scotia during the Seven Years' War, surveyor of the St. Lawrence River and the Newfoundland coast, the first European to map Australia's east coast and the islands of New Zealand, Cook was among the most accomplished explorers of the golden age of European discovery. Already he had sailed *Resolution* on the first recorded human crossing of the Antarctic Circle and circumnavigated the frozen continent. He was no stranger to uncharted seas and unknown shores.

Resolution sailed south to Table Bay on the Cape of Good Hope, where it rendezvoused with a second ship, *Discovery,* and together the two boats journeyed east. They became the first European ships to drop anchor at several of the smaller Hawaiian islands in January 1778, and then sailed onward to the west coast of North America, finally reaching the Bering Strait—and an impasse—in the first week of August. On August 18, 1778, off a spit of land they named Icy Cape, their boats trapped in water thick with ice and teeming with what they called "Sea Horses"—walruses—ice hanging from their rigging and their noses, Cook and his crew gave up the quest to find the Northwest Passage. The forbidding Arctic climate had denied Cook his prize after two long years of sailing, and in consolation he set a course for still more *terra incognita,* returning to that half-known volcanic archipelago in the middle of the Pacific.

Cook reached the Big Island of Hawaii—another new discovery—in November. Fearful of repeating the fiasco of his crew's visit to the other islands in the chain on the outward journey, which had led to a spate of venereal disease among the female inhabitants, Cook decided to forgo a landing. Instead, he plied up and down the island's east coast, trading his exotic iron for pigs and fruit among the natives who rowed out to meet them, and inventing a drink—a "strong decoction" of sugar cane and hops—in the hope of placating his crew. But the men didn't much like this strange beer, and *Resolution* sprung a leak, and so on the morning of January 17, 1779, the boats dropped anchor in Kealakekua Bay and the crew prepared to go ashore for a welcome beyond anything even James Cook had ever seen.

"I have no where in this Sea seen such a number of people assembled at one place," Cook wrote in his diary that morning. The scene that had so moved him was this: a bay crowded with 800 canoes, then a thousand; one observer reckoned there were 1,500 boats on the water by mid-afternoon. A high priest came aboard *Resolution* and presented Cook with a red cloak, more pigs and fresh fruit, and then they went ashore, the islanders prostrating themselves as Cook passed. He was led onto a stage of piled stones 10 metres high, its front edge adorned with a row of skulls. Cook had arrived during the feast of Lono, the god of fertility and harvest. The Hawaiians, seeing his great ship pass by in the previous weeks, had taken Cook to be no less than Lono himself, or one of his avatars or minions, or anyway a man "partaking something of divinity," as Cook's second lieutenant summed it up.

I can only wonder what it was like to be a Kealakekua villager in 1779, can only speculate at the kind of mental revolution inspired by the sudden presence, in flesh and blood, of a long-prophesied god. I'm pretty sure, though, that I've never felt anything close to it, and even to try to equate the minor deities of my time with Cook's arrival in Hawaii would seem not so much to diminish Lono's grandeur as to dangerously overinflate the importance of its transient modern-day analogues. Still—same as it ever was—the human spirit continues to hunger for something more profound than the here and now, and so the Anthropocene Era is not without its mythic landscape, limited as it might be, and it provides its own idiosyncratic strains of revelation's delirious intoxication.

Like a movie.

Exactly: like a movie. A great many of the genuinely transcendent experiences of this age are in movies or other media spectacles, or feel at any rate so beyond everyday reality as to be out-of-body and dreamlike and larger than life—like a movie. More precisely, like one of those signature cinematic Big Reveals: a tight-focus shot pulls back and back to expose a world of unimaginable scale, or something new enters into the frame to dramatically recalibrate the proportions of the film's universe. One of the most influential movies on the mental landscape for us kids of the Anthropocene Era* was *Star Wars,* and it opens with a moment like this. After the bombastic opening fanfare—the horn-driven theme song, the mythic text-on-screen prologue ("A long time ago, in a galaxy far, far away") scrolling upward into infinite space—after all that, only empty starry sky remains. A briefly commonplace sight, until the camera pans down to reveal not one but two moons on the horizon, the surface of a vast orange planet below, and then a sci-fi spacecraft in flight. There's at most a moment or two to absorb this otherworldly scene, when suddenly the *top* of the screen fills completely with the underbelly of another craft. It's passing overhead, this ship, and it's so impossibly big that it makes the first ship look like a dugout canoe in the wake of a great English vessel in full sail. The larger craft fills the screen for what feels like *days.* In reality, it's about fifteen seconds—still a fairly long time in cinematic terms—but I remember the sense of time stretching on forever. Like everyone who ever lived must've been on board, with God himself at the helm, and the world had been somehow altered by its passing. ·

It's been the subject of many gallons of spilled ink and many reels of talking-head pontification, this *Star Wars* phenomenon—this conundrum of how an unevenly acted, clumsily scripted sci-fi B-movie got inflated to Homeric scale in the minds of a generation of viewers. What it comes down to, I think, is this: *Star Wars* filled a critical void in the mythic landscape of the Anthropocene Era. It charted *terra incognita,* populated it with heroes and villains, plucky white-robed underdog good and blackest machine-tooled imperial evil. It climaxed at a dark fortress the size of a freaking *moon,* armed with a cannon that could incinerate whole planets. And there came a hero—a shepherd boy, more or less, guided by a godlike presence—who destroyed it with a single volley from a sci-fi slingshot. The film's subtitle, it warrants mention, was *A New Hope.*

---

* As previously noted, "Anthropocene" refers to an era that began with the dawn of the industrial age. Hereafter, however, I'll use it as a shorthand for the generation that came of age cognizant of the existence of anthropogenic climate change.

And I mention all this because I can name almost to the minute the first time I truly felt that sense of boundless possibility as an adult, my first encounter with real Anthropocene hope—the kind that makes you swivel your head around wide-eyed to make sure you're still on the same planet you were on a moment before. That hits you with enough propulsive force to send you on a round-the-world mapmaking journey.

It was a quarter-century later. October 16, 2000. A Monday, mid-morning, overcast and unseasonably cold. I was in Montreal. I was staring at drops of dew on a man's open palm.

It was—*listen*—it was a goddamn miracle.

A GODDAMN MIRACLE

It happened on a strip of blacktop alongside the Gilles Villeneuve Circuit, a racetrack on Île Notre-Dame, an artificial island in the middle of the St. Lawrence River. (It was built by dumping more than 20 million tonnes of earth into the river as part of the preparations for Expo 67.) This was the marquee media event of the 17th International Electric Vehicle Symposium & Exposition—EVS-17— an annual meeting of the Electric Vehicle Association of the Americas. The scholarly sessions and trade show were ongoing at the Palais des congrès downtown, but the press had been bused out to Île Notre-Dame to take a few spins around the track in what were purportedly the latest and greatest electric-powered vehicles on the planet. There were cars of famous make (a Toyota Prius and a Honda Insight, a Nissan ultra-compact called the Tino), big trucks and glorified golf carts, scooters and even electric-motor-assisted bikes—all of them lined up in this pit area next to the racetrack. A handful of journalists and windbreakered technicians from the various manufacturers were buzzing around each vehicle, and every so often an Insight or a little golf-cart fartbox would go zooming past and out onto the track with no more fanfare than the burbling hum of its futuristic electric engine.

Right up at the front of the line was a white Ford sedan, a slightly stretched-out version of the Ford Contour that went by the trade name P2000. (The standard-issue Contour, *Motor Trend* noted, was "a strong entry in the family friendly sedan class.") I joined a large knot of gawkers, all of us looking down at a man in a navy-blue

Ford windbreaker who was squatting next to the car's exhaust pipe. A bit later, this man would sit next to me as I drove the Ford P2000, bearing witness as I learned that the car worked about the way you'd expect a strong entry in the family-friendly sedan class to work. And after I pulled back into the pit, he'd hand me a card identifying himself as Ronald D. Gilland, a propulsion systems engineer at Ford Scientific Research Laboratory in Dearborn, Michigan. At this point, though, this Ronald Gilland was simply squatting there, making a joke about how cold it was.

What I mean by all this is that it was an ordinary day, just another trade-show meet-and-greet nice-weather-we're-having sort of day. Not even a glimpse of an impossibly scaled mast on the horizon to foreshadow the coming of the divine.

Gilland was squatting there, making his joke about *you Canadian freaks call this a brisk fall day?* The Ford P2000 was running, but I couldn't hear a sound from it. Thin, vaporous clouds puffed out of the tailpipe next to him. Someone asked about those clouds.

Gilland said, "It's pretty much like the outflow on a clothes dryer."

He held his hand in front of the exhaust pipe for a few seconds, then held it up for inspection. We all leaned in for a closer look. His hand was dotted with drops of water. After a few seconds of mildly impressed muttering—about the same as you'd expect if he'd held up a new style of keychain with an extra button that turned off the headlights or something—the crowd dispersed, and Gilland wiped his hand dry on his thigh.

I stood there awhile. Probably fifteen seconds, but it felt like days.

This was a car. A prototype, sure, but a Ford sedan nonetheless. It had an electric motor, and that motor got its power from a hydrogen fuel cell—a proton-exchange-membrane fuel cell, specifically, a Mark 700 Series fuel cell manufactured by Ballard Power Systems of Vancouver, B.C. There was a hydrogen tank in the trunk and an air compressor up front, and when the hydrogen from the tank and the oxygen from the air compressor combined in the fuel cell, they generated electricity, and their waste was pure water.

And like that—whatever this P2000 cost to make, whatever the sticker price ten years from now if you made a million of them, whatever its wheelbase or peak torque happened to be—like *that,* one of

the most pervasive and symbolically heavy contributors to anthropogenic climate change was fixed.* It was less than zero-emission: it
emitted something useful. *Sure is cold for October, and by the way
this here fully functional Ford sedan spits potable water out its
exhaust pipe. Any colder and it'd be snow, har-de-har, wanna see?*

For weeks afterward, months, that moment stayed with me. It
was what I thought about when I wanted to believe a better world
was just around the corner: drops of water on an engineer's hand,
water from the exhaust pipe of a Ford sedan. Water clean enough to
drink. It was an amulet, a thing to be held aloft against the darkness.

In the days after EVS-17, though, I saw no banner headlines about
the P2000, no breaking stories on the cable news, not even a mention
in the thick weekend automotive supplements. I would periodically
find articles about climate change—items about the increasing certainty of its existence, others nearly as sure that humanity lacked the
tools to even begin to apprehend it—but there was never a word
about the goddamn miracle I'd witnessed. I searched with more
rigour and found mention of demonstration projects in California,
and of showpiece buses powered by Ballard fuel cells in Vancouver
and Chicago—Chicago Mayor Richard Daley purportedly drank a
glass of exhaust from one of those—and of a hydrogen-driven transportation future ten or twenty or fifty years off, regardless of whether
the story was datelined 1993 or 1999. I'd talked to engineers back at
the Palais des congrès who'd said the same thing. A couple of them
mentioned California's pioneering zero-emissions laws, which were
supposed to mandate whole fleets of P2000-style cars by 2003, but
you could hear the winking skepticism in their voices, like they knew
California wasn't *really* going to enforce those laws. In 1997, Daimler-
Benz had entered a $350-million partnership with Ballard, boasting
at the time that it would have 100,000 fuel-cell cars on the road by
2005, but as of that blustery day in Montreal, three years after the
announcement, the launch date seemed no closer on the horizon. I

---

* I'm obliged to note that hydrogen fuel cells are not, in and of themselves, a complete fix.
The most common way to produce the hydrogen they require is through electrolysis,
which requires an exterior electricity source. Any given fuel cell is thus ultimately only as
clean as the power plant feeding this process, although it eliminates the greenhouse gas
emissions from the car's propulsion system in any case.

even spoke to Firoz Rasul, Ballard's chairman and CEO, and he told me I'd see fuel cells in my house—in a generator, that sort of thing—before I'd own a car that ran on one.

The problem, I learned, was multifaceted, but it came down to scale. The current generation of fuel cells—the ones that had powered my spin around the track on Île Notre-Dame—required quite a bit of platinum, a precious metal that came at a dire price. And there was the distribution problem: hydrogen is an energy-storage medium, not a pure fuel source, and it requires manufacture from other sources, trucking to distribution points, compression and secure storage. There was much more to it than simply adding a hydrogen pump at the corner gas station. And there were other high-efficiency cars—Toyota's celebrated gas-electric hybrid Prius, in particular—that were free of all these infrastructure obstacles and thus far closer to mass market than the P2000.

In the years that followed, the skepticism all proved well-founded. California eased up on its zero-emissions policy, and fuel cells remained the focus of test projects (a growing number of these installed at large industrial operations, powering forklifts and the like). The P2000 vanished into obscurity. A friend of mine bought a Prius, and I drove it a few times and was duly impressed with how little gas it burned. But the thing was that the Prius did not drip clean water from its tailpipe. It was an evolution, not a revolution. And so I clung as long as I could to the image of those dewdrops on that engineer's hand, and when my grip finally slipped, my hope started to slide into despair.

I'd seen something miraculous, but the vision soon dissipated into the known world of budgetary constraints and infrastructure troubles—a bitterly cold and turbulent but ultimately mundane sea. *Here there be serpents* still. The great sailing ship remained trapped in icy waters, the Passage tantalizingly close but out of reach, maybe forever out of reach.

Or maybe the fuel cell wasn't like a boat stuck in ice at all. Maybe it was more like a god turned flawed and mortal flesh.

RUNNING ON EMPTY

In the days after the ceremony that welcomed James Cook to the Big Island of Hawaii as an authentic representative of the divine Lono, he and his men enjoyed the most generous hospitality they'd ever encountered. They were brought roasted pig each night and sere-naded by priests as they ate. But even the Big Island of Hawaii did not have a limitless supply of hogs and fruit, and even Lono could overstay his welcome. Barely two weeks after they came ashore, Cook and his men were obliged to return to their ships and renew their voyage. *Resolution* suffered major damage to a mast just a few days out of port, however, and Cook was forced to turn back to Kealakekua for repairs. The sudden return confused the Hawaiians—how could a ship of such divine providence have failed on its journey back to the heavens? Relations between visitors and hosts soured quickly. A pair of armourer's tongs—that magic tool by which the wondrous iron was forged—went missing; the islanders had decided, apparently, that they could try their hands at fashioning those heretofore holy treasures themselves. Others tossed stones at a party of sailors fetch-ing water. And then, on the night of February 13, 1779, *Discovery*'s cutter, its largest landing craft, was stolen. The next morning, a furi-ous Captain Cook stomped up and down the shore, searching for the boat; he went to complain to the village chief, breaching local custom several times in the process. Lono, the god from across the sea, was revealed to be little more than an angry and disrespectful man. In a mob scene on the beach, amid thrown stones and musket fire, James Cook was clubbed on the head and stabbed in the back. He died face down in a gathering pool of his own blood in Kealakekua Bay.

The Ford P2000 came to an end nowhere near as dramatic. It simply became frozen in a moment that receded into the past and then faded away, like a picture of an unrealized future in an old mag-azine. Still, I mourned the P2000's passing like I'd lost something sacred. I remember 2002 and 2003 as dark times—many of us do, I think—and amid the swirling entropic vortex of terrorist attacks and pre-emptive war, I all but abandoned hope for a sustainable future. And I carried that image of the stillborn fuel-cell family sedan with me like one of those prayer cards from a funeral, as a heartbreaking symbol of the world we needed but would probably never build.

Around the same time, I went and found a copy of a song called "Running on Empty" by Jackson Browne. It was lodged in my head, and I had to get it out. It was a song I knew from childhood but never loved, the kind of thing that would come on the radio in my parents' car in those same years that *Star Wars* was colonizing my consciousness. On repeated listens, I think I figured out why it had come back to me after twenty-odd years. It's a ragged song, decadent and sloppy, lurching for seventies AM rock's trademark self-assuredness and falling just short. It's the sound of someone who thought he knew exactly where he was going just as it dawns on him that he's lost the trail:

> Looking out at the road rushing under my wheels
> I don't know how to tell you all just how crazy this life feels
> I look around for the friends that I used to turn to to pull me
>   through
> Looking into their eyes I see them running too.

Turns out Browne produced the entire album *Running on Empty* while on tour. A handful of the songs were recorded in motel rooms, another on a bus "somewhere in New Jersey." Rock & roll has always mated well with the car culture it grew up with, but on *Running on Empty* Jackson Browne may have taken it to some kind of symbiotic apex: it's a *literal* road album. And so it's not much of a stretch to think of it as a great seventies gas-guzzling monster—one of those Cadillac land yachts, sharp-edged and over-chromed—out on the open highway, burning cheap gas with no destination in mind, and then one day passing a gas station with a lineup around the block.

To listen to "Running on Empty" a generation later, in the spring of 2003, as war raged in the sand above one of the world's last proven crude-oil reserves, was to hear a prophesy fulfilled. And to wonder, finally, what to do with this sacred image of a car that burned no oil at all. The Anthropocene's denuded mythic landscape barely had room for the apocalyptic scenes beaming in from the Middle East, let alone a meticulously detailed tight-focus shot of a hand glistening with dew from the tailpipe of a Ford sedan. It just wouldn't fit. Better to hope that some day, some way, it could be restaged somewhere else.

CHINATOWN

Singapore must have the prettiest inner-city expressways in the world: wide and smooth, almost fully canopied in spots by expansive spider-limbed tropical trees. Towering palms line the medians, and the overpasses are garlanded with industrial-sized flower boxes planted with pink bougainvillea so lush it overflows, dangling above the highway like fine drapery. Thick, snaking green vines cover the retaining walls. Modern Singapore was built to the exacting specifications of its founding father, Lee Kuan Yew—until recently its only prime minister—and his vision of a "Garden City" on the southern tip of the Malay Peninsula is in full flower along the controlled-access ring roads that circle the city-state.

I got a good long look at a stretch of this thick foliage along the Ayer Rajah Expressway, from the passenger seat of an A-Series Mercedes, riding in air-conditioned comfort as the searing equatorial sun overlit the sights. I had a dapper and helpful guide behind the wheel—one Nelson Chu, the guest-services manager of the Conrad Centennial, a deluxe downtown hotel. Plus there was the added bonus of riding a little higher than you would in a typical hatchback, because the Mercedes had had its seats raised to make room underneath for hydrogen tanks.

Singapore is unique among Asian metropolises for the conspicuous absence of gridlock on its highways—we'll come back to this later—so it was a smooth and fairly quick drive as well. And uncommonly silent: the car's fuel-cell engine made only a sort of breathy whistle, like strong wind through trees, which increased in volume and pitch when Chu cranked the a/c. He was luxury-hotel meticulous about pointing out the landmarks along the way, but I was there mainly to see the final destination.

We were bound for a brand-new filling station just a little way off the expressway. It stood on the edge of a huge new technology park, its bright green and yellow logo the same as you'd find at any other BP station. It had a motorized security gate—which Chu opened by typing a code into an ATM-style keypad—because it was an unmanned station, and more to the point because it was the first unmanned, on-site-generating hydrogen filling station on the planet. It was wired to the city grid, and in a fully automated process it pulled electricity in, ran it through a state-of-the-art electrolyzer to create hydrogen, compressed it to 420 times atmospheric pressure, and then stored it, about 10 kilograms at a time, in a squat white shed at the station, there to wait for the likes of Nelson Chu to come refill his Mercedes. Which, with no technical expertise and only a hiccup or two more procedure than any other hurried driver's rest stop, he did.

It went like this: Chu entered his code onto another keypad mounted on a BP-logoed pump of more or less standard size and shape, pulled off the hose (the nozzle of which, it warrants mention, bore a striking resemblance to the handle of a Jedi knight's light sabre) and locked it into his car's intake. The system then automatically ensured that a full seal had been made between pump and car, checked to make sure there were no leaks anywhere down the line, and then filled the tank with about a kilogram of compressed hydrogen gas, enough to allow Chu to take curious hotel guests on about 150 kilometres of sightseeing. It took five minutes, about the same as a regular fill-up.

When we were ready to leave, I asked Chu if he would mind doing me a favour, and he (ever the four-star concierge) of course obliged. And so he waited while I trotted behind the car and hunkered down by the exhaust. Once I was in position, he started up the engine. There wasn't much sound, but the tailpipe spewed water droplets like a dolphin clearing its blowhole, forming a puddle on the sun-bleached pavement. After that, a thin mist was visible for a few seconds, and then nothing at all. I held my hand to the exhaust. Even in Singapore's steamy air, I could feel a warm, moist, steady blast against my palm. I gawked for a moment, and then—I couldn't help myself—I licked my palm. I tasted warm water. Six years later and half a world away, my awe was undiminished.

There were any number of caveats and qualifiers to the process I'd just witnessed. There were, for example, only six cars in all of Singapore rigged up to use the station, and there were only about ten tankfuls of gas at the station at any given moment, and this limited efficacy had cost more than $1 million. Who knows how much the cars would've cost if they weren't subsidized by BP and the Singapore government, and even then they were viable only as vehicles for high-end hotels and multinational corporations. (Japan Airlines and DaimlerChrysler were among the other businesses that had added a modified Mercedes to their local corporate fleets.) And like any hydrogen fuel-cell system, BP's electrolyzer pulled its juice off Singapore's fossil-fuelled grid, and so it was ultimately only as sustainable as the city itself.

"Have you ever been to a dog race?" This is S. David Freeman, energy adviser to Jimmy Carter back in the last big green-energy push of the late 1970s, offering some wry, hard-earned wisdom in the 2006 documentary *Who Killed the Electric Car?* "You know, there's the mechanical rabbit that's out in front, and the dogs never quite reach it. Well, the fuel cell is the equivalent of the mechanical rabbit. We're going for it—for the last fifteen years, they've been telling us the fuel cells are ten to fifteen years off."

But wait—hadn't I just laid my hands on that elusive rabbit on a patch of bleached pavement in Singapore? Wasn't the P2000's faded promise renewed—amplified—by the spectacle of a fastidious concierge in a dark suit routinely refilling the tank of his fuel-cell Mercedes? And yet it *did* feel oddly stillborn—another mission frozen in sea ice, the elusive Passage to untold renewable riches still as yet not fully charted. "We think that in twenty years the internal combustion engine could be obsolete," said Koh Kim Wah, president of BP Singapore, at the pilot program's launch in 2001, citing the seemingly immovable time horizon that was always attached to fuel-cell activity.

And so consider one last time James Cook's futile, fatal attempt to find that damned Northwest Passage—and what came after. Brave explorers carried on with his quest into the nineteenth century—most famously Sir John Franklin, whose doomed 1845 expedition from the Atlantic side ended with his ship trapped in ice while he and his crew wandered desperately to their deaths across the frozen arctic wastes. A couple of other expeditions crossed the Arctic by both sea and land in the 1850s, but nobody navigated the Passage by ship alone until the legendary Norwegian explorer Roald Amundsen turned up in Alaska in 1906 after a three-year east-to-west voyage. By which point the Passage was essentially redundant: railroad track now crisscrossed the continental land mass, offering a faster, more reliable year-round transit route for goods, and the U.S. government of Theodore Roosevelt had begun construction of the Panama Canal while Amundsen was at sea. Upon the canal's completion in 1914, the flow of global seafaring was forever altered. Great changes—technological, social and commercial—had doomed the Northwest Passage to irrelevance.

I don't regret my sojourn with the hydrogen fuel-cell car. I may still see a day when I drive my own water-dripping hatchback to the local hydrogen station. But I have to wonder if it isn't of a kind with the Northwest Passage expeditions—magical, even epic in its way, but ultimately a sidelight, eclipsed by bigger shifts in other places, using other tools. One in particular: another of the cars I first drove that day on Île Notre-Dame.

THE HIP HOLLYWOOD HYBRID HALF-STEP

I'm sure the Toyota Prius no longer requires much in the way of introduction. While hydrogen-powered vehicles have been languishing in the backwaters of Southeast Asian pilot projects and public-transport demos, the Prius has become one of the most talked-about and sought-after automobiles of its time. It was launched in the United States to minimal fanfare in 2000 (after a slightly more extravagant rollout in Japan). A modest 20,000 Priuses were sold in the United States in 2002, and 24,000 in 2003. And then, around 2004, the car conquered the popular consciousness like a mass Viking raid, and Prius sales exploded amid stories of long waiting lists at Toyota dealerships across North America. By 2006, Toyota's annual sales estimate for the United States alone was more than 100,000.

There are a handful of solid reasons for the Prius's extraordinary success. Most of them are purely practical, owing much to the fact that the Prius is, from the owner's point of view, a car more or less like any other. You refill its tank with regular gasoline from any old gas station when it's empty, and you don't have to do so as often as you do with other cars, because its hybrid engine uses electric batteries— recharged by the kinetic energy given off during braking—to augment its internally combusted power, greatly improving its fuel efficiency. This indeed has been central to Toyota's marketing strategy for the Prius: it's the most fuel-efficient car on the market, which incidentally reduces your automotive greenhouse gas emissions by as much as 90 percent but mainly saves you a lot of money at the pump. It's no coincidence that the Prius boom has directly coincided with the biggest spike in gas prices since the last OPEC crisis. And because the gas-electric hybrid engine is so practical and its bottom-line benefits so easy to spell out, the Prius's success has been quickly mimicked across the automotive industry. There are now trim little Honda Civic hybrids and hulking hybrid Ford SUVs, luxury Lexus hybrids and meat-and-potatoes hybrid GM trucks. Compared to a water-dripping fuel-cell vehicle, the hybrid's a half-step, but it's one that average consumers by the hundreds of thousands have been willing to take.

There's one other reason why the Prius has caught on so rapidly, a reason at least as crucial as its vaunted fuel economy but nowhere near as practical: the Prius has become, in a few short years, something verging on the defining symbol of twenty-first-century environmentalism. And that has happened in large measure because the Prius got Big In Hollywood. Brad Pitt drives one, and so do Julia Roberts and Cameron Diaz and J.Lo. Big-shot movie director Rob Reiner owns a Prius. Larry David and Leonardo DiCaprio own two apiece (as Toyota's website proudly notes), and Harrison Ford showed up at the 2003 Oscars in a chauffeur-driven Prius. *Han Freakin' Solo* is a Prius man. Ironically enough, so is "Running on Empty" composer Jackson Browne. "It's the hottest car we've ever had," Toyota's U.S. division president told a *Fortune* magazine reporter in February 2006.

The Prius was already a hot item in certain segments of the green-minded populace, but once the celebrity machine got hold of it, it became something much bigger: a mass-market, worldwide phenomenon, a hip accoutrement for anyone enamoured of the lifestyles of the (socially conscious) rich and (concerned) famous. A star was born, as it were, and what's more it was saddled with the slightly ironic weight of an environmentalist's badge of honour. What a funhouse-mirror time is this Anthropocene Era, when possibly the most recognized symbol of climate change activism is a gasoline-burning car.

A strange symbol to suit confused and uncertain times, I guess, and at any rate the Hip Hollywood Hybrid Half-Step has offered no shortage of such odd sights. One of the most pathetic scenes in the documentary *Who Killed the Electric Car?*, for example, depicts Arnold Schwarzenegger—the former action hero turned California's head of state, the Governator himself—pulling up to a photo op in a fuel-cell Hummer to inaugurate his "Hydrogen Highway." The film has done a spectacular job to this point of making its case for the viability of the purely electric car, particularly GM's late, lamented EV1, which earns on-camera endorsements from a handful of Hollywood stars. The pivotal moment for the electric car—its death warrant, more or less—was California's decision to abandon its pioneering electric-vehicle mandate in favour of the California Fuel Cell Partnership. This came barely three months after George W. Bush's rhetorical endorsement of a distant hydrogen-powered transportation future. And finally here was Arnie, committing California to building a network of hydrogen fuelling stations for cars that weren't even in production yet.

It isn't that Schwarzenegger has no business playing at being green—he has fought hard, for example, for solar power, and under his guidance California recently passed North America's most ambitious climate change regulations—but rather that he's a man so deeply linked, literally and symbolically, to the largest and most wasteful passenger vehicle of our time. AM General, the manufacturer that originally transformed the gargantuan gas-guzzling Hummer from military-personnel carrier to mass-market automobile, did so in part at Schwarzenegger's suggestion. He was the Hummer's first and remains its most famous driver; he purportedly owns a fleet of eight. And here he was, in a GM-made Hummer, dancing on the grave of GM's discontinued electric car in a fuel-cell rainmaking ceremony. If Schwarzenegger and the most fossil-fuel-friendly former oil man ever to occupy the White House were the leaders of the chorus singing hydrogen's praises, that was enough all by itself to bring into question its utility in the climate change fight.

Meanwhile, another sort-of-sad spectacle from the Hybrid Half-Step was being screened on the other side of the Atlantic, courtesy of Greenpeace UK. The British arm of the prominent global environmental group had devoted considerable resources in 2005 to chastising drivers of suvs, tucking leaflets under their windshield wipers and attaching fake tire clamps to their wheels that proselytized in favour of higher taxes for high-emissions vehicles. In April 2006, Greenpeace proudly declared victory: one of its leaflets had convinced English actress Thandie Newton to sell her suv and buy a Prius. A mid-level celebrity had taken the decisive half-measure of switching to a more fuel-efficient car. This evidently amounted to a breakthrough worthy of a press release.

As part of the same campaign that had won Thandie Newton's heart and mind, Greenpeace UK also commissioned a TV commercial. It was a slick and whip-smart ad, shot in stylish black-and-white and set to a moody acoustic guitar score. It depicts a pointedly average bloke going through the motions of a typical day at his white-collar office job. Something's clearly amiss, however, because everywhere the poor sod goes, he's subject to withering ridicule. His co-workers meet his greetings with rolled eyes, a woman spits in his coffee before bringing it to his desk, and an aerial shot of the company cafeteria finds him seated for lunch with a huge table to himself in an otherwise jam-packed room. He heads for home at the end of the day—a sign surreptitiously taped to his back reading I AM A PRICK—and when he reaches the parking garage we finally learn the cause of his ostracism: a big black SUV sits waiting for him. Cut to white text on a black screen: "The city gas guzzler / What does your car say about you?"

Look: we're talking about cars here. Overgrown and lunkheaded as SUVs might seem, the people behind the wheel see them as extensions of the all-pervasive and deeply enticing automotive culture they've always known. A culture of ubiquitous and useful, frivolous and fancy, souped-up, custom-painted, fetishized and madly adored cars. A half-century of blissful postwar mobility. Drive-in movies and burger joints. Car chases on the big screen, Formula One and NASCAR races on the small one. James Bond in a white Lotus to match his dinner jacket, Steve McQueen in a Mustang as dark green as the dirty money he's chasing, Archie Andrews in a jalopy to suit his goofy smile. The open road, pedal to the metal, Bruce Springsteen on the stereo.

One of the most powerful symbols of individual liberty in the free world.

And to compete with all this: a British art-house actress and a KICK ME sign? Bloody 'ell, mate. If that's the other option, *I'd* take the Mustang.

CAR CULT (I): THE MYTH

My first car was, in fact, a Mustang: a 1981 Ford Mustang hatchback, a black four-cylinder clunker, way past whatever prime it'd ever had. It was sluggish and not terribly sporty by the Mustang's high historical standards. It overheated if you even attempted a pale, third-rate imitation of Steve McQueen in it. It was a pain in the ass, and I cursed its name many times, but in truth I adored it. I learned to drive in northern Ontario, and let me tell you, if you didn't have a girlfriend or a buddy with slick enough fake ID to buy a case of Molson Ex, the most fun you could have as a sixteen-year-old on a snowy winter Saturday night in northern Ontario was behind the wheel of car—even a piece-of-shit four-cylinder Mustang—in the local shopping mall's empty parking lot. You could find a big empty section with half a foot of fresh powder and take 'er up to maybe 80 kilometres per hour, and then you'd slam those brakes and spin the wheel and you were off on a yippee-ki-yay of a skid that lasted for weeks. And when you finally came to a stop, you could just leave the wheel cranked and floor it, and just like that you were on the best tilt-o-whirl in all Creation. Yippee-ki-yi-fuckin'-yay!

Further back—in northern Alberta, on a military base just south of the oil sands—I was, for a time, in the thrall of a shiny black Camaro. I was fourteen years old, and it belonged to this slightly older guy I knew. He'd dropped out of high school to go work in the oil sands, as many aimless teenagers did in that part of Alberta. Made a bundle as a rig pig—the bottom-tier labourer in an oil-drilling operation, still ridiculously lucrative by any teenager's standards—and came back behind the wheel of that brand-new Camaro. He liked to flirt with a couple of the girls I hung out with, so he'd come by the school at lunch hour and take us all roaring and screeching down the back roads. Like any serious muscle car, this guy's Camaro had a booming stereo, and he'd pop a tape in and play the same song over and over at top volume as we drove:

> James Dean in that Mercury '49
> Junior Johnson runnin' thru the woods of Caroline
> Even Burt Reynolds in that black Trans Am
> All gonna meet down at the Cadillac Ranch

He sometimes had a buddy with him, and they'd howl along to the chorus. After a couple of rides, I knew the lyrics too, so I'd join in from the back seat when it came to the part about that shiny black Cadillac chewing up the highway like "a big old dinosaur."

The song was "Cadillac Ranch" by Bruce Springsteen, just one of the Boss's many passionate odes to the American highway and the cars that roar down it. Just thinking about it, I get those old chills down my spine, the ones that come when you're a little scared but mostly elated, drunk with the freedom of a fast car on an empty stretch of road.

So if we're going to talk about a sustainable world and the place the automobile will play in it, we need to confront that incomparable thrill head-on, like it's a back-road game of chicken.

Globally, transportation—increasingly by private automobile—accounts for 21 percent of greenhouse gas emissions. It's one of the fastest-growing emissions categories, projected to expand by as much as 92 percent over 1990 levels by 2020; even greening Europe has seen its transport emissions shoot up 32 percent from 1990 to 2004. This data alone would make transportation a critical system in the fight against climate change. But it's the singularly huge symbolic power of the automobile that's ultimately the larger issue. A significant wedge of the resistance to reconfiguring our societies along sustainable lines—possibly the biggest slice, particularly in North America—is couched in terms of preserving our "standard of living" and maintaining certain kinds of "lifestyle." And this rhetoric has resonance because it speaks to people's deep affection for big houses on huge lots, for wide controlled-access highways and vast paved shopping plazas, for the cottage out at the lake or the condo up in the mountains, for a sense of unfenced freedom and limitless mobility—all of it symbolized and personified and indeed *enabled* by the car.

By far the dominant player in the shaping of postwar Western culture (and the fragmented "global" culture that now travels worldwide) has been the United States, and the version of American culture that has proven most alluring to the rest of the world has been its individualistic, hyper-consumerist pop culture—a culture by, for and in many ways about cars. Fast-food restaurants and shopping malls were invented to provision people who ran their daily errands by car, and they were initially situated only in suburbs built specifically to maximize driving comfort. (The typical suburban street is so broad and curving because planners wanted it to be safe to drive at 50 miles per hour.) The car chase has long been the centrepiece of the typical Hollywood action movie, possibly the most widely exported American film genre. The archetypal rock & roll song—the marching cadence of this culture's global conquest—is about driving around in a car trying to meet girls.

Pretty much all of this incomparable allure is encapsulated in that great heavenly meeting described in Springsteen's "Cadillac Ranch." There's James Dean: the progenitor of brooding American cool (along with a motorcycle-riding Marlon Brando), catapulted to fame in a film that climaxes with a drag race, only to die at age 24 in a tragic car crash and pass into legend. Junior Johnson: a bona fide American outlaw hero, whose exploits as a bootlegger running moonshine and dodging police roadblocks along the back roads of North Carolina made him a regional superstar, and whose similar heroics on a NASCAR racetrack brought him national fame. And, yes, even Burt Reynolds, star of numerous brain-dead and massively popular movies in the late 1970s and early 1980s, movies (such as *The Cannonball Run* and *Smokey and the Bandit*) that were essentially nothing but car chase. And where else can this holy trinity of American car culture find its eternal peace but in a "Cadillac Ranch" immortalized in a rock & roll song?

It was Junior Johnson who was foremost in my mind as I sped along U.S. Route 421 into the Blue Ridge Mountains of North Carolina one fine spring day in 2006. I was behind the wheel of a rented Chevy, on my way to meet an organic farmer up in one of those backwoods hollows formerly known for tobacco-growing and bootlegging. From there, it was south to Georgia, where possibly the world's most ambitious experiment in sustainable industry was well under way, and then I'd be pushing on to see an equally bold effort in pedestrian-oriented sustainable living down in Florida. In between, though, lay a slice of heaven, no less rapturous for the fact that it was unsustainable as all hell: hundreds of miles of highway and a stack of mixed CDs.

I had one of those CDs cranked on the Chevy's stereo as I headed up Route 421 toward Wilkesboro, past a sign informing me I was on the "Junior Johnson Highway," and then past the Junior Johnson Speedway a short time after that. "The hardest of the hard chargers"—that's how Tom Wolfe described Johnson in his mythmaking 1965 *Esquire* profile. Johnson's father had been the proprietor of one of the largest whiskey stills in Wilkes County—"the bootleg capital of America"—and his son had first risen to fame as the most daring driver in hills so heavily populated with bootlegging hotshots that even their cars' nicknames were the stuff of legend.

Going legit as a stock-car racer only expanded the size and reach of the hard-charger myth. "Junior Johnson," wrote Wolfe, "was like Robin Hood or Jesse James or Little David or something." For decades to come, in suburban garages and on four-lane main drags and, yes, snow-covered northern Ontario parking lots, several generations of kids grew up chasing Junior Johnson's version of life, liberty and the pursuit of happiness. And now here I was, finally, roaring down his namesake highway in a blissful car-culture trance. The miles rolling by, hills out the window blanketed in the green of early spring buds, rock & roll on the stereo like an aural cocoon, maybe a coffee at the next exit to keep my energy up—there was a part of me that lived for this scene.

Somewhere along the way, though—maybe it was the three-bucks-a-gallon fill-up in South Carolina, or else the maniac gladiatorial traffic on the I-285 bypassing Atlanta—it occurred to me that I was on a kind of holiday. This was an amusement park ride, a fantasia. The kind of thing I might take my daughter on years from now, but only as a nostalgic treat, a blast from the past. Because there was a roadblock in the distance not even Junior Johnson could beat.

CAR CULT (II): THE REALITY

The trouble with car culture is not strictly a question of reducing emissions. Some hyper-efficient next-generation hybrid will almost certainly come along to tackle that problem adequately. If I've still got the wherewithal fifty years from now, I have no doubt there'll be a vehicle capable of hurtling me down the Junior Johnson Highway at 90 miles per hour on a fifth or a tenth or a hundredth of the amount of gas it would take today, even in a Prius.

In fact, some of these vehicles appear to be nearly roadworthy. A German company called Loremo, for example, has developed a super-light turbo-diesel car that gets *157* miles per gallon—more than triple the Prius's fuel efficiency—and it has stated that it will begin its first production run of ten thousand in 2009, with a sticker price of less than $15,000. Out in California, meanwhile, a start-up called Tesla Motors has been wowing journalists and Silicon Valley millionaires with its Roadster, a purely battery-powered rocket of a sports car with a 250-mile range that accelerates faster than a Porsche Turbo. The first hundred Tesla Roadsters have already sold—at $100,000 apiece—before production has even begun.

There will surely be newer, better cars—more efficient, lighter in weight and more aerodynamic, with batteries that take a charge quicker and hold it longer than anything we've seen to date—but they will still be cars. And the damage wrought by car culture extends far beyond the amount and composition of the exhaust coming out its tailpipe.

In his profile of Junior Johnson, Wolfe described the hard-charger's hometown of Ingle Hollow (the place was just a crossroads, really), lingering on the social scene at a little general store called Anderson's. The store was the centre of Ingle Hollow's social activity, a place where locals gathered to sit by the gas pumps out front and shoot the shit, telling the sorts of tales that built Johnson's legend. Wolfe recounted Johnson's arrival on the scene: "Junior goes inside and gets a Coca-Cola and rings up the till himself, like everybody who goes into Anderson's does, it seems like." This was simply a bit of local colour in 1965—the crossroads grocer where you ring in your purchase yourself—but forty years on, it has about it a sepia-toned bygone vibe and an undertone of quiet, Hollow-scale tragedy. Because thanks to the car-scale world Johnson's myth helped to create, there are precious few Anderson's stores left in the Carolina hills or anywhere else. On my visit, I stopped at a chain gas station where you had to pay in advance, and then I carried on a little further into the hills past Junior's Wilkes County home, and I arrived at a spot called Old Mans Hollow, where weekend-getaway condo development was swallowing up failing farms up and down the valley.

It was the same story throughout the South—as it is, to greater or lesser extents, across North America. Farmland and small towns devoured by suburban tract housing and strip malls, controlled-access highways lined at tidy intervals by gaudily logoed franchise development, the off-ramp near Wilkesboro essentially identical to the one in suburban Atlanta or exurban Colorado. I was stuck one night at a prime specimen of this species next to the I-40 outside Burlington, North Carolina. This stretch of interstate was miles from the nearest town, and about all there was at the exit was my chain "suite" motor inn, another chain motel a half-mile off and a Wal-Mart strip mall a mile beyond that. My evening dining choice, if I didn't want to drive anywhere, came down to a bleak traverse across several parking lots to arrive at either a Steak & Shake or a Hooters. I went with the pulled-pork sandwich at Hooters, seated at the bar in front of two ceiling-mounted TVs. One was showing a NASCAR race in Las Vegas, with sound, the roar of engines and crowds as dining music; the other, soundless, broadcast a *60 Minutes* report about the war in Iraq.

So it went throughout my driving tour of the Deep South. In South Carolina, I saw a gated community of 3,000-square-foot McMansions on multi-acre lots spilling down the steep slope of a hill at random, as if the valley had recently been ravaged by an exurban upper-middle-class landslide. It was a dozen miles from anything else at all, but I guess it was ostensibly a bedroom community for Greenville, a half-hour down the highway. I drove Route 331 south out of Montgomery, Alabama, through town after town of half-empty crumbling brick main streets and peripheries overgrown with bustling big-box franchises.

The day I passed through LaGrange, Georgia, several pages of the local newspaper were filled with ecstatic talk of the decision by Kia Motors of South Korea to open a manufacturing plant just up the highway in West Point. For the low price of between $250 and $400 million—the range of estimates for the value of the state's incentive package, which included tax breaks, free land, a new highway interchange and a job training centre—Kia had agreed to employ 2,500 or so locals to build some of its cars. And I was left to sit at the off-ramp Waffle House, jotting down calculations on my paper placemat to figure out the length of time the Georgia government could have paid those workers at Kia's average annual salary of $50,000 if it'd simply given them the money (about three years). And wondering what a loyal Chevy driver like Junior Johnson would think of this phenomenon—his Southern brethren more or less bribing a Korean discount automaker to set up shop there. And, for that matter, what he'd think of off-ramp Waffle Houses and all the rest of it. Actually, maybe he'd just think they'd all be good places to sell his Junior Johnson–brand barbecue pork skins in the handy snack-sized bags, because that's the sort of business Johnson's in these days. And maybe it's a better racket than running whiskey down dirt roads in the dead of night, but still you've got to wonder at the price of it all.

Estimates of the price of it all do, in fact, exist. A 1998 study by the International Center for Technology Assessment in Washington entitled "The Real Price of Gasoline," for example, added up "the many external costs of using motor vehicles." The study tallied up everything from the oil industry's tax subsidies to the costs of protecting supply lines to the environmental, health and social costs of running all those millions of internal combustion engines, and it came up with a cost—per year, in the United States alone—of between $558.7 billion and $1.69 trillion, which equates to $5.60 to $15.14 per gallon at the pump. Around the same time, *Natural Capitalism*—the ground-breaking tome on sustainable economics by Paul Hawken and Amory and Hunter Lovins—was first published, adding some other figures to the accounting: 250 million Americans maimed or injured over the course of the twentieth century; pavement enough to cover all of Ohio, Indiana and Pennsylvania and require $200 million per year in maintenance; massive increases in asthma, emphysema and bronchial infections; 7 billion pounds of solid waste added to landfills each year. A 2001 Cato Institute study estimated that the United States spent $60 billion every year by the 1990s just on the military protection of Persian Gulf oil supplies—this before the trillion-dollar war in Iraq was added to the bottom line.

A more recent study by an economist at the U.S. National Defence Council Foundation included the cost of the invasion of Iraq, and came up with a price per gallon of $8—spiking to $11 per gallon for Middle Eastern crude, if you costed it separately. I came across this stat in a four-part story by Paul Salopek that ran in the *Chicago Tribune* in July 2006. The series traced the legacy of a tank of regular unleaded from a suburban Chicago gas station to its origins the world over, Salopek's reporting overflowing along the way with haunting images of the global impact of car culture. Here were oil operations built to unearthly· scale (*30,000 miles* of pipe, for example—more than enough to circle the earth at the equator—"tangled like spaghetti" on the bottom of the Gulf of Mexico to enable oil drilling there). Karina tribespeople in tiny Venezuelan villages buying their first cars with the country's newfound oil wealth (Salopek noted "a weakness for old Yankee gas guzzlers" among the Karina, surely one of the strangest field notes in the annals of cultural anthropology). An Iraqi oil field littered in rusting Baathist Army gear, guarded by an embittered ex-Baathist who frets over his son's jihadist sympathies and travels to the Basra airport by armed convoy to escape to the United Arab Emirates for a little R&R.

There was one scene, though, that stuck with me the longest: a Nigerian fisherman by the almost comically resonant name of Sunday Jeremiah, coming home at the end of a long day of desperate fishing amid dwindling stocks in the estuaries of the Niger Delta, the night sky above him lit "an angry orange" by the gas flares from the copious drilling operations there. The flares were just one element of the vast apparatus by which Nigeria exports about 2.3 million barrels of crude oil each day. And here's a statistical correlation that's even harder to shake: 2.3 million barrels of crude oil produce about 45 million gallons of gasoline, which is about the amount of gasoline burned in America every week *by idling vehicles alone.* The night sky over the Niger Delta turned permanently orange, then, to fuel a week's worth of heavy American traffic.

GRIDLOCKED

It is estimated that idling vehicles—primarily those piled up bumper to bumper in stagnant traffic—burn through 2.3 billion gallons of gas in the United States every year. For a couple of days in March 2006, I idled through a few gallons of my own in the relentless stop-and-go traffic of County Road 30A east of Fort Walton Beach, Florida. CR-30A runs parallel to a long stretch of fine Gulf Coast sand on the Florida Panhandle, but despite its obvious charms, this piece of coastline remained sparsely populated enough that a "county road" served its traffic needs just fine until recently. For generations, there had been little vacation cottages tucked amid the fishermen's shacks on the bluffs overlooking the beach, but nothing that proved too much for the two-lane county road to handle. This was the "Redneck Riviera," far enough north and far enough away from Florida's major population centres that it attracted mostly weekending Georgians and Alabamans. By the early 1980s, however, condo and resort towers had filled seemingly every other available inch of prime beachfront property in the rest of Florida, and developers turned their attention to the beaches backed by CR-30A.

One of the first of these new developments was a place christened "Seaside," a collaboration between a developer who'd spent his childhood summers in the area and a pair of forward-thinking architects based in Miami. Seaside, built to resemble an idyllic Southern town circa 1950, was the first experiment in a massively influential school of urban design known as "New Urbanism." So unprecedented was Seaside among Florida's carbon-copy holiday-condo sprawl that it helped drive up property values all along CR-30A, amplifying the Gulf Coast building boom already in progress. By the time of my visit to

Seaside, the former county road was an all-but-unbroken strip of dense new development for miles in either direction. Wherever there weren't condos, there were strip malls thick with fast-food joints and beach-wear shops or other resort communities still under construction.

One of Seaside's biggest draws was that it had been consciously built to the scale and needs of people instead of their cars. Its cottages and condos were packed tightly together along narrow streets with wide park-like medians and cobblestony interlocking-brick surfaces, which together forced motorized traffic to move at a walking pace. Its main shopping and dining area had been intentionally laid out as an outdoor bazaar, parking-lotless and directly abutting CR-30A. This had created a holiday setting so unique and beguiling (not to mention world-famous—it served as the living stage set for the Hollywood movie *The Truman Show*) that it attracted day trippers from all those other, less charming resort communities down the road. Indeed, so magnetic was this pedestrian oasis that—in its ironic crowning achievement—it had almost completely clogged CR-30A with traffic trying to reach it (and its handful of nearby imitators).

The curse of traffic is not at all unique to the Florida Panhandle, nor even to the car-obsessed U.S. of A., and the paradox I faced in Seaside was one I ran into again and again on my travels. Motor vehicle traffic was my constant companion, far more endemic to this geography of hope than windmills or solar panels, and it was the Achilles heel of even the most ambitious experiments in sustainability. Even on the awe-inspiring Danish islands of Samsø and Aerø, the question of the CO_2 emissions from automobiles was the only one that hadn't been fully solved (Samsø's offshore-wind-farm offset strategy was, at best, a stopgap measure).

The maddening absurdity of the global traffic curse reached something like a crescendo, however, on the streets of Hyderabad, India. I was in Hyderabad to see one of the world's greenest buildings, but to reach it I first had to negotiate the broad boulevards and narrow lanes outside my hotel near the railway station—all of them choked with clanging, growling, belching traffic that I found to be superlatively godawful even by the formidable standards of rapidly urbanizing India. Hyderabad's traffic unnerved me completely. There were bigger and more sprawling Indian cities, but none I'd ever seen that had so completely outgrown its transport infrastructure. There were not enough lights, not enough stop signs, nothing even vaguely resembling order. To cross the street in front of my hotel to use a phone kiosk or flag down an eastbound rickshaw, I had to hike up the block to the nearest intersection and then wait—sometimes five minutes or more—for a gap in the westbound traffic. I'd stay there, motionless, until enough locals had joined me to give me at least the illusion of a system to participate in. The gap would finally come and we'd all sprint to the median, and by then the eastbound traffic would usually have started back up. Again we'd all wait, perched in a precarious row on a concrete divider a half-foot high and three inches wide, as buses coughed black exhaust directly into our mouths and scooters piled high with families of five zipped by mere inches from our noses. At the next gap, we'd all sprint again.

Once, on a suburban thoroughfare in one of the more prosperous parts of the city, I was so intensely focused on finding a break in the traffic that when one finally came and I darted out, I was levelled by a bicycle that had been forced onto the dirt shoulder by all the motor vehicles. My fellow pedestrians growled curses at the bicyclist as a courtesy, but I could tell this kind of thing was as common to Hyderabadi life as a plate of idlis or a monsoon rain.

Now, to be fair, the chaos of Hyderabad's inner city isn't much more than a baroque embellishment on the usual madness of the contemporary Indian metropolis: a few more trucks and overflowing buses per square kilometre like automotive filigree, an extra lane or two of buzzing motorbikes as two-wheeled gilt, the screech of the supplemental, hand-squeezed arrooga horns preferred by Hyderabad's rickshaw wallahs bleating out a kind of overwrought fanfare. (One popular brand of these horns emits a piercing screech that sounds uncannily like a small child wailing in agony.) And like the Florida Panhandle's CR-30A, Hyderabad's downtown streets were not an ominous sign of deepening squalor but an emblem of bustling prosperity. The city, once a mid-sized burg best known as the historic stronghold of Muslim culture in otherwise deeply Hindu South India, had been stampeding toward megalopolisity for nearly a decade on the strength of a massive high-tech boom. Hyderabad's 2001 population was estimated at around six million (up from three million or so a decade earlier), and it has undoubtedly grown far beyond that in the intervening boom years. And every last Hyderabadi in this burgeoning bunch seemed to be in a perpetual struggle to drive, bike or bullock-cart it crosstown on a system of roadways laid out in 1948 to serve a city of 500,000.

This was Progress. It was a central and inescapable component of the apparatus by which an Indian city, or any other, developed its way onto the map of the modern world. It was, that is, the very essence of Modernity—or, more accurately, the downside of Modernity's Faustian bargain, brought to reeking life in yellow-brown clouds of smog and writ large in the form of umpteen lanes of bleating, lurching, barely moving traffic. It was a pathetic Keystone Kops parody of freedom's promise of unlimited mobility. And it was, moreover, a kind of ultimate case in point for the argument that car culture is, in general, much less than its mythic hype. The dream entices with visions of adrenaline-soaked romps up empty winding mountainside roads—the kind so beloved by the makers of car commercials—but the reality is much more often stop-and-go, lurch-and-stomp, honking screeching road-raging gridlock. It would be one thing to suggest an overhaul of the status quo in global transport if it consisted mainly of Junior Johnson thrill rides, but who would size up Hyderabad's madcap free-for-all or CR-30A's bumper-to-bumper crawl and suggest it was chugging briskly in the right direction toward a bright liberated future?

What I mean is this: even if you take the millions of tonnes of carbon dioxide spewing skyward out of the equation, this is still a cat-astrophically unsustainable wreck of a system that simply begs for change. The automobile was the reigning monarch of twentieth-century progress, but its kingdom is on the brink of ruin. It's long past time for a palace coup.

THE POST-COMBUSTION MAGNA CARTA

There's a particularly pointed irony to the fact that I found the planet's most ambitious zero-emission automobile project in bliss-fully gridlock-free Singapore: there may not be another city in the developed world more avowedly hostile to the private automobile. To buy a car in Singapore, you must first obtain a "certificate of entitle-ment." These are strictly limited in number and sold at auction, and they can add as much as $45,000 to the price of a luxury vehicle. Registration fees are high and subject to frequent hikes, and there's an additional levy for the privilege of driving into the Central Business District during working hours on weekdays.

None of these are recent initiatives. There have been steep import levies on new cars in Singapore since 1970, and the "area licensing" scheme that restricts downtown traffic dates to 1975. And when these measures proved insufficient to limit automobile ownership to the desired level, strict quotas on new-car sales were introduced in 1990. Singapore's opposition to the car cult is as old and dear to the city-state's famously zealous planning regime as its bans on gum and public spitting. And it's just another part of Lee Kuan Yew's vision of a modern, orderly "Garden City," which was born around the same time that most of the West was racing to enmesh its countryside in ribbons of freeway and ring its cities with ever-more-distant, car-centred suburbs.

It's worth noting the mess the city-state was in when it first achieved independence in 1965, with Lee as its first prime minister. Singapore had been a key British colonial outpost (and opium supplier) in the nineteenth century, but after years of brutal Japanese occupation during the Second World War and then benign neglect by the bankrupt British empire in its aftermath, it had fallen into filthy, teeming squalor. Over the course of a single generation, under Lee's meticulous, micromanaged guidance, Singapore transformed itself into one of the tidiest and most prosperous cities in Asia or anywhere else, a fierce Asian Tiger with a mammoth container port and a booming service economy heavily invested in high finance and high technology. It's barely democratic—Lee and his successors in the People's Action Party since he stepped down in 1990 have always wielded a heavy authoritarian hand—but it's also an undeniably liveable city. Among other world-class amenities, it boasts a state-of-the-art, profit-turning transit system—first launched in 1987, against the best advice of the World Bank, and regularly expanded ever since—which ferries upward of 40 percent of the city's populace on its daily commute. And you don't need to spend very long in the perpetual gridlock of Bangkok or Kuala Lumpur or Manila before you start to suspect that no small part of Singapore's extraordinary success rests on its steadfast refusal to make a high priority of the automobile.

Bangkok provides a particularly revealing counter-example. The sprawling capital city of another Asian Tiger economy, Bangkok boomed in parallel to Singapore for much of the 1980s and 1990s, and a trip to its modern retail heart, Ploenchit Road, reveals a dense corridor of the same sort of upscale shops and multilevel malls that line Singapore's Orchard Road (Southeast Asia's answer to Fifth Avenue). The two districts are light-years apart, however, when it comes to the quality of the experience. The enormous shopping palaces of Ploenchit are often separated by long stretches of parking lot and wide side streets dense with a dozen lanes of screaming traffic. The brand-new SkyTrain looms high above—a transit network far too small and expensive for the sprawling city, its wide track creating a concrete canopy over Ploenchit that traps the exhaust of the endless rush of motor vehicles below.

Compare this dreary scene to Orchard Road: wide sidewalks dotted with fountains, an endless series of cafés fronting the retail complexes on either side. Many of the cafés are tucked into mezzanines slightly below the road's grade or on terraces a level above, which along with the burble of the fountains blocks out most of the traffic noise from the street itself. And any number of them provide a great place to knock back a Tiger beer or two and watch the constant parade of pedestrian shoppers stroll by. Whatever traffic there is on Orchard Road is far away and irrelevant, and when you're ready to stumble back to your hotel, there are subway stops at tight intervals from which you can zoom off to within walking distance of pretty much anywhere in the city. The most striking thing for me, at first, about driving around in that hydrogen-powered Mercedes was simply the novelty of being in a car on an expressway in Singapore—I'd barely noticed that the city even *had* expressways.

Of course, an autocratic city-state can pull off feats of planning and growth that less regimented regimes can't manage. And so, fittingly enough, it is to England that we turn for the real post-combustion Magna Carta. To central London, more precisely, which starting in February 2003 fell under the authority of the car-obsessed West's first "congestion charge": a steep £5 fee to drive a motor vehicle into the heart of the city between 7:00 a.m. and 6:30 p.m. on weekdays. In the face of worldwide attention (including deep skepticism and even hostility at home and abroad), London's bold traffic-control experiment has been, by almost any measure, a resounding success. The city's technocrats are so pleased with the 18 percent reduction in traffic it has precipitated that they've upped the fee to £8 and (as of February 2007) expanded it to the West End. The many vested business interests that fretted over its impact have been reassured by an Oxford-Cambridge joint study that found its effect on commerce to be "broadly neutral." Even the stodgy *Financial Times* saw fit, by 2006, to call it a "a broadly welcome measure." It's also a huge money-making engine for the city, of course, though the purpose of the newfound cashflow has received less publicity: the net revenue is being used to fund mass transit.

On the surface, the congestion charge might appear to be a uniquely London phenomenon, a double-decker bus of a local ordnance, built on the arrogance of one of the world's biggest and most distinctive cities to solve a problem specific to its dense core of narrow pre-industrial streets. The same could be said of the Magna Carta: the joint declaration of a bunch of pissed-off, infighting English barons, speaking to obscure thirteenth-century squabbles over Breton territorial rights and the proper way to choose a new Archbishop of Canterbury. Fair enough, but it also contained the first written guarantee of due process—a cornerstone of enlightened legal systems the world over and the fulcrum upon which the balance of power began its long swing from the divine right of kings to the civil rights of citizens.

It remains to be seen whether London's congestion charge, with its redress of the urban imbalance between automotive and human scale, will be as epochal in import. There's already evidence, though, that it may soon be welcomed as a liberator far and wide. Even in the very heart of the car's empire—in the fabled open spaces of the American West—the independence movement is under way.

TRANSIT CULT (I): FREEDOM TRAINS

"Well, Portland, Oregon, and sloe-gin fizz / If that ain't love then tell me what is, uh-*huh*."

That's Loretta Lynn, an old-school country singer belting out a honky-tonk tune of recent vintage. I like to think of her rolling into town on a train to order up her ecstatic highball. There are almost as many trains as cars in the folklore of American music—mystery trains and freedom trains, slow trains coming and night trains gone, Wabash Cannonballs and Chattanooga Choo-Choos, fantastical freight trains hauling boxcars full of hobos bound for the Big Rock

Candy Mountain—and so it'd just make sense for Loretta Lynn to fall in love with Portland at the end of a train ride, because it is America's first great train city of the Anthropocene Era.

This new freedom train isn't a big ole Union Pacific freight or anything like that. It goes by the name of light rail transit—the LRT, a catch-all term that includes both underground and above-ground urban commuter trains—and it came to Portland decades before London's transit Magna Carta in a rejection of car culture just as categorical. Portland's LRT system (the MAX by name) traces its origins to a wave of grassroots activism in the early 1970s. Portland was in the midst of a wave of ambitious "urban renewal," and as in most North American cities of the era, that meant bulldozing derelict downtown buildings to make room for freeways. Portland's citizens finally drew the line, however, at the proposed Mount Hood Freeway, which was intended to run roughshod through several historic inner-city neighbourhoods. After several years of intense political battle, the freeway plan was scrapped, and the millions of dollars earmarked for it were instead pumped into mass transit, which in 1986 birthed the MAX.

In the years since, as the plague of sprawl-fed gridlock has spread to city after city, Portland has emerged as every contemporary planner's shorthand for how to build a city right, and it perennially tops surveys and expert-ranked lists of America's most desirable cities in which to live. There were many other enlightened elements critical to Portland's singular success—I'll come to those later—but for the moment the key point is this: its origin was in a decisive choice of transit over more roads.

Portland's change of direction—when the freeway idea was shelved in 1973, even in 1986 when the MAX system debuted—was so out of step with contemporaneous trends in the United States that the city may as well have hired Don Quixote as an LRT conductor. Times, however, have emphatically changed. "Light rail," *The Economist* observed in a September 2006 article, "is suddenly booming across America." The story went on to detail big new LRT projects in Dallas, Charlotte, St. Louis—even Phoenix, possibly the most car-oriented city on the planet. And the Denver metropolitan area has embarked upon a project called FasTracks ("one of the most ambitious urban transit projects in the nation's history," decreed the *New York Times*), which will see 120 miles of track laid on six new lines by 2016; by the time it's finished, Denver's LRT will be nearly triple the length of Portland's pioneering MAX network.

The train craze extends well beyond America's borders. Not so far from Singapore—and stifled by the perpetual traffic jams it so pointedly lacks—Bangkok and Kuala Lumpur have both inaugurated LRT lines in recent years. There's also talk of light rail transit in smog-choked metropolises across the Indian subcontinent. Delhi recently opened a subway line, and there are plans already afoot to extend it to the booming high-tech hub of Noida. Even Hyderabad (which I introduced as the chaotic traffic raja of India) is making noise about an LRT. But perhaps the most revealing plan is the one that had its foundation stone laid in June 2006 in Bangalore.

Bangalore has earned world renown in recent years as the epicentre of India's impressive high-tech boom, and it has taken considerable pride in its emergence as the youngest, fastest paced, most Westernized and fastest growing of Indian metropolises. Less highly publicized is the strain this growth has put on the city's decrepit infrastructure, from roads to water mains to power stations. "Bangalore today is in a shambles," announced *Business Today*, a prominent Indian business magazine, in an August 2006 article that estimated the average speed of a Bangalore commute to be 10 kilometres per hour (or just barely double a healthy adult's walking pace). A year earlier, *The Economist* had described Bangalore as a city "choking on its own success" in a feature that opened with a detailed description of an abandoned, half-completed overpass on the highway leading in from the airport—this in a city where the two largest IT firms were adding a thousand employees every month between them. *The Economist* could've also noted (but didn't) that Bangalore has been planning a new airport for *seventeen years,* a process stalled repeatedly by petty bureaucratic squabbles between the state and federal governments.

All of which serves to underscore the significance of the fact that Bangalore has begun construction on two new LRT lines—33 kilometres in total, the first to be completed by 2009 and the second by 2011. Fearful of losing its lucrative pride of place in India's high-tech sector to gridlock, Bangalore is off—at breakneck speed, by local standards—in pursuit of a little piece of Portland. A freedom train, if you will, for the Deccan Plateau.

It's almost enough to inspire a folk song—or a romantic ballad.

TRANSIT CULT (II), OR HOW I LEARNED TO STOP DRIVING & LOVE PUBLIC TRANSIT

I like to think I come by my membership in the transit cult honestly, inasmuch as I certainly wasn't raised in it. I'm not sure how old I was when I first set foot on a subway car, but I'm pretty sure I was old enough to drive. After I finished university, though, I moved to Toronto. My old shitbox Mustang was several years in its grave, and I had nowhere near the means with which to buy even another shit-box. To my surprise and delight, I soon discovered I didn't need one. For most of the next decade, I never lived more than a five-minute amble from a subway or streetcar stop. I got in the habit of making more frequent grocery trips for smaller bundles of purchases, grew to like reading a magazine article or a few pages of a book on my way somewhere, all but forgot the hassles of finding parking, paying for routine maintenance, choosing a designated driver.

A few years ago, I moved to Calgary—a much younger and smaller city than Toronto that did most of its growing after the Second World War, in the suburbanized automobile era. For all that, Calgary is ostensibly a leading light in the transit boom: not only is the city laced with two modern LRT lines, but the system gets its power exclusively from wind farms south of the city. It's possibly the greenest LRT network on the planet—if Calgary were a different kind of city, this might be its pride and joy, the centrepiece of its civic brand, the slogan on the WELCOME TO sign out by the airport. Alas, Calgary already has a brand. It's a freewheeling Wild West town of ranchers and cowboys (historically) and oil barons (currently). Most Calgarians, I'd wager, don't even know that their LRT is powered by renewable energy. Calgary's extensive transit network, which includes hundreds of bus routes in addition to the flagship C-Train, is exceedingly well used (overcrowding and insufficiently frequent service are the chief complaints against it), but the city is both culturally and functionally a car town.

My wife and I own a house in one of the city's oldest neighbourhoods, on the edge of the inner city. We live a brisk fifteen-minute walk from two C-Train stops—a walk either alongside a busy commuter road bereft of street life or across a parking lot shared by the Calgary Stampede grounds and the Saddledome arena, a vast asphalt expanse that is similarly lifeless except during the two weeks of the annual Stampede (the city's wildest party and biggest claim to international fame) or on the night of a Calgary Flames hockey game. There's also a shuttle bus that comes to the nearest corner of our street once every forty minutes to ferry residents to one of the C-Train stops. Neither the trains nor the shuttle, however, takes us anywhere near our essential services (the nearest grocery and hardware stores, the health clinic, our favourite Vietnamese joint), and the closest commercial strip is a good half-hour walk or fifteen-minute bike ride— sometimes manageable for maybe seven or eight months of the year, but pretty much out of the question in the sub-zero chill of winter. Most of the practical stuff of a functional neighbourhood has moved to the suburban strip malls and big-box plazas. All of which is to say that despite our best efforts—despite having so fully shaken the car habit that I actively miss the transit ease of Toronto every time I climb behind the wheel to embark on a twenty-minute drive just to buy a few screws or a new notebook—we've again become car-dependent.

To find out why this was the case, I paid a visit to my friendly neighbourhood urban geographer—Byron Miller, a professor at the University of Calgary—who explained to me why the mere existence of the C-Train wasn't enough to make Calgary a transit city. He noted the concrete wastelands that surround the majority of the city's LRT stations, hallmarks of the historic indifference of the city's broader planning scheme to its transit plan. And he related two telling anecdotes about how a truly transit-oriented cityscape works.

The first involved his time as a graduate student in Germany. Miller was studying in Freiburg, a small city in southwestern Germany blessed by a postcard-perfect, pedestrian-friendly medieval downtown *and* one of the best transit networks of any city its size anywhere. He recalled that many of his fellow North American students arrived in Freiburg with plans to buy cars, on the routine assumption that modern life was unbearable without one. Within weeks, the pedestrian scale of Freiburg and the quality of its transit changed their minds. Miller: "I can't think of a single one of my North American friends— who grew up in a culture of suburban North America, automobile-based North America—can't think of a single one of them who purchased an automobile when they lived in Freiburg."

 Miller's contrasting anecdote was about his stint as a grad student at a university in suburban Phoenix, Arizona, a few years later, and about an Italian friend who came to study there, a young man accustomed to the human scale and multiple transportation options of European cities. He arrived intent on using Phoenix's transit system, which he assumed would be as adequate as any Italian one. "About two or three weeks later," Miller said, "after experiencing the horrible public transit system in Phoenix—taking two hours to get from his home to the nearest shopping mall and then two hours to get back, and getting stranded one evening because the buses stopped running at seven o'clock—he decided he had to buy a car. And he bought a car, and he never used public transit in Phoenix again. And the point I want to make here is that people respond to the opportunities that are presented to them. And they respond to what works best for them, what's most efficient, what's most cost-effective, what's most enjoyable, and so on. And if you present people with opportunities that are better than what they have now, they *will* switch."

Miller's worst case of Phoenix popped up as well in a 2004 *New Yorker* essay by David Owen on green living. Transit, Owen argued, is not a one-size-fits-all solution. Running LRT lines out to distant low-density suburbs may just encourage further suburban development, which will likely wind up car-dependent. He cited Phoenix as the most extreme example of a city that transit alone couldn't help—it was all but irredeemable, a rapidly metastasizing suburban tumour on the Arizona desert where twice the population of Manhattan had blobbed across two hundred times the land mass. The resulting population density was so low, Owen said, that "no transit system could conceivably serve it."

The main subject of Owen's essay was the "utopian environmentalist community" he lived in as a young man, a place better known as Manhattan. "By the most significant measures," Owen wrote, "New York is the greenest community in the United States, and one of the greenest cities in the world." Manhattan consumes gasoline at a rate last seen in the rest of the country in the 1920s, and 82 percent of its residents commute to and from work by transit, by bicycle or on foot. The city's tightly packed and toweringly stacked apartments greatly reduce the amount of energy needed to heat each residence. Calculate its environmental footprint by surface area, and Manhattan looks like an overconsuming disaster, but calculate it per capita, and it turns bright green. By virtue of a handful of happy accidents—a physical geography that forbade sprawl, a street system laid out by merchants who valued the efficient movement of goods over the aesthetics of broad, curving tree-lined avenues, and a density so great by the early 1900s that it couldn't be reconfigured for cars—Manhattan was, however unintentionally, "a model of environmental responsibility."

It's a surprising point, but one I find hard to refute, especially from the point of view of transport: most of what we love about cars—freedom of movement, ease and speed of travel, plain old fun—applies in Manhattan mostly to sustainably biased transit. In place of the celebrity-piloted Prius on an L.A. freeway, Manhattan offers a less jarring symbol of ecological virtue: an urban environment whose "green" features have been invisibly woven into the social fabric and where transit is a deeply engrained, all-but-unavoidable feature of daily life.

Green has long been a common find-and-replace term for ecological awareness, and environmental activists have always been most vocal and visible in their defence of pristine nature. When the movement has talked about the urban environment at all, it has been deemed a necessary evil at best. What's more, a "green" city—insofar as this oxymoron was even reconcilable to the movement's veneration of untouched wilderness—was one that tried to mask its urbanity behind a façade of expansive parks and tree-lined streets. Singapore, for example, predicates its pretences to greenness on its "Garden City" trappings, its ample parkland and manicured waterfront promenades and expressway bougainvillea planters. It could instead take greater (and more valid) pride in the fact that it functions smoothly with one-sixth the per capita automobile traffic and eight times the transit ridership rates of smoggy Los Angeles. The Prius, particularly one driven by an L.A. resident, has come to symbolize climate change action despite being a half-measure verging on a cop-out to the car-culture backbone of our unsustainable social order. So why not replace it with humble, workaday public transit, which can make its case as the cornerstone of a sustainable city without such shuck-and-jive contortions?

Start, perhaps, with this: there is no truly world-class city without great public transit. Consider the twin metropolises that have ruled over the past two hundred years of fossil-fuelled modernity: London and New York. Congestion-charging London is so inextricably linked with its Underground mass-transit system that the Tube's red-hoop-and-blue-bar logo is the de facto seal of the city and a perennial tourist postcard and T-shirt favourite. New York's subway looms similarly large in the city's public image—so much so that its name and iconography have been co-opted by the world's most prominent chain of New York–style sandwich joints. (The interior walls of many Subway sandwich shops are plastered with wallpaper collages of newspaper articles from the early days of New York's subway system.) Many of the world's other great metropolises yield similar iconographies. The stunning art nouveau station signage of the Paris Métro, for example, is better known than all but a handful of the Louvre's treasures. The cable car is synonymous with San Francisco, and Toronto's distinctive red-and-white streetcars are central to its persona. Hip-hop artists may have embraced the suv as a pimped-out status symbol in recent years, but the art form's roots are forever entwined with graffiti-covered New York subway cars. And in the popular computer game series *Civilization* (an elaborate simulation of the rise and fall of great societies), the appearance of mass transit is as sure a sign as any that the cities in a given civilization have truly reached the modern age.

Here's what I'm driving at: there is already a significant mythological backstory to public transit. It just needs an Anthropocene update: a sense of purpose, an air of urgency, and most of all a Prius-like boom in the pop consciousness. Which is not to say that the sustainable order we need to build won't include cars—it surely will—but that it won't be *for* cars. Transit may never be Hollywood hip, but it can at least come to seem essential. Recycling, possibly the greatest success story in the history of environmental activism in terms of participation, works on precisely this level: no one thinks of it as the best part of urban life, but its absence increasingly scans as a glaring deficiency and a public embarrassment.

The way forward, then, isn't a hard-rockin' tune with a passionate Bruce Springsteen vocal and a title like "LRT Farm," or dramatic footage of bicycles racing at full speed down hillsides or even through rush-hour traffic. It would be foolhardy to confront the car cult head-on, to try to beat it at the game it created and mastered. Propaganda works best when its claims—however grandiose and overstated—build upon a basic truth. And the basic truth is that driving a car *is* sometimes a wild thrill ride, and sitting behind the wheel of a certain kind of automobile *does* make the driver more desirable to some eyes. Transit's virtues are, for the most part, the exact inverse of the car's. They speak to the veneration of the public sphere over the private sector, and of social cohesion over personal sovereignty. Collective efficiency over individual consumption. Sustainability over depletion. If the car is a delirious backseat seduction with no thought of its consequences tomorrow, then transit is a pleasant stroll in the park with someone you plan to spend the rest of your life with. Try to sell the latter as sexier than the former, and you don't stand a chance. Much better to build a new vocabulary with which to sing transit's praise.

THE GEOGRAPHY OF HOPE IN TRANSIT

Mostly by necessity and occasionally by preference, my cartographic journeys involved damn near every mode of transport there is. I travelled the greatest distances by airplane, of course, and air travel is even more intractable, from the perspective of CO_2 emissions, than the automobile: there's not an emissions-free passenger jet to be found on anyone's drawing board. It might well be that oil, no matter what the price, will forever remain the fuel of air travel, in which case the true cost of it will undoubtedly become part and parcel of flying, prompting a return to exclusively luxury-priced flights.

Back down to earth, I rode long-haul trains and commuter trains, two- and three-tiered sleepers and packed standing-room-only subway cars. I rode long-distance buses and airport shuttles. I sailed on ferries and small motorboats, rented cars and motorbikes, hired taxis and rickshaws. I pedalled bikes, walked, sometimes sprinted to catch a departing LRT. Without a doubt, fossil-fuelled motor vehicles provided some of the greatest thrills—the kind derived from bombing down the Junior Johnson Highway in a rented Chevy, but also the more visceral sort that come from the wrenching turns and miraculous near-miss deliverances of an autorickshaw madly slaloming through Hyderabadi traffic. I finagled a ride on a private yacht in southern Thailand, a mix of onboard motor and sail that I guess amounted to a seafaring hybrid and at any rate was a singular pleasure. But there was a unique quality to the most sustainable kinds of travel, something less adrenalized but ultimately more lasting, the kind of contentment that comes from participating in a mass ritual or a public improvement project—or both.

On Bangkok's SkyTrain, for example, my wife and I often had our daughter with us, grinning from a hip-mounted sling or baby backpack, and the old Thai ladies already seated on the cars would invariably begin motioning to hold her before the train had pulled out of the station. We could spend the rest of the ride consulting maps or guides or doing nothing much at all as our daughter bounced along on some fawning Thai woman's knee. (Bangkok's LRT system is also much safer, healthier and faster than a tuk-tuk ride down on the smog-clouded, overcrowded streets.)

The seamless integration of Copenhagen's public transport was its own kind of quiet thrill. Find a free bike outside the central train station, pop a coin in the slot, and head off on a leisurely ride through the car-free inner city. Join a train of biking commuters to pedal past the gilt palaces and baroque parliament buildings in dedicated bike lanes with their own traffic lights. Find a metro stop, lock the bike back up and reclaim the deposit, and then head down into the subway to find a digital sign broadcasting news of a train arriving in a minute and a half to whisk you back to your hotel or anywhere else in the city you need to go. The transit system in Copenhagen is so thorough and efficient it would seem like a ridiculous mix of decadence, stubbornness and folly to bother with a car.

Such are the mythic proportions of public transit: it doesn't electrify you with speed, but when it's done right, it can lull you with its calm, efficient rhythms. Though the technology (and civil engineering) is often plenty sophisticated, there's rarely much of the heat and flash associated with a sleek new car's whiz-bang gadgetry. Transit isn't a muscle-bound action hero, it's the dignified lead in a redemptive drama. The LRT-car manufacturer may not show up in some down-at-heel town proffering 2,500 jobs the way a Korean car company does, but a 1999 study published in the *Journal of the American Planning Association* found that "access to public transit is a significant factor in determining average rates of labour participation"; the more of a city's population within walking distance of transit, in other words, the more people can hold down steady jobs of all sorts. By contrast, a World Bank study estimated that every car in Bangkok spent an average 44 days stuck in the city's notoriously awful traffic by the mid-1990s—a staggering productivity drain that finally convinced the city's civic leaders it needed an LRT. Transit might not be exciting, but its efficiency gains are bottom-line practical.

The same principle holds true even when the subject turns to the enormous, industrial-scale network of private transport that moves goods around the world by the millions of tons. Seaborne shipping, for example, consumes about 5.5 million barrels of oil every day, 80 percent of it in the form of high-emissions heavy fuel oil. In lieu of a fleet of futuristic hydrofoils speeding into port to save the day, a German company called SkySails offers a marvel of pre-industrial science, an oversized version of a ubiquitous child's toy. A kite, that is. SkySails calls its invention a "towing kite system," and what it entails, more or less, is attaching an enormous, precision-guided kite to the front end of an industrial freighter. Once the boat is up to cruising speed, the SkySail unfurls, leveraging wind power to greatly relieve the burden on the ship's engines. A 140-metre cargo ship from the fleet of Beluga Shipping of Bremen, Germany, made the first commercial purchase of a SkySail in 2007; the SkySails company predicts savings of 10 to 35 percent on fuel costs, and it reckons that if its kites catch on worldwide, they could breeze their way to CO_2 emissions reductions of 130 million tonnes per annum.

Improving upon the spectacular inefficiencies in the world's existing transport systems has long been the fanatical focus of the Rocky Mountain Institute (RMI), one of the world's top sustainability think tanks, which was founded by Amory and Hunter Lovins in the ski resort village of Snowmass, Colorado, in the 1970s. "The contemporary automobile," they reported (along with Paul Hawken) in their 1999 book *Natural Capitalism,* "after a century of engineering, is embarrassingly inefficient: Of the energy in the fuel it consumes, at least 80 percent is lost, mainly in the engine's heat and exhaust, so that at most only 20 percent is actually used to turn the wheels. Of the resulting force, 95 percent moves the car, while only 5 percent moves the driver, in proportion to their respective weights. Five percent of 20 percent is 1 percent—not a gratifying result from American cars that burn their own weight in gasoline every year." A startling stat. Surely an error. And indeed, after further review—of energy wasted on idling and air conditioning, of energy that made it to the tires but got used up heating the tire surface and the road below, and on and on—Amory Lovins had to revise his estimate in 2005: it was more like 13 percent of a car's fuel that was converted into propulsive force, and *less than* 1 percent that actually moved the driver.

Perhaps not surprisingly, Lovins and his colleagues at RMI have been at work for years on the construction of a prototype of an ultra-lightweight, hyper-efficient car, which they've dubbed the Hypercar. Alas, the major American automakers have proven reluctant to confront the 99 percent-plus inefficiency of their core product, and the Japanese car companies have been focused on improving their fuel economy with the gas-electric hybrid engine of Prius fame. So it may well be that the most significant achievement of RMI's first three decades—at least in terms of volume and visibility—is its recent contract to carry out the comparatively mundane task of maximizing the efficiency of Wal-Mart's trucking fleet. And when the world's largest retailer announces that its stated goal is to double its fuel efficiency across the board by 2015—thereby affecting supply chains that circle the globe and involve 7,200 trucks in the United States alone—even the most trivial of tweaks yields a certain statistical awe. One of the first glaring inefficiencies RMI uncovered, for example, was the fuel wasted by truckers who left their engines idling all night, which they did so they could run lights and small appliances off the battery without draining it. By outfitting the trucks with auxiliary power units, Wal-Mart will save $26 million in fuel costs. Add in a few minor adjustments to the tires and axles and the wind-dragging trailer, and the savings tick up to $52 million. Just a few of the incidental, incremental ways by which Wal-Mart intends to eliminate 13 million tons of CO_2 emissions by 2020.

A trucker watching a late-night sitcom rerun on a portable TV next to an anonymous strip of highway: this is not sexy; it doesn't make your heart race or take your breath away. It might be the most effective way to begin the process of containing anthropogenic climate change, but it sure isn't James Cook welcomed as a god or them engines roaring their way to the Cadillac Ranch. Hell, it can't even pretend to the genteel charms of a train ride.

And so let's return, circuitously, to the rails: the most photogenic side of sustainable transport, the most enticing in its way, the one that most readily ascends to the shared memory of myth. I spent a lot of time on trains when I was in Germany, and like most travel it entailed long stretches of nothing much at all, but there were snapshot flashes of an existence more memorable than anything I've ever experienced on an interstate. A regional commuter train out of Hamburg: I was tapping out some notes on my laptop, which caught the attention of a German teenager across the aisle, and then we talked for a while in his broken English and my rudimentary German, and when he got off a while later I felt like I knew a little more about where I was. An overnight high-speed express from Berlin to Freiburg: sitting at the bar in the sleek dining car just before bed, sipping a glass of draft Pilsner that would be the pride of any pub anywhere, sharing solitude with a half-dozen fellow night-owl passengers, central Germany passing by in alternating blurs of bright light and inky darkness, an air of black-and-white old-movie romance wafting through the car like smoke. Freiburg to Heidelberg: by foot from my hotel to the Freiburg station—no heavy labour in pedestrian-scaled Freiburg—to reach a crowded platform at five o'clock on a holiday Friday and board a packed northbound express, my Austrian seatmate offering me a can of his beer to leaven the mood before hopping off in Mannheim to catch a regional commuter train to Heidelberg in five minutes flat. Transit at its best: multiple integrated layers, ready to accommodate all but the most irregular of travel requests, comfortable and semi-communal and completely relaxing in a way that I've found no car trip to be since I was involved in a serious highway collision at the age of fifteen.

And let's not forget Freiburg itself: buying the reasonably priced all-day unlimited-ride pass from an automated kiosk, the streetcar-like LRT tram whirring slowly through the medieval gate like it'd been built to accommodate modern transit, stepping onto the tram in the middle of a cobblestone square with no more thought or effort than ascending the steps of a cathedral.

Catch the No. 3 tram south to Vauban. Ten minutes to a station in the southern suburbs where grass grows between the rails. Wait till you see what kind of *houses* they've got in Freiburg.

FOUR

HOME, GREEN HOME

[sustainable housing]

THE SUNNY SIDE OF LIFE

Downtown Freiburg is a pretty accurate approximation of the mental image conjured up by the term *Europe* in your average North American's imagination: an Altstadt of narrow, cobblestone streets and half-timbered houses encircled by medieval stone gates, footbridges lined with flower boxes over babbling brooks, bakeries and cafés with little circular tables out front lining compact squares. The traditional highlight of a tour of Freiburg is the Münster, the city's towering Gothic cathedral, an imposing edifice of spike-crowned buttresses and leering gargoyles in red-brown sandstone that looms over a broad square in the centre of the Altstadt. Completed in 1513 after three centuries of construction, its 381-foot spire testifying to God's glory and the engineering genius of medieval Europe, the Münster is the quintessence of the high art and refined culture of its time. But I didn't come all the way to southwestern Germany by intercontinental jumbo jet and superfast train to gawk at another old church.

Instead, I caught the No. 3 tram down on Kaiserstrasse, passing smooth and electric-quiet through the thirteenth-century gate to a southern suburb called Vauban. Here I found a new landmark, a temple for the worship of both ancient sunlight and hypermodern science: Heliotrop. A house, actually, but some other kind of house entirely: three storeys high and tubular in shape, a sleek glass drum perched upon a stout pole, wrapped in translucent pipe and crowned by a bank of reflective panels. Heliotrop looks like the misplaced centrepiece of a "Homes of the Future" exhibit at the 1939 World's Fair or a stage set for a live-action version of *The Jetsons*. The house was completed in 1994 after much less than three hundred years' work by a visionary architect named Rolf Disch, as a place for his family to live and as living proof of his big idea, which he calls *das Plusenergiehaus*. Which idea, if you can't parse the *Deutsch,* is this: the plus-energy house, the house as power plant. Heliotrop, then: the first home in Germany—maybe the first anywhere—that produces more energy than it uses.

The name, from the Greek, means "tracking the sun"—heliotropes are plants whose flowers turn toward the sun's rays. And that, for starters, is what the house does: it spins on its stilt-like perch so that its triple-glazed, light-welcoming glass front can face the warming sun in winter and its sun-blocking, heavily insulated rear can repel it in summer. When supplemental heating is required, a geothermal heat exchanger makes use of the warm ground below, and hot-water heating comes from the translucent solar thermal vacuum tubing that snakes around the building (which doubles as balcony rail). The antenna-like protrusion on the home's roof is a bank of PV panels, which rotate independently to maximize their solar exposure, thereby generating something like five to six times this 2,000-square-foot, intensely naturally lit home's electricity demand. Beyond this, there's a rainwater catchment system for the washing of dishes and clothes, on-site composting and chemical-free sewage treatment. Greenhouse gas emissions are essentially nil.

Heliotrop's price tag was €1.5 million, with some of that coming from the Baden-Württemberg state government. Disch has built two others in Switzerland as "demonstration buildings" (neither of which is lived in) since he finished his own. Which is kind of incidental, because he has already refined his concept for the mass market on a site just up the street, as a sort of gateway to Vauban—quite possibly the first great model suburb of the Anthropocene Era.

Sustainable Vauban was born of a transformation nearly as quick as the fall of the Iron Curtain that set the stage for it. Until 1991,

Vauban was a French military barracks, a legacy of the Second World War turned Cold War relic. After the French went home, it passed briefly through the German government's hands to the City of Freiburg, which in 1993 began the launch of an ambitious redevelopment plan for the old barracks blocks. The core of this new neighbourhood is found at the wide, plaza-like intersection where the southbound No. 3 tram makes a hard right off Merzhauser Strasse into the reclaimed military lands, and it's at this corner where you'll find Rolf Disch's more recent designs: Sonnenschiff ("sun ship") and Solarsiedlung ("solar settlement").

Sonnenschiff is a five-storey, block-long complex lining Merzhauser, tight to the wide sidewalk and tiled in smooth slate grey, its upper-floor windows bracketed by little flashes of pastel cladding like exuberant shutters. As of the overcast spring day in 2006 when I first laid eyes on it, Sonnenschiff's ground floor was occupied by an organic grocer and a pharmacy, with the far southern bank of storefront windows covered over by a billboard-like display reading ZUKUNFT—"Future"—in bright red lettering on a white background, like it was the gateway to a new world. Sonnenschiff's second and third floors are used as office space, and at the very top, perched on the main building at intervals, are nine two-storey luxury condos. And atop these lies Disch's signature crown: roofs paved entirely in photovoltaic tile. Sonnenschiff is a bit of a laggard by Disch's astronomically high standards—it produces only about 55 percent of its energy requirements—but then its main purpose was to bring mixed-use life to the street and provide a visual and aural buffer between the busy boulevard and the cozy car-free neighbourhood tucked behind it.

That neighbourhood is Solarsiedlung: fifty-nine townhouses tightly packed in five neat rows out back of the Sonnenschiff. Each unit is decked out in bright siding—red, then yellow, aqua green, then vivid primary blue—and each has its own balcony and small patio and wee patch of garden. More importantly each is hyper-insulated and triple-glazed-windowed and topped in a sloping south-facing bank of solar panels, so that each is, like Disch's own green home, a net energy producer. Simple and utilitarian. *Plusenergiehaus*-ing for the masses.

In Solarsiedlung's far northwestern corner unit, which is clad in pale gold like the sun, I found the offices of Architekturbüro Rolf Disch. Disch and his wife, Hanna Lehmann, met me in his second-floor conference room at the end of a hallway littered with showpiece examples of the top of the line in high-efficiency windows and solar panels. We had coffee and little snack-sized Ritter Sport chocolate bars—the latter because the Ritter family, a major backer of sustainability projects throughout Germany, helped finance Solarsiedlung.

For thirty years, Disch explained, he'd been pursuing this model of total sustainability. He'd experimented, built models, tested new materials and concepts. His houses, he said, were intended not just to provide shelter now but to be ready for the next fifty years, the next hundred. "When you build a house"—this in his wife's translation—"you have a responsibility for the whole society." Now, three decades on, the results were in. What was Solarsiedlung—each unit generating about 7,000 kilowatt hours per year when the average German home needs but 2,000 or 3,000, and heating itself with a tenth of the fuel at the same time—if not incontrovertible proof? Disch, again in translation: "It's not a question of the *Technik*"—the technology—"we have the *Technik*. Of course, the *Technik* can develop more and more. But it's a question of the mind, and to do it. We have a problem to *do* it. We have no technical problems anymore." It was, in other words, a problem only of will.

At one point in the conversation, we came to one of those notoriously hard-to-translate German words, a word Disch had used to summarize his work: *Herausforderung*. My *Langenscheidt's Standard German Dictionary* translates it as both "challenge" and "provocation," and I like to think of Disch's houses as a little of both: as challenges overcome, leading to a provocation for a world in desperate need of more sustainable housing everywhere *now*. Houses that produce more energy than they consume, gone beyond green, ready for the next century or the one after that. *The house as power plant*—why build a house any other way?

There was already tacit affirmation of Disch's approach elsewhere in Vauban. The redevelopment of the French military barracks encompassed a 42-hectare site across the boulevard from Disch's Sonnenschiff that would eventually be home to five thousand residents, the core of which was a series of multistorey flats built from a variety of sustainably-minded designs.

When the city of Freiburg embarked on Vauban's rejuvenation in 1993, its goal was to build a sort of living school of enlightened urban design, which it called "Planning That Learns." What it got was something even more than that. Urban planners across North America have lately become enamoured of a planning philosophy that often goes by the name of "Smart Growth" and argues in favour of pedestrian-scaled, mixed-use, community-oriented neighbourhoods. Vauban has emerged as a living, breathing, German-speaking embodiment of these principles. It's almost as if it slid directly off the page of some high-minded planner's wish list onto a derelict military base in Germany fully intact—except that one of the keys to Vauban's success is that it was planned not by one inspired mind but by hundreds. Early in the planning stages, a public interest group called Forum Vauban formed among the future residents of the neighbourhood to guide community participation. From its deliberations emerged a grander scheme, which in the unwieldy German-to-English translation is dubbed "Sustainable Model District Vauban." What Forum Vauban recommended—and what is now manifest—was a neighbourhood of mixed-income, mixed-use, hyper-efficient and (mostly) sustainably powered flats.

Any given apartment in these Vauban blocks uses between zero and 30 percent of the energy of a standard German dwelling, and 65 percent of that power comes from renewable sources. There's a district heating plant fired by a mix of 80 percent wood chips and 20 percent natural gas. There are solar panels on some roofs, and green vegetation on others. Forum Vauban decided that the spaces between rows of flats would be strictly for people—park-like, kid-friendly—and so there are no cars, not even any roads, just green space laced with walking paths and dotted with park benches, playground equipment and assorted other communal property, as chosen by the residents. (Hiking across one field between two rows of buildings, I stumbled upon a hulking brick-and-iron baking oven.) For those who do own cars, there's a huge parking garage out by the main boulevard, its roof carpeted in solar panels. But 40 percent of the residents have opted out, instead using the tram that runs past and pocketing the steep price of a parking spot (reportedly as high as €17,500) as a sort of tax rebate.

For all of this conformity to high sustainability standards, the flats themselves are highly eclectic. A few are repurposed barracks, trimmed now with balconies and ivy-clad wood siding. Most of the

rest were built from scratch, funded by the residents to their specifications, many of them under a "co-building" scheme that permitted
relatively low-income families to participate. Any given row of them
might yield a half-dozen distinct architectural styles. One building,
which calls itself Passivhaus, grew out of a few conversations between
prospective residents into a green marvel of passive solar heating
and hyper-efficiency, complete with a biogas reactor fed by the flat's
vacuum toilets and on-site chemical-free wastewater treatment. (On
the Passivhaus website, one resident proudly boasts that his annual
heating bill for 2004 was €114.)

Walking through Vauban, I found myself even more amazed and
bewildered than I'd been amid the net-energy-producing townhouses
of Solarsiedlung. I tried—and failed—to figure out which buildings
were retrofitted army barracks. I watched residents tend their gardens and kids pedal by on bikes, the quiet broken only by the call of
human voices and the semi-regular distant *whooshing* sound of the
tram, and I felt utterly transported. There was a creek trickling by in
a bucolic wood, lined by a walking path. This was a *military barracks*
fifteen years ago; the former officers' mess is now a community centre. It was like walking through a stage set almost, not because it felt
overly constructed or artificial but because it seemed too . . . *perfect.*
Workaday real, but also dreamlike. *Mein Gott,* man: Why build
houses any other way?

All this would be easier to shrug off, of course, if it was just a
German thing. But the first *Plusenergiehaus* I'd ever seen wasn't in
Vauban, wasn't even in Europe. It was in Bangkok. In Thailand, of
all places.

CHÂTEAU MANGO

So there's a Thai architect by the name of Soontorn Boonyatikarn. A
cheery guy, quick to smile, loves to point out all the fun and romantic
details on the houses he builds and make gentle, self-deprecating
asides about the lengths a man will go to in order to please a woman.
Takes a lot of pride and joy in what he does, is what I'm saying. And
so it's not hard to picture him wearing a wide, satisfied grin as he
settled into a comfortable chair outside his new home one fateful
day circa 1998 to treat himself to a mango. He'd built the house himself, and it was a hyper-efficient, green-minded marvel that used just

15 percent of the usual energy supply for a Thai home of its size and vintage—a pioneering piece of design in a country where ecological concerns were heretofore immaterial to the field of modern architecture. He'd surely earned a lazy afternoon of fresh fruit and job-well-done contentment.

This Dr. Soontorn, as his students and acolytes called him, hadn't strolled easily to this moment of satisfaction. As a young architect keen on introducing new ideas to Thailand back in the 1970s, he'd encountered nothing but resistance and indifference, so he decamped to the United States. He picked up a Ph.D. and an abiding interest in environmentally friendly design (inspired in part by a meeting with Amory Lovins of the Rocky Mountain Institute), and he spent almost twenty years teaching at the University of Michigan. He returned to Bangkok in the early 1990s, planning to stay just a year to care for his ailing mother, uninterested in working in a country where all the money and prestige were in importing designs wholesale from the West and throwing them up with naked contempt for Thailand's torrid tropical climate. But then Chulalongkorn University—Bangkok's top school—offered him a teaching position. He took the job and went to work on building Thailand's first modern green home. Despite continued resistance and skepticism—even outright disbelief—he built his green house, and it immediately earned him a handful of awards and vaulted him to the front ranks of Southeast Asia's building trade.

"I was so proud of myself at that time," Dr. Soontorn told me. "I thought, 'Oh, I've done a good job.' And one day I sit down and eat a mango, and I throw the seed to the next door."

We were seated, he and I, in a pleasantly cramped cafeteria at Chulalongkorn University, the clank and murmur of students at breakfast our white-noise soundtrack. He leaned back and looked off toward the aisle next to our table like he was appraising the discarded mango seed, watching it take root and grow, a bountiful tree emerging from his presumptive refuse. He blinked hard and threw his head back, as if dumbstruck. "I am so stupid! Look at the mango. It doesn't consume energy. It uses nothing. However, it produces fruit for me to eat. And the next-generation home should be like the mango."

Thus humbled, Dr. Soontorn had returned to his drawing board.

A few days later, I headed out to a northern suburb of Bangkok to see what he had come up with next. Dr. Soontorn met me there, on a quiet residential street lined with new homes, several still under construction. The house modelled on a mango was midway down the block, a tan stucco structure with a steep-pitched roof that extended far past its frame, like the house was wearing an overlarge hat with an extra-wide brim pulled low on its head. The south-facing side of it was covered almost entirely in PV panels. Dr. Soontorn had dubbed it the "Bio-Solar Home." He used it as a part-time residence and a full-time showpiece, frequently taking visitors on guided tours because few people would simply take his word for it that he'd built a house that produced more power than it needed.

The Bio-Solar Home is about 1,500 square feet in size, but it is high-ceilinged, open concept, zealously airy and as naturally lit as Dr. Soontorn could possibly manage without permitting too much heat gain, so it feels larger than that. He started my tour in the ground-floor great room, a living/dining/kitchen combo bedecked with sleek cream couches, IKEA-like built-in dark wood shelving and a legless kitchen table that protrudes from the wall to hover modernistically above a handful of round moulded plastic space-pod chairs. The overall effect is intercontinental, hypermodern with traditional trim, a sort of Euro-Thai fusion style. Dr. Soontorn was particularly pleased with the "sun room" extension—a small leisure space with a glass floor that thrusts out over the outdoor pool in the yard. When the light's right, the pool shimmering below, the floating effect is magical—so he assured me. We moved upstairs to the two bedrooms—a small child's bedroom and a master bedroom with ensuite bathroom, skylights in the ceiling of each with automated retractable covers. Dr. Soontorn got downright syrupy describing the romantic vibe in the moonlit bedroom. This was, in a sense, the "bio" part of the Bio-Solar Home: he intended it to be a welcoming living space as well as a feat of future-tense green engineering.

As for the technical wizardry, it was best viewed from a small nook on the staircase landing, where a computer workstation had been installed to monitor the various systems by which the Bio-Solar Home had been rendered essentially self-sufficient. Here were charts and graphs and digital dials monitoring the whole operation in real time, from water harvesting and storage to interior and exterior temperature. The elaborate self-replenishing, closed-loop water system was particularly impressive: the Bio-Solar Home, as you might expect, harvests rainwater, but it also gathers the steady drip of condensation from the air conditioning system (which can yield up to 40 litres over the course of a hot day), and its roof is coated with a paint engineered to keep its surface two or three degrees below air temperature, causing dew to form at a rate of about 80 litres per day. All of this—stored in a tank buried in the yard—earns the Bio-Solar Home complete independence from the municipal water supply. The home's non-sewage wastewater, meanwhile, is used to irrigate the lawn and gardens, and the sewage is fed to bacteria in an on-site septic tank for detoxification.

The real showstopper on Dr. Soontorn's monitor, of course, was the pair of counters tracking power production and consumption; during my tour, the 6.2-kilowatt PV array on the roof was selling power back to the state power company in a 700-watt stream. This wasn't so much a triumph of photovoltaic technology as a credit to the fanatical approach that had been taken to energy efficiency, the details of which Dr. Soontorn eagerly pointed out at every turn on the tour.

It started with the walls, which had been tailor-made in Thailand to properly insulate against the hot, wet local climate. This might not sound all that revolutionary, but so enamoured were Thai architects of Western imports that a great many modern buildings in Thailand had been built essentially inside out, with insulation designed to *retain* heat in weather that rarely dips below 30°C. "They thought it's so good because they imported technology from overseas to Thailand," Dr. Soontorn explained. "But it's *wrong*. The same as you import the maple tree to Thailand: the maple never change the colours on the leaves." Dr. Soontorn instead took an advanced German insulation system and in effect inverted it: the *outer* layer of the Bio-Solar Home's walls is made of insulating foam 6 inches thick, keeping heat and moisture out. This is backed by a layer of fibreglass and a pocket of air to further reduce heat transfer.

Several other design elements help the walls do their job. The windows, made of heat-blocking glass, are carefully arranged and shaded by the overhanging roof to allow ambient light in while keeping direct warming sunlight out. The house is also laced with a web of condensation-coated air ducts, which channel what little outside breeze there is, providing what's known as "indirect evaporative cooling." The Bio-Solar Home's air conditioning requirement has thus been reduced to less than 10 percent of the Thai norm—a massive decrease in the overall power demand. All that natural light, meanwhile, means the house needs only about a quarter of the electricity used by a conventional home for artificial lighting.

Dr. Soontorn also obsessed over price, using only low-cost and readily available materials and easily installed fixtures. (By way of random example, the master bathroom's shower enclosure is a simple glass frame sealed directly into the floor tile.) And so, despite the fact that he'd built a house that was several generations ahead of the rest of the country in its design and execution, the price tag was about US$125,000—a bit more than your average upper-middle-class home in Bangkok, but still competitive—and Dr. Soontorn reckoned he could reduce it by 60 to 70 percent if he was building Bio-Solar Homes by the score. He wasn't quite there yet, though he had taken orders for about a dozen houses of similar design—a couple more in Bangkok, the rest elsewhere in Thailand.

At the same time, he'd become a highly sought-after architect. He'd recently designed a college campus on the outskirts of Bangkok and an office complex in Malaysia, and he'd started discussions with the United Nations Environment Programme about the feasibility of building a sustainable-city prototype in Bangkok as a larger showcase for the Bio-Solar concept. "In the near future," he told me, "we have to do more. Single home is not enough. We have to do neighbourhood. That would be approaching a true sustainable concept for the future." He still ran into constant skepticism, he said, about the Bio-Solar Home. He compared it to the dawn of the age of flying machines, how people needed to see them with their own eyes—sometimes repeatedly—before they accepted the incontrovertible truth that people had learned to fly. He thought maybe a whole village of Bio-Solar Homes would go a good way toward doing the same for energy-producing houses.

The architect himself is, at any rate, intimately familiar with such skepticism—he'd had to work to dispel some of his own. Dr. Soontorn turfed a mango seed, and by the time it hit the ground he had found cause to dismiss his first attempt at designing a green home. The key breakthrough was his conclusion that he hadn't taken his design far enough, hadn't made it so extraordinarily efficient that it became self-justifying. This is a result prophesied in *Natural Capitalism* (a book co-written by Dr. Soontorn's long-ago inspiration, Amory Lovins). The process is referred to therein as "tunneling through the cost barrier"—a sort of working hypothesis of sustainable economics that posits that small, incremental gains in efficiency eventually fall victim to diminished returns, but much more radical efficiency improvements ultimately (and paradoxically) start to *reduce* overall costs. A resident of one of Dr. Soontorn's Bio-Solar Homes, for example, might never again pay an electricity or water bill—which alone would reduce the net cost of the structure to nothing over its lifetime. The tricky part, then, is to push beyond that initial barrier—whether it's an intimidating price tag or a disarming mango seed—to the place where the real wonders lie.

And so the best lesson to take from Dr. Soontorn's career thus far—beyond the specifics of how to build a house in the tropics that produces more energy than it consumes—is simply that it is possible. It can be done. Even in Thailand: in a country with a per capita income about 20 percent of America's; a country utterly bereft of the long-standing environmentalist traditions and abundant green-building incentives of, say, Germany; a country, moreover, in which architects routinely build structures inside out to impress their clients, and in which ambitious plans routinely turn into irredeemable boondoggles. It can be done—it *has* been—and it took only one driven architect with enough cheery tenacity to make it happen.

That first morning at breakfast, I listened to Dr. Soontorn get so wound up about the potential embedded in his work that he felt compelled to mangle John F. Kennedy's "Ask not what your country can do for you" line trying to explain why he knew his approach was righteous and true. (What he was driving at was that you shouldn't ask how to change the environment to fit your needs, you should ask how to change what you're doing to suit—and indeed harness—nature's will.) And then practically in the next breath he was on about mangoes again: "We have to take advantage of the light, the wind, the sun and everything, and use it like a mango tree. And that, you know, that is the starting of a new concept. And from now on, I think—when I see the garbage, I see newspaper—this is energy.

This is *money*. Because I can recycle, I can reuse, remodify and convert into energy. Every single thing."

Every single thing: this is an easygoing fiftysomething Thai architect speaking in the voice of a starry-eyed radical. This is the voice of a man who saw a potential future and then went and built it. A house that produces more energy than it consumes, a house like a mango tree, *every single thing:* this is more than even the grooviest green builders have aimed for anywhere else.

It makes you wonder why their ambitions are so modest, actually.

THE HIP MODERNIST-BOXY HALF-STEP

Around the same time Dr. Soontorn was putting the finishing touches on his Bio-Solar Home, ground was broken on a new residential community in a town called Okotoks, not far south of where I live, with the intent of revolutionizing the typical North American suburban tract house. The development—Drake Landing by name—was in several respects the most ambitious sustainable-housing project anyone had ever mounted in Canada. The dwellings that would make up this new neighbourhood were being outfitted with all manner of green trappings, from wood frames made of sustainably harvested lumber to top-of-the-line insulation and ultra-efficient appliances and solar hot water heaters. The truly pioneering aspect, though, was the solar thermal district heating system, the first of its kind in North America: a network of garage-mounted solar panels, linked by insulated pipe to a storage facility at the edge of the community, that would trap the heat energy of the area's three-hundred-plus annual days of sunshine to provide the fifty-two houses with all their heating needs. Seventy to 80 percent of the average Canadian home's greenhouse gas emissions come from heating—mainly from the individual oil- or gas-fed furnaces in most Canadian basements—and Drake Landing's solar thermal system promised to erase 100 percent of those emissions in one giant leap. The technology was far from brand new—it was more or less identical, for example, to the much larger district heating system I'd seen littered in sheep droppings on the Danish island of Aerø—but this was nevertheless a potentially huge innovation for North American space heating and a powerful new weapon in the battle against climate change in my home and native land.

Not that anyone talked about it in those terms. A sizeable consortium of organizations large and small, public and private—the Calgary-based developer and builder, the municipality it was located in, one of the province's largest energy distributors, even the Canadian government—had slapped their logos with apparent pride upon the COMING SOON placard at the entrance to the new subdivision, but I was hard-pressed to find even a mango seed's worth of Dr. Soontorn's infectious enthusiasm for the task. Drake Landing was, at its core, a run-of-the-mill suburban-style housing development, and pains had been taken to emphasize the nothing-to-see-here veneer. The builder had even insisted that the solar thermal panels be placed on the tops of back-alley garages, where they were less likely to freak out your average prairie home buyer, rather than on outsized south-facing roofs as initially planned. Standard-issue floor plans and starter-home prices from the low $220s, free five-foot white vinyl fences out front—as much as humanly possible, Drake Landing was to be just another pocket of everyday suburbia.

Maybe this was all for the best. Maybe the best way to introduce Canadians (especially the legendarily conservative-minded ones who inhabit small-town Alberta) to sustainable homes was to make them pointedly bland. After all, this was a demonstration project, and who in their right mind would want to dump their life savings into a *demonstration project?* This was $19.1 million in government grants and R&D money, feasibility studies and test runs and a final assessment report at the end, and for all that the municipal government of Okotoks still had to go and set up a not-for-profit corporation to assume all the risk before they could convince the energy company to sign on to manage the solar thermal system.

Like the rest of the Southern Alberta prairie, Okotoks is endowed with a climate of almost desert-like aridness. As development encroaches and climate change shrinks the glaciers in the mountains to the west, the health of the region's aquifers grows ever more precarious with each passing year. And so the *main* reason Drake Landing was built in Okotoks wasn't the ample sunshine so much as the dearth of water—or, more precisely, the presence of a local government that had chosen to account for this problem. While many of the other small towns on Calgary's fringe have gone for quick-buck breakneck suburban development, the municipal government in

Okotoks decided, based on intensive consultations with local residents in the mid-1990s, to chart a different path. It christened itself "Sustainable Okotoks" and introduced a comprehensive new planning regime that included not just zealous water management but a host of other energy-efficiency and zoning guidelines besides. Out of these came, among other things, a small local boom in solar power, and it was this nascent local expertise that brought the town to the attention of the federal government when it went looking for a partner for its solar thermal demonstration project.

By rejecting business-as-usual suburbia, Okotoks had become a hotspot for solar-energy innovation, the handpicked site for a pioneering solar thermal system—which was doing its damnedest to don the guise of grey suburbia. I wonder how freaked out the residents of "Sustainable Okotoks" would have been, really, by overlong south-facing roofs. And wouldn't something totally unexpected—a few rows of primary-coloured whimsy like Rolf Disch's Solarsiedlung, for instance—have a certain value-added cachet in the sea of conformity that is Calgary suburbia? But no: the call for a solar-heated Dullsville carried the day. It was an odd fit, a bit like trying to stuff a geodesic dome into a regimented modernist box.

In a sense, it was the tarnished legacy of the geodesic dome that drove Drake Landing's developers to conduct their experiment in the guise of factory-produced, blandly modernist conformity. The geodesic dome: one of those indelible symbols of the haphazard 1960s experiment with eco-friendly living, as antithetical to contemporary middle-class values as a Volkswagen microbus. It was a tragic irony, really, because the dome's inventor, Buckminster Fuller, missed out on the role of suburbia's godfather by a hair's breadth of bad luck and inescapable circumstance, and his version of the cookie-cutter housing development would have left us several generations ahead in the sustainability game.

Fuller, at any rate, was one of the most famous and successful inventors of the twentieth century, the holder of twenty-eight patents and forty-seven honorary doctorates, a *Time* magazine cover boy in 1964, one of the few genuinely household names in architecture—and all this with no formal training in architecture or design. Fuller was a relentless and prodigious idea machine—not so much an architect, one of his biographers said, as "a philosopher of shelter." He was an early advocate of renewable energy—he'd seen solar energy as the future source of power for his dwellings as far back as the 1930s—as well as a pioneering spokesman on behalf of conservation and recycling.

In the early 1930s, Fuller launched his first groundbreaking design, a cheap, lightweight, durable prefabricated shelter intended to be delivered by zeppelin and assembled quick and easy anywhere there were paying customers. He called it the Dymaxion house (from *dynamic maximum tension*). It was hexagonal, made primarily of new-fangled aluminum, built around a central stainless steel strut. The interior was to be stuffed with the latest in automated appliances, a waterless toilet made of sheet metal and a hyper-efficient "fog" shower that recycled its wastewater. The Dymaxion was poised to become the Model-T Ford of modern housing: mass-produced, affordable, ubiquitous, revolutionary. Beech Aircraft of Wichita, Kansas, entered into an agreement with Fuller toward the end of the Second World War to handle the factory-scale production. By 1946, a prototype with a widely affordable price tag of $6,500 (about the same as a new Cadillac) had been built at the company's Wichita factory. It drew prospective buyers from across the country; by one estimate, there were thirty thousand orders on the books—mostly unsolicited—when internal political machinations at Beech killed the Dymaxion house dead. In the end, only two were manufactured. One of these now stands, fully assembled, at the Henry Ford Museum in Dearborn, Michigan, as if to underscore the potential scope of the future that might have been had the Dymaxion house become as integral to postwar life as a shiny new sedan.

Fuller, for his part, simply shrugged it off and went back to work on the design that would become his signature: the geodesic dome. Built by mounting a series of interlocking triangular panels on an aluminum frame, with no need for internal support struts no matter how large the sphere grew, the geodesic dome seemed to be limited in size only by the ambitions of its builders; Fuller envisioned enclosing entire cities in them. As a 1988 *American Heritage* magazine retrospective on Fuller's life noted, the shape mimics almost perfectly a form that recurs countless times in nature, from the protein shells of certain kinds of virus to microscopic sea creatures to the human cornea. Fuller's dome has proven strong enough to withstand mountaintop winds and the brutal climate of the high Arctic. It quickly became the covering of choice for remote radar installations, and it was also the centrepiece of the American exhibit at Expo 67 in Montreal. It's estimated that there are, today, about 300,000 geodesic domes on the face of the earth, and the design's meteoric rise in the architecture world of the 1950s and 1960s launched Fuller to international superstardom. A marvel of geometry, a full-blown revolution in strength-to-weight ratio, the geodesic dome is quite simply one of the most influential design breakthroughs in modern history.

For all this, the geodesic dome has endowed a mixed blessing upon the current era of sustainable housing. At the peak of Fuller's fame in the 1960s, his simple, easily copied design became the do-it-yourself darling of the counterculture. It was always prone to leakage, mainly because a structure with that many joints is very hard to seal completely. Smart, careful construction was usually able to overcome this flaw, but the amateur version with the sieve-like roof was one of the geodesic dome's best-known incarnations. Like bland brown rice and Mao's little red book, the geodesic dome became inextricably linked with eccentric, impractical, alternative living in the mass consciousness. Never mind that Fuller was, as I mentioned, not a trained architect, certainly not an elite mechanical engineer, but a philosopher of shelter—of what it should do and what it was for. Nor that the unconventional *shapes* of his designs weren't, until they acquired the hippie stigma, enormously enticing to a wide range of people from many walks of life. And never mind that those shapes were essential to the efficiency and other technical advantages offered by the overall design. Never mind all that: instead, avoid novel shapes at any cost.

And so we are affronted now by the spectacle of "green" housing hidden behind the façades of woefully inefficient suburban tract houses (the habitation pattern preferred by modernist urban planners) or glammed up inside a sleek box of concrete or glass (the preferred shape and building materials of doctrinaire modernist architecture). Anything at all, anyway, to avoid the scent of patchouli or the feel of fringed buckskin, even if it means avoiding sustainable foundations in favour of more stylish ones that aren't sustainable at all.

"Green Goes Mainstream," trumpeted the cover of the September 2006 issue of the stylish home design magazine *Dwell,* by which they mainly meant that Green was going Modern. Indeed, *Dwell*'s cover image was of a suburban Barcelona home called Villa Bio that was almost nothing but poured concrete and plate-glass boxes. The walls on both sides: raw, grey, windowless concrete. The floors: raw, grey concrete. Plate-glass boxes hung off the back of the building and squatted awkwardly atop the cantilevered roof of the garage. An accompanying schematic diagram revealed the interior to be a series of gently sloping, switchbacking ramps—an apparently unintentional homage to the concrete slabs you trudge up and down to get into and out of major sporting events. I read the accompanying text twice, and still the only overtly "environmental" detail I could find was a hydroponic rooftop garden.

Other features in *Dwell*'s Green Issue included an Arizona home featuring still more plate-glass boxes and an interior littered with Corbusier chairs, and the new Santa Monica home of an environmental building adviser that undermined its own industrious efficiency measures by building its frame out of expensive, resource-intensive steel and perching the living space on expressed-structural stilts to make room for a ground-floor multi-vehicle carport. And lest there be any remaining doubt about what kind of green architecture *wasn't* worth talking about, there was this unequivocal opening paragraph in the magazine's "Editor's Note": "In early 2000, when the not-yet-launched *Dwell* began to take shape editorially, we decided to introduce 'Off the Grid' as one of our regular features. At that time, it was nearly impossible to find well-designed, modern, sustainable homes to publish. The bulk of our searches yielded projects that fell squarely into the old paradigm of eco-consciousness—lots of hilltop yurts with batik curtains and purple carpeting." (Really? *Lots* of hilltop yurts?) Anyway, how terribly *gauche*. Thank *god* sustainable houses have finally got an outfit hip enough to wear in decent twenty-first-century company—by draping themselves in designs that were last actually avant-garde in 1920s Paris.

And—*really*, now—what an extraordinary event the 1925 Paris Exposition must have been. I mean, who knew the weird dude in the barn-owl glasses, spouting the deranged manifesto about houses being "machines for living," would still be telling practically the whole of the Western world what kind of homes to build in 2006?

I'll come back to the 1925 Exposition des arts decoràtifs et industri-
ales modernes in Paris. First, though, I want to introduce Le
Corbusier properly, as I first met him, on a vast empty plaza of
cracked concrete on the edge of the Ganges plain, under an Indian
sun so witheringly hot it made time seem to warp and melt beneath
it, stretching moments into delirious hours. Particularly while I was
crossing this ridiculous, overwide, shadeless fucking *plaza,* which
was the centrepiece of possibly the grandest project ever built by
Charles-Édouard Jeanneret, a man better-known to the adoring
world of highfalutin' architecture as Le Corbusier, godfather of the
modernist box. "*Corbu!*" as Tom Wolfe wrote of him, "the way Greta
Garbo was *Garbo!*" And here, in India, on the border between the
states of Punjab and Haryana, was the capital he built for both of
them out of empty pastoral nothingness in the 1950s with the fervent support of Jawarhalal Nehru, the modernist-worshipping
Indian prime minister. *Chandigarh!*

Chandigarh: India's first city of the modernist future. Unabashedly
admired, it must be noted, by many a middle-class Punjabi, because its
flawlessly gridded extra-wide boulevards, endless rows of mid-rise
machine-for-living apartment blocks and carefully placed parklands
create an illusion of tidy, futuristic order. Chandigarh is like no other
Indian city. It doesn't have teeming bazaars with meandering alleys
and dusty paths. It doesn't even have neighbourhoods; it has neatly
numbered "sectors." Corbu imagined them, neatly arrayed in a long
rectangle, as the "body" of his mechanistic city, and the head is an
administrative complex of poured concrete office blocks at the very
top. The legislative and administrative buildings are on one side, the
judicial block is on the other, and in between is, I guess, the brain: a
great yawning communal hive mind rendered in wide concrete slabs.
A plaza, I mean, featureless save for the sculpture of the bold new
city's emblem, also of Corbu's design—a big abstract hand-shaped
thing that looks quite a bit like a heavy metal fan's raised-pinkie-and-
forefinger devil horns, or perhaps a surfer's "hang ten" gesture.
Something spectacularly, inadvertently banal, anyway. Which monumental banality you have plenty of time to contemplate as you perilously traverse the plaza upon which it stands, a kind of horizontal
Everest face in the 46°C heat of the hot season, each step extending

elastically away from you like you're the clueless fool the joke's on in this particular modernist cartoon.

This is how I met Corbu—on a May afternoon a few years ago, as I was trying to get from the administrative block to the courts—and it was the right way to meet him, I think. Because no matter how many sleek modernist façades I'd encounter thereafter, and no matter how cool and enticing these buildings looked on the covers of magazines, I would always have this object lesson in their utter disregard for real sustainable human life. For the environment and climate and the readily observable everyday fact of the goddamn weather. Chandigarh is perhaps the most modernist city on the planet, the crowning glory of Le Corbusier's career. And it never occurred to the great modernist demigod—inspiration for nearly a century now of cutting-edge architecture, the altar image in front of which you must genuflect even today if you want your sustainable house to appear on the cover of a trendy design magazine—it never occurred to this *Corbu!* that Chandigarh is not very well suited to wide, shadeless plazas, because for several months of the year it is one of the hottest inhabited places on earth.

This is why I've been carrying on like this about modernist boxes: because they are inherently, indeed preeningly, unsustainable. If sustainability means anything to architecture, to the construction of human shelter, it means accounting for and harnessing regional climatic conditions, planning for and guarding against extremes of local weather, treading lightly upon the earth and using its bounty to the fullest. The one-size-fits-all modernist-box approach to design is not just ignorant of or indifferent to this concept. It is *responsible* for the mess we're in—as much so, in its way, as the coal-fired power plant and internal combustion engine for which it has long provided stylish window dressing.

I should get back to the Paris of the mid-1920s to begin to explain why this is the case. The 1925 Paris Exposition (sometimes called the Art Deco Exposition) was a vast trade fair for the decorative arts— furniture, sculpture, architecture and especially fashion—intended to reinstate Paris's long-standing reign as the world's premier taste-maker, the undisputed capital of the authentic avant-garde. (Vienna had made claims to this throne just before the First World War, and America was now coming on strong.) For the most part, the Expo was an expansive celebration of all things tasteful, refined, bourgeois and *au courant*. But no self-respecting Paris art show was without its scandalous *enfant terrible*—Manet and Gauguin, among others, had first made their marks by outraging the masses at such expositions—and in 1925 that role was filled by a manifesto-scribbling architect-intellectual from Switzerland who called himself Le Corbusier.

Corbu's Pavillion d'Esprit nouveau was an unadorned white box set up in a remote corner of the vast fairgrounds. It contained a full-scale model of the stark worker's home of the future—the austere cube Corbusier called "a machine for living," a dead ringer for the stuff that still stares back at us flatly from the covers of design bibles—and embodied a categorical dismissal of the notions of decoration, adornment, fashion. Inside was an even more outrageous affront to Parisian decency: Corbu's Plan Voisin de Paris, an elaborate redevelopment scheme that proposed razing a wide swath of outdated downtown Paris to the ground, to be replaced by a utopian future cityscape consisting of row upon row of featureless concrete high-rise apartment buildings separated by lush greenery and linked to each other and the city by hypermodern elevated roads built exclusively for automobiles (a scheme he later named the "Radiant City"). The local design authorities were so insulted by Corbu's pavilion that they literally tried to hide it from view, hastily erecting a 20-foot fence around it. (The fence was later removed.) They needn't have worried: the Radiant City would never be built in Paris. Instead, it hopped the pond, became the inspiration for a North American architectural philosophy dubbed the "International Style," and was transformed into the one-size-fits-all blueprint for urban architecture and design across the continent for many years to come.

By the end of the following decade, modernism was ready for mass consumption. It introduced itself to mainstream America at the 1939 New York World's Fair in a huge and heavily hyped exhibit called Futurama. Designed by Norman Bel Geddes and proudly sponsored by General Motors, Futurama was a vast model of the city of the future that took Corbu's Radiant City, gave it the art deco trim so prevalent in the rest of the 1925 Paris Exposition's exhibits, and declared itself a car-centred American paradise. Futurama envisioned the city as an enormous grid of sleek high-rise towers linked by raised concrete pedestrian thoroughfares that floated above an extensive road system dense with automobile traffic. The exhibit sported broad car-covered suspension bridges, multilaned elevated freeways snaking through empty countryside and past elaborate amusement parks, and colossal cloverleafs where mammoth fourteen-lane freeways intersected. Squint at a picture of the exhibit today, and you'd swear you were looking at an aerial photo of Atlanta or Anaheim or the kaleidoscopic interchange north of Toronto where the twelve lanes of Highway 401 meet the ten lanes of Highway 400.

Nowadays, most of us encounter modernist-boxy architecture primarily in office parks and cubist metropolitan skylines, and it's easy to forget that its stated intention was to be the ideal egalitarian shelter of the proletarian masses. Tom Wolfe explains what happened in *From Bauhaus to Our House:*

> It was not that worker housing was never built for workers. In the 1950s and early 1960s the federal government helped finance the American version of the Dutch and German Siedlungen of the 1920s. Here they were called housing projects. But somehow the workers, intellectually undeveloped as they were, managed to avoid public housing. They called it, simply, "the projects," and they avoided it as if it had a smell. The workers—if by workers we mean people who have jobs—headed out instead to the suburbs. They ended up in places like Islip, Long Island, and the San Fernando Valley of Los Angeles, and they bought houses with pitched roofs and shingles and clapboard siding, with no structure expressed if there was any way around it, with gaslight-style front-porch lamps and mailboxes set up on lengths of stiffened chain that seemed to defy gravity—the more cute and antiquey touches, the better—and they loaded those houses with "drapes" such as baffled all description and wall-to-wall carpet you could lose a shoe in, and they put barbecue pits and fish ponds with concrete cherubs urinating into them on the lawn out back, and they parked the Buick Elektras out front and had Evinrude cruisers up on tow trailers in the carport just beyond the breezeway.

As an exclamation point, Wolfe relates the pathetic saga of the Pruitt-Igoe projects in St. Louis, completed in 1955 from a plan by celebrated modernist Minoru Yamasaki (who later designed the World Trade Center). Corbusier had recommended covered walkways—"streets in the air" akin to the ones in the Futurama model—linking his machines for living. Pruitt-Igoe had those, and they'd quickly become dens of enough virulent strains of vice to spin Dickens in his grave at least twice. In 1971, a task force rounded up Pruitt-Igoe's residents to decide what to do with the awful buildings. "The chant," Wolfe writes, "began immediately: 'Blow it . . . up! Blow it . . . up! Blow it . . . up!'" So they did, with dynamite, a year later.

It's hard to imagine a style of architecture that has been a more abject failure by its own stated goals: a machine prone to breaking down inside of a generation that no one—least of all the working class it was intended for—wants to live in. Alas, the responses to its excesses and evident failures have been pure baroque: bigger still and even weirder, downright proud of their disdain for practicality. Consider the latter-day "starchitects," among the most prominent of whom are Frank Gehry, with his undulating metal waves in Bilbao and Los Angeles, and Daniel Libeskind, with his improbable spire on the World Trade Center's ruins and his crystalline addition to the Royal Ontario Museum in Toronto. There's not necessarily anything *wrong* with their designs. Such stunning, singular *forms,* certainly. Such uncompromising visions. But I can't find even passing mention of ecological or efficiency concerns in the adoring reviews they inspire. How does the Bilbao Guggenheim keep itself warm in the chilly Basque winter? From what source would Libeskind's 1,776-foot Manhattan tower have drawn its monumental power load?

This is not an architecture in need of tweaking. It can't be remedied by high-efficiency light bulbs, and it won't be redeemed by rooftop gardens alone. It needs to be rethought from the ground up. Begin, perhaps, with modernism's extraordinary ability to generate garbage. Take its ruins, its discarded shards, form uneven piles and rounded shapes, and begin to build something better.

THROUGH A CRACKED POT (BRIGHTLY): THE OFFBEAT CURVEBALL SUSTAINABLE MODERNIST TRADITION

One of the most pointed rebuttals to the excesses of modernism was assembled, appropriately enough, from the refuse of the masterpiece of the greatest of the Great Masters. In a quiet corner of Corbusier's Chandigarh lies the city's most popular tourist attraction, far more heavily trafficked than any given sector's assigned parkland or even the heatstroke plaza. It's a sculpture garden made entirely of debris: piles of melded gravel and great stacks of busted bangle chips, clay humanoid figures smoking crockery-encrusted hookahs, countless thousands of smooth quadrangular stones cobbled together into multi-tiered amphitheatres populated by dense eclectic rows of sculpture. This is Nek Chand's Rock Garden, a walled-in, treed-over labyrinth of scavenged shapes tucked between the governmental head of India's model modernist city and its sectored, squared-off residential upper torso, like Corbusier's grand figure has something permanently lodged in its throat. It's a blessedly shady place, this garden, inviting visitors to linger awhile and consider the curious little fairy tale of how one tenacious Indian bureaucrat built a miniature city (with a population of more than five thousand individual sculptures, most of them humanoid) in gentle, multihued, asymmetrical reproach to the grand design of modernism's vaunted Silver Prince.

Like millions of Indians, Nek Chand Saini was born in what is now Pakistan. Flung into motion by the wrenching subcontinental partition of 1947, Chand crossed into newborn India as a refugee, making his way eventually to the region of eastern Punjab where the vast construction site that was to become Chandigarh lay—a new capital for the Indian state now that its historic capital of Lahore lay across the freshly drawn border. In 1951, Chand found a job as a roads inspector, a junior bureaucrat in the vast apparatus soon to begin work on Corbu's "City Beautiful." A couple hundred labourers toiled under Chand, building new roads and repairing or dismantling old ones, and he began to fixate on the rubble and debris that were the constant companions of his crews. Sometime around 1958, he started to spirit away bits of this refuse, piling it in a hilly patch of jungle centred around a monsoon gorge not far from the site of the new capital buildings, then still under construction. Initially, he thought to build a simple garden, encircling it in piles of scavenged stone and concrete. But there seemed no end to the trash generated by the City Beautiful—busted crockery and smashed tile, shiny red shards from broken bangles, electrical fittings and fluorescent tubes, bottle caps and rags. He built a retaining wall out of discarded oil drums and began to populate his garden with human forms—he thought of them as the gods and goddesses of a sort of lost kingdom. Chand remained, by day, a cog in the bureaucracy that churned up all the junk; at night, in secret, he tended his garden. It became known to certain officials—among them the city's chief architect, a fawning admirer of "the Great Master" Corbu—by the mid-1960s, but although it was on land set aside as green space, none of them wanted the hassle of dealing with it, and so Chand was left to carry on with his strange hobby.

The question of what to do with the odd, obsessive roads inspector came to a head around 1975, and the Chandigarh Landscape Advisory Committee decided summarily that it was an illegal development, a tumorous blight on Corbusier's precise master plan, and had to be destroyed. Word of this garden of recycled wonders hit the press, however, and locals soon began to trek by the hundreds to see it for themselves. Under mounting public pressure, the bureaucracy relented, and in January 1976 Nek Chand's Rock Garden was given official approval and formally opened to the public. Chand was installed as "Sub-Divisional Engineer—Rock Garden," and given a small staff to help him continue his sculpture work. The city even set up depots around the city to collect busted crockery and rags and other scraps to supply the project.

Over the course of three phases—the last of which was finally completed around 2003—Chand expanded his little patch of jungle into a meandering 25-acre park that now greets somewhere between three thousand and five thousand visitors a day. Chand's work appeared on a one-rupee stamp in 1983; more recently, he received the city of Paris's Grande médaille de vermeil and the Folk Art Society of America's Lifetime Achievement Award. Through it all, he has remained so unassuming that you'd be forgiven for thinking, after a cursory scan of his press clippings, that his official title was "humble former roads inspector." He's not an artist, he invariably explains—certainly no "Great Master"—just an engineer with an idea. "It is my belief," he told an Indian reporter a few years back, "that any conflict between nature's will and man's design is bound to lead to an overall destruction. The dimensions of the essential harmony between man and nature can be economic, social, political and aesthetic. My own effort is to explore the aesthetic dimension. The natural environment, trees, water, soil, birds, rocks are the major participants in my work."

I have to assume that Le Corbusier admired symmetry, and so I wonder if he'd appreciate the perfect symmetrical harmony of Chand's shady remnant garden and the grand baked concrete plaza at the head of his City Beautiful. The greatest fault of Corbu's brand of modernism, I'd argue, is its extraordinary arrogance, its intrinsic assertion that the architect's inspired vision, driven by a supremely rational mind, transcends its context. That it is *above* the mundane concerns of nature somehow. How else to account for the guiding principle that a standard-issue mass-produced box could be plopped down virtually anywhere, strung with electric lines and garlanded with paved roads, and perform the same function in Chandigarh as it does in Paris or St. Louis? Not to mention the notion, implicit in Chandigarh's master plan, that the architect's symbolic purposes were more important to a central public space than the comfort of the public for whom the space was ostensibly intended? And how better to right this imbalance between the public's needs and the creator's ego—both symbolically and literally—than to build a far superior public space out of the flawed plan's rubble?

The European modernists of the 1920s and their acolytes the world over argued repeatedly in favour of the idea of "starting from zero." There was a certain youthful wisdom to this, and a huge appeal to avant-garde artists and socialist politicians everywhere, hamstrung as they often were by leaden traditions and outdated ideas. The modern world they apprehended—still bruised from an industrial-powered war's impossibly outsized destructive scale, riven by endemic social unrest and epidemic disease, its economic system on the brink of a near-total collapse—certainly seemed to be desperate for a fresh start. Wipe the slate clean, tear the whole ruined house to the ground, and put the smartest people to work on the reconstruction. "If you were young," writes Wolfe, "it was wonderful stuff. Starting from zero referred to nothing less than re-creating the world."

What the modernists forgot, though, is that zero is a mathematical abstraction, that no structure built by human hands actually begins from nothing. Nature provides an immediate and essential context for any building. Nek Chand understands this, not just in his inclusion of his local environment's varied elements as "major participants" in his work, but in the nature of that work itself—in his use of readily available materials and tools, in the way his sculptural amphitheatres rise and fall with the contours of the ground beneath them. Chand is, in this sense, a "vernacular" architect in countless ways Corbu never was, and it's pretty much the first principle of sustainable architecture that the traditional pecking order of vernacular and academic architectural styles be inverted. The ideological, manifesto-born stuff must drop to the bottom rung, and the vernacular—the baseline requirements imposed by the immediate natural context, that is—ascend to the top spot. Bring ideological or aesthetic or symbolic principles to bear on a design, certainly, but figure out, first, what the weather's like in May wherever you intend to execute it.

This concept was implicit in the stillborn vernacular styles of architecture and art in America in the early twentieth century—the ones modernism so fully supplanted. The most lamented of these in many circles is Frank Lloyd Wright's Prairie Style, an approach to housing design characterized by wide, low profiles and heavy materials—this in homage to the flat American Midwest, born of Wright's desire to articulate a wholly American vision of shelter. Wright was just about to launch an affordable mass-production version of his Prairie houses (called the "Usonian" house) when the International Style washed ashore to reset everything to zero, erasing the vernacular styles from American architecture like so many forgotten sandcastles on the beach. Wright's houses were far from flawless from the point of view of sustainability—they were built facing away from the street and were ultimately as car-dependent as any modernist box—but they were at least *informed* by their context. Place them in a sort of curio-shop parallel-modernist tradition alongside Nek Chand's whimsical junkyard scarecrows, and you begin to fill in the contours of a multivalent movement that, if it didn't always point in the same directions, often pointed at the same tools: an enthusiastic embrace of the immediate environment, a deep respect for local materials and a bias toward reusable ones, an overarching goal of harmony with the natural setting.

Or maybe they all *did* point in the same direction after all: to a time and place far in the distance, way out west. Across Wright's beloved prairie on the dusty Santa Fe Trail, then swooping south into the Sangre de Cristo Mountains. Arriving, eventually, at a wide mesa on the lip of the deep Rio Grande Gorge, where an architect who has been stripped of that title has evolved a design that trumps them all—Corbu's white Esprit Nouveau cube and Wright's horizontally stretched Usonian ranch house, even the solar-powered marvels of Rolf Disch and Dr. Soontorn. If sustainable shelter has a fountainhead, a pavilion at the 1925 exposition, then it is found here, outside Taos, New Mexico, a manifesto written over several strange and practical books and brought to 3-D life on a high sagebrush plain littered with odd low buildings by the dozens. Perfectly self-sufficient, totally sustainable dwellings. A radical new way of thinking about what a house *is*.

But I don't want to get ahead of myself. Let's not even name it yet. It only begins to make sense once you've become acquainted with Taos.

FAR OUT & DOWN TO EARTH: THE RADICALLY PRACTICAL, SUPER-SUSTAINABLE MESA MODERN TRADITION

The Taos Valley of New Mexico is a wide desert plain 7,000 feet above sea level, a dramatic landscape of flat sagebrush mesas and panoramic mountain vistas, hemmed in on one side by the towering peaks of the Sangre de Cristo range of the Rocky Mountains and on the other by the deep Rio Grande Gorge. The first non-indigenous artists arrived in the valley by horse-drawn wagon in September 1898, at a time when there were perhaps twenty-five English-speaking residents in the whole region. There were two of them— Ernest L. Blumenschein and Bert Geer Phillips—and they were immediately transfixed by the stark terrain they encountered. They were soon joined by a steady stream of artists and dreamers from back east, drawn by the valley's famously clear and varied light, captivated as well by its deep and diverse human history: Taos is home to one of the most ancient human habitats in North America, a major population centre for the Anasazi and their descendents since at least

1000 AD, home since the middle of the fourteenth century to one of the largest pueblos in the region, and a major Spanish ranching outpost from the 1600s onward.

Taos soon found a small but permanent role in the cultural life of America. It was the birthplace of several subgenres of modern art, an intellectual hotbed, a countercultural haven. In the 1920s it was home to a vibrant salon culture, and in the 1960s it hosted communal experiments by the dozens. In their wake, Taos emerged as a major landmark of the New Age, a place of holistic healers and elegant spas, artists' studios and writers' retreats. Today it is home to a solar-powered radio station and an annual solar-electric sun-worshipping music festival, and it's the fashionable address of one of the world's most ecologically friendly luxury resorts and the most exhaustively stocked natural-food supermarket I've ever seen.

It would be easy to reduce contemporary Taos to caricature—to sketch it as the archetypal crunchy-granola hippy-dippy spaced-out station, an artists' enclave gone so far out it splits apart and dissipates in a fairy-dust cloud of ephemera and gibberish. The morning after I arrived, I was sitting with a coffee at a downtown café/bookstore/healing centre when a woman draped in loose robe-like vestments burst through the door in evident distress. The establishment's proprietor met her in the entryway, took both of the discombobulated woman's hands in her own, and talked her down in soothing New Age aphorisms. "This is *change*," I heard her declaim at one point. "This is entering into your power years and becoming the grandmother of the world." On the way out, I found a glossy handbill next to the cash register advertising the Solar Logos Activation Retreat ("The SOLAR energy is the inherent seed of Cosmic Awakened Consciousness within every human being. . . . The LOGOS is the creative word force that stems from our personal connection with Source Consciousness"). Or there's this from Phil Lovato, the deceased former mayor of Taos, quoted in an otherwise straightforward account of the valley's history: "Taos is not a city, Taos is not a town, Taos is not even a place. Taos is a state of mind and a power centre of the universe."

So I might as well get it out of the way right here and now: I was staying on the outskirts of town in a dwelling known as the Suncatcher Earthship, and I was in Taos, yes, to learn how to build one. An Earthship. It's a damn shame about the name. I frequently find myself wishing their inventor had called them *anything* other than Earthships, something that sounds less like a vehicle you might rent to take you on an activation retreat, because Earthships are much more revolutionary in their architectural significance—and far more representative of Taos's down-to-earth flipside—than the name suggests.

It might just be, in other words, that Taos *is* a kind of a power centre of the universe, a transcendent place where the far-out excesses of intellectual hypothesis and dreaming mind find down-to-earth resolution in the life-or-death practicality of survival in a harsh desert climate, in the mud-brick architecture that has hugged the landscape here for six hundred years, in the eternal but ever-changing light that inspired generations of painters. Consider the uniquely Taoseño take on modernist art. The same starting-from-zero ideology that conquered American architecture also came to dominate its visual arts, but it never completely colonized Taos. As David L. Witt noted in *Modernists in Taos,* there was something about the place that seemed to rein in the more extreme and alienating forms of abstraction that came to characterize modern art elsewhere after the Second World War. Indeed, Taoseño artists tended to think of themselves as simply modern—informed by the art world's intellectual currents but not completely committed to the European schools of thought, never fully modern*ist*—and even when their work veered onto more abstract planes, it remained tightly connected to the light and shape of the Taos Valley's landscape and the deep traditions of its culture. The Taos Moderns seemed to recognize that even an abstraction had a natural context, and a Taoseño abstraction was thus not the same as a Parisian one.

This painterly Bohemia gave way to the 1960s counterculture, and by 1970 there were, by one estimate, twenty-seven full-fledged communes in the Taos Valley. And this was but the most overt manifestation of a migrant hippie population of maybe 2,000, at a time when the population of the town itself was only 3,500. There were back-to-the-landers and smash-the-state revolutionaries, Weathermen and Hell's Angels, Puerto Rican and Dominican radicals, and tuned-in, turned-on dropouts of every other imaginable stripe. Taos became a place of peyote-fuelled rituals and acid-tripping outlaws, where manifestos were issued and revolutionary rhetoric was frequently invoked; there was even something like a blood feud between the pueblo-worshipping communards and the dirt-poor, militant Hispanics. Amid all this high life, it was surely hard to see much down-to-earthiness at work. And so when a dude by the name of Michael Reynolds rolled into town, circa 1969, he must've seemed like just another easy rider in the lunatic parade.

Reynolds arrived fresh out of the University of Cincinnati with a Bachelor of Architecture degree to his name, but he'd come mainly to race motorcycles and avoid the draft, and as it turned out he needed to go even further out than most before he again found terra firma beneath his feet. He would write, years later, of sleeping in pyramids of his own construction out in the desert, of visitations by ancient ageless wizards. Somehow, in the midst of all this, he discovered his true calling: to develop, through thirty years of constant experimentation and hard labour on a hardscrabble mesa west of town, a 100 percent sustainable human dwelling, totally self-sufficient, completely off the grid, capable not only of generating its own electricity, heating and cooling itself, supplying its own water, treating its own waste and growing its own food—all accomplished in high-altitude desert conditions—but also of being replicated essentially anywhere on earth. He called his house an Earthship, and we've already been through what a problematically far-out name that is for a design so down-to-earth that it's literally half-submerged in dirt.

So let's meet this Mike Reynolds and see what these Earthships are all about.

The Greater World Earthship Community—the third and largest of the Earthship communities built by Reynolds and his fellow travellers in the Taos area, and the site of the headquarters and visitors' centre of his home-building business, Earthship Biotecture—sits on a wide, parched plain 12 miles west of Taos on Highway 64, just beyond the vertiginously deep Rio Grande Gorge. Westbound out of Taos, there's very little to see from the highway—a handful of odd adobe-like mounds in the distance, the glint of the blinding New Mexico sun off a wall of glass. If you're watching for it, there's a dusty clearing of a parking lot just off the highway and a small sign reading SOLAR SURVIVAL ARCHITECTURE.

The sign fronts a cluster of bizarre structures that resemble a life-sized diorama combining Luke Skywalker's childhood farm on

Tatooine with the Bag End home of the beloved ring-bearing hobbit Frodo Baggins, seemingly assembled from adobe and the contents of the local landfill. There's a rounded, somewhat southwestern vibe to the main building, whose north façade is submerged beneath a sloping mound of earth. Its unburied walls are studded with the multicoloured translucent circles of wine bottles. Squatting next to this building is a small dome-shaped hut sporting empty aluminum cans where the bricks should be. This is the Earthship Visitors' Center, a fully functional demonstration Earthship built ten years earlier, the public face of Mike Reynolds's life's work, and the conference space out of which he runs his weekend-long hands-on building seminars. This was my reason for being in Taos. As I'd soon learn, it was consistent with Reynolds's approach to the more ornamental aspects of architecture and the field of public relations that he introduced himself to all and sundry with a cluttered, semi-finished, somewhat out-of-date and still utterly fascinating muddle of a welcome mat.

The seminar began on a typically warm Friday evening in June with a meet-and-greet dinner and orientation session at the visitors' center. I arrived, with my wife and daughter and an anthropology professor friend from Manhattan in tow, just as the sun disappeared over the distant western edge of the mesa in a blaze of muted reds and oranges right out of a Taos Modern painting. In the dusty clearing between the demo Earthship's side door and the pop-can dome, a couple of Reynolds's work crews had gathered. They were drinking beer and smoking hand-rolled smokes and looking to all the arriving seminar attendees like Central Casting had sent over an assortment of counterculture archetypes to set the tone for the weekend: elaborately bearded young dudes and older, wirier greybearded guys, twentysomething women with multiple piercings and even more tattoos. Dreadlocks and torn T-shirts abounded, and an assortment of dogs, some with bandanna collars, darted in and out.

We made our way inside to a classroom-sized space near the entrance to the visitors' center where the walls and built-in shelves were lined with pictures, books and other sundry info on the life and times of the Earthship. An orientation video ran on a small TV. Our fellow students were mostly middle-aged or older and comfortably upper middle class, the kind of people who'd gone into early semi-retirement and were wondering what kind of country retreat to build for themselves. Work-crew members and their dogs sauntered through periodically as we sipped at the complimentary microbrewed beers and organic sodas and traded glances indicating a generalized mood of anxious confusion. *Why are* you *here? Why am* I*? Is this some kind of cult? Do I have the right place?*

A buffet dinner was served, at which point, without any fanfare whatsoever, Mike Reynolds showed up to chow down, surprisingly against type, on meat-stuffed lasagna. He installed himself on a plastic chair next to a small table where a slide projector had been set up, and tucked into his dinner. Reynolds has a great untamed mane of thick grey-black hair and white scratchy stubble, and he was dressed in his standard work outfit: heavy cotton workpants, a ratty T-shirt and construction boots, all of them caked in paint and dust. Two pairs of glasses—granny-style reading glasses and sleek extreme-sporting sunglasses with lenses of orange metallic tint—were perched on his head like a sort of semaphore communiqué of the paradoxical mix of wise older gent and wild-eyed radical that defined him. As dinner was about to wrap up, one of the dogs knocked over the table next to him, sending the projector crashing to the floor. While Reynolds and a couple of his colleagues futzed with it, the assembled seminar crowd came alive with the tense, querulous chit-chat of people who are starting to think they've been had.

I mean, there we were, dusty and sun-baked, stuck in a strange land with few familiar bearings and not much of a map, seated on cheap plastic chairs or cross-legged on the bare floor. In a sort of adobe cavern tinged with the portentous scent of patchouli, we waited for a dishevelled dude with two pairs of glasses tucked into his funky hair to fix a projector some damn dog had kicked over. This was emphatically *not,* we all knew, what it was like to go hear Gehry lecture on the Bilbao Effect. This wasn't even what it was like to visit the show home of some third-rate cookie-cutter cul-de-sac maze. I smiled sheepishly at our friend from New York as she fixed me with increasingly pointed what-the-*hell*-kind-of-nonsense-have-you-dragged-me-into? glances. And this is a woman who does most of her field research in rural India—I can only imagine what John and Judy Investment-Portfolio across the way were thinking.

That's what made what came next all the more remarkable: Reynolds got the projector working, and within five minutes the room was his. We were summarily *mesmerized*. Reynolds walked us through his big ideas in a crystal-clear, logically flawless lecture, accompanied by a series of well-organized slides, the almost professorial tone of it balanced by wicked-funny anecdotes of hard-won victory over bureaucratic myopia and by his distinctive drawl. (*Hwut thuh hayul's goin' awn?* is about how he'd intone his amazement at some pain-in-the-ass bylaw he'd encountered.) What the hell's going on, indeed. By the first break forty-five minutes in, I could feel a kind of delighted, half-incredulous surprise pouring off nearly everyone, a product of the dawning recognition that we were in the presence of authentic genius. My friend and I stepped outside for a much-needed breath of fresh air, and the first thing she said was something to the effect of *Why isn't every building on the planet constructed this way?*

So maybe the name's a little weird, and maybe the venue isn't quite a fancy pavilion, and no one will ever confuse a mesa west of Taos with the heart of gay Paree. So the *hayul* what? I'm fairly sure Mike Reynolds doesn't care, because it's abundantly clear that Mike Reynolds is, in his far-out down-to-earth way, starting from the only approximation of zero that exists in nature: the ground beneath his feet, the building materials he can pick up and shape with his bare hands. He lives in a house of his own battle-tested design that he built himself, mainly out of dirt and scavenged junk, in the middle of a flat patch of scrub populated by scorpions and venomous spiders that sees 100°F heat and sub-zero cold and maybe 8 inches of rain every year. Crazy-stubborn and well versed in the fine art of political compromise, a starchild dreamer who's more of a hard-facts realist than all of the world's name-brand starchitects combined, Reynolds is the kind of hyper-individualistic frontier-pushing rebel-yelling psychedelic cowboy that has always been at the centre of American innovation.

I'd come to Taos with much apprehension. I'd felt silly even saying the stupid name *Earthship* out loud, and right up until the moment the projector whirred to life, I was secretly almost certain there was nothing to see on this bone-dry mesa except a southwestern-style take on the leaking handmade geodesic dome. But after forty-five minutes in a room with him, I was convinced that Mike Reynolds was among the most important architects on the planet, and the most potentially revolutionary force in the philosophy and practice of human shelter since at least ole Buckminster Fuller himself. Reynolds has not tried to figure out ways to make modernist boxes more efficient, nor how to heat a suburban tract house with the sun. Wide awake to the cold, hard facts of the natural world, its changing climate and our place in its grand design, he has *begun* from the premise that a house must be self-contained, zero-emissions, waste-free. An Earthship, prepared to "sail on the seas of tomorrow." Something, anyway, fit for crossing the great tumultuous sea of anthropogenic climate change dead ahead. Sounds hokey, I concede, but then again so did "machines for living," and odds are you currently live or work (or both) in a building modelled after one.

At the next morning's lecture, Reynolds spoke in a sort of editorial "we" about the connection between his houses and the stormy Anthropocene. "These buildings are not just our idea of how things should change. They're our logical response." It didn't matter, as far as he was concerned, how much we *liked* the way things currently were— how attached we'd become to ranch-style wood-frame McMansions or clean-lined modernist cubes—because there was no way they could handle the rough waters up ahead. A new kind of dwelling was essential. "It's more necessary than tradition," he said, his tone matter-of-fact, ready to get on with it. "Tradition is baggage at this point."

Okay, then: So what the *hayul* is an Earthship?

An Earthship is the refinement of thirty years of tinkering out on the mesa into a single simple, replicable, scalable, mass-producible structure. Reynolds: "Basically we're making a vessel, we call it, that deals with shelter, of course, energy, food, water and air. Almost like on Walden Pond—those were the things Thoreau said people needed. Well, we need them, but we need them without nuclear power plants, we need them without power lines, and we need them without destroying the earth's aquifers. We need to provide them in each unit that we build. And that's the idea that we're dealing with here. And so we're providing food, shelter, power and sewage treatment, all in one unit." Just like that? *Wayll,* no.

The Earthship began, Reynolds readily conceded, with "a contrived effort to recycle." He started playing around with old beer cans back in the early 1970s, to see if they could be made into building blocks, which they readily could. But Reynolds soon realized they also *were* building blocks, easily mortared into place, more versatile than nearly any other common building material, capable of being formed into interior walls, vaults and arches, almost anything. Around the same time, another realization: tires. Everywhere you went in the world, on the outskirts of seemingly every burg from Taos to Timbuktu: *Tires!* Heavy, sturdy, ready-to-be-stacked rubber tires. So Reynolds hatched another contrived recycling project: he built a one-room shack out of tires (a sort of tire-brick adobe, more precisely) and he brought out the state building inspectors to see it. In his introductory slide show, he proudly shows off the photo of how he convinced them it was structurally sound—it depicts a cement truck parked atop his little tire cottage.

In the lurching, haphazard way of any far-out futurist's laboratory, Reynolds's building concepts steadily progressed over the following years. He toyed with little vertical-axis wind turbines, installed solar panels, built beer-can pyramids and tire domes, started half-burying his structures in the dusty ground, just as the Anasazi had done with their pit houses on the same land a thousand years ago. In time, the basic building form standardized into a deep tire-wall U, its north side buried under an earth berm, its south-facing opening fronted by a glass greenhouse. Line up several of these Us in a series, with a plant-lined hallway along the front, and you had a house.

Along the way, totally by accident, Reynolds discovered the concept around which his design would coalesce. The concept is thermal mass, and it was delivered to him, providentially, by beer truck. Reynolds had found a brewery in Tucson, Arizona—this was still in his contrived-recycling-exercise phase—that would make sealed cans of water for him without pop-tops, forming little water-filled beer-can bricks. The water in the cans would heat up a bit on the drive from Tucson, and one time when Reynolds had the truck driven into a chilly Taos warehouse to unload, he noticed how the stored heat in the cans warmed the room. This is the simple science behind thermal mass, and Reynolds came to realize it could do more for his buildings than a thousand state-of-the-art solar panels. "It was like a total revelation for me," was how he recollected it. Thereafter, thermal mass became the *sine qua non* of a Reynolds design (of course, he'd probably refer to it as something like *the nitty-gritty*). And as luck would have it, a thick wall made of old tires, their hollow insides pounded full of hard-packed dirt, was a staggeringly effective way to amp up a building's thermal mass. "I've said it a thousand times," Reynolds told our seminar for the thousand-and-first. "If I was paid, in a grant, $30 million to invent two of the best building materials I could invent, I would invent tires and cans."

Reynolds likes to describe himself as a miner of knowledge, and he's definitely something of an accidental archaeologist, because he stumbled on a building concept nearly as old as human civilization. Indeed one of the most radical pre-industrial exercises in thermal mass occurred not far from Taos, at the Anasazi village of Mesa Verde in southwestern Colorado. Nearly a thousand years ago, members of the most technologically advanced civilization of the American Southwest built an elaborate settlement in a sort of notch in the middle of a cliff face, which took advantage of the great stone wall's passive heating and cooling, as well as the shade of the rock overhang. (It's not known if this was the motivation for situating the Mesa Verde settlement hundreds of feet up the face of a cliff, but it's certainly one of its more notable consequences.) Much more recently, Frank Lloyd Wright's Usonian houses featured thermally massive concrete floors and other passive solar details. Some of Wright's ideas have been resurrected by green-minded latter-day architects— the Santa Monica modernist cube featured in *Dwell* magazine's 2006 Green Issue, for example, relies on a thermally massive concrete slab floor for much of its vaunted energy efficiency. What distinguishes Mike Reynolds from this pack, though, is that he has made thermal mass his *first* priority. From this choice, form has followed function to produce the Earthship design now found scattered across the Taos Valley and in hundreds of other places around the world.

In a 1996 primer on the uses of thermal mass for designing "energy-conserving buildings," Bruce Haglund and Kurt Rathmann of the University of Idaho outlined a handful of critical elements that read like academic translations of the results of Reynolds's single-minded, unconventional field research. "Ideal thermal mass," they wrote, is found in materials with "a high heat capacity, a moderate conductance, a moderate density, and a high emissivity." This rules out a number of the modern world's most common building materials, including wood (which neither stores nor conducts heat well), steel (which reflects too much heat and conducts what it does absorb too quickly, resulting in a "storage cycle" of mere minutes) and glass (which is also too reflective and doesn't trap certain kinds of heat energy at all). "Concrete and other masonry products," they concluded, "are ideal." As are old tires stuffed with compacted dirt.

Reynolds, for his part, acknowledges that concrete and other more conventional stuff will do the job, but they fall short of his beloved tires in terms of cost and structural integrity—he likes to point out that his Earthships are earthquake-proof—so he builds his dwellings with thermally massive load-bearing tire walls. The "cardinal rule," Haglund and Rathmann argued, is that the thermal mass be placed "inside the insulated skin of the building." Hence the earth berm that hugs every Earthship. The resulting thermal-mass system functions "both diurnally and annually," as it's phrased in Haglund and Rathmann's ivory-towered prose. By which they mean that the tire walls store the day's heat to warm the house at night and they also trap the heat of summer to warm up the winter. This is the central organizing principle of the Earthship: the idea that thermal mass, properly applied, with careful consideration of local climate, can reduce artificial heating and cooling needs to virtually nil. And this, all by itself, eliminates the lion's share of a typical home's energy load.

By the latter half of the 1980s, Reynolds was ready to conduct his most radical thermal-massing exercise yet. He needed a house of his own, so he combined his most successful experiments into a unified concept, and thus was born the Earthship. Pounded-tire Us were built against an earth berm, sufficiently thick and dense and subterranean to provide the house with all of its heating and cooling in the Taos Valley's wildly varied climate. To these were added interior walls of beer-can mud brick, a greenhouse along the front fed by the house's wastewater, a roof carefully constructed to channel every drop of infrequent rain into a cistern, and a small bank of PV panels for the building's meagre electricity needs. Fruit and vegetables—even bananas—grew robustly in the greenhouse, at 7,000 feet, even in snow-blanketed winter. More or less complete self-sufficiency, then. Well, almost. "It's difficult for me because I haven't figured out how to grow bacon"—so goes Reynolds's only serious lament.

Designwise, everything about an Earthship builds out from its thermal-mass core. The slightly sloped glass of the south-facing wall is precisely angled to allow very little heat gain to penetrate to the thermal-mass core at the peak of a hot summer and to maximize heat retention when the sun is low in the sky in the depths of winter. Gravity-operated skylights toward the rear of the building's rooms allow the venting of interior air, which aids both heating and cooling. And the PV array on the average Earthship's roof needs only six to ten panels, testimony to the efficiency gains that accompany thermal massing. Energy needs thus summarily taken care of, Reynolds has designed an elegant water-management system in which damn near every drop of rain that falls on an Earthship is channelled by the roof's contours into a cistern for use on demand. The greywater from dishwashing and showering is cycled through the greenhouse to feed its plants before being run back through the toilet. Post-flush, this "blackwater" is piped through a bacterial treatment pond to a small garden plot out front, where it feeds seasonal crops and emerges, detoxified, into a septic field.

This, in experimental form, is what Mike Reynolds built for himself on that mesa west of Taos. And like *that*—it was the late 1980s, climate change still a half-formed cloud on most people's horizons—some mad-scientific genius of an architect invented the first fully self-sufficient, globally applicable housing design the world had yet seen. A house that, in the middle of a desert that sees near-Saharan heat and near-arctic chill, allows its interior temperature to fluctuate maybe 10°F or so. In the years since, the only changes to the Earthship have been minor refinements to reduce that temperature fluctuation another degree or two, stylistic improvements and design tweaks to fine-tune the concept for other climates. "That's all we've been doing for thirty years—experimenting," Reynolds explained. "And something that works good, we keep repeating it, and, you know, after doing that for thirty years, we looked around, and we're building fully sustainable housing. And it's tried and true."

That first Earthship is still standing, still provides self-sufficient year-round shelter out on the unforgiving mesa. The design has evolved, but even the prototype did the job it was built to do from the moment it was completed.

Reynolds's timing was, from a certain angle, impeccable: in November 1989, around the time he was settling into his second winter in his half-built Earthship, there occurred a gala opening at Ohio State University that the *New York Times* described as "one of the most eagerly awaited architectural events of the decade." This was the unveiling of Peter Eisenman's Wexner Center for the Arts, a gallery and performance space in his signature "deconstructivist" style, which was considered a bold and experimental leap forward, using Le Corbusier's International Style as its springboard. The Wexner Center's skylight began to leak within a couple of years, and the windows of its several glass façades were placed in such a way as to encourage sun damage to the artwork hanging within. Its interior also suffered from temperature fluctuations of as much as 40°F. In the last couple of years, it has been given a $15.8 million retrofit to correct the Eisenman's many glaring oversights. Eisenman, asked for comment by the *New York Times* in 2005, quickly pointed out that similar problems had plagued the "experimental" designs of Frank Gehry and Mies van der Rohe and even old Corbu himself. As if to say, I suppose, that you couldn't expect a Great Master to fuss over such incidental details.

By comparison, I stayed in the second Earthship that Reynolds built—his first commercial commission, which came shortly after he'd begun work on his own house. It was a 700-square-foot cottage on the outskirts of Taos. Its first owner named it the Suncatcher, and she liked it enough that she had a bigger one built up the hill from the first, so the Suncatcher was now a rental unit. We arrived at the Suncatcher in the blazing 90-degree heat of a June afternoon, and it was refreshingly low-70s inside. We slept in high-60s comfort as the temperature outside plummeted 15 or 20 degrees below that level. We showered and shat, cooked and ate, kept our daughter's milk in the refrigerator, turned on lamps against the dark at night. Lived, that is, about the same as we would have in any rental condo. The interior—deep, rounded, U-shaped rooms, adobe-like walls, cool stone tile—reminded me quite a bit of Mediterranean villas I'd seen, though I'm sure it had more in common with the numerous southwestern-style pueblo revival homes surrounding it. The Suncatcher, at any rate, was *just fine*.

This was Reynolds's idea of "experimental," which for him also meant fully functional. Even the Earthship Visitors' Center, built several years later and also lacking in obvious systems failures, was to his mind out of date, desperate for a retrofit. The "packaged" Earthship designs he now sells for your low-cost off-the-shelf convenience and the "hybrids" that combine the packaged version with his custom designs—these are marked improvements on what was already a pretty solid concept. The Suncatcher—the inaugural version—is still plenty comfortable fifteen years on. This is worth bearing in mind as we consider how little Mike Reynolds has been granted in the way of Eisenmanesque Great Master leeway in the years since he unleashed *his* bold new idea.

Reynolds would at any rate probably refuse such special dispensations; he's never taken the easy road. In fact, the first major development he embarked on, beginning at the start of the 1990s, was a whole community of Earthships built several hundred feet up the face of a mountain north of Taos. Maybe it was the fact of a Mesa Verde parallel too perfect to pass up, or maybe it was that land was cheap when it was on a 45-degree slope, but more than anything I bet it was that Reynolds is just that kind of stubborn, the kind of guy willing to do the *nearly* impossible just to prove it isn't, in fact, impossible, and what's more he could do it blindfolded with both hands tied behind his back and nothing even vaguely resembling the infrastructure of modern development. Anyway, he did it, and it's called REACH—short for Rural Earthship Alternative Community Habitat. And although it won't be expanding any time soon, the simple truth of it is that a dozen completely sustainable, totally off-the-grid homes have been providing shelter and heat and fresh produce at 9,500 feet above sea level and a healthy hike from the nearest road for more than a decade now. A second Earthship community, STAR— short for Social Transformation Alternative Republic—got going in 1992 on a particularly remote patch of mesa west of Taos. And the Greater World Community, where Reynolds and his building firm are now located, was inaugurated on a slightly less remote patch two years later.

Meanwhile, propagated by a couple of volumes of a how-to manual, countless seminars and some disaster-relief work, tires have been pounded full of earth, cans formed into staircases, and Earthships thus erected the world over. There are fully functional Earthships in Belgium and Bolivia, in the snowy mountains of British Columbia, in dreary Scotland and in sunny St. Lucia. The most famous one, for a long time, was the million-dollar multilevel, mansion-like "Earth Yacht" built by former *Gunsmoke* star Dennis Weaver in the mountains of Colorado. Reynolds built a kind of modified Earthship to house the power plant for Taos's solar-powered radio station (thus avoiding the construction of a $20,000 road to the transmitter, which would've been necessary so propane could be trucked in to keep it from freezing up in winter). Earthship Biotecture just finished building a house in Brighton, England, and if the advocates on the local council there get their way, it will be the first of a community of sixteen, which will become the largest commercial build Reynolds has ever undertaken.

So then: as of the seminar I attended in June 2006, Reynolds was sixty years old, a man with maybe a thousand or more of his novel houses up and running, and for all his fringe-dwelling, building-halfway-up-a-mountain efforts, he was a sort of éminence grise of sustainable shelter. "I used to wish there was some guy with white hair to tell me what to do," he told us as the second day of class began. "Well, I just had to wait long enough and I'm that person." And then he explained, in maddeningly funny detail, how unfathomably hard it'd been to get to that point. It had very little to do with the Earthships themselves—the core engineering of which, as I've mentioned, has been solid since at least the second one he built. "I've spent 75 percent of all my time, all my energy, and all my money getting permission to do all this stuff," he said.

The bureaucratic squabbles are the stuff of broad farce. There was the building inspector in Ventura, California, for example, who walked into a brand-new Earthship on one of the coldest days southern California ever sees, removed his coat, embraced the home's warmth, and then demanded to see the code-mandated heating system. When attempts to explain why Earthships didn't need such things failed, Reynolds ran out and rented some electric baseboard heaters, set them up at strategic points throughout the house and invited the inspector back. He didn't even bother to plug them in. He got his permit. Reynolds was invited to address the Scottish Parliament on the issue of a national crisis in home heating costs, only to realize once he got there that there was no earthly way to build an Earthship to standard Scottish building codes.

Back home in New Mexico, meanwhile, Reynolds fought a protracted battle with the state government over his licence to practise architecture, primarily over his obstinate refusal to stop designing homes that might be, according to state guidelines, unfit for human habitation. He cites the example of a rule stating that a home must be capable of holding a room's temperature steady at 73°F at a height of 41 inches off the floor; his off-the-shelf Earthships, as a written testimonial from one delighted owner attested, can maintain a temperature of 68°F to 74°F year-round with a $47-per-year utility bill (exclusively to feed a natural-gas cooking stove), but they couldn't meet the state's demands. At the urging of a supportive lawyer in the state attorney general's office who worried the fines would bankrupt him, Reynolds voluntarily surrendered his architecture licence and continued building quite possibly the most certifiably sustainable houses on the planet without it.

An even messier legal squabble erupted in 1996 with the arrival in Taos of a new county planning director, who vetoed previous permits and special variances, declaring all three of the county's Earthship communities to be illegal subdivisions. After a couple of years of legal battle, attempting among other things to argue that a stand-alone Earthship was surely a smaller burden on county infrastructure than a conventional grid-connected home, Reynolds and the other Earthship dwellers decided the fight couldn't be won. They spent the next several years painstakingly bringing their otherwise self-sufficient houses into compliance with the one implacable tentacle of the grid—its bureaucracy.

There's just something about Earthships, I guess, that makes people *want* to dismiss them out of hand. It might be the Age of Aquarius name. Or maybe it's Reynolds himself—his audacity, his complete and unwavering certainty in the righteousness of his work, his disdain for the more frou-frou elements of style. The way he dismisses pretty much the whole of modern architecture as the practice of erecting monuments to the egos of its creators. "It's like making a beautiful boat that doesn't float," is how he puts it. (Design, as far as he's concerned, should be an incidental minor at architecture schools, only useful—if at all—after you've mastered biology and physics.) For all their revolutionary import and tried-and-true functionality, Reynolds's Earthships have become a sort of shorthand in some circles for the kind of far-out freak show people *don't* want when they choose a "sustainable" house. The notoriety the Earthship gained through Dennis Weaver's fame, for example, hasn't always been to its immediate credit. "'Gunsmoke' star built mansion out of tin cans," went the headline on one obituary when Weaver passed away in early 2006. The *New York Times,* meanwhile, most recently discussed Earthships alongside such oddities as singer-songwriter Carole King's handmade, collapsing Idaho ranch as part of a feature on "intriguing vacation homes."

It follows, then, that when *Newsweek* devoted a July 2006 cover story to answering the question of "Why Environmentalism Is Hot," it had no trouble finding an executive type in Charlotte, North Carolina, to supply a quote about how he'd gone to some lengths to ensure that his new green house would resemble a *normal* house, not "a yurt, or a spaceship, or something made out of recycled cans and tires in the middle of the desert." Never mind that until maybe ten years ago nothing on the planet had ever resembled the McMansions I saw scattered up a hillside near Charlotte, or that even the standard-issue split-level ranch house would've looked freakishly alien if it had been a pavilion at the 1925 Paris Exposition. The crux of it is that there's only one member of this guy's far-out trifecta that I'd even *consider* letting my daughter sleep in for a week, and once I did, it was very hard to comprehend a mindset in which the massively wasteful, hopelessly grid-dependent suburban tract home could seem a more desirable norm than the one Mike Reynolds was pointing toward.

Anyway, the somewhat maligned Reynolds simply sat there in the visitors' center's U-shaped meeting room, in his stained T-shirt and heavy black Carhartt workpants—because, unlike many celebrated architects, he *builds* things—and got on with it, explaining the unimpeachable technical details of his misunderstood housing concept with the hippy-dippy name and the enviable ecological footprint. This was day two of the building seminar, a day given over mostly to examining each of the various systems that provide Earthships with their self-sufficiency. Reynolds ran through it all in his matter-of-fact drawl, as if every house heated itself by the warmth of its walls and treated its own sewage. His conclusion: "It is *insane* not to build thermal mass into a home." Not for him, really, to wonder why people found his ideas hard to swallow. He was off to give a seminar in Hawaii the next day, and over to England to push the Brighton project forward a short while after that, and what the *hayul* did it matter whether his Earthships were pretty?

Actually, he'd addressed that question, briefly, toward the end of the first day's slide show. "They will take care of you," he said. "A lot of people think that to be off grid and all sustainable and everything, that you have to be living in a tepee." He clicked the controller in his hand, and a slide of the plush interior of one of the more elaborate Earthships he'd built appeared on the screen. "Well, this is *far* from a tepee."

It bears repeating: Earthships *are* far from tepees, and just as far from yurts. The Earthships I saw—from the Suncatcher to more refined latter-day buildings—had a singular charm, a mix of earthy, soft-edged warmth and future-tense funkiness. Let's call it Mesa Modern, and let's take a moment to look at it purely from an aesthetic angle, because clearly there are some national-newsweekly-scale misconceptions about its defining elements.

The morning of the third and last day of the Earthship seminar consisted of an extensive tour of the Greater World community. This included realtor-style walkthroughs of a handful of Earthships, representative samples of Mesa Modern living that demonstrate an impressive versatility in styles of decor and levels of creature comfort. There are certain universal elements, of course—particularly the overall floor plans, which are limited to the fused Us and dome-like circles of the home's basic building blocks, and the adobe-style interior walls of smooth mud or concrete mortar, which conceal the tires, cans and bottles that give them their shape and structural integrity. Beyond that, though, there are no obvious limits. Some homes seem enamoured of the "expressed" bottle wall, in which the bottoms of the glass-bottle bricks are left exposed, creating a stained-glass effect. One owner has clearly embraced the hobbit-like elements of the design; this Earthship has arched doorways, floors of irregularly shaped stone, petrified wood beams in the middle of the living/dining area, and kitchen cabinetry in knotted wood with lacquered twig inlays. Another Earthship leans toward contemporary southwestern styles, with floors of squared stone in desert sunset hues, cool blond wood panelling on walls and ceilings, stove and fridge in matte stainless steel, and dual free-standing deep freezes under one kitchen counter. Some Earthships have TVs and satellite dishes; others have wireless internet. Some greenhouses are more elaborate than others, but in all cases they are no more intrusive on the living spaces than a double-wide plant-lined windowsill. There is no discernable odour of wastewater being treated, and there is, as advertised, at least one fruit-bearing banana tree.

These are very nice homes, comfortable and cozy, even elegant and stylish in their way. These seem like ridiculously trite things to say, but as long as the perception remains that the Mesa Modern life is in any way equivalent to yurt-dwelling austerity, I guess the point needs belabouring. To live in fully sustainable homes—even the first of them, the ones largely built by hand, often by their owners themselves, homes as yet unseen by professional designers or the editors of upscale decorating magazines—is not, in any substantial way, to live *less*. It is, certainly, to live quite a bit *different,* but the arc of sustainable shelter's trajectory from leaky domes and modern-primitive tepees to the Mesa Modern Earthship has been a rapid ascent through several centuries of technology, so that it has arrived today at roughly the same place as any old house. Or, I'd argue, at a point a few enviable steps ahead.

At one stop on the tour, I watched the whole process condense into the lifespan of one resident. It was like a fast-forwarded time-lapse photograph or a cinematic montage, a dizzyingly quick acceleration from a bit of exotica spied in the pages of *National Geographic* to a global villager's funky Mesa Modern pad.

The Earthship in question was still having finishing touches applied when we arrived. It was the home of Kirsten Jacobsen, a thirtysomething jack-of-all-trades employee of Earthship Biotecture. Jacobsen is the company's education director, she keeps the visitors' center humming smoothly, and she hops over to England periodically to oversee the construction of the Brighton Earthship. Plus she's been known to swing a mean sledgehammer to pound dirt into tires herself—most rewardingly for the walls of her own home, which is as handmade as a modern dwelling can get, the product of a quietly monumental career arc that found Jacobsen standing in her kitchen, explaining how she'd come to build herself an ultra-customized Earthship in the New Mexico desert. And seeming, by the end of the tale, like the first citizen of the Sustainable Age.

The house itself is impressive enough in its own right, overflowing with elegant touches, singular details, startling juxtapositions. Sustainably harvested bamboo flooring and a fabric drop ceiling in the bedroom. A couple of paintings, Taos Modern maybe, propped on a shelf. Eight car-stereo speakers strategically placed throughout, broadcasting mellow grooves from her iPod. A cheap IKEA-style wardrobe rack. A circular bathroom, the upper half done as an exposed bottle wall, one particularly striking section entirely in blue glass. (A friend of Jacobsen's had to drink a heroic amount of the cheap white Zinfandel that came in said blue bottles to facilitate the construction.) Her dog, a big yellow-black German shepherd cross named Dreyfuss, was curled up next to the bathtub. The concrete floor had been finished in a special sort of ultra-durable burnished bronze paint. And Jacobsen stood in the middle of her bedroom with a cup of tea, running a hand through her sun-bleached blond hair, her arms showing the wiry muscle tone of someone who's swung many sledgehammers indeed, explaining the elaborate, painstaking process that brought about that burnished bronze effect and all the rest of it.

The most captivating detail for me was a crinkled computer printout of an old photo that sat casually on a table. It was a picture of Jacobsen and Dreyfuss standing in the doorway of a beer-can dome in the middle of the windswept desert. The tops of the cans were still exposed, the dome's mortar a wet-cement grey, Jacobsen had an arm around her dog and a determined smile on her face. It looked like a still from *The Road Warrior* almost, post-apocalyptic and survivalist, the opening shot in the story of an Anthropocene nomad's hard-won triumph.

"There were some cold, cold, *cold* times," Jacobsen said, appraising the photo, recalling that first long Taos Valley winter in the dome she'd built herself. "You know, it gets dark at five." We'd all walked past the dome on the way in; the rest of the house had grown up around it, enveloping it, and now it was a sort of antechamber of a much larger living/dining/kitchen area with an elaborate greenhouse planted with fruit tree seedlings. "When I took all my stuff out of the dome and moved here," she told us, meaning the spacious bedroom she was standing in, "it was just epic."

Like many Anthropocene kids, Jacobsen began her epic tale with a childhood marked by an unsettling, inchoate sense that something was deeply, intractably *wrong* with modern life. For her, it finally took solid shape and clear resolution on the pages of *National Geographic*. It was an issue from 1983, a picture of one of Mike Reynolds's beer-can domes. Jacobsen: "It's something I remembered for a long time. There was a picture of a woman in a dome that was made out of cans, and it was just a striking photograph and an interesting idea, 'cause I think I always kind of sensed that the way we lived on the planet, even when I was young, was just"—a rueful chuckle—"not harmonious. I mean, if you look at power lines or a power plant or a polluted lake, I think people have an intuitive sense that that's not natural, or that it's wrong. So that kind of struck a chord with me."

Almost a decade later, Jacobsen—who was born in New York, raised in San Francisco—was at New College of California, a small school with an activist bent, learning the art of screen printing by making social-justice campaign paraphernalia. A fellow student started talking about Earthships, and it clicked with her old memory of the magazine. Her classmate had one of the Earthship how-to books and a copy of a 1993 *New York Times* feature that described Reynolds as "a one-man Monkey Wrench gang of architecture" who built strange homes from discarded tires—"the detritus of twentieth-century civilization and building blocks of a new utopia."

Jacobsen came to Taos later that year, planning to volunteer on a work crew for a month and write a paper about it for school. She's never really left. She worked as a sledge-swinger on the building crews for several years, one of the few women, working harder and longer to prove her worth. "It was exciting to me, as a woman, to learn some of these building skills that—I don't think anyone told me that I *couldn't* do it, but no one ever told me that I *could*." Once the REACH community was finished, she rented one of those mountainside Earthships for a couple of years—a mile and a half from the nearest road, hauling dog food and clean laundry up the hill by hand. "I felt like I was in training for something when I lived there," she told me, "but I wasn't quite sure what it was."

Maybe it was the next phase, which was to build her own place out on the Greater World mesa. This was in the mid-1990s, before Taos County forced subdivision status on the place. It was still a land-use association, and Reynolds was practically giving away lots to crew members who wanted to build an Earthship. Jacobsen began with a dome—starting casually, picking away at it in her spare time, piling beer cans, mixing concrete and mud in a wheelbarrow, stirring it with a hoe. She was living in town by then, but sometimes she'd stay the weekend, camping out in a sleeping bag and mixing cement by hand. Around 2000, pressured by friends who thought she might never finish it, she moved into her dome full-time. She lived with her dog in a 120-square-foot room, posing at some point for the picture in the doorway as if she'd stepped into that old *National Geographic,* body and soul. She made modest expansion plans, and then Reynolds talked her into a more substantial dwelling, and before she knew it she was building a whole damn house. Even had to get the bank involved to finance the last chunk of the construction, which, for someone who'd been living outside the mainstream for as long as Jacobsen had, equated to a partial surrender to Ozzie-and-Harriet-ville. "It feels pretty cush and, I don't know, *middle class* to me," she explained. "Where I was just such a nasty little mesa hippie for so long. It's weird."

We were talking by phone now, nearly half a year after I'd first met her on the tour. She was just back from Brighton, and it was the first time she'd returned to a completed Earthship of her own making. The houses in England, she said, even the expensive ones, had struck her as intrinsically substandard. Because they weren't Earthships. "This morning," she told me, "it was negative-eleven degrees after the sun was up. There's snow everywhere. It's minus eleven. And inside my house, it's 75 degrees, and I'm standing around in a T-shirt—with no heating system. When I opened the door to the outside, this crazy ice mist just blew in the door, because it was so freezing cold outside and it was so warm inside that the air was just instantly freezing and crystallizing"—she started to laugh—"from the temperature difference. It was crazy."

It was more than that: it was amazing. *Powerful.* A bicoastal cosmopolitan woman—born and raised in big cities she still misses—living in a house she built herself on a desolate mesa. With her bare hands, practically. If the worst of the worst-case scenarios about climate change are right, then Kirsten Jacobsen is as well equipped to survive the fallout as pretty much anyone on the planet, and if they're wrong, then she simply owns a sturdy house in a ruggedly beautiful valley, a place perfectly fitted to her needs that she could live in forever, never wanting for anything. Powerful—even quietly heroic in its way. I don't need to build my own house by hand out in the desert, necessarily, and neither do you, because Jacobsen and people like her already have. They are the Anthropocene's pioneers, and we will, in time, benefit from their work out in the wilds.

The afternoon of the last day of the Earthship seminar was the hands-on workshop. Reynolds was midway through construction of the most colossal, luxurious Earthship he's ever built (not counting Dennis Weaver's), a sprawling place called the Phoenix, and that was where we went to learn to pound tires and stack beer cans. There *is* an art to these techniques, but not much of one. If the apocalypse was a week away, you could still learn enough to save yourself, even if what you built turned out nowhere near as pretty as the Phoenix. One bedroom of the Phoenix, already completed, resembles a cross between a Taos pueblo and the Playboy Mansion, all rounded adobe half-staircases and cushioned banquettes, burgundy velvet and bottle walls, a flat-screen TV and a pedestal bed. A stone path meanders along the front of the building, through a double-wide greenhouse; it's like walking through an indoor arboretum.

Reynolds's intention—or at least one of them—was to build a showcase so grand and luxurious that it laid to rest forever the notion that sustainable living equates to grim sacrifice. The argument is solid, but I'm skeptical that Reynolds will be the one who makes it most convincingly. There's a unique and impressive skill set that leads a guy to build completely autonomous homes in the desert, to defy conventional wisdom and flout building codes and push against every boundary he encounters, and I'm inclined to think it's not the same skill set that makes a guy a good marketer. If it was, I doubt these amazing houses would still be called Earthships. It's probably up to someone else to figure out what Reynolds's designs mean for a mass audience, to design the Earthship equivalent of the split-level ranch house, to figure out how best to bring thermal mass to sprawling suburbia. The result may or may not look like a low-slung, glass-fronted pueblo. Reynolds has freely admitted that he cares more about physics than style, so it stands to reason that a more aesthetically oriented designer will one day figure out the full potential of his technical achievements.

In the meantime, I was about eight swings into my first tire-pounding exercise when an almighty wind starting howling across the mesa. The sky had gone Biblical—big, menacing clouds towering everywhere with bright rays slanting in through the gaps, catching the dust the wind had thrown up. We pulled up collars and pulled down hats and tried to keep at it, but then someone spied a huge dark fan of swirling debris on the horizon, burnt orange in colour and surely ten storeys high: a massive dust storm heading our way. We all stopped to watch its progress. One of the tire-pounders—an easy-going dude with dreadlocks tied back and a bandanna pulled up over his mouth and nose—mentioned the Double D, a ranch to the north of the Greater World Community that had been cleared of all its sage to permit the grazing of livestock. He reckoned that was Double D topsoil roaring our way. "A lesson in the trouble with overgrazing," he noted wryly, "right before our eyes."

Just then it started to rain, and we all ran inside the Phoenix for shelter. There was a status quo ranch out there and a bunch of strange pioneers squatting in Earthships hereabouts, and there was no question left in my mind as to which group would still be here a couple of decades hence. I'll never live on an overgrazed agribusiness ranch, but I just might reside in an Earthship one day. I know which one has a future.

FIVE

TAJ MAHAL 2.0

[sustainable design]

CERTIFIED PLATINUM

In the beginning, there was LEED.

Actually, that's overstating it. Architects have been working on sustainable design since long before the U.S. Green Building Council was born and even further in advance of the development of its Leadership in Environmental Engineering and Design rating systems, much as Greek doctors were saving lives before Hippocrates swore his oath and Babylonians obeyed other codices before that most famous legal code issued forth from the throne of Hammurabi. There was Frank Lloyd Wright with his passive solar Prairie houses, to name one, and Buckminster Fuller with his geodesics and Dymaxions, to name another. And there was the English architect Norman Foster, inspired by both of them and a collaborator with the latter in Bucky's last years, and Foster's been obsessed with natural light and hyper-efficiency ever since. (His late-nineties retrofit of the Reichstag in Berlin, for example, generates its own power from vegetable oil, yielding a 94 percent reduction in CO_2 emissions.) Even further back, before the Industrial Revolution cleaved the natural from the manufactured in human societies, there was an intrinsic sustainability to all manner of building designs. The Anasazi had their thermally massive cliffside pueblos, the Bedouin were masters of natural ventilation, the Moghul Empire brought the Indian subcontinent its first emissions-free air conditioning, and all of it was as finely tuned to its environment (and as biodegradable) as the mud and cloth and stone from which it was built. But the dawn of the Anthropocene Era—or, more accurately, our awareness of its dawning—brought an enormous urgency to the task of rediscovering sustainable design practices, and there has probably not been a greater catalyst to this process in the building trade than the formulation of the LEED codes, which first went public circa 1998.

It wasn't the looming cataclysms of the Anthropocene, however, that gave birth to LEED. It was a different and more specific kind of disaster: the collapse of the skywalks linking the towers of the Hyatt Regency Hotel in Kansas City in 1981, a design failure that killed 114 people and injured hundreds more and sent the building's shell-shocked designer, Bob Berkebile, on a haunted hunt for more sustainable methods of construction. Berkebile's soul-searching expeditions took him to top green-design think tanks—among them Amory Lovins's Rocky Mountain Institute—for extensive meetings. Out of these discussions, Berkebile helped form the American Institute of Architecture's National Committee on the Environment, which morphed into the U.S. Green Building Council (USGBC) in 1993. Five years later, the council introduced its LEED certification, which aimed to provide the first universal, standardized measure of a building's sustainability.

After a trial run of pilot projects under the inaugural v1.0 of the LEED standards, a second draft (v2.0) emerged in late 2000, codifying the LEED certification process into a sixty-nine-point scoring system tallied in six categories: Sustainable Sites (the location of the building, its proximity to public transport, whether it represented the rehabilitation of derelict urban space or contaminated "brownfield" industrial land); Water Efficiency (its frugal use and reuse); Energy and Atmosphere (from efficiency measures to on-site renewable-energy generation to emissions levels); Materials and Resources (the use, reuse and recycling of local, non-toxic building materials); Indoor Environmental Quality (from "low-emitting" carpeting and paint to ventilation, temperature and natural light); and Innovation and Design Process. In addition to the general LEED certification, which would be awarded to any building with a score of twenty-six or higher, there were also Olympian gradations for truly exemplary buildings: Silver, Gold and the coveted Platinum.

Shortly before LEED v2.0 emerged, v1.0 bestowed its very first Platinum award upon the Philip Merrill Environmental Center in Annapolis, Maryland. An elegant, low-rise office building constructed to house the headquarters of the Chesapeake Bay Foundation (a prominent regional conservation organization), the Merrill Center was a fitting inaugural candidate for LEED Platinum: a well-heeled old-school environmental group, a showcase structure intended as a sort of living model of the emerging sustainable architecture movement, an Earth Day march of a design project. Which is to say that the centre was, as its LEED case study notes, nothing less than "one of the 'greenest' buildings ever constructed." It was built on the site of an old inn; the old building's materials were diligently reused and the new Merrill Center constructed atop the footprint of the defunct hotel's pool and pool house. The Merrill Center faces south, overlooking Chesapeake Bay, maximizing its passive solar properties. Its exterior is clad in recycled galvanized siding; the south-facing façade was also outfitted with photovoltaic cells, and the roof crowned with a solar hot water heater. The floors inside are recycled rubber and fast-regenerating cork. The Merrill Center diligently collects its rainwater and captures its waste in composting toilets, reducing overall water use by more than 90 percent. There are geothermal wells tapping the earth below it for heating and cooling. The total cost of the construction was $7.5 million, an estimated 28 percent more per square foot than a conventional building, but the foundation estimated that it would recoup the added costs within seven or eight years through the dramatic reduction in energy use. The Merrill Center was, in short, a poster child, a prototype, an architectural collage of the latest and greatest in green building techniques. The very definition of LEED Platinum. A fine start.

LEED's popularity quickly exploded among forward-thinking builders in the United States in the first years of the new millennium. It was just the thing for campaigning environmental groups and enlightened institutional and corporate chiefs who wanted to demonstrate their concern about ecology in a nation whose new government refused to acknowledge the existence of anthropogenic climate change. In Europe, guidance might be coming from on high—elected federal officials, new national legislation, stringent new sustainability-minded building codes—but in America it had to come from the grassroots, and it helped that it came with an embossed plaque you could proudly display above the reception desk. Among the first Platinum buildings under v2.0 were the Chicago Center for Green Technology, the offices of the Aububon Society and the Natural Resources Defense Council in southern California, and the marquee headquarters of the next-generation biotech firm Genzyme next door to MIT in Cambridge, Massachusetts. LEED Gold went to the Institute of EcoTourism in Sedona, Arizona; city halls in the liberal hubs of Austin and Seattle; a Starbucks outlet and a Toyota port facility in the vicinity of Portland, Oregon; and the showpiece headquarters and educational centres of dozens of other green non-governmental organizations and socially responsible corporations.

LEED was not—and still is not—without its critics. The certification process was more bureaucratic than some would like, and more costly. It applied uniform measurements in disregard of actual ground-level results, placing the goal of certification ahead of proven sustainability, which necessitated cutting significant corners in a system as elaborate and variable as the earth's climate. Its criteria overemphasized some practices over other equally valid ones, and it was geared more toward big builds than toward a house or two. The result, as one disgruntled assessment put it, was "a few super-high-level eco-structures built by ultra-motivated (and wealthy) owners that stand like the Taj Mahal as beacons of impossibility."

Notwithstanding such seeming tokenism, the LEED gospel soon spread beyond the usual suspects, becoming a blueprint for the expanded foundations of what was imminently possible. The USGBC updated its standards a couple of times as new lessons were learned in the field, and it introduced new LEED rating systems for retrofits of existing buildings and for commercial interiors. The list of certified projects climbed into the hundreds, and they began to make their own friends. The case of Alberici Constructors, Inc., a construction firm based in St. Louis, Missouri, is highly instructive—both because the company's new headquarters, completed in 2004, scored the highest total in LEED history (a certified Platinum 60), and because there's nothing especially green-minded about Alberici Constructors, Inc.

When Alberici went looking for a new corporate headquarters a few years back, it was simply one of the oldest and biggest construction firms in St. Louis. It didn't specialize in green construction, and even today, the word *sustainability* remains absent from the company's mission statement. But one of its vice-presidents had been to Ford Motor Company's headquarters in Michigan for a conference, and he'd been impressed by the auto giant's vocal commitment to sustainability—Ford's new headquarters was being planned just then by green-design guru William McDonough, who I'll introduce more fully a bit later on—so he decided to attend a LEED workshop.

Out of this workshop emerged Alberici's pursuit of something beyond the usual suburban office pod. A decrepit office building and metal manufacturing plant were found near an interstate bypass in the St. Louis suburb of Overland. The offices were demolished, their materials reused, and the old plant was outfitted with a series of sawtooth-shaped extensions to maximize its southern exposure. A rooftop wind turbine and the *de rigueur* solar hot water system were installed. Mostly, though, the new headquarters accumulated its record-breaking LEED score not with eye-popping technical innovations but by the careful implementation of sound, time-tested principles. One of the partners of HOK, the lead design firm on the project, explained it like this to a St. Louis business magazine: "With green buildings, you don't make them more complex, you make them more primitive. Use daylight instead of artificial lighting. Ventilate a building naturally instead of sealing it up tight." The result was 109,000 square feet of certifiably sustainable office space for an otherwise conventional construction company, about $540,000 per annum in energy savings, and a stellar example of the uses of the LEED approach to sustainability even to organizations not given to principled stands on ecological issues.

The recent boom in sustainable architecture extends well beyond the LEED-certified ranks. About one-third of *all* the electricity generated in the United States is used to heat, cool, ventilate and light commercial buildings, and the increasing sums needed to pay for all that power have opened the ears of procurement VPs and CFOs to the messages of formerly fringe-dwelling efficiency zealots. "As Power Bills Soar, Companies Embrace 'Green' Buildings," read an August 2006 headline in the *Washington Post*. The article used as its case in point a Pittsburgh-based financial services company that had moved to sustainable design practices midway through the construction of an operations centre and was now planning to do all its new branches in sustainable, money-saving green.

The same feature also discussed what it called America's "flashiest green building," the new Bank of America Tower on Sixth Avenue in Manhattan, soon to become New York's second-tallest tower and easily its greenest. The building's architect, Robert Fox, also designed the twin skyscrapers around the corner at 3 and 4 Times Square, which weren't LEED-certified, in part because they were completed before the formulation of LEED v2.0. The tower at 4 Times Square—the headquarters of publishing powerhouse Condé Nast—was previously the Big Apple's flashiest sustainable structure, its top nineteen floors encased in a curtain of solar panels, a pair of natural-gas-fed fuel cells on its fourth floor providing most of its nighttime power and using their waste heat to warm the building, the remaining heating and cooling provided by an arsenal of hyper-efficient on-site absorption chillers. Unlike the Times Square projects, the Bank of America building will seek LEED certification, and its builders expect a Platinum award.

For all this, green architecture has remained the exception to the rule, the notable deviation from the wasteful norm. It is exotic and future-tense, luxurious in its way, like the vacation home with the solar-panelled roof or the showpiece Prius at the red-carpet Hollywood opening. LEED is, after all, *American*—a salve to the guilty conscience of the world's most oil-addicted and overconsumptive society, a gaudy medal to wrap around the neck of a dubious champion as he hurriedly exits the arena ahead of the next round of climate change talks. What good does it do to erect a vainglorious eco-friendly spire amid the wanton burning of a quarter of the world's oil? In the absence of America's singular wealth and power and its exceptional resistance to climate change action at the national level, was there any real purpose to LEED?

A tough question, and one that would seem to be all but answered by a quick scan of the list of the twenty-seven projects currently certified as Platinum at LEED's website. Twenty-three are in the United States. There is one in Dubai—that Vegas-like monument to fossil-fuelled affluence on the edge of the Arabian desert. But then there is also the startling appearance on the same list, in the three remaining slots, of this unexpected geographical designation: *India*.

A TAJ MAHAL IN SUSTAINABLE GREEN

Visit some of the world's most celebrated monuments, and it's not uncommon to be just a little let down by the reality after so much hype. The Eiffel Tower, so often the set dressing for cinematic romance, might strike you as smaller than you were expecting, especially if you're accustomed to the vertical wonders of North American cities, and there's nothing all that romantic about milling around amid gawking package tourists and pushy postcard hawkers. The Sistine Chapel might be more diminutive than you imagined, and all that shuffling along in endless lines detracts from the awe of contemplating the moment of Creation depicted above. Big Ben isn't actually all that big, either, and neither is that "giant" Hollywood sign (and half the time you can barely see it through L.A.'s smog). Toronto's CN Tower *is* all that big, but it's also kind of bland and pointless, and it amazes you only with the added intensity of the vertigo that accompanies staring down from its observation deck.

The Taj Mahal, however, is one of those rare buildings that is *more* than you anticipated. Notwithstanding the countless photos, despite its name being pretty much synonymous with luxury and elegance and exotic romance, *nothing* prepares you for the sensory fact of it. The Taj is surrounded on three sides by a wide courtyard enclosed by a high ornate wall of red sandstone, so you can't see it from a distance. The first time I visited, I was walking along a path alongside the wall; I glanced through an opening, and there it was. I felt the air leave me in an awed gasp, and for the first time I fully understood why beautiful things are described as breathtaking.

The Taj Mahal is many things. It is a singularly flawless example of the genius of Mughal architecture and engineering, a testament to the extraordinary technological achievements of seventeenth-century India. The precise, multilayered symmetry of the structure and its grounds is head-spinning. The acoustics of the interior are themselves a sort of scientific miracle, and the delicate inlay of precious stones that covers the outside walls staggers the imagination with its volume and painstaking care. The Taj is a mausoleum, the final resting place of the emperor Shah Jahan and his deceased wife, who was taken from the emperor in childbirth, and for whom, heartbroken, he had the monument constructed. And so it is also a shrine to the idea of enduring human love—"a tear on the face of Eternity," as the great Indian poet Rabindranath Tagore described it in an oft-repeated aphorism. Above all, the Taj is an open statement of defiance, phrased not as a battle cry but as a heart-rending ballad: for a beloved spouse, for fragile, precious life, for the near-impossible feats humanity can achieve with the right combination of indomitable will, fantastic imagination and kind intent—incontrovertible proof that there are fewer natural limits to what is possible than you might think.

It was much harder, at least at first glance, to imagine such limitless possibility from within the claustrophobic confines of an autorickshaw trapped in the grinding crush of a traffic jam in inner-city Hyderabad. More than one thousand kilometres south and several centuries of mixed-blessing progress ahead of the elegant Taj Mahal, I was lurching my way past the Andhra Pradesh state legislature building on a broad boulevard, my perturbed rickshaw wallah leaning on his horn and weaving around city buses packed to overflow and belching black exhaust into the rickshaw's windowless cabin. He would buy us another 10 metres of passage, and then we would sit and wait and choke, watched over by the large statue of Mahatma Gandhi on the legislature lawn—an iconic bronze depicting India's most revered modern prophet seated in cross-legged, meditative repose, looking like the only person in the whole city who'd found any peace. Up around the next bend was a tall fence draped in banners, one of them advertising the Earth Charter Exhibition under a blaring slogan: *Are we the last generation on this planet???*

After some time—and never was that imprecise Indian-English phrase more apt—we worked ourselves free of the downtown bedlam and headed up a narrower avenue into the hills west of the city. We chugged past desultory rows of concrete-walled, monsoon-stained motorbike repair shops and dingy chai stalls, past whole half-blocks of rubble and junk that looked positively bombed out. It was as if the teeming, traffic-clogged inner city was encased in a grimy layer of its own wreckage. Somewhere along the way, lane markings began to appear on the street. At first they seemed an absurdly optimistic joke, but they were soon joined by traffic circles and concrete medians planted with tidy flower beds and neatly spaced trees, and a comparative calm slowly emerged. "Clean and Green— Plant Trees to Reduce Pollution," suggested a series of civic-minded signs. The roadside scene morphed as well, the concrete-bunker stalls of downtown Hyderabad replaced by upscale Starbucks knock-offs (Barista Crème, Café Coffee Day) and computer stores. These were the harbingers of my ultimate destination: a commercial district whose designers have given it the clumsy name of "Hyderabad Information Technology Engineering Consultancy City" (i.e. HITEC City). It's better known, however, as Cyberabad, the suburban software development hub that had drawn all those inner-city throngs to hunt for a trickle-down drop of the boom's overflowing largesse. Just up ahead was the very heart of this HITEC City: the sleek, curvaceous Cyber Towers, all golden brick and smoked glass, the centrepiece of a vista sufficiently postmodern and prosperous that it could convince a visiting Western business executive or a blinkered *New York Times* columnist that all India was a branch plant of the global information economy and the world was thus flat.

Beyond the Cyber Towers, Cyberabad seemed to quickly recede. Wide, boulder-strewn expanses of blessed emptiness stretched away from the boulevard on either side, populated by only a few diligent cows and the half-formed skeletons of a couple of standard-issue poured concrete office blocks crowned in naked stalks of rusted rebar. The landscape looked a bit like the setting of a post-apocalyptic sci-fi film, but through an optimistic squint I guess it could look like the city's next frontier, bursting with promise. This, anyway, was the way it was intended to meet the eyes of the dignitaries who gathered at the Cyber Towers in March 2000 to look out across this rocky waste and declare it the birthplace of a bold new movement in Indian architecture and a massive leap into the front ranks of sustainable design. Within a few years, there would rise on this site possibly the most significant building project the subcontinent had seen since Shah Jahan broke ground on his wife's mausoleum: the Confederation of Indian Industry's Sohrabji Godrej Green Business Centre—the CII-Godrej GBC, as per its unwieldy official abbreviation—the first LEED-certified Platinum building ever erected outside the United States and only the fourth in the world at the time of its completion in 2004. The Taj Mahal, v2.0.

Not that the potentates who gathered in the exhibition hall of the Cyber Towers for a staid ceremony that day in 2000 had anything anywhere near this ambitious in mind. The event was, in fact, little more than a photo op, the centrepiece of U.S. President Bill Clinton's visit to Hyderabad, itself merely one of many courtesy calls on his whirlwind tour of the subcontinent. Clinton had come to India to talk development, trade and regional security, and he'd included Hyderabad on his itinerary mainly as an acknowledgement of the enormous role played by Indians in America's high-tech boom (both in the front ranks of Silicon Valley and, increasingly, in the rank-and-file drudge work of outsourced software development). It was the first time a sitting American president had ever visited the city, so the streets were duly lined with smiling Indian children waving the Stars and Stripes, the Cyber Towers draped with banners reading "Well.com Mr. President."

An impressive roster of corporate chairmen and senior ministers was assembled to listen to a little speechifying and applaud the president with earnest enthusiasm. First to the podium was the chief minister of Andhra Pradesh, Chandrababu Naidu, an ambitious populist who styled himself not as his state's premier but as its publicly appointed CEO. Naidu orated enthusiastically on his state's prospects for "leapfrogging into the future," evidence of which he enumerated in a list of brand-name multinationals—Microsoft and Motorola, DuPont and Pfizer—with facilities in the region. And then Clinton, quick-witted and charismatic as always, took the stage and charmed the room with lavish praise for India's high-tech leadership before sliding in a cautionary note or two. "Millions of Indians are connected to the internet," Clinton declared, "but millions are not even connected to fresh water." With that, he pledged $5 million in funding from the United States Agency for International Development (USAID) to accelerate the transfer of miraculous technologies from bountiful America to the Indian heartland. Then came more high-minded talk—of the promise of biotechnology to fight the diseases that still plagued modernizing India, of moratoria on poverty and the poaching of tigers. Almost in passing, Clinton noted that his visit marked the beginning of a new partnership between India and the United States to develop a green business facility, an Indian undertaking to be enabled by USAID expertise and thus to account for climate change, at least symbolically, as India charged ahead into a techno-utopian future. Just a few hours later, Clinton was back at the airport, a ceremonial shawl draped around his neck, leaving the vagaries of this green building plan to his hosts.

In short order, the Andhran chief minister issued a vague buck-passing pledge of his own: 5 acres of barren, rocky land near the Cyber Towers, bequeathed to the Confederation of Indian Industry (CII) along with the full co-operation of his government in whatever capacity was deemed suitable when the time came. The CII, an esteemed business association whose membership comprises a wide swath of India's industrial might, then canvassed its ranks looking for backing, and thus was the House of Godrej—a Bombay-based, diversified corporate behemoth, manufacturer of everything from hair dye to forklifts—convinced to donate 50 million rupees (a little over $1 million in U.S. greenbacks) to the cause from its charitable Godrej Foundation. In this offhand way, the ad hoc group that would build India's first LEED-certified structure was cobbled together.

In due course, a research team was assembled—architects, engineers, a handful of CII executives—and they travelled to the United States on the obligatory fact-finding mission. Accompanied by USAID advisers, they met with officials from the U.S. Green Building Council, toured the brand-new Platinum-certified headquarters of the Chesapeake Bay Foundation outside Washington, and returned to Hyderabad determined to duplicate its unparalleled achievement on a barren ridge in South India. This was not much different, really, from an eighteenth-century English trade mission returning to the court in Georgian London hellbent on building a Muslim mausoleum of white marble and precious-gem inlay on the banks of the Thames. It wasn't that it couldn't be done, but that it was almost comically optimistic to think that it simply *would* be. Who in India knew how to build such a thing? Where would they find the proper materials? And what kind of woefully naive ambition was involved, in a country whose top tech hub had spent almost two full decades waiting for a new airport, to think the greenest building on the planet could simply be thrown up in a couple of years?

Which is why it was about as throat-catchingly amazing as a visit to the Taj Mahal itself to come sputtering along the boulevard past the Cyber Towers in an autorickshaw a few short years later and find the cii-Godrej GBC open for business. It was a mirage, an oasis, a future-tense vision of harmonious, smogless calm.

It is, for all of this—well, yes—just a single building: a modest 8,000-square-foot office complex, with a low profile, built of grey brick with patches of red brick lattice, arranged in partial concentric circles of unequal height like a series of interlocking parentheses. The roof is swathed in a checkerboard of green grassy foliage, save for the south-facing section, which is sloped toward the sun and carpeted in solar panels. It's flanked by two square, whitewashed, chimney-like towers perforated with narrow vertical slits, like some funky mix of medieval battlements and a mosque's minarets. The overall effect is a little bunker-like and unquestionably modern. The cii-Godrej GBC is not quite elegant and not exactly beautiful, but it is truly striking, especially compared to the bland boxes of concrete and glass that usually serve as modern office blocks in India. And it is also, as I mentioned, one of the finest examples of sustainable architecture on the planet. Standing—just to be crystal clear—on the rocky soil of a nation ranked 159th in the world in per capita income.

It was a fine February day—blindingly sunny and just beginning to crawl above 30°C, still pleasantly balmy by South India's intense standards—and I arrived to find the building's cool, cavernous interior awash in late-morning shadows and whisper-quiet. The developing world is littered with well-meaningly progressive, technologically overwrought projects built with misguided foreign aid money, structures and installations devoid of real purpose and gathering dust that's wiped clean only for the occasional dignitary's visit. And certainly the prospect of state-of-the-art sustainable architecture on the fringe of a city verging on infrastructural collapse was ripe for such a role. The place seemed almost abandoned, actually, and I started to wonder whether I'd entered the empty belly of some futuristic white elephant.

The reception area was spacious and well-appointed. There were official commendations and an artist's rendering of the building on the walls, a rack and a coffee table littered with glossy brochures. I checked in with the bored receptionist, took a seat on a comfortable couch and perused a pamphlet, its cover bedecked with logos—cii, usaid, a major Indian bank—and its text littered with well-intentioned banalities ("Centre of Excellence," "client-driven," "interactive").

A short while later, I was joined by Air Cmdre (Retd.) S.C. Kumar, a senior adviser for the CII and the CII-Godrej GBC's project manager. He settled into an easy chair across from me and almost at once launched into an orientation lecture as trim and tidy as his haircut. Kumar had the slightly regal bearing and florid quasi-British accent typical of the senior Indian military officer he used to be. His delivery was polished to a bullet-pointed sheen worthy of a PowerPoint presentation and peppered with the baroque vocabulary endemic to India's bureaucratic elite (*mooted as a possible area of co-operation . . . as per auspices . . . I'll just expand it by an example*). He quoted precise, unrounded-off statistics from memory and spelled out acronyms without prompting. There was indeed plenty about Air Cmdre (Retd.) S.C. Kumar that appeared to confirm the notion that this Green Building Centre was merely a meticulously executed vanity project.

There was much else, though, that hinted at something more substantial. There was Kumar's evident enthusiasm, for starters, and his reluctance to boast. Sure, he wanted me to know that he and his team had never aimed for less than Platinum, and he was happy to tell me exactly how many points the CII-Godrej GBC had scored on the LEED scale (fifty-six of sixty-nine) and where it placed in the ranking of the all-time worldwide highest scores as of the mid-2004 tabulation (first). And yes, he spoke readily of the higher purpose that had always been at the core of the project: "When the building was being conceived, even right in the beginning, one of the areas of our activity was to promote and facilitate and work as a catalyzer for the green building movement in this country." Kumar also told me that the president of India was among the first converts—his private residence in New Delhi now roofed in PV panels, all new federal-government buildings decreed by his office to include sustainable elements in their design—and that there were LEED-certified projects now in the works for several of the firms in CII's heavyweight industrial ranks.

But Kumar also readily acknowledged that green architecture built of local materials remained a hard sell for that enormous segment of the Indian populace that had yet to enjoy steady electricity from any source, that was desperate to cast off biodegradable mud huts and the recycled building materials of the scavenged urban slums at any cost. Perhaps the escape from abject poverty could be theoretically fused, with a Clintonesque rhetorical flourish, to the adoption of state-of-the-art technologies, but on the ground there would surely be much more in the way of slapdash development by any number of paths of least resistance before anything like an Age of Sustainability swept the subcontinent. "So this awareness," went Kumar's modest conclusion, "is gradually growing. It's not very massive—it will take a long time."

In the meantime, he was happy to show off the fine details of the remarkable CII-Godrej GBC itself, so off we went. The structure is built around a circular central courtyard, with two storeys of office space, conference rooms and a small auditorium surrounding it. These spaces provide working areas for the GBC's staff of thirty-five—mostly architects and engineers—plus meeting spaces for its densely packed schedule of training sessions and conferences. (I later learned that the preternatural quiet I'd encountered on arrival was an exception owing to the fact that most of the staff had gathered in a second-floor meeting room that morning to watch a big India-Pakistan cricket match.) The courtyard itself is leafy and amply shaded by undulating overhangs, which are supported by slim pillars encrusted with mosaics of broken crockery (an apparently unintentional homage to humble former roads inspector Nek Chand up in Chandigarh). Small framed displays at regular intervals explain how the building functions, augmenting Kumar's more comprehensive elucidations.

The CII-Godrej GBC had certainly earned its boastful plaques: there's real genius in the details. The primary building material, a large rectangular stone-like brick, resembles cinder block, but it's composed of 30 to 40 percent fly ash—the recycled waste of coal-fired energy production, not to mention a superb insulation material. Fully 80 percent of the GBC's building materials are recycled and recyclable, including every last chunk of the 4,000 cubic metres of rock removed to prepare the site for the structure itself. The structural steel is reclaimed, the ceiling tiles are recycled gypsum, and the furniture is made of a composite material derived in large part from a limitlessly renewable sugar-cane fibre called *bagasse*. The roof channels rainwater to irrigate the lush grounds, with wastewater treated on site in one garden-like section. And on it goes: the rooftop greenery helps cool the building, whose interior is sufficiently naturally lit that electric lighting demand has been reduced by 90 percent over a conventional building. Overall, the building's energy use is half the norm, and about a quarter of the power it does require comes from the PV array on the southern section of the roof. There are waterless urinals, special welcome mats to reduce the amount of dust tracked inside, even a charging station for electric vehicles near the front entrance.

Maybe the most inspired part—and definitely the most eye-catching—is that pair of minaret-like chimneys. These are, in fact, "passive cooling" towers: ventilation ducts whose walls drip with steady trickles of water, which cool incoming air by almost 10°C before it reaches the building's air conditioning units. The concept bears some resemblance (though Kumar didn't mention it) to the porous, water-saturated sandstone walls installed in the buildings at Fatehpur Sikri, the short-lived Mughal capital built from scratch 40 kilometres south of Agra by Shah Jahan's grandfather in the 1500s.

Midway through the tour, Kumar brought me into the CII-Godrej GBC's largest hall, which was crowded with information kiosks and product displays like a trade-show floor. He pointed out a cross-sectioned triangle of window, the centrepiece of an installation on high-performance glass sponsored by Saint-Gobain, a French manufacturer. The window—like the ones installed in the building itself—was double-paned, tinted and coated with a microscopic layer of metal, this to allow 75 percent of available light but only 25 percent of incoming heat to pass through. This glass is ideally suited to the architectural needs of South India, but it was virtually unknown on the subcontinent until it was first imported to outfit the CII-Godrej GBC. There was now enough regional demand that Saint-Gobain had set up a manufacturing plant down in Chennai—just another small but crucial step in the direction of Indian-style sustainability. "We are not trying to deliver a punch, per se," Kumar told me, "but we are caressing the people to get involved."

Many of the newly minted sustainable-design experts employed by the CII-Godrej GBC work in an open-concept office space on the second floor of the building. The area is half-cubicled and populated by energetic young Indian architects and engineers hunched over keyboards. My tour ended here, Kumar entrusting me, with a semi-formal adieu, to the good graces of two of his subordinates. Employees were ducking in and out of the conference room, where a blaring TV was broadcasting the cricket match. They called out scores to each other, then switched gears moments later to talk about this consultation or that design plan. The vibe was decidedly dotcom-like: youthful, informal, electric: I sat with an architect named Prasad Jadhav and a design consultant called Selvarasu as they guided me through a PowerPoint presentation on the robust green building boom inspired by the cii-Godrej GBC's example and the evangelism of its staff. This lovely white elephant, they explained, had birthed a whole herd.

The siring process, in the ground-level version of the story told by Selvarasu and Jadhav, was considerably messier—and much more exciting—than the official summary I'd heard from Kumar. The cii-Godrej GBC's Platinum goal, for example, had been set immediately upon the fact-finding mission's return from the United States. "Even without knowing," Selvarasu wryly noted, "what is 'LEED' and 'Platinum.'" The team's first design scored only seventeen on the LEED scale, not even enough for basic certification. Selvarasu, in quiet, clipped understatement: "So there was panic." In the ensuing scramble, suppliers were somehow located, manufacturers of the raw materials educated on what the GBC team needed. I thought of the stalled and abandoned building sites that clump around fast-growing Indian cities like concrete shrubbery, all those patches of bare rebar protruding from their unfinished roofs like an invasive species of weed, and I was amazed anew at what an uncommon feat it was that a Platinum wonder had emerged from the boulder fields of the Hyderabadi hills. And moreover that it began to spawn LEED-certified progeny even before it was complete.

Prior to the cii-Godrej GBC's improbable construction, Jadhav explained, glass cubes were all the rage among the big tech firms in India, who were willing to trade the astronomical costs of cooling them for the appearance of hypermodern prosperity. But the LEED system, with its list of precise guidelines in six straightforward categories, proved highly appealing to the Indian technocrat's mindset. It was a refreshingly easy sell, especially after the doors opened on the living laboratory of the GBC itself. "When this building is done," said Jadhav, "we can see the whole thing in totality." Which totality proved very persuasive.

The GBC's impact was clearly demarcated in a handful of tidy charts on Selvarasu's computer monitor, which quantified the embryonic nationwide boom in sustainable construction, still small in size but increasingly ambitious in scale. There were two more Platinum buildings already up and running in the techie enclave of Gurgaon, north of Delhi, each of them more than eight times the size of the CII-Godrej GBC. One housed a software development facility for the Indian IT giant Wipro; the other was a corporate office for a company called ITC, better known until recently as the Indian Tobacco Company, whose Platinum-winning design required a fairly elaborate finesse of the LEED guidelines in order to permit the inclusion of a smoking lounge. Chennai was home to two Gold-certified office complexes, and there were another dozen or so buildings with Gold and Platinum ambitions in the works in Indian metropolises from Bangalore to Bombay to Calcutta. The GBC was also helping with the design of a pair of new structures in Dubai. And every last one traced its origins to the GBC—to its staff of LEED-accredited consultants, its many training sessions, its trailblazing work in the introduction of green materials, the sheer fact of the place.

Beyond the construction sites, there had also emerged under the CII-Godrej GBC's roof an Indian Green Building Council, which was in the process of modifying the LEED system into a score sheet more reflective of the subcontinent's unique climatic features. (Because India suffers from widespread water scarcity, for example, the Indian LEED ratings will award up to seven points for sustainable water use instead of the five mandated by the original LEED system.)

It was in these moments, sitting there listening to the past, present and bright future of green architecture in India, that I found myself at my most awestruck. It was a subtle sort of awe, but no less deep or lasting or hopeful for it. It had little to do with the facts and figures of LEED's infiltration of urban India, or with the sight of the CII-Godrej GBC's ingenious cooling towers. It was the quality of the conversation, in a sense, its optimistic buoyancy: Selvarasu with his stoic, spreadsheeted certainties; Jadhav the architect, who was moved to a sort of formal, businesslike giddiness as he described his work. He was developing a sustainable-design curriculum for a number of major Indian architecture schools. He also gave students tours of the GBC—"the bulk" of the building's visitors, he claimed, were students—and advised them on their in-depth studies of green buildings. Sustainable architecture, Jadhav said, was a lot like the internet, like the sudden ubiquity of mobile phones. "We have the luxury to learn from abroad," he told me, fixing me with a stare both sober and quietly jubilant. "And not repeat the same mistakes."

I took my leave shortly thereafter, and within the hour I was back on the roadside in downtown Hyderabad, sucking in more black exhaust as I waited anxiously for a break in the anarchic traffic so I could cross the street. It would be an overstatement to say the scene had been transformed by my visit to India's first Platinum edifice. "Green Buildings (as on Jan 06)" had been the heading on the charts in Selvarasu's slideshow, and the total number of projects listed below was just nineteen. I'd had to focus pretty tightly on the facts and figures on the screen to keep the crush of India's billion-strong population from overwhelming them, and now it came rushing back, a dozen lanes wide, arrooga horns screaming. Hyderabadi traffic remained its anarchic, unnerving self. But it no longer seemed inescapable. It wasn't the only game in town.

I left Hyderabad two days later on an overnight train bound for Bangalore. As the train pulled out of the station, my fellow passengers took final calls and tapped out messages of departure or impending arrival on their mobile phones. In Bangalore—the capital city of India's IT boom, but not its green one—I met up with a friend who ran a small business that did IT consulting for non-profit groups. We went to his favourite tavern for far too much battery-acid Indian whiskey and heady conversation with a pack of his friends. The talk was of social justice, defending the legal rights of Indian widows and stateless Tibetans, waging a war of liberation on self-serving Western notions of copyright. It was another head-spinner, a sort of extension of my talk with the green builders in Hyderabad.

One of my friend's colleagues—Chinese-Indian, born and raised in Calcutta—was a lawyer who worked on human rights issues. He told an anecdote about a conference he'd attended in the Netherlands, where he'd found himself stuck in condescending conversation with a Dutch bureaucrat who'd been to India and wanted to marvel at its chaos. How, the Dutch guy wondered, could you even *begin* to talk about issues of any real import amid such ceaseless madness? "Well, to begin with," the Indian lawyer replied, "you'd have a larger audience."

THE PLASTIC FANTASTIC RECYCLING TRAP

Here's another curious scene from an Indian train. On the overnight express to Bangalore, a cleaning man came hustling through my car as it waited to leave the station. He set about hurriedly wiping down tables and seats, spurting out a few squirts of pink liquid from a bottle and wiping them away with a tattered cloth. The bottle was an old plastic water bottle, but it wasn't quite standard issue. Bottled water in India is generally sold in dirt-cheap, paper-thin plastic containers that barely hold their shape for one use and quickly spring holes and tear apart after they're emptied. This was a slightly sturdier bottle, closer in quality to the Western standard, perhaps brought aboard at some point by a Western tourist toting her own Evian. The cleaner had presumably recognized its unique worth amid the piles of onboard trash. Salvaged it, poked a hole in its cap, turned it into a makeshift spray bottle. It was performing the new task just fine.

Insofar as "recycling" exists in India, this is what it looks like. Slums are made from scavenged tin and vinyl and cloth. Household staff in wealthier homes zealously hoard the highest-quality bottles and cans for repeated use. Professional scavengers go biking by in the streets, toting impossibly balanced loads of plastic containers for resale. The designer, the manufacturer, the wholesaler, the original buyer—none of them thinks for a minute about where their products will end up. And I suppose it's fair to ask why they would need to. Owing to India's vast population and widespread poverty, there's little doubt that anything of any use will be scrounged and reclaimed by someone or other.

Shorn of its subcontinental trappings, the process is actually not much different in even the world's wealthiest and most ecologically conscious enclaves. You might do your own separating of irredeemable trash from biodegradable compost and blue-box treasure at the curbside, and some enterprising company likely takes responsibility for the job of figuring out how to turn your recyclable waste into something useful, but the trajectory remains mostly downward, and the entirety of the product's life cycle up to the moment the item is turfed remains completely contemptuous of its final destination. It's the unstated underlying assumption of modern design: everything made by human hands, no matter how gracefully constructed or deeply desired or seemingly essential, will eventually outlive its worth. A rare few items are so effective at their task or so solidly designed that they're deemed worthy of refurbishing, and certain others are so beautiful or so freighted with memory that they become treasured antiques, but almost everything else becomes junk.

The useful life of things has seemed to constrict particularly quickly during the Anthropocene Era. Which is ironic, because we're also surrounded more than ever by items that will live on essentially forever. By plastic, that is: the most ubiquitous petrochemical byproduct of the age of oil and a common symbol of both its enviable standard of living and its existentially hollow and poisonous down-side. Starting with the consumer-culture explosion of the 1950s, the nature of the West's unparalleled prosperity was sometimes summed up with the phrase *plastic fantastic,* invoking a wondrous new poly-merized age of Bakelite appliances and E-Z-clean laminated sur-faces, vinyl records and polyethylene hula hoops, and later of life-saving plastic implants in hearts and image-enhancing ones in breasts, nylon shoes and polyester suits, stain-resistant nylon carpet and waterproof polytetrafluoroethylene (i.e., Gore-Tex) jackets—all of it shrinkwrapped for your safety and packed in polystyrene for your convenience. I tap on plastic to write this line, and you likely bought this book with a plastic card and carried it home in a plastic bag. Durable, inexpensive, ubiquitous, seemingly limitlessly multi-purpose plastic. Fantastic.

It's easy, nevertheless, to forget about plastic, for nearly the same reasons we don't walk around thinking about each and every breath we take. It just, you know, *is.* Something like 80 percent of the plastic ever manufactured is still extant, but it's often hidden: buried in a landfill, gone sailing far out into the deep blue sea, or (at best) ground down to pellets and reformed into a lawn chair. Aside from noting the curious tendency of plastic bags to get caught in tree branches, we don't generally spend much time contemplating all the plastic we use just once and throw away.

So it was in India that I was first overwhelmed by the transcen-dent fact of plastic, its prevalence and agelessness, the sheer immo-bile *volume* of the stuff. This was in the spring of 2000, on a ridge in the Himalayas. The capital-in-exile of the Tibetan people is usually said to be Dharamsala—another decaying British hill station—but most Tibetans actually inhabit McLeod Ganj, a ridge-top village farther up the mountain. At the north end of the ridge, a wide paved clearing serves as a makeshift town square. Buses arrive here, packed with pilgrims and tourists and Tibetans returning from errands in the larger town below, and there are several restaurants in the immediate vicinity, travel agencies, a taxi stand. The main road to Dharamsala angles down to the northwest, and a narrower footpath leads up the hill to the northeast. At the time of my visit, the steep slope in the joint between these two roads was a sort of town dump, covered almost entirely in empty plastic bottles. They formed a wide translucent blanket, a petrochemical snowfall that stretched from the roadside at the top of the slope all the way down to the low brick building at the bottom, gathering against its rear wall in a great drift-like pile.

Plastic was still relatively new-fangled in India, and no one had even begun to think in any serious way about what to do with it all. It tended to be most prevalent in places where Western visitors congregated—they had the greatest thirst for certifiably safe drinking water and the money to pay for it—and so in McLeod Ganj, where so many of them came in search of deeper meaning, they were helping to bury the place in plastic. It felt like the physical manifestation of some great modern demon; it had an air of prophecy about it.

It's a demon we like to think we've slain. We recycle, after all—some of us with the diligence of zealots—and isn't recycling the greatest success story in the past few decades of environmental activism? Has there ever been a more widely adopted mass ritual of ecological stewardship than the great curbside vigil of the blue boxes? Take, just for instance, the Canadian province of Nova Scotia, land of my maternal ancestry and home of my retired parents. Economically devastated by the wholesale collapse of one of the greatest fishing industries in human history (the decimation of the Atlantic cod population), and more recently home to one of the most ambitious and successful recycling schemes in North America. As Silver Donald Cameron reported in *Canadian Geographic* in 2001, Nova Scotia transformed itself in a single decade from a place mostly lacking even in blue boxes into the first province in Canada to eliminate a benchmark 50 percent of its solid waste.

It began with the provincial capital of Halifax, which realized in 1990 that its landfill was half a decade from full. The municipal government put the problem to a public debate. "As it turned out"—this in Cameron's summary—"the citizens were far ahead of the government in their thinking. Governments were chasing technological solutions because they didn't think people would change their behaviour, but the citizens believed the key was, precisely, changing behaviour. If you don't want a lot of stuff in the dump, they reasoned, then you shouldn't put it there. And you shouldn't think of the waste stream as garbage; you should think of it as a supply of valuable resources." Out of these public consultations there emerged in 1995 an ambitious list of recommendations: a total ban on organic materials from the landfills, plus prohibitions of aluminum, tires, tin cans and hazardous waste. The proposed solution required considerable trust in the general public, as it asked them to sort their trash to an unprecedented extent. If the idea hadn't come from the voters themselves, it's hard to imagine a government in the free world that would have taken on such a potential political liability.

The Halifax recommendations became province-wide regulations in February 1996. I remember visiting my parents not long after. My father flew fighter jets in the Canadian Air Force, and his sole experience with environmentalists to this point (not counting the rants he occasionally endured from his son) had been cursing them for closing the road into the base we lived on in northern Alberta back in the mid-1980s to protest cruise missile testing. When I'd taken that summer job with Greenpeace just a few years before, my parents had treated it like I'd gone and joined the circus or something, and my dad worried for his security clearance. They were not, shall we say, ecologically minded by nature. So imagine my surprise to find them diligently sorting their garbage into five separate containers. They even had this handsome new blond wood chest out in the laundry room that they'd bought from some enterprising local craftsman. It was waist-high, wide and narrow like a credenza, and it had four small lids on top, one for each new breed of recyclable material. It was much the same story across Nova Scotia: widespread participation, formerly landfilled compost sold for profit to local gardeners, new businesses springing up to turn newspapers into household insulation and tires into car parts. *Canadian Geographic* estimated that the recycling scheme had created six hundred new jobs—no small beer, as they say, in a province cursed by endemic unemployment, where every business closure is treated as another portent of impending doom.

And so—verily, it would seem—the waste demon was banished forever from the land of my forefathers. Victory was surely at hand. But it was at best only partial, destined to be undermined. A couple of years after the new regulations came in, for example, my mother took up swiffering. It was a new and seemingly benign habit she shared with many other North American consumers. So many, in fact, that in only a few short years, they'd turned a nifty new product—the Swiffer Sweeper, a household broom filled with disposable electromagnetic cloths, manufactured by the consumer goods behemoth Procter & Gamble—into a verb. Where once they had swept their floors, now they swiffered. P&G, keenly attuned to market breakthroughs and what to do with them, soon introduced a wet-mop version, a duster and a thing called the CarpetFlick (a sort of swiffering riff on the vacuum cleaner). In place of a handful of durable goods that lasted for years—mops and brooms, dust cloths and scrub brushes—there were now thin single-use sheets by the twenty-four-count refill package. P&G calls these things "cloths," perhaps to convey the comforting notion that they're little rectangles of biodegradable fabric, much like the ones that have always occupied our cleaning closets, but in fact each Swiffer cloth is made of a few grams of all-but-indestructible polyester and polypropylene. Plastic, that is. And there is not as yet a single recycling program on the planet equipped to deal with it. It's just more trash, and it has the potential to remain in whatever landfill it eventually finds itself for millennia.

This, alas, seems intrinsic to the nature of our overexcited consumer society. For every altruistic community waste-reduction program or ambitious municipal recycling plan, there are any number of products emerging from the tireless and resourceful activity of the corporate manufacturing world to chip away at their effectiveness. This damage is rarely (if ever) intentional, and certainly not malicious. It results from a catastrophic design failure, but not at the level of any particular corporation's R&D department. The Swiffer, for example, is by almost any existing measure a resounding success. Its patented electromagnetic polymers, attached effortlessly to the end of a Swiffer broom, perform the task of removing dust and dirt with the sort of miraculous thoroughness and ease that made the plastic fantastic era so exciting in the first place. It is, from this angle, inarguably better at the job than a whisk broom and dustpan.

Point being: it's not really P&G's *fault* that it doesn't consider the ultimate fate of its products. The failure is in the design of the whole system. This is the essence of the recycling trap: a socioeconomic order in which the responsibility for the repercussions of a product's design falls to the end users (or their advocates in government), and does so only *after* it has been produced, is bound to be unsustainable. It reminds me of one of those old-school open-ended videogames I spent so much time with in the 1980s—games like *Centipede* and *Missile Command*—in which deadly debris fell relentlessly from the sky. I'd execute some frantic, dexterous feat of joystick manipulation and rapid-fire button work to clear the screen, and with barely a pause another great load of shit would come tumbling down—faster now, stronger, augmented by new and more virulent species of threat. No matter how skilled I became at the physics of the game, I would eventually lose. There would be no end to the falling garbage, no way to zap *all* of it into oblivion.

So pervasive is the recycling trap—so intrinsic to the design structure of this fossil-fuelled age—that it plagues even some of the greatest of the sustainability movement's triumphs. The simple, ingenious compact fluorescent light bulb (CFL) is a revealing case in point. The initial design for the CFL emerged from the brief, frenetic period of R&D work inspired by the energy crisis of the 1970s. With energy conservation suddenly in vogue, the world's consumer-goods giants began to churn out power-saving prototypes of any number of everyday household items. Light bulbs were high on this list— particularly fluorescent ones, which require far less energy than the standard incandescent bulbs. The long fluorescent tube that adorns countless institutional hallways had been brought to market by General Electric in the late 1930s, but there was not yet a household equivalent, nothing that would fit the countless millions of table lamps and light sockets already in use in homes around the world. For a time, designing a CFL ready for this task occupied many of the industry's top R&D labs.

In 1976, Edward Hammer, a researcher at GE, came up with one of the more elegant and practical designs: a small, swirled tube roughly the size of a standard bulb, in a shape reminiscent of a soft-serve ice cream cone, that threw out a glow similar in size and quality to that of an incandescent. It was difficult to manufacture with existing apparatus, however, and GE decided that the development of new manufacturing equipment was too costly. Besides, the whole conservation craze had started to fade.

Even when several other companies dusted off the old design in the 1990s to see if it could compete with existing bulbs, the future of the swirling CFL remained dim. It didn't put out enough light, for one thing. Plus it took a few flickering seconds to amp up to full power, it was prone to such flickering even at maximum strength, it emitted a low hum, and it still couldn't be installed in standard fixtures. And the price tag was something like a dozen times the cost of an incandescent bulb. The CFL was the home-lighting equivalent of a leaky geodesic dome: inconvenient and impractical, more good intention than great design.

This remained a reasonable take on CFLs until just a couple of years ago. And then, seemingly overnight, the kinks in the design were gone and the light bulbs were hanging in eight-piece blister packs in every big-box hardware store in the free world. I work by the light of a CFL that cost me maybe four times as much as the cheapest generic-brand incandescents. It comes on in an instant and doesn't flicker or hum. Once it's encased in a shaded lamp, the slight variation in the quality of the light is, to my eyes, negligible. (Hanging from a bare socket, a CFL casts a glow slightly more bluish and a tiny fraction less intense.) But most important, it uses a quarter of the electricity of an incandescent and lasts ten times as long.

"Swirl bulbs don't just work, they pay for themselves," gushed an ecstatic article in the next-generation business magazine *Fast Company*. The story's title was "How Many Lightbulbs Does It Take to Change the World?" and it drew its enthusiasm from an announcement made by Wal-Mart that it hoped to sell one CFL to every one of its American customers in 2007. That would be enough of these amazing swirls, *Fast Company* observed, to double U.S. sales and save enough electricity to power Dallas, Texas. Wal-Mart's partner in the venture was General Electric, which—thirty years after it had abandoned the CFL design—was preparing to set up "light-bulb education centers" in every Wal-Mart in America to make the case for them.

The meteoric rise of the CFL from the lip of history's dustbin to the starring role in a special display in the aisles of the world's largest department store chain would seem to be the very embodiment of an unqualified success in sustainable design. This was certainly *Fast Company*'s conclusion. By way of introduction, the article asserted that the CFL "cuts to the heart of a half-dozen of the most profound, most urgent problems we face. Energy consumption. Rising gasoline costs and electric bills. Greenhouse gas emissions. Dependence on coal and foreign oil. Global warming." This is all more or less true; it's incontestable, for example, that the best household light bulb on the market from the point of view of climate change abatement is—by far—the compact fluorescent.

There is, however, a catch. A tripwire, if you will, set by the all-pervasive recycling trap. The problem is this: a CFL bulb, like any other fluorescent, generates light by using an electric current to agitate a tiny dollop of mercury, which in turn sets the phosphorescent coating of the swirled tube to glowing. And mercury is one of the most toxic heavy metals in general commercial use today. Manufacturers have already made great strides in reducing the total amount of mercury needed in each bulb: in 1990, 23.6 tons of the stuff were used to produce 500 million bulbs in the U.S., whereas 650 million were produced in 2003 with only 7 tons of mercury. Mercury is also readily recyclable; indeed, the "Lamp Section" of the National Electric Manufacturers' Association in the United States has been amping up its public-awareness campaign on the need to keep CFLs out of landfills in concert with their booming sales. Still, as of November 2004, at most 22 percent of the total mercury used in fluorescent lamps in the United States—and barely 2 percent of the mercury in household fluorescents—was actually being recycled. (In Canada, the figure is about 7 percent for home and commercial lamps combined.) The CFL, for all its laudable efficiency and its enormous potential to enable major strides toward the reduction of greenhouse gas emissions, is as intractably stuck in the recycling trap as the most frivolous of Swiffers.

THE GREAT ESCAPE

There are at least two reliable ways out of the recycling trap. The first—easier to implement, but far less thorough—is to force producers themselves to account for the recycling of the goods they produce, a strategy that goes by the name of Extended Producer Responsibility (EPR). The European Union pretty much invented EPR, and its program remains the most ambitious. EU regulations mandate the recycling of almost all major appliances and electronic devices, and they are accompanied by a near-total ban on a handful of the most problematic heavy metals—including mercury. CFLS and other fluorescents containing sufficiently tiny amounts of the metal are exempted, however, and are instead covered by the recycling plan. (The EU's goal was to recycle 80 percent of "lighting products" by 2006.) Copycat EPR schemes in Korea and Taiwan have also forced manufacturers to reclaim their dead bulbs. (In the case of Taiwan, 87 percent of CFLS were being recycled at last count.) British Columbia was one of the first jurisdictions in North America to adopt EPR regulations; at present, the B.C. scheme covers some kinds of electronic equipment, lead-acid batteries, tires, paint and solvents—but not CFLS. Even in the matter of a readily recyclable material, in other words, EPR is far from a complete solution.

At any rate, EPR in no way disables the recycling trap. It just removes the burden from the consumer and clamps it onto the producer. The intent, at least rhetorically, is to subtly persuade producers to rethink their designs. A manual published by the Organization for Economic Co-operation and Development (OECD), for example, argues that EPR sends "an implicit signal" to manufacturers to abandon their wasteful ways. In practice, however, companies whose products fall under EPR regulations must simply "recover" them—remove them by some means or another, that is, from the waste stream. Some items can be refurbished for reuse in something very close to their current form, others recycled into new products built of the same materials, still others broken down into their barest raw materials and fed back into production cycles as feedstock. Old computers can sometimes be wiped clean, gussied up and sold (or donated) to people or organizations that can make do with less than the state of the art. Old tires are ground into tiny rubber pellets called "crumb" and reformed into shoe soles or rubber hoses. Old TVs and monitors are dismantled, the half-dozen toxic metals in their cathode ray tubes stripped away for reuse or careful disposal by professional hazardous-waste handlers, the remaining glass and plastic recycled. In no case will any of these items ever again be a top-of-the-line modern consumer product of equal worth to its predecessor. The efforts are generally admirable, the resulting items useful, but the trend remains downward.

"Downcycling" is the term coined to describe this process by the architect William McDonough and the chemist Michael Braungart in their sustainable-design manifesto *Cradle to Cradle: Remaking the Way We Make Things.* "Most recycling," they write, "is actually *down-cycling;* it reduces the quality of a material over time." In their view, even the most ambitious of recycling regimes is merely an emergency measure—not a permanent solution but a stopgap against many decades of inferior industrial design. "In a world where designs are unintelligent and destructive," they argue, "regulations can reduce immediate deleterious effects. But ultimately a regulation is a signal of design failure. In fact, it is what we call a *license to harm:* a permit issued by a government to an industry so that it may dispense sickness, destruction, and death at an 'acceptable' rate." It's an iconoclastic argument, to be sure, but one confirmed by the impact thus far of the EPR regulations in Europe. Rather than inspiring European manufacturers to develop products that are readily reusable—rather than eliminating the waste stream entirely, that is—Europe's ambitious EPR program has instead precipitated a boom in the "reverse logistics" industry, a business category consisting of subcontractors entrusted with figuring out how to divert the same old stuff from the Continent's landfills.

In lieu of more elaborate stopgaps and more vigorous go-betweens, McDonough and Braungart pointed beyond the recycling trap toward the *real* great escape: a whole new design paradigm, considerably trickier and much more idealistic, but infinitely sustainable and potentially even restorative. (In interviews, McDonough frequently mocks the term *sustainable,* arguing that if you described your marriage that way, you wouldn't be very happy with it.) They variously refer to their approach as "eco-effectiveness" and "cradle-to-cradle" design—the latter referring to an endless circular pattern in place of the linear cradle-to-grave progression that governs the overwhelming majority of modern design. They offer the example of the earth's vast population of ants, millions of years old and greater in biomass than all humanity, whose productive activity not only sustains their ranks and produces no useless waste but enhances the lives of other living things in the ecosystems in which the ants live.

What McDonough and Braungart are thinking of is something akin to Rolf Disch's *Plusenergiehaus,* extended to every aspect of design: a whole new industrial order of human habitats and human products that not only provide us with the things we need to survive but generate only useful surpluses.

Eco-effectiveness, they explain, means approaching design with not just the product's primary purpose but its whole life cycle and the larger system it interacts with in mind. They argue that it will result in true sustainability, wherein a product's active life involves beneficent emissions and its death yields new life for something else. Their example is a cherry tree—its growth yielding an excess product (oxygen) that is essential to the lives of others, its "wasteful" overproduction of blossoms and seeds littering the ground with nourishing fruit, its corpse returning life-giving nutrients to the soil it stood in.

As design paradigms go, cradle-to-cradle is almost deliriously idealistic. It sounds impractical, ethereal. A fantasy. At least until you see it in person.

THE HIDDEN POWER OF MICROBIAL FARTS (& OTHER FANTASTIC TALES FROM THE SONS OF THE SUSTAINABILITY PIONEERS)

John Bradford is about as far from ethereal as any guy you're likely to meet. He's a corporate vice-president, an engineer and a born-and-bred Alabaman. He's sharp-minded and quick-witted; polished, methodical and crystal-clear in presentation style; given to goofy, gently scatological similes. Also fortysomething, square-shouldered and solidly built, with close-cropped side-parted hair. On the day I met him, he was clad in business-casual khakis and a golf shirt. Throw in an easygoing nature and a *Deep* Southern accent, and Bradford could pass effortlessly for a college football coach.

In fact, Bradford is the overseer of the mind-warping, paradigm-shifting technical details of possibly the most thorough and widely admired corporate sustainability program on the planet. He's the vice-president of research and development for Interface Flooring Systems, one of the world's largest producers of commercial carpet tiles, which since 1994 has been hard at work on becoming its first fully sustainable multinational corporation. Interface's dramatic reconfiguration arose from an epiphany that struck its founder, Ray

Anderson, while he was reading a book called *The Ecology of Commerce* by Paul Hawken (who later went on to co-author *Natural Capitalism* with Amory and Hunter Lovins).

I'll examine the full import of Anderson's moment of clarity a couple of chapters from now; for our present purposes, the critical thing to note is that one of Anderson's first actions in its wake was to assemble an all-star team of green-business thinkers to figure out how to transform a company whose chief product was made almost entirely of plastic—nylon thread fused to a bed of polyvinyl chloride (PVC)—into a model of ecological commerce. William McDonough was one of the blue-chip idea guys drafted onto that team, and the manufacturing system I'd come to talk to Bradford about was possibly the best example the world has yet seen of cradle-to-cradle industrial design.

Bradford works out of Interface's main R&D facility on the outskirts of a small city called LaGrange, Georgia, near the Alabama border, which is also home to a large Interface carpet tile manufacturing plant. Bradford, meticulous engineer that he is, had first walked me through the plant's vast, hangar-like space, explaining in minute detail how every possible scrap of waste had been systematically eliminated from the production process in place there. After that, he took me to a smaller plant adjacent to his lab, the place where vinyl backing is applied to the carpet after it comes off the other production line. There, he talked me through one of the key battles in Interface's "war on waste."

Bradford was standing next to an industrial backing machine, a great long conveyor-belted contraption that roared like a jumbo jet and reeked of burnt rubber. He leaned in to point to a spot where several streams of oozing black goo—liquid PVC—were being squirted onto a flattened roll of Interface carpet. This was the previous generation of machine, the one that seemed just fine before Ray's epiphany, and it was here that Bradford's tour moved fully into McDonough territory.

"If you really do your homework on plastics," Bradford said, hollering a bit over the noise of the machine but maintaining his smooth flow, "you find out that all plastics come from a cracked oil molecule, which starts out as a thing called a monomer. Which is basically a kamikaze molecule that is out there seeking anything to connect with. And very high energy. If it connects with a human, it can cause cancer.

Okay? And that's not just vinyl. That's polypropylene, polyethylene, polyester, PVA—anything that is a poly-poly-poly-poly-poly, which is a manmade cracked oil molecule, starts out as a monomer." He paused, like it was halftime and he was about to explain a tricky new play-action fake he wanted to bring in for the third quarter. He wanted me to *completely* get it. "So . . . this . . . *discussion* about vinyl—in *any* of its states—is a discussion of perspective. Okay? Our position is that if it's bad when it starts and it's bad when it's finished, then keep it in the loop and recycle it. Definitely do *not* cast it aside and say, 'All right, now I'm dooming you to death,' which is automatically saying, 'I'm taking you to a bad place.' And pick up another plastic that starts out just like vinyl does. How *stoopid* is that?"

I nodded in complete assent. All kinds of stoopid, Coach. But how come none of the other teams look at it this way? And what exactly was it that happened down here in LaBoondocks, Georgia, that got a no-bullshit engineer such as yourself talking about precisely the same things—the same priorities, the same themes, even some of the same *phrases*—that I was used to hearing from placard-carrying members of the anti-corporate eco-radical fringe? What in the Sam Hill had happened to convince *you?* Was it just that a straight-talking detail-oriented person such as yourself didn't need *convincing*—not on an ideological level, anyway—so much as a clean, clear shift of the design parameters? Something that would give you a big, juicy fixed-target problem to throw the whole of your engineer's mind at? *Coach?*

Bradford didn't actually want to talk about any of this, I'm sure, and anyway he didn't leave me much time to ask any of it, because he was leading me around the corner to see his pride and joy. It was another industrial backing machine, another conveyor-belted mass of heating ducts and valves the length of a basketball court, which was fed backless Interface carpet spools at one end and rolled them out the other fused to a thick layer of rubbery no-slip backing. Its exterior was painted a Day-Glo teal green; Bradford and his design team had dubbed it Cool Blue. It was the contraption that closed the loop.

There were several big teal green dumpsters with "Cool Blue Food" stencilled on the side next to the backing machine. They were full of tiny grey plastic pellets. These had been produced by feeding used or defective carpet tiles—backing and all—into an industrial shredder. The thin strips of carpet that emerged were then forced through an enormous 50-horsepower spaghetti machine—it had actually been manufactured, Bradford said, by a pasta machine maker, and it had "Cool Blue Food Processor" stamped on its side—that spat the little grey pellets into the bins. The process began with formerly landfill-bound carpet tiles made of non-biodegradable plastic as an input, and it finished with top-quality backing on spools of standard carpet tile. It did essentially the same job as the old machine, to basically the same specifications. The main difference was that it had replaced a ruthlessly carcinogenic raw material with stuff that had previously been treated as pure waste. At the time, Cool Blue used its own company's trash, but it had been designed to produce backing from nearly any kind of plastic feedstock. Eco-effective, cradle-to-cradle, 100-percent sustainable.

It was only a couple of strides across a factory floor to get from business as usual to Cool Blue, but the path from one process to the other had of course been far less direct. It began with the new parameters set by Ray's epiphany, and with Bradford then asking his designers some hard questions about the way Interface manufactured backing, which accounted for 40 to 60 percent of the volume of materials required to produce its tiles. Bradford: "The dilemma in this plant has always been that it used virgin raw materials. So the vinyl operation runs vinyl for our backing, and has for fifteen years. About five years ago, we took a lot of our really great engineers and machinery designers, pulled 'em into a room together, and kinda said, 'All right, we were all taught in school to have a given on every project that the raw materials are abundant and consistent.' That was a given in a problem statement for an engineering student designing machines. And my proposal to those guys at the time was, 'What if that's not true? What if ten years from now raw materials aren't abundant, and they're not consistent? They're recycled, mined from a landfill and variable. Now what?'"

Interface's first solution—Cool Blue v1.0, I guess, though nobody's ever called it that—suffered from the same kinds of problems that a lot of first-generation "green" systems do. It was unwieldy and expensive. It could be fed only about 2 percent of the world's range of extant plastics, and it took six steps to do a job formerly done in one. "We had created and incubated a little developmental backing technology that was like reaching over your head to scratch your rear end, actually," is how Bradford put it. If not for the unwavering commitment prescribed by Ray's epiphany, Interface might well have abandoned its cradle-to-cradle goal then and there. Instead, it sacrificed economic imperatives to sustainability goals, and it bought into this awkward bum-scratcher of a backing production line, which in 2005 churned out about a million yards of carpet backing.

Meanwhile, Bradford and company toiled ceaselessly on v2.0. "All the while," he explained, "our goal was to reduce the footprint of all of those different steps. And to design a machine that would do it in one. And that would also open up the fishing pond to just about any plastic. That line is Cool Blue. And that's the line that we designed and built over the last five years."

Bradford's baby was birthed in November 2005. It tripled Interface's potential recycling capacity, and it replaced the old feedstock—virgin PVC—with waste plastic. There had been a great many eyes rolled elsewhere in the industry when Interface and its starry-eyed founder first articulated this goal in the late 1990s. The price of PVC has shot up 38 percent since then. "Now we look like geniuses," Bradford told me with a well-earned shit-eating grin.

Simply having a completely closed-loop and nearly waste-free manufacturing process was not enough for Bradford, however. A touchdown was zero waste and total sustainability. "If you take sustainability from a technical standpoint," Bradford told me, "then sustainability is converting your raw materials to either recycled or renewable and converting your energy streams to either waste energy streams—things that are already here that you can't do anything about—or renewable energy streams. And that's where all of our technical activity is focused." So Bradford's been "playin' around" with an organic plastic made from corn starch by the name of polylactic acid (PLA)—and by "playin' around," he means using the largest volume of it in the entire carpet industry—and waiting for the petrochemical giant Cargill to come up with a version of it better suited to large-scale carpet manufacture.

Another thing Bradford did was he went to meet with municipal officials in LaGrange to explain about microbial farts. He set up a meeting, and then another and another, until they understood what he meant. Understood that the big eyesore of a landfill they had out near the industrial park where Interface manufactured its backing was in large part a great writhing pile of feasting micro-organisms, and that all those microbes gave off a waste gas by the name of methane—farted it out, more or less. And Bradford made it clear to the folks down at city hall that methane was an absolute evil if you left it sitting there in the landfill—a greenhouse gas twenty-three times as destructive as CO_2 that would eventually be released skyward—but that if you soaked a capped landfill in water and then ran a vacuum tube into it and sucked out all the methane, it could be a fuel source. Bradford: "The thermal energy on Cool Blue, which is a little over half of the total energy, is completely heated by methane gas from the landfill here in LaGrange. Took us about two years to convince the city that that was the right thing to do—after many, many engineering meetings and validation from different parties, different groups, we ended up with a win-win-win system with the city." So now the city of LaGrange had a fifty-year source of all-but-free biogas, some of which it was selling to Interface at 30 percent below the going rate for natural gas to facilitate the melting of recycled plastic onto its carpets, and the methane's potency as a greenhouse gas was being reduced by a factor of twenty-three in the process. *Win, win, win.*

Alas, when you're a sustainability pioneer, this kind of robust symbiosis is exceedingly rare. At the core of the cradle-to-cradle design philosophy is the idea of embracing and encouraging a diversity and interconnectedness among industrial processes that attempts to imitate the rich web of co-operative life in a natural ecosystem. *Biomimicry* is what this is called, and it cannot thrive in isolation. A single carpet company, even one as committed to sustainability as Interface is, cannot succeed on its own. Much as a single building, even one as innovative as the CII-Godrej GBC or any other LEED Platinum wonder, will not by itself redeem the city it stands in. But bring enough of these buildings together with such factories, arrange them carefully in the right kind of landscapes, and something greater than the sum of its parts can emerge.

The real grunt work of sustainability—labour that yields some of the greatest opportunities—lies in the spaces in between.

SIX

GREEN SPRAWL

[sustainable metropolis]

THE SPACES IN BETWEEN

The city of Kalundborg looks at first like the farthest place you could find yourself from this nascent sustainable world order and still be in greening Denmark. It's a small port city, and despite its twelfth-century cobblestone downtown, Kalundborg is mostly a dour industrial burg. It hugs a small inlet of the Kattegat, and on the shore opposite the city centre looms a massive coal-burning power plant and Denmark's largest oil refinery. A giant pharmaceutical plant and a good-sized plasterboard factory squat a bit farther south. Kalundborg would seem, then, a textbook example of the ecological wreckage that has accompanied industrial growth: a harbour lined with smokestacks and sea container cranes, a lapping surf of tarnished brown, a downtown promenade peopled in the late evening by bellowing drunks kicking over trash cans. But probe deeper, and even Kalundborg reveals the depth and breadth of change that starts to occur once a society has moved far enough along a sustainable path.

It's an inescapable fact that we are not in any way starting from zero. So whatever the Sustainable Age ultimately looks like, vast swaths of it will surely continue to look like the world we've already built. And Kalundborg, in its modest way, demonstrates just how much potential there is even amid the mess of our oil-powered world. Enormous opportunities linger in the spaces in between.

Case in point: a weed-strewn lot midway between the power plant and the pharmaceutical plant, a quiet patch of land ribboned with four huge lengths of pipe the diameter of oil barrels, their steel exteriors painted varying shades of deep green. I'd come here on a bright, chilly fall Sunday morning with my host, one Noel Brings Jacobsen, a soft-spoken, earnest young academic who specialized in the study of the uses of such spaces. More precisely, Jacobsen was just then working on a Ph.D. in the newborn subject of industrial symbiosis, which had been more or less invented amid the tall wild grasses that separate Kalundborg's hulking industrial installations.

Industrial symbiosis describes a sort of mutual backscratching on an industrial scale—the trading of wastes and byproducts between factories engaged in divergent activities, thereby boosting the efficiency of all involved—and these pipes were its most visible sign in Kalundborg. It wasn't so much cradle-to-cradle as a breed of particularly inventive downcycling. But it was, for all that, quite a feat, and it provided a refreshing new perspective on the smoke-spewing industrial landscapes that litter so many of the world's cities.

It works like this: the power plant—Asnaes Power Station, a 1,500-megawatt coal-burning monster—serves as the symbiotic network's central node. The excess steam from its power generation is sent next door to Statoil's refinery, where it provides 15 percent of the refinery's "process steam" (for the heating of oil tanks and pipelines, for example). The power station's enormous surplus of heat, meanwhile, feeds a district heating system that warms the Novo Nordisk pharmaceutical plant down the way, the Novozymes enzyme production facility next door to that, and around 4,500 households all over Kalundborg. The power plant's smokestacks have been outfitted with scrubbers to remove toxic sulphur dioxide from their emissions, and the chief byproduct of this process is gypsum, which is shipped to BPB Gyproc, the nearby plasterboard factory, where it has supplanted trucked-in Spanish gypsum as the factory's primary raw material. The desulphurization process yields a handful of smaller-volume nitrogen-rich byproducts as well, which are used as pig feed and fertilizer on local farms. Finally, the Asnaes plant's wastewater feeds an adjacent fish farm. And the maze grows only more intricate—and more rewarding—from there.

Over at the oil refinery, the excess gas from the refining process (which is simply flared off at most of the world's oil refineries) is in Kalundborg piped to BPB Gyproc to power its production line and to the Asnaes power plant as the starter fuel for its boilers. The power plant also uses the refinery's cooling water to supply its boilers. Down at Novo Nordisk, the production work, which yields half of the world's raw insulin, generates a huge volume of contaminated water, so the company sends it to the enzyme manufacturer, where both companies' wastewater gets an initial cleaning before being sent to the municipal treatment plant for a more complete scrub along with the city's own wastewater (increasing the efficiency of the process for all three). Novo Nordisk also creates a substantial amount of waste sludge and slurry, which is used as fertilizer.

The mind already reels, I'm sure, and these are simply the major symbiotic pathways. The overall schematic is a spider web of arrows in seventeen colours, one for each distinct stream of traded waste. All told, there are about twenty constituent projects in the Kalundborg Centre for Industrial Symbiosis, which have reduced overall water usage by a quarter and total oil usage and CO_2 emissions by 45,000 and 175,000 tons per annum, respectively. Not long after naming it a global model for industrial co-operation, the United Nations Environment Programme (UNEP) estimated the total cost of it all at about $75 million by 1999, generating $160 million in savings by the same date. Each separate project recouped its costs within an average of five years.

Jacobsen and I strolled casually alongside the massive pipes as he sketched the key aspects of this network. I thought of the steam and gas and surplus water rushing past us, and every so often I would follow their snaking path off into the distance, where they reached out to embrace the smokestacks and cooling towers on the horizon. The scene morphed a little with every few steps and each new branch in Jacobsen's labyrinthine sketch, until eventually it looked almost as much like a brighter future as a smog-clouded disaster standing there on the horizon. Here were four green tubes to carry things we'd once thought worthless across land we'd previously deemed useless. If this grim setting could be salvaged, even partially, then almost any landscape could. It had taken a couple of decades to transform Kalundborg's busy harbour this way, but then again one of the most encouraging things about it was that it had happened piecemeal, in little trickles—organically, if you will—and it has emerged as much from corporate self-interest as from stern regulatory measures.

"In a way," Jacobsen told me, "it started with water." More specifically Denmark's scarce groundwater, which even when Statoil built its refinery back in 1961 was a zealously hoarded commodity. So the refinery drew its water instead from the regularly replenished surface of nearby Lake Tissø, a much less plentiful source that had to be carefully managed. The first thread in the symbiotic web, therefore, was a pipe carrying Statoil's wastewater to the power plant. The gainful use of the refinery's flared gas came next. Then, in response to the increasingly stringent Danish environmental regulations that came in the wake of the energy crises of the 1970s, the coal plant moved into the district heating business in 1981. Bit by bit, other strands emerged to expand the web. This growing assortment of efficiency measures was given its "Centre for Industrial Symbiosis" moniker only in 1989, well after it had generated its own self-perpetuating momentum. There were certain intrinsic details that perhaps predisposed Kalundborg to symbiosis—the physical proximity of the various plants, in particular—but the only truly unique feature was the commitment to hunt for mutually beneficial collaborations.

A UNEP case study warned against top-down approaches to duplicating Kalundborg's symbiosis, but nevertheless ambitious prefab "eco-industrial parks" have been plopped down in recent years on many city fringes—in Germany and the Netherlands, but also (make that particularly) in the United States and China. Jacobsen duly noted that Chinese planners had been frequent visitors to Kalundborg. (This was a refrain I heard all over Denmark; the Chinese appear to be studying Denmark's sustainability breakthroughs more closely than anyone else.) Jacobsen fretted a little over it all, concerned that symbiosis might become "just a label."

We were walking across the wide inner courtyard of the Asnaes Power Station, where the plant plucked its fuel from the decks of enormous container ships and prepared it for combustion. A mountain of black coal three storeys high loomed behind Jacobsen as he talked. "How do these kinds of things come together, and how do they encourage sustainability?" he said. "That is the lesson to be learned from this district. It's about collaboration, communication and partnership." It was a site-specific process, not a universal scheme; a continuum, not a set of fixed principles. But it could travel almost anywhere, had the potential to do much in the way of smoothing the path between the fossil-fuelled status quo and true sustainability. Organic— yes, in its way—like native weeds bursting through cracked pavement in a vacant lot.

DERELICT CHIC & SUSTAINABLE URBAN RENEWAL

"Don't it always seem to go, that you don't know what you've got, till it's gone / They paved paradise, and put up a parking lot." So goes Joni Mitchell's most famous lament. And the choir sings, *Shaa-oooh, bah-bah-bah-bah,* and surely everyone listening knew, in those *Silent Spring* days of its debut, exactly what sort of irretrievable loss had inspired Mitchell's ironically buoyant chorus. "Big Yellow Taxi" came out in 1970, by which point Rachel Carson's *cri de coeur* had become canonical in the circles Mitchell travelled in—the song's third verse beseeches farmers to discard their DDT—and it's a representative example of that generation's critique of modern urbanization. There was a downward ecological spiral under way, and it began with trees and bees and everything else that made pristine Wordsworthian Nature so grand, passed through the Machine Age and the smoggy asphalt A-bomb present, and ended in some ultra-urbanized, over-populated nightmare landscape in which the trees were all gone and no flowers bloomed and the human soul had been reduced to something no more vibrant than any old bourgeois appliance. (In 1982, the grim sci-fi film *Blade Runner* came along to provide the default cinematic template for this scenario.) If there was a way out of this mess, surely it involved, at a minimum, jackhammering through the asphalt of a good many parking lots to unearth and rebirth the paradises beneath.

This might be the case, metaphorically speaking, but the regenerative process may not be quite what Joni Mitchell had in mind. The global population rocketed past six billion a few years back, and it's forecasted to reach at least eight billion before it reaches anything like a peak, so a sustainable future (unless it involves culling half the herd or more) is an urban future. We will redeem the Anthropocene Era—*if* we redeem it—by redeeming the metropolis.

By the time "Big Yellow Taxi" was released in 1970, Joni Mitchell was living in Los Angeles, but she'd cut her songwriting teeth in the smoky coffee houses of Yorkville, the epicentre of Toronto's 1960s counterculture. In those days, Yorkville was a tight knot of old Victorian homes on narrow streets, just a few square blocks in all, tucked into the elbow formed by the intersection of two of Toronto's most important thoroughfares. It was mostly working class, dingy and crowded; the proprietors of the coffee houses that incubated Mitchell's career (and countless others) were often recent European immigrants. Yorkville was, in other words, just the kind of unsightly urban blight that had helped inspire the ongoing middle-class flight to the suburbs in Toronto and across North America. But barely a decade after Mitchell had decamped for L.A., her old neighbourhood had been transformed from a hippie enclave into one of Toronto's most desirable addresses. Today, Yorkville is a luxurious neighbour-hood of designer boutiques, celebrity hairdressers, million-dollar condos and the hotel where all the biggest stars stay when they're in town to shoot a movie or attend an opening gala.

What happened to Yorkville was merely a particularly dramatic example of a process that has become so deeply engrained in the evolution of modern cities that it might as well be in the building codes. Even as Yorkville was trading love beads and marijuana roaches for diamonds and Cuban cigars in the 1980s, a new generation of artists, musicians and scenesters initiated the transformation of Queen Street West just a few subway stops south. The rejuvenation of all-but-derelict blocks of that avenue then skipped westward along Queen until it couldn't go much farther, and now it's bounding east from the original starting point. This same phenomenon has chased waves of bohemian culture all over New York, from Greenwich Village south to the derelict warehouses of SoHo and TriBeCa (both now among the most valuable real estate on the planet), eastward across Manhattan, then over the East River to Williamsburg and Park Slope in Brooklyn and westward over the Hudson to Hoboken. And so it's gone in cities big and small throughout the Western world: the decrepit warehouses of East Berlin made over into fashionable cafés and live/work spaces; London's old working-class neighbourhoods gone posh one after another; Sydney so completely fancified that even young professionals lament the vanished possibility of ever owning a home downtown.

If the story of the Western metropolis since the Second World War can be reduced to two overarching themes, the first of course would be the explosive rise of suburbia—just the sort of paradise-paving that had Joni Mitchell so bummed out. But the other theme, later to emerge but increasingly prominent, would be this massive reinvestment in urban spaces, the rebirth of value in the all-but-discarded cores. The common name for this phenomenon is "gentrification," which verges on pejorative and implies a more singular and linear phenomenon than the multivalent process at work in many cities. Let's call it instead "derelict chic"—the transformation of industrial trash into civic treasure.

The emergence of derelict chic is neither uniformly positive nor inherently sustainable. It is, however, more readily adaptable to both of those conditions than the suburban alternative (which I'll come back to a bit later). If, in many of its current incarnations, it encourages a reduction of diversity and the evaporation of affordable inner-city housing, if it seems more consumerist style than sustainable substance, it should be noted that these qualities are not intrinsic to its nature (whereas overconsumption, for example, *is* intrinsic to the nature of suburbia, which I'll also come back to). The transformation of old warehouses into expensive lofts with *au courant* bistros and high-end furniture stores on their ground floors might be the current norm, but it's not the only way a city can reimagine itself. Derelict chic can be more than a species of gentrification; it can be a template for the building of a sustainable metropolis.

Consider what happened to one Yorkville-style bohemian enclave whose leading lights never ran off to L.A. It's a place called Christiania, a 34-hectare expanse of prime real estate just across the canal from the palace-studded heart of Copenhagen. Constructed under the reign of Christian IV in the seventeenth century, Christiania was an important naval fortification until the late 1960s, when it fell into disuse. The working-class residents of the surrounding neighbourhood began to poke holes in its fence to get at the ample parkland and forested canal banks within, and they were soon joined by countercultural idealists from communes across Denmark.

The fences came down for good in 1971, and the newly arrived communards set about converting the sturdy old warehouses and barracks into apartments and building new homes of whimsical design along the canal. By the mid-1970s, Christiania was a fully functioning, semi-autonomous urban village—it called itself a "Free City"—and it was legally sanctioned to carry on as a "social experiment" until such time as the Danish government commissioned a public competition to decide its ultimate fate. That competition was repeatedly delayed while a succession of mostly left-leaning governments vacillated on what to do with the Free City, in concert with a range of obscure legal battles over its fate. The contest finally materialized in 2003, by which point Christiania had become a landmark on Copenhagen's map nearly as prominent as the Tivoli Gardens. (One Christiania café boasted that it had become the third most popular tourist destination in all of Denmark.)

It had also become a sort of living model of grassroots urban renewal and direct local democracy. Christiania had a self-financed, self-regulated municipal government, its own postal service, its own currency. It had a single communal trust for the entire neighbourhood in place of private property, and it was largely self-policed. Christianites established Copenhagen's first comprehensive recycling program, and they managed it themselves. They set up a kindergarten, a daycare, a health clinic. Christiania was home to theatre groups and resident artists and filmmakers, architects and entrepreneurs, blacksmiths and plumbers. Most famously, it was also home to a handful of marijuana-friendly smoking cafés and Europe's most vibrant and conspicuous hashish market, which practised its trade out of a row of semi-permanent hawkers' stalls along the main pedestrian thoroughfare. Owing in no small part to this last feature, the conservative Danish government that came to power in 2001 set about systematically dismantling much of the social and legal apparatus that made Christiania unique. By 2005, when I visited, the hash market was gone, patrols by city police in riot gear were constant, and the future of the place was uncertain and highly contentious. The government's latest plan, as of late 2006, would open Christiania to comparatively conventional residential redevelopment. After fighting (sometimes physically) to keep the community they'd constructed intact, the Christianites may have no further options.

Christiania would lose a significant piece of its soul in such a bargain—possibly the most critical part—because the key to its uniqueness was that it was purely the product of its residents. They'd turned abandoned military land into one of the most fascinating urban quarters I've ever set foot in, along the way precipitating the transformation of several of the largest brick buildings into airy open-concept lofts with high ceilings, exposed beams and on-site office/studio spaces—the preferred post-industrial dwelling of the contemporary Western hipster. Absent the hash market, the main drag in Christiania was an artist's conception right out of a big-money condo developer's fanciful brochure, a teeming pedestrian live/work promenade replete with handicraft shops, offices for social services and political activists, cafés and pizza stalls, an excellent bakery. There was an extensive network of walking paths through the nearby woods, playgrounds and pastoral village greens, a skateboard ramp. The *style* of all of this was hippie-radical funky—Day-Glo paint and graffiti, thrift-store trim, groovy names like Meadow of Peace and Café Woodstock—but its substance was a functioning, self-sustaining model of the exact kind of vibrant urban community that every warehouse-loft developer in the free world claims to be trying to build.

This isn't just a Danish thing: like-minded souls have come together to carry out successful grassroots redevelopments of even more dilapidated urban spaces in other metropolises. In Berlin, for example, about a hundred activists occupied a shuttered film studio slated for demolition in 1979. This was ufaFabrik, the former home of Universal Film AG (which, in a bit of convenient and potent symbolism, included the sound stage where Fritz Lang created his nightmarish *Metropolis*). The people who came to salvage ufaFabrik replaced those memories of future dystopia with a modest utopian community, the cultural heart of its neighbourhood. Today, ufaFabrik is home to about thirty people and a work and social space for thousands of others. It has been retrofitted with a theatre, a community centre, a free school, a petting zoo, a café and bakery and natural-foods store, green roofs and solar panels. Like Christiania, it styles itself as a sort of laboratory for a new and more holistic way of life. It might just be the polar opposite of the back-breaking labour and subterranean squalor that Lang prophesied for Germany's working class, and it is at any rate a model for a kind of urban redevelopment that embraces and revitalizes the community that surrounds it.

On the surface, Toronto's newly refurbished Distillery District would seem to be kith and kin to these older, more measured redevelopments. Tucked into a denuded industrial area near Toronto's old port, the Distillery District is a sort of self-contained urban village built on the site of the Gooderham & Worts Distillery, once the largest liquor factory in the whole British Empire, a sprawling complex that closed up shop in 1990. It was acquired by a handful of enlightened corporate developers and lovingly restored during the first few years of the new millennium. They filled it with artists' studios, elegant public sculptures, hip cafés, a brew pub. Walled and gated, with pedestrian lanes of cobblestone and grand old brick edifices dating as far back as 1859, the Distillery District has become one of the most atmospheric neighbourhoods in the city. A glass condo tower now rises to a height of thirty-two storeys above one of the old distillery buildings, and there are several more condo developments just outside the original complex. All the elements of a funky urban neighbourhood have been thus assembled.

Although it might be too soon to assess its merits, there's nonetheless a slightly antiseptic quality to the Distillery District at present. In the decade between its closing as a working distillery and its rebirth as a mixed-use neighbourhood, it was frequently used as a shooting location for Hollywood movies, and that stage-set vibe still pervades. Maybe it's because the redevelopment was so thorough, but anyway there doesn't seem to be much room left in which the residents can invent an authentic community. There's nothing left to be created, few purposes yet to be determined.

"Even the most startling cultural and economic developments do not arise out of thin air." This is Jane Jacobs, one of the most prominent thinkers in the annals of urban planning, writing in the *New York Times Magazine* in 2004. "They are always built upon prior developments and upon a certain amount of serendipity and chance. And their consequences are unpredictable, even to their originators and the pioneers who believed in them and initiated them." One of the central goals of Jacobs's life and work was to carve out spaces in the modern metropolis that encouraged this process, which she viewed as heavily analogous to the growth of a natural ecosystem. Jacobs had cut her activist teeth opposing the catastrophic excesses of postwar urban renewal, leading the fight to block the construction of modern expressways through the hearts of historic neighbourhoods, first in Manhattan and then in Toronto. She loathed the careless blacktopping of paradise even more than Joni Mitchell did, and it's likely she'd have seen an abandoned distillery as exactly the kind of place where an Edenic urban garden could one day bloom. And so let's not dismiss the Distillery District out of hand. It's certainly one of the most ambitious and best realized developer-driven retrofits you'll find anywhere—in many ways a pacesetter in the world of derelict-chic design. What remains to be seen is whether it can learn, progress, become more than the sum of its parts.

That Jacobsian alchemy by which streets and buildings evolve into neighbourhoods and communities is one of the primary engines of culture, and it is the essential prerequisite for a sustainable metropolis. In recognition of this necessity, an urban-planning tool called "mixed use" has emerged in recent years with the avowed goal of providing a catalyst for this alchemical process. Prior to the advent of modernist zoning, mixed use was a city-building technique so dead obvious it didn't even have a name—it was a seemingly immutable part of the social order at anything larger than village scale. Workplaces were established near the labour pool, and merchants opened shops close to their customers' homes, and if they had spare rooms upstairs they rented them out at affordable rates. Starting in the 1920s, however, single-use zoning emerged as a reaction to both the filth of industrial production and the revolution in human mobility enabled by the automobile. Home, work, shopping, recreation and the arts were assigned to strictly delineated zones—the elements, in a sense, confined to separate flasks, reducing those serendipitous reactions of disparate forces essential to a healthy society to potentially fatal infrequency—and the sum soon became much less than its parts.

Thanks in no small measure to the advocacy of Jacobs herself, mixed use has been returned in recent years to its rightful place at the core of urban design. And just in time: though this wasn't its original intent, the establishment (or re-establishment) of mixed-use space is the city's best first response to climate change. It is, to begin with, an effective method of recycling—even *upcycling*—the built urban environment. It wages war on car dependency and creates sufficient population density for mass transit. It reduces the energy footprint of individual residences and businesses, while encouraging a more active civic life that negates the apparent sacrifice implied by this loss of space. Most critically, mixed use moves beyond the technical apparatus of energy production and emissions reduction to create a *social* context for the growth of sustainable communities. These are most durably constructed at village scale, and mixed-use zoning encourages the degree of social freedom and community investment necessary to begin building those urban villages promised in the glossy brochures of warehouse-loft developers and made manifest in places like Christiania.*

An obvious question: Can such an enlightened approach to planning produce a sustainable cityscape more or less from scratch? Moreover, can it do so on the panicked timeline of the Anthropocene? On the Øresund shore directly opposite Copenhagen, a Swedish city—Malmö, the country's third-largest urban centre—has launched an experiment to answer these questions. For centuries, Malmö thrived as a major shipbuilding centre, but much of that industry has moved east to Korea in recent years, leaching 40,000 jobs from a city of 265,000 and rendering its old port and harbour lands economically redundant. Not content merely to mend its wounds, Malmö has set itself a much more ambitious goal: "From industrial site to a new sustainable city district." So declares the banner headline in a brochure outlining the dramatic redevelopment under way in the city's Västra Hamnen ("Western Harbour"), a swath of reclaimed waterfront that was still gaining new area via landfill as recently as 1987 to provide space for the bustling shipbuilding trade.

---

* Put another way, the goal of mixed-use planning is to create pockets of the kind of urban landscape I found *everywhere* in Freiburg. The redevelopment of Vauban was actually *less* ambitious in this regard than many of its North American "Smart Growth" cousins, in part because the rest of the city had never been carved into single-use chunks, was indeed such a model of mature mixed-use urban living that Vauban didn't need to be much more than a residential community with a light dusting of commercial and retail space. Its residents already have a sustainable city at their disposal.

For decades, the harbour's skyline had been dominated by a towering white crane capable of lifting 1,500-ton boats. In 2002, the crane was dismantled and freighted away to join the rest of the shipbuilding business in Korea. It has since been replaced by the Turning Torso, an elegant twisting tower of residences and offices 190 metres high, designed by Santiago Calatrava. Constructed as a stack of five-storey cubes, each separated by one recessed storey, hyper-efficient and powered by renewable energy, the Torso is a curvaceous, futuristic symbol of Malmö's bold transformation. The surrounding neighbourhood has been morphing rapidly as well, with efficiency retrofits to 1950s-era apartment buildings and almost six hundred new residences built by twenty-two separate firms, all of them sustainably powered by wind and sun and heated in part by a biogas plant fuelled by the organic garbage stuffed down those houses' own sinks.

By such means has Malmö turned a patch of partially contaminated land next to a down-at-heel port into the core of the "Ecological City of Tomorrow." And it has done so in less than a decade. Equally conscious of the stifling homogeneity that has often accompanied urban redevelopment projects of this scale, the city's planners worked hard to create as richly varied and potentially unpredictable an environment as possible on such a tight schedule. The employment of those twenty-two different firms to build the new homes, for example, was an attempt to encourage the kind of spontaneous inter actions of disparate elements so beloved by students of the Jane Jacobs school of urban planning. "Diversity characterises the area," the official Western Harbour brochure declares, pointing out the new seaside park and promenade, ready to play host to everything from sunbathing to "musical happenings." The brochure makes note as well of the "exciting structural mix of individually designed streets, pedestrian walks, alleyways and open squares."

All in all, it's a stunning plan, and the prospects for its success are surely as high as any. The key, though, may not be what kind of buildings and plazas Malmö's planners thought to build but what they allow to happen in between them. City planners aren't *that* much closer to perfect foresight than anyone else, and one of the critical features of a sustainable metropolis might just be how it reacts to the consequences it least anticipated.

UNDERCROFTS, UNINTENDED CONSEQUENCES & URBAN RENEWAL BY SKATEBOARD

Here's a scene that would definitely please Jane Jacobs: A posh café on the south bank of the Thames, with a broad riverside promenade visible out the big picture windows. The walkway is crowded with strolling tourists, hustling commuters, hawkers and gawkers and all the other teeming masses of humanity that give thrumming life to this, one of the world's pre-eminent cities. The promenade out there, that's the Queen's Walk—one of the most monument-dense riverside strolls on the planet. Hang a left and head southwest past Waterloo Station to the London Eye, where there's a lovely view of Big Ben and the Parliament buildings, or turn right and saunter due east to the hulking Tate Modern and Shakespeare's storied Globe Theatre and, eventually, legendary London Bridge. Or find a welcoming leather banquette inside the café, take a seat and pause for a moment to absorb it all, and understand that if English-speaking urban culture has an epicentre, you're pretty much seated on top of it.

But the real Jacobsian heart of this grand scene was, to my mind, the discussion at one of those comfortable banquettes one fine autumn morn. I was seated there with the proprietor of a local skateboard shop and a pair of officials from the South Bank Centre—the massive multivenue arts complex whose ground-floor café we were meeting in—and we were talking about unintended consequences, unexpected opportunities, great gaffes in the history of urban design and the serendipitous correctives to same. The South Bank Centre's ongoing rejuvenation, I discovered, was a case study in the spontaneous, unpredictable creation of vital urban space. And it was the product of the accidental intersection of two vectors that had started their journeys far apart, separated by continents and decades, converging now on the south bank of the Thames as a powerful lesson in the ways of redemption for the contemporary metropolis.

The first of these vectors is one we've already discussed: the ascension to paramount prominence of the modernist school in urban architecture and design. Owing to the devastations of the Second World War and the privations of its aftermath, modernism arrived a bit late to the banks of the Thames. But when it did, it came with a ferocious zeal. Pretty much the first modernist edifice in England was the Royal Festival Hall, constructed in 1951 for the

Festival of Britain. The festival was intended to inject some optimistic energy into the country's gloomy postwar mood, and the Royal Festival Hall was conceived as a reincarnation of the Queen's Hall, which had been destroyed during the Blitz in 1941. It was the only permanent structure built for the event, and it later became the cornerstone of the greater South Bank complex.

In the years after the festival, the idealistic avant-garde in British design joined the rest of the world's cultural elite in its enthusiastic embrace of modernism. Commissioning officers around London favoured a particularly austere form first demonstrated by Le Corbusier in the construction of his Unité d'habitation, an apartment building in Marseille that was completed in 1952. With Unité, Corbu introduced raw concrete—*béton brut*—as the preferred building material of the fully purified Great Master. This spawned a subsect of the modernist church whose work came to be known by the accidentally evocative English term "brutalism"—a derivation of the French name for the unadorned and dutifully expressed structural material it favoured. The most notorious of London's brutalist slabs was the Trellick Tower, a residential building in west London designed by the Hungarian-born architect Ernö Goldfinger and erected in the late 1960s. The Trellick's sterile concrete spaces soon became such a welcoming home for violent crime that the London tabloids nicknamed it the "Tower of Terror." Around the same time as the tower's construction, London's original modernist edifice, the Royal Festival Hall, received a pair of brutalist additions: the Queen Elizabeth Hall and the Hayward Gallery. These were in turn fused to nearby Waterloo Station by a series of wide terraces and raised walkways, all in spartan *béton brut*. This vast cultural warren came to be known as the South Bank Centre.

The design concept underpinning this expansive institution—"Britain's most important cultural complex," in *The Observer*'s esteemed estimation—was lifted pretty much directly from Corbusier's original "Radiant City" plan. Here were concrete pathways in the sky between great expressed structural cubes and rectangles. Here was a true utopian vision of the liberated urban proletariat—indeed, part of the appeal of brutalism in postwar London was its promise of informal spaces unbound by historic class distinctions, a public architecture restarting from zero to build a whole new social order. But here, alas, was brutalism's massive blind spot, brought to desolate life in the spaces in between the various grand halls of the South Bank Centre, which many pedestrians found cold, unwelcoming, even a bit creepy. In particular, there was the empty expanse of shadowed pavement beneath the Queen Elizabeth Hall's wide terrace—the Undercroft, people called it. And they hated it. They disliked the concrete, were put off by the austere, forbidding emptiness, didn't care much for brutalism generally, to be honest (in the mid-1980s, Prince Charles dismissed another proposed brutalist project as "a monstrous carbuncle," sounding the movement's death knell to vigorous agreement far and wide), but they *really* loathed that accursed Undercroft. Wouldn't go near it. "Slack space" was the term used to describe it by a royal commission on the South Bank Centre's future. This was one in a series of studies conducted throughout the 1980s and 1990s to examine what could be done to salvage the centre and transform its environs into viable public space. There were suggestions—serious, studious suggestions—that it should simply be razed to the ground and replaced, and, with the exception of the nostalgic Royal Festival Hall, it's doubtful there would have been much in the way of mourning for the demolition of all that *béton brut.*

Meanwhile, right around the same time that all those brutalist carbuncles were being erected along the Thames, a solution for the problem they would create was being formulated amid the concrete wastes of distant Southern California. This is the second vector in the Jacobsian convergence I witnessed decades later, and its origin lies in the dead space of another kind of failed utopian experiment: an amusement park. Pacific Ocean Park, a gaudy fantasia erected in the 1950s upon an enormous pier on the Pacific shore in Santa Monica, was for a brief time the embodiment of a particular breed of postwar American dream. It was a sort of Coney Island of the West, a bustling 28-acre playground of midway rides, life-in-the-future installations and hot dog concessions under the warm sun of sainted California. For a few short years, Pacific Ocean Park was an attraction to rival nearby Disneyland, welcoming more than one million paying customers in 1959 alone.

By the 1960s, however, Santa Monica had begun to experience some of the same decay that plagued nearby Los Angeles, and the city embarked upon an ambitious urban renewal scheme of blighted-neighbourhood demolition and concrete freeway construction, a short-sighted and ill-conceived strategy typical of its era in American urban planning. The widespread construction made it exceedingly difficult to get to Pacific Ocean Park, and the stretch of beach it inhabited was growing increasingly seedy—"the last great seaside slum," in one former resident's recollection. By 1966, admissions at the amusement park had plummeted to barely a third of their late-fifties peak. It locked its gates for good in the fall of 1967. Anything of value was auctioned off the following summer, and the fantasia's skeletal remains were left to slowly rot and collapse atop their grand pier.

A funny thing about the great pilings upon which that pier stood, though: they enclosed a small cove of choppy seas and created a sort of aquatic obstacle course, thereby producing a *killer* surfing site for a certain kind of thrillseeker. And when the surf wasn't quite right, some of those adrenaline junkies took up the next best thing: surfing the local asphalt on skateboards. The neighbourhood was known to these surfers as Dogtown—the wrong side of Santa Monica's tracks—and the cash-poor, adventure-hungry kids who congregated at Dogtown's Zephyr surf shop took to mapping the city's terrain by skateboard like it was a new kind of amusement park laid out in sporadic patches just for them.

"Two hundred years of American technology has unwittingly created a massive cement playground of unlimited potential. But it was the minds of 11 year olds that could see that potential." That's Craig Stecyk, one of the original Dogtown skaters, assessing the scene at its peak from the pages of *Skateboarder* magazine. The line appears again in the 2001 documentary *Dogtown and Z-Boys,* a loving, hagiographic chronicle of those seminal years of concrete surfing, which was directed by another of its pioneers, Stacy Peralta. (Stecyk co-wrote the film.) The Z-Boys (short for "Zephyr Boys," from the surf shop's name) spent the early 1970s hunting out dried-up culverts and oddly banked asphalt school grounds. When drought descended upon southern California in the mid-1970s, water rationing compelled wealthy residents to leave their backyard swimming pools to dry up, and the Z-Boys took to hopping their fences to skate the steep walls of those *béton brut* bowls. The half-pipe, that ubiquitous skatepark adornment, was a direct copy of an empty suburban swimming pool. The Dogtown skaters turned trespassing into a kind of liberation, created art from trash, practised urban renewal by skateboard.

Before long, the Z-Boys became the rock stars of the skateboarding world. They founded skateboard companies, sold T-shirts by the truck-load, toured America and Europe. They would have passed through London on any number of occasions, and I don't know for sure if any of them ever skated the infamous Undercroft, but by the early 1980s it had become London's premier venue for Dogtown-style street-urchin skateboarding. The Undercroft proved perfectly suited to the sport: a wide, empty expanse of concrete paving stones, protected from the ceaseless English rain by the terrace above, with thick concrete pilings to swerve around and a recessed lower tier with sloping ramp-like sides. It was like the Pacific Ocean Park pier's underside remade in *béton brut.* The unplanned, unexpected convergence of brutalist archi-tecture and skateboard culture brought life to an urban dead zone and meaning to the lives of a generation of English kids.

And here, seated across from me in a knit cap and a paint-splattered shirt at the South Bank Centre's stylish café, was one of those Undercroft veterans: Richard Holland, now in his early thirties, co-founder of a skate shop near Waterloo Station and an artist and sculptor by primary trade. Holland was sipping tea and listening quietly as the bespoke-suited, greying gent sitting next to him—Mike McCart, South Bank's director of partnerships and policy—recounted the history of the facility's fractious relationship with skateboarding. Every so often, McCart would pause to allow Holland to tell the story from its street-level flipside, as if they were business partners. Which, in a sense, they were. "I suppose our relationship with the skateboarding community as an institution sort of went through three phases," McCart explained. "The first was sort of absolute confrontation. We weren't going to have them on the site." The centre's highbrow crowd initially viewed skateboarding as noth-ing more than a new strain of delinquency; it didn't help that certain of the skaters' favourite tricks took them up a concrete ramp to bounce off the wall of the Queen Elizabeth Hall auditorium, which created an audible thud inside, sometimes right in the middle of a recital. And so the South Bank management dutifully took to installing railings and other deterrents throughout the Undercroft.

Holland, his accent soft and lilting, his tone deadpan: "It's quite interesting, the actual skate-stopping devices which they put up there became obstacles to skate. All the bars around the small banks, you know, that was then the challenge—who could do something over the bar. And like it was world-renowned—that bar, that gap, was really world-renowned."

By the late 1980s—returning to McCart's telling—the centre and the skaters reached a tentative truce, "a period of co-habitation, really," while the South Bank management wrestled with what to do about the whole brutalist mess in a protracted series of committee meetings, studies and redesign proposals. In 2002, the South Bank Centre hired an Australian by the name of Michael Lynch away from the Sydney Opera House to oversee the centre's reinvention. And it turned out that Lynch—more serendipity—had himself been a skateboarder as a teenager. McCart: "He was the first chief executive who really understood that arts centres, if they were going to be successful, had to be rooted in the community, and that the skaters were as much a part of that community as anyone else."

Holland, meanwhile, had co-founded The Side Effects of Urethane (TSEOU), an art collective with three full-time members and a much larger network of occasional collaborators. The collective's "sole purpose," it explains on its website, "is to explore and promote the symbiotic relationship between skateboarding and art/photography/design/architecture." TSEOU had mounted installations of what it called "skateable sculptures" in a couple of temporary gallery spaces in London, converting them for short periods into artful indoor skate parks. The goal, Holland explained, was to provide a counterweight to the dominant image of skateboarding as an aggressive "extreme sport" for over-adrenalized nihilists (often cynically employed as a corporate branding tool).

Around this time, Mike McCart began to investigate ways the South Bank Centre could get neighbourhood kids more involved in the life of the facility. He got to talking to a woman named Natalie Bell, who ran a nearby community youth group, and she introduced him to Holland. In short order, they were pitching the centre's august board of governors on the idea of a semi-permanent installation of TSEOU's skateable sculptures in the Undercroft. "There were two things I put to the governors, really," McCart said. "One is an agreement to put these 'Moving Units' in for a period of time. But the other was to say that, in doing this, you had to recognize that there must also be a long-term commitment. Because if we have aspirations to develop the site, then we should be building in some sort of skate plaza or some environment for the skaters."

"Moving Units" is the name Holland and his collective gave to their South Bank installation. It consists of a handful of low, backless concrete benches and sloping ramps strategically placed around the Undercroft—an overt homage to the modern office plazas and other underused urban spaces that have been colonized by skaters worldwide in recent years. The installation debuted in August 2004, and the plan is to leave the sculptures in place until the entire centre's redevelopment—which will include ample room for skateboarding—is complete. For Holland, though, the real accomplishment was demonstrating, in a highly visible manner, the creative and social energy skateboarding brings to the metropolis.

After the meeting, Holland took me out to the Undercroft to show me the sculptures. There was a low platform-like rise in the centre, a gently pitched ramp overlooking the sunken section of the space, a rectangular slab the size of a park bench marking the border between the Undercroft and the open-air plaza beyond. The sculptures' top edges had been chipped and worn down from countless rail slides, and their grey *béton brut* sides had been covered over in elaborate graffiti, which echoed the tag-covered walls at the rear of the Undercroft, creating a unified space, harmonious and even inviting. Some skater had tagged the front face of the park bench "Moving Unit" with the words SOUTH BANK in funky hip-hop script, almost like a welcome sign.

Holland told me about other exhibitions that he and his TSEOU crew were involved in—an installation just finished at a prestigious museum in Finland, another upcoming in France. He spoke as well of great public spaces in cities across Europe where skateboarding was a key feature. Barcelona's Museum of Contemporary Art is particularly renowned in skateboarding circles. The imposing white slab, designed by the celebrated modernist architect Richard Meier, is skirted by a broad, austere concrete plaza, where hot-shot skaters gather to wow the loitering crowds in a continuing and constantly reinvented exhibit that might be more famous than any of those mounted inside the building. "Pretty much everywhere in the world where there's a contemporary art gallery, there are people skating at it," Holland observed. As punctuation, there came an echoing clatter from the lower level of the Undercroft. A couple of kids were skating the ramps, grinding Holland's concrete sculptures, executing elaborate balletic kickflips. One of the skaters had just flubbed a trick, sending his skateboard skittering noisily across the barren space. Breathing life into the brutalist gloom.

If this troubled space could be redeemed, I had to wonder if there was hope even for the metropolis's most pressing problem, its least sustainable landscape. If skateboards could pound life into the cracks in brutalism's downtown façades, what might come along to salvage suburbia?

THE BIG EMPTY

For two years in the early 1980s, my family lived in Aurora, Colorado. Aurora was, at the time, one of the fastest-growing municipalities in the United States: its population had more than doubled in the preceding decade, and it was on its way to doubling again by 2000. (It reached 276,000 that year, up from 75,000 in 1970.) Aurora was an archetypal post-industrial edge city, one of those exploding tract-house suburbs filling up with refugees from downtown Denver and the rapidly declining industrial cities of the East as fast as developers could slap wood frames and aluminum siding together to house them. My brother attended middle school in a nearly windowless clover-shaped concrete bunker—a sort of suburban take on brutalism, I guess that was so overcrowded that the students were being taught in two shifts. Aurora was my introduction to modern suburbia: my first cul-de-sac, my first split-level ranch-style home, my first daily commute by yellow school bus, my first Chuck E. Cheese's birthday party.

My father was a military officer and my mother had been a teacher in military schools before they met, and their careers took them to a number of unfamiliar and unwelcoming places: remote northern Alberta, even more remote Labrador, small-town New Brunswick and southwestern Germany. My mother will tell you today what she knew within months of moving into that split-level on East Gunnison Place: Aurora was the worst place she ever had to live.

On a fine sunny day in the summer of 2006, I returned to Aurora with my wife and daughter for the first time in more than twenty years, navigating a rented minivan from our downtown Denver hotel by the faded, disjointed memory of a nine-year-old. We drove east along Colfax Avenue, which I half-remembered as an endless strip of chain-link and barred windows. Although Colfax was historically the primary artery linking Denver's east side to its inner city and the mountains beyond, we didn't use it very often when we lived in Aurora. This was partly because we didn't go downtown much, but also because Colfax had become the commercial heart of one of the city's most crime-ridden slums and because there were wide Interstate bypasses circling the downtown to get us where we wanted to go with much greater speed. What I didn't know as a kid was that the decay of that stretch of Colfax was a direct result of more than half a century of deliberate planning, which in Denver had been strongly favouring automobile-enabled decentralization since the city's first master plan in 1929.

As we cruised along Colfax in search of my childhood home, I noticed there were more taquerias than I remembered. I'd heard as well that a large new branch of Denver's most prominent independent bookstore was opening soon on East Colfax as a key element of an ambitious revitalization scheme, which had local officials cautiously optimistic about the avenue's future. But I also noticed that many of the windows of the businesses along East Colfax, including an amazingly large number of pawnshops and payday loan offices, were still hidden behind grids of thick iron.

We continued east on Colfax under the I-225, the north-south bypass my family had used for most of our day-to-day travels. A little while later, I spied a cross street—Chambers Road—whose name bore a faint echo of familiarity. I turned south, and a half-dozen strip malls later the cross streets again began to resonate in my memory. Left on Iliff, left again on Buckley, back to Buckley and further east to Tower Road. I backtracked, turned into one subdivision and then another. The names triggered increasingly intense waves of recognition, but still I couldn't find my old neighbourhood. I retreated to the corner of Buckley and Iliff, pulled up to the strip mall gas station and bought a map. I was parked on a patch of tarmac less than a mile from my childhood home, and I had no idea, really, where I was. It turned out there was not one Evans Avenue but several curving arms on the same latitudinal axis. Colorado Drive ended every few blocks, only to start again on the far side of another handful of intermittent curving avenues and dead-end spurs. There were five East

Gunnison Places, five separate little cul-de-sacs scattered across the map. I found my brother's old middle school and traced the memory from there to figure out which one was mine.

We went past the quasi-brutalist school building (a few windows had been punched into it at some point) and then a few twisting blocks farther to East Gunnison. The cul-de-sac seemed smaller than I remembered, our old house a little larger. My wife took a quick snapshot for posterity, and then we drove off. There was no point lingering: I felt nothing at all for the place. We took our daughter to play on the jungle gym at my old elementary school, and when she tired of it we headed back to the minivan. My wife got a little choked up in the parking lot, thinking about my mother stuck here all those years ago, but I still felt not a thing. No trace of nostalgic affection, not even a sighing relief at having left it behind.

Actually, that's not right. Aurora did evoke a response in me, something all its own. It wasn't indifference—not the absence of emotion—but a sense of feeling and memory being sucked away, vacuum-like, before they could find any purchase. It was profoundly hollow, quiet but not calm. The big empty. I thought of that scene in the film *Grosse Pointe Blank* where the protagonist— a sardonic hit man by the pointed name of Martin Blank, played with deadpan nihilistic zeal by John Cusack—returns to his childhood tract home to find it replaced by a convenience store. He pulls out his cellphone and calls his therapist, but gets only an answering machine. "I'm standing where my living room was," he barks with a sort of resigned exasperation, "and it's not here because the house is gone and it's an Ultimart." A brief pause, considering. "You can never go home again. . . . But I guess you can shop there."

A few scenes later, Blank and a rival assassin cross paths at the same Ultimart and engage in a cartoonishly lengthy, twin-fisted gun battle, Blank escaping just ahead of a bomb that reduces the convenience store to rubble. The barely concealed subtext of the scene is that pointless ultra-violence is the natural analogue to suburbia's numbness. Or maybe, more delicately phrased, that there is a dangerous strain of despair that can thrive on quiet cul-de-sacs, a derangement that sometimes mutates into murderous rage. Indeed, the places I knew as a child in suburban Denver have been particularly prone to violent outbursts in the years since I moved away. One night in December 1993, a man walked into the Aurora Chuck E. Cheese's restaurant, where I had attended a couple of birthday parties, and shot and killed four of the staff. A few years later, in the nearby suburb of Littleton, whose minor-league hockey team I used to play against, two students marched into Columbine High School and murdered twelve of their classmates and then themselves in one of the most brutal school shootings in American history. I was shocked, as everyone was, by the news of the Columbine massacre. There was one aspect of the collective astonishment I didn't share, however, and that was incredulity at the location of the murders. This awful thing, it was repeatedly noted, had happened at an *affluent* high school in an *affluent* suburb. The implication was that this setting rendered these senseless murders more intensely shocking. Wasn't it the very heart of the suburban ideal, after all, that suburbs were good places to raise a family? What were they for, if not to insulate their residents from this kind of brutality?

A HAPHAZARD CATASTROPHE

The day after my uninspiring homecoming, I paid a visit to the Aurora History Museum. I was curious about how you told the history of a suburb, not to mention a little surprised that Aurora even *had* a history museum.

The museum was tucked around back of one of the smaller buildings at the colossal Aurora Municipal Center complex, which was a mile down the parkway from Aurora's second-largest mall. The Municipal Center mimicked the city it served in general design scheme, sprawling across a 35-acre "campus" that wrapped around a wide parking lot and trim lawn. Its dominant feature was the new Municipal Center itself, a hulking five-storey city hall in pale concrete brick trimmed to look like old-school stone masonry. I arrived early in the afternoon on a weekday to find the vast open space between the buildings largely deserted. Every now and then, a car would pull into the parking lot and a figure or two would emerge, often clutching a handful of documents, to wander tentatively across the empty square in search of the right office. A wrong turn would mean a five-minute backtrack across the mostly shadeless grounds.

The museum was in a low building opposite the parking lot. It was a somewhat cramped space, its exhibits spread through several small rooms the size of classrooms. Strewn among the old photos and displays highlighting "colorful characters" from Aurora's history was a random assortment of geographically indistinct artifacts. An old wood-cabinet console TV and easy chair stood in for 1940s Aurora. For the 1950s, there was a Tupperware catalogue and a "Family Radiation Measurement Kit," and for the 1970s a Swanson TV dinner, a few eight-track tapes and an Apple II-E computer. The sign introducing the section on Aurora's most recent history read: "Malls, McDonalds and Movie Theaters."

The urban design critic James Howard Kunstler has called the suburban explosion "the greatest misallocation of resources in the history of the world," and Aurora offered evidence of this almost immediately. Incorporated in 1891, the fledgling streetcar suburb promptly ran out of water a few years later. This was to become a recurrent theme in Aurora's history—perhaps the dominant one—as each new wave of expansion saw the city swell even further beyond the parched land's ability to supply it. Aurora's growth was slow and steady until the end of the Second World War, and then it exploded. From 1950 to 1990, a period during which the population of downtown Denver expanded by a mere 12 percent, Aurora's population grew *twentyfold*. And it did so, as it always had, with almost no foresight whatsoever. In the museum lobby, a pamphlet issued by the municipal utilities department during the record drought of 2004 testified to the ongoing search for yet more water. "Even if we stopped all growth," the pamphlet read, "we'd still have to conserve water through watering restrictions. . . . That's because growth is not the cause of the problem, drought is." This was a line of argument so disingenuous it was kind of magnificent in its way—akin to blaming the lava flow from one particular eruption for the destruction of a community built at the base of an active volcano.

A similar unwillingness to consider consequences appears to have governed Aurora's land-use planning. One exhibit at the museum, for example, celebrated the arrival of the gargantuan Aurora Mall in 1975, before noting in the museum-display equivalent of the next breath that it "dealt a death-blow to Colfax businesses." This devastation was still in abundant evidence as of my cruise down the avenue in the summer of 2006, and Colfax's resurrection had become an urgent project for metropolitan Denver. A business improvement association had formed in 1989, and the governments of its three largest municipalities (the city itself, plus its two largest suburbs, Aurora and Lakewood) had begun pooling resources to aid the fight in 1994, but it only now seemed to be yielding results. In addition to the fancy new bookstore, East Colfax had also recently witnessed the construction of its first new residential development in eighty years: Chamberlain Heights, a mixed-use condo development that had gone up only after a protracted dispute over the necessary rezoning. A couple of decades late, Denver's elites had realized that their city couldn't work without a viable main street, and now they were scrambling to make up for all those years of neglect.

The old Aurora Mall—the first real indoor shopping palace I'd ever known—had nearly suffered the same fate as the stretch of Colfax it had supplanted, falling into its own downward spiral by the late 1990s. Like a lot of suburban construction, it hadn't been built with the future in mind. It was cheaply made, poorly lit, trapped in a design scheme that was on the verge of being eclipsed by the new big-box-village style of shopping plaza. This is a problem endemic to malls of its era; according to a 2000 study by PricewaterhouseCoopers, 19 percent of North America's shopping malls are "dead" or "dying." On the verge of joining those ranks, the Aurora Mall had just undergone an emergency facelift, a $100-million renovation, after which it was rechristened the "Town Center of Aurora."

I headed to the Town Center when I was finished at the museum. I'd dropped my wife and daughter there on the way in, watching them hike off toward a building I recognized even less than my old neighbourhood. It had been completely redone inside and out, and its elegantly appointed new concourses elicited only that now-familiar twinge of big emptiness. I was nowhere I'd ever been before, even though I had.

I found my wife and daughter in the Town Center's elaborate children's play area. My daughter was reeling around in a toddler's ecstasy: the place was crammed with kids, who were climbing all over each other and the assorted installations of child-sized cars and crawling mazes. The perimeter benches were packed with parents. It was a glorious summer day outside, brilliantly sunny but not too hot, and it was abundantly clear that the concourse of the Aurora Mall was still the best place in town to take your kids.

It was surely a scene like this that Kunstler had in mind when he asserted that, "the tragic truth is that much of suburbia is unreformable." This was in his 2005 book *The Long Emergency*, a bleak assessment of America's "converging catastrophes." Suburbia, he explained, "does not lend itself to being retrofitted into the kind of mixed-use, smaller-scaled, more fine-grained walkable environments we will need to carry on in the coming age of greatly reduced motoring." True to form, Aurora had done nothing more than change the aesthetics of its ailing shopping centre. It was still a sprawling single-use resource hog, built primarily, if not exclusively, as a place to be driven to and from. It was the path of least resistance: no tricky zoning debates, no anxious locals, most of all no hard questions about what a city—especially a hollowed-out, water-starved edge city—was supposed to be.

On the other hand, I knew of a place on the other side of town that defied Kunstler's assessment. It was the reason I was back in Denver in the first place, and I'd soon learn that Kunstler knew of it too. I wondered if it could change his mind. After all, he'd given its developer a powerful and unambiguous nickname: "the redeemer."

THE NEW URBANISM & SUBURBAN REDEMPTION

In upstate New York, the surname Falcone is inextricably linked to prosperous business as usual in the property development business. Indeed, the Michael J. Falcone Center for Entrepreneurship at Syracuse University now provides eternal testament to the business acumen of Michael J. Falcone, co-founder of the Pyramid Companies, which in the 1960s and 1970s amassed an impressive portfolio of shopping plazas and office parks worth $250 million. Falcone later founded the Pioneer Group, and his enterprising sons spun off their own Pioneer Development Company. In 1987, they merged into a conglomerate (the Pioneer Companies) that develops strip malls and big-box retail plazas in sixteen states.

Grand Traverse Crossing in Grand Traverse, Michigan, was a Pioneer build, and so was Berkshire Crossing in Pittsfield, Massachusetts. (Each of them was outfitted with its own cavernous Wal-Mart and

Home Depot.) The Saratoga Mall in Wilton, New York, just over the town line from Saratoga Springs, was an earlier Falcone project, when he was still at Pyramid. It was built in the 1970s—around the same time as the Aurora Mall—and its effect on stately old Saratoga was almost identical to the Aurora Mall's evisceration of East Colfax. Thanks to Michael J. Falcone and hundreds of developers like him, and to countless pliant, myopic city councils continent-wide, the predominant pattern of urban development in the second half of the twentieth century was a monumental shift of the centre of gravity from the core to the periphery. From urban to suburban, from pedestrian to car-driven, from sustainable to unsustainable.

The momentum of this approach is such that it has often taken tremendous force to reverse its course, even just enough to allow for a single modest project. The case of East Colfax's Chamberlain Heights is very much in keeping with the norm: overwrought zoning battles, nervous and intransigent locals, unimaginative bureaucrats and politicians, each of them another lumbering weight to be pushed back in a sort of serial re-enactment of Sisyphus's futile struggle with his rock against the force of gravity.

There are, however, signs that tireless Sisyphus is no longer pushing his boulder to the top of that damn hill all by himself. There's the rising cost of gas, of course, and the ever-more-inescapable fact that suburbia, as currently conceived, cannot persist in the face of anthropogenic climate change. (It will either reconfigure itself, implode or hasten a wider catastrophe. These are, at any rate, the last days of the stand-alone big-box store.) Perhaps just as important, though, has been the extraordinary alienation felt by many of us Anthropocene kids who grew up in the Big Empty. As members of the first generation to live in some cases our entire childhoods in the most sprawling suburbs, we appear to be far less convinced of the authenticity of the suburban ideal, and thus far more likely to choose the decrepit fixer-upper in the gutted downtown neighbourhood as a starter home. (Colfax Avenue's greatest success to date has been just such a renaissance in its historic Capitol Hill neighbourhood.)

The sins of the fathers, in other words, may not be visited upon the sons. This, anyway, is one way to look at how Mark Falcone, son of the aforementioned shopping-mall baron Michael J., became the property developer that Kunstler has purportedly called "the

redeemer," and how he turned another dying shopping mall in suburban Denver into the birthplace of a new kind of suburbia, teeming
with mixed-use promise. For Mark Falcone is a committed acolyte of
the New Urbanism, and in his first great work he appears to have
found his true calling—and perhaps as well the greatest redemptive
potential embedded in that philosophy.

First, though, to the prodigal son's conversion, which began, por-
tentously, in the very birthplace of the Renaissance—in the Tuscan
capital of Florence in the early 1980s. Falcone: "I spent a year in college studying in Florence, thinking up to that moment in time that
I had been dealt an extremely luxurious hand of cards in my life. I
really had a great family and a really wonderful childhood, my parents had been very successful. And yet I lived in a small apartment
behind the train station in Florence for a year, and the quality of my
life was significantly better than my own life, you know, than the circumstances that my own life provided. And I remember coming
back thinking, 'You know, here we are, the richest nation in the
world, and we can't do better than what we're doing?'" Where was
postwar America's Uffizi, its Ponte Vecchio? Where indeed even a
few decent piazzas or a palazzo worthy of the name? And—
Madonn'—what were we doing building all these shopping malls?

After graduation, Falcone went to work for the Rouse Company,
an ambitious developer that was by then almost two decades into an
attempt to build a new kind of suburb in Columbia, Maryland, on the
fringe of Washington DC's sprawl—a cluster of "urban villages" in
place of cookie-cutter subdivisions. It was an impressive project but
far from flawless, not quite Florence on the Potomac. "There were
some tools and some skills that were clearly missing," Falcone recalls.
So, in the late 1980s, he returned to his father's fold, and it was not
long after his reintroduction to the New England shopping mall business that he discovered the tool kit he'd been missing: the urban
design philosophy known as New Urbanism.

As I've already noted, New Urbanism was born on the sandy
banks of the Gulf Coast of Florida in the early 1980s. It began with a
deep-pocketed, nostalgically bent developer named Robert Davis,
who wanted a beach community built to pedestrian scale, with simple cottages like the ones he remembered from his youth, streets
where kids could play safely, maybe a town common. He hired a

husband-and-wife team, Andres Duany and Elizabeth Plater-Zyberk, to design the place. The result was Seaside, a self-contained urban village that became the birthplace and showpiece of the design revolution its creators dubbed "the New Urbanism."

Duany and Plater-Zyberk's pioneering work soon attracted acolytes, imitators and like-minded visionaries: architects, developers and city planners by the score who'd long felt the same bewilderments and frustrations that Falcone had brought home with him from Florence. In 1993, they united into a body called the Congress for the New Urbanism, which issued a practical manifesto—the Charter of the New Urbanism—three years later. It read in part:

> We stand for the restoration of existing urban centers and towns within coherent metropolitan regions, the reconfiguration of sprawling suburbs into communities of real neighborhoods and diverse districts, the conservation of natural environments, and the preservation of our built legacy. . . .
>
> We advocate the restructuring of public policy and development practices to support the following principles: neighborhoods should be diverse in use and population; communities should be designed for the pedestrian and transit as well as the car; cities and towns should be shaped by physically defined and universally accessible public spaces and community institutions; urban places should be framed by architecture and landscape design that celebrate local history, climate, ecology, and building practice.

The New Urbanists were the sworn enemies of the kind of office parks and shopping malls that had made the Falcone family fortune. They deplored the single-use zoning that separated home from store and store from workplace. The metropolis, they argued, was "a fundamental economic unit of the contemporary world," and its design, though it would still allow room for cars, would have to learn to do so without infringing on the primacy of pedestrians and public spaces. There was nothing overtly nostalgic about the movement—in fact, there was much about it that was future-tense utopian—but in practice it was at least partially a return to the state of urban design before the ascent of modernist planning and car culture. Indeed, its founding premise was predicated on the belief that the postwar approach to urban design had been a total disaster.

This was all music to Mark Falcone's ears. For a short time, he tried to convert the rest of his father's business to the cause, but that proved a *truly* Sisyphean task, so he struck out on his own. He moved to Boulder, Colorado, and started taking courses in urban planning at the University of Colorado. He was in town barely half a year, though, before he began to notice the state of affairs in the sprawling metropolis to the south, which seemed overripe with promising real estate and desperate for fresh ideas. So he called back east to Syracuse and invited a few of his associates to join him in Denver, and together they founded Continuum Partners in 1997. Before long, Continuum was building 16 Market Square, an elegant throwback to 1920s Denver in the heart of Lower Downtown—LoDo—a neighbourhood on the edge of the inner-city core that was rapidly being revitalized. The building was in many ways a textbook New Urbanist build: a classic stone office block, with ground-floor retail, four floors of office space and a couple of dozen luxury condo units on top, perched on the corner of a busy pedestrian square. It won a handful of awards—including the National Association of Office and Industrial Properties' best new building honour—and served as a boldface calling card for Falcone's firm.

Now, the reversal of half a century of the property development trade's standard operating procedure is no effortless task, and the first wave of New Urbanist building has often found its most welcoming space where there are fewer long-standing building codes or arcane zoning bylaws to contend with: out on the suburban fringe. By one estimate, there were more than two hundred major New Urbanist projects scattered across North America by the year 2000, and a great many of these were suburban neighbourhoods. Surrounded by split-level sprawl and encircled by controlled-access freeways, these new developments did what they could to carve out oases of mixed-use life in desolate suburbia. Tight rows of front-facing prewar-style homes went up on gridded streets with wide sidewalks, their garages tucked around back along downtown-style alleys. Townhouses and low-rise apartments were sprinkled throughout, in keeping with the New Urbanist principle of encouraging people of mixed incomes and varied backgrounds to live side by side. The neighbourhoods were festooned with town squares, village greens and pedestrian shopping streets—the small shops even crowned with rental units in the best examples.

There are practical limits, of course, to what can be done in a given set of pre-existing circumstances, immovable obstacles sometimes lodged in the zoning bylaws or the municipal planning office. Still, an idealistic urban designer has to wonder: What if just the right kind of official was sitting across from the ambitious New Urbanist developer at the planning table? A suburban mayor, say, who'd attended one of the Congress for the New Urbanism's many seminars and then taken a look around at his gutted mess of a suburb and realized that a rezoning redeemer was *exactly* what he needed. What would you get then? Turns out you'd get Belmar—a downtown to fill up the Big Empty.

Lakewood, the west-side analogue to Aurora, is a fast-growing suburban blanket that stretches from Denver's western edge all the way to Golden in the Rocky Mountain foothills. With a population of 145,000, it's quite a bit smaller than Aurora, and it's also a good deal younger—Lakewood was incorporated as a city only in 1969. It put itself on the map, however, a few years before that, in 1966, with the inauguration of the most colossal shopping mall the Great Plains had ever seen. This was Villa Italia: 1.4 million square feet of retail space on 104 acres, which soon became the commercial and social heart of a rapidly expanding suburban community.

By the early 1990s, however, Villa Italia had fallen into a rapid and terminal decline. Sales revenues peaked at the mall in 1994 and then dropped off a cliff. By the late 1990s, the overall occupancy rate had dipped to 30 percent, and the concourses and half-abandoned parking lot had become a haven for crime and drug activity. In 2000 and 2001, three of its largest stores closed. Villa Italia stood at the end of a stretch of Alameda Avenue lined with pawnbrokers, auto-body shops, old motels whose signs spelled out decay in busted neon. It was a worn-out building housing an outmoded species of retail trade—the very definition of a "dead" mall. And what to do with the corpse became one of the chief concerns of the occupant of the shiny new city hall across the boulevard from it.

"Malls don't die short distinct deaths, they just—they strangle. They just keep ratcheting down." This is how Lakewood Mayor Steve

Burkholder recalls the state of his city's biggest landmark at the dawn of the new millennium. The way Burkholder saw it then, he had three options. The first was the path of least resistance later chosen by, for example, the Aurora Mall. "We'll put a new fresh coat of paint on it and everything'll be okay," is Burkholder's shorthand version of this option, which he dismissed out of hand. The second, really a parallel fork on the same path, was to demolish the old mall and build in its place a standard-issue big-box village of the sort then in vogue. The last option—the one that puts a twinkle in the mayor's eye even now—was much more dramatic, a suburb's collective Sisyphean shove back against the tumbling boulder. "I kinda got brainwashed a few years ago when I went to a Congress of the New Urbanism meeting," Burkholder explains, "and said, 'Wait a minute, what is this new thing called *mixed use?*'"

Not only did the Congress have a few ideas about what to do with Villa Italia, it even had a name for what it had become: a *greyfield.* Greyfields are "large, uncontaminated developed sites that are due for redevelopment," and their rebirth as prime mixed-use civic space had been under way in isolated pockets for a decade or so. In Boca Raton, Florida, the decrepit Boca Raton Mall had been transformed into Mizner Park, its shops and restaurants reconfigured along gridded, pedestrian-friendly streets and joined by nearly three hundred houses, 262,000 square feet of office space and a museum. In suburban Los Angeles, a mostly vacant shopping centre called Ontario Gateway Plaza had been extensively renovated and outfitted with a seniors' housing complex, which had helped bring its occupancy rate from 30 percent to essentially full. Similar schemes were afoot in St. Paul, Minnesota, and suburban Chicago. Unlike brownfields (contaminated industrial sites), greyfields require no expensive soil remediation; they simply need a daring city council, nimble land-use regulations and an enlightened developer.

This, Burkholder decided, was what Lakewood needed: not another million square feet of retail space with prettier trim, but a bold plan to build a downtown for a city that had never really had one. It would require a developer of enormous ambition, someone willing to take a risk on something far outside the norm. So Burkholder went calling on the most ambitious New Urbanist he could find in the Denver area: Mark Falcone of Continuum Partners.

They immediately agreed on what needed to done, how to do it, *why*. They were under no illusions, however, that it would be effortless.

Falcone: "It does take a pretty significant commitment of will to shift the paradigm. And, you know, we can all sit here and identify the thousand little things that conspire against it. And I can assure you, in the path of progress, those thousand little things show up, and you have to wake up every day with the commitment and the will to simply overcome them. And to not just seek the path of least resistance."

Fortunately, the newly minted partners in Villa Italia's redemption had a few advantages working in their favour. There was the fact that Continuum was a privately held company, meaning there were no nervous shareholders to get in Falcone's way. There was Lakewood's tireless city manager, Mike Rock, who would be the lead bureaucrat guiding the project through its obstacle course, and whom all involved now describe with a reverence reserved for someone who has performed impossible miracles in broad daylight. The city also had a handful of policy tools on its belt. The bureaucrats used the law of eminent domain, for example, to expropriate the land, sell it to Continuum and help clear out the mall. A failing office building adjacent to the mall, which had such awful drainage infrastructure that a dentist working out of a ground-floor office reported watching rainwater trickle right through it during big storms, was condemned. Probably the most powerful measure, however, was the designation of the site as a "metropolitan district." This was a special planning policy category created by a 1947 Colorado statute, and it was an enormously powerful instrument: once a parcel of land was so designated, its developer was entitled to rights that allowed it to skip over complicated zoning ordinances and finance itself with municipal bonds.*

Once the old Villa Italia lands were thus redesignated, it was relatively easy to tweak the taxation that would occur once the

---

* There was an exquisite irony to using the "metropolitan district" statute to combat sprawl, because it had been one of the primary tools used by developers to build Denver's expansive suburbs in the first place. As Owen D. Gutfreund reports in *Twentieth-Century Sprawl*, Aurora's breakneck growth in particular was fuelled, at a policy level, by the creation of metropolitan districts. (For example, the Denver Tech Center, a vast single-use office park on the southern tip of Aurora, had been built by stitching together eleven of these districts.)

redevelopment was finished, thus to give Continuum sufficient resources and reassurances to undertake a wholesale New Urbanist revival. The district's sales tax, for example—the main tool in a Colorado suburb's revenue-creation arsenal—was cut from the Lakewood standard of 2 percent to 1 percent, and a 2.5-percent "public improvement fee" brought in to replace it. The money collected by the site's merchants under this levy would go to paying off the debt Continuum accrued during its construction of state-of-the-art infrastructure. (This procedure was a Lakewood version of a much more widely used development-generating technique referred to generically as tax increment financing.)

Deep in Lakewood's history, back when it was a place where rich city folk built their country homes, there'd been a grand estate nearby called Belmar, and so the project found a name as well. In late 2001, Villa Italia was demolished, and Continuum gathered together a range of designers and architects and broke ground on Denver's first great suburban downtown—maybe the first place of its kind in all of North America's yawning suburbia. Belmar was laid out in a tight grid of twenty-two blocks and outfitted with new roads and sewage and state-of-the-art telecom, at which point it was ready to acquire all the necessities of a full-service urban neighbourhood. The heart of Belmar remained, on its surface, devoted to shopping, but it was now arrayed along pedestrian-friendly high streets, with the stores flush with the sidewalks, office or residential space installed above, and curbside parallel parking. (One of the nastier squabbles Mayor Burkholder would eventually have—and win—with his council was over the introduction of metered street parking, which struck some of the council members as downright unsuburban.) Condos and townhouses were scattered throughout, bringing permanent residents to the site for the first time. Once the entire project is completed in 2012, there will be 1,300 homes in Belmar, assembled by multiple builders in a range of architectural styles in an effort to avoid a theme park's artificial unity.

Something like 90 percent of the original mall's scrap was recycled on site, and 160 of its old trees were preserved. On its own initiative, Continuum brought in the International Dark Skies Association to design the streetlights, and spent lavishly on low-intensity lamps that intrude as minimally as possible on the night sky above them.

Burkholder kind of gushes talking about just how much his faith in Falcone and his firm has been rewarded. "These guys are so great. I mean, the principles belong to the Nature Conservancy. They built a LEED-certified building—*on spec.* I mean, it's *amazing.*" Burkholder presided over Belmar's grand opening in May 2004, and the first few dozen stores and restaurants opened that spring.

I arrived in Belmar two years later, on the Sunday afternoon before the Fourth of July, just in time to catch the last hour or so of the farmers' market that takes over a couple of blocks of one of its prime shopping streets every weekend. I got myself a couple of top-notch homemade tamales from one little stall and washed them down with a fresh-squeezed lemonade from another. My wife bought a belt made from recycled tires at a booth that dubbed itself Cruelty-Free World, which was run by a recently married and stridently vegan gay couple from nearby Wheat Ridge. Other stalls offered up fresh produce, homemade jams and salsas, organic honey, the works. One of the organic-fruit sellers said business wasn't bad, though people weren't yet in the habit of buying whole cases of apricots the way they did in Boulder. The lemonade ladies, for their part, couldn't say enough about how much had been accomplished in a place where that "disgusting" gang-ridden mall had been not five years earlier. It was a warm, sunny summer day, a great day to stroll through a market, chat with the merchants, cut a deal on some fruit at the peak of its ripeness. It was pretty much everything a suburban shopping mall wasn't.

I came back to Belmar the next day for a more thorough tour. My guide was Bob Hayner, Continuum's development director for the Belmar project. Hayner was golf-shirted and chino'd, pointing out the sights with avuncular and energetic enthusiasm as we ambled leisurely down the sidewalk of Belmar's main commercial artery. He drew my attention to the disco-style bowling alley and the Century Theatre, a modern megaplex tricked out in throwback art deco. A second layer of New Urbanist life rested atop many of the retail establishments: office space, which was filling up rapidly with eager tenants, "funky urban lofts" selling briskly, a banquet facility that could serve a party of 1,400. In another part of Belmar, Hayner noted, another developer had recently finished the construction of 142 townhouses. "Those," he said, "sold as fast as they could build 'em." None of it was more than three years old, but the street already felt lived in, alive, a natural part of the city's fabric. Mayor Burkholder had described the overall aesthetic of Belmar as European scale infused with the feel of a bustling small town in Kansas or Nebraska, but to me the vibe was quite a bit like Disney's "Main Street U.S.A."—or, better, like the patchwork of authentic, three-dimensional, fully functioning communities that had inspired Disney World's builders half a century earlier, if they'd actually been a single place and not a fantasia. I mean that mostly as praise, not scorn: Belmar was simultaneously old-timey and modern-age, and just a little like something impossible brought to life.

A few blocks south of Alameda Avenue, the sidewalk opened onto a wide plaza. It was enclosed on two sides by upscale cafés with tables out front, on the other two sides by construction hoardings. Behind one of these, Hayner told me, a sixty-two-unit condo with ground-floor retail space was under construction under Continuum's auspices. Hayner took a moment to marvel at the phenomenon: they'd pre-sold their first batch of fifteen units in a couple of weeks, some for as much as $330 per square foot. "Which is not unusual for downtown Denver," Hayner said. "But in Lakewood, there's nothing that has ever come close to that."

Well, and who wouldn't snatch up a residence on suburban Denver's only Florentine piazza? You had cafés and pubs at your doorstep and a movie theatre across the street. A patch of the plaza was frozen in winter so you could go skating, just like at Rockefeller Center in oh-so-urbane Manhattan. A brand-new Whole Foods had just opened across the way for all your organic grocery needs, and there was the farmers' market on the weekend, of course, and the first major line of the extensive FasTracks LRT network was expected to pull into a new station a short bus ride north of Belmar in 2013.

This had been, five years earlier, the parking lot of a megamall. It was surely the nearest anyone had yet come to building a living, breathing embodiment of the ideals contained in the highfalutin' Charter of the New Urbanism.

Actually, not quite. There was that item in the charter that went like this: "cities and towns should be shaped by physically defined and *universally accessible public spaces*." The emphasis is mine, and that particular clause was on my mind as I stood looking over Lakewood's nifty new piazza with Bob Hayner, and so I had to ask. The piazza, I wondered. It was Continuum land, right? *Private* property?

"It's kind of a quasi-public space," Hayner replied. "Because we didn't want to have to deal with the kind of things that could happen in a public space, we decided to keep it private. Even though it's in part of the district, we decided to keep it private so we could control the programs and the activities in this space. And so it was a trade-off. I mean, there were benefits to making it public, but I think we felt the liabilities and the loss of control over what could happen in here swayed us toward keeping it private."

"Right," I said. "And is that mainly toward, you know, criminal activity, things of that nature, or . . . ?"

"Well, if somebody wants to have, you know, a gay rights parade—you know, we don't want to do that. You know? How would we stop it? So there's things that we think are, you know, more appropriate and beneficial to the community, and those things that would rather become a platform for somebody else's agenda that wouldn't necessarily be consistent with ours. We just didn't want that."

Look: Bob Hayner struck me as a decent fellow. Heart in the right place, live-and-let-live, all that. It was maybe even a poor choice of words, a bad example delivered clumsily in the heat of the moment. And even if *he* didn't think Belmar's elegant piazza should be open to unpopular free speech, that did not mean it would be closed to such things forever. This was a flexible space in any number of fundamental ways that Villa Italia's parking lot was not and never could have been. It was nearly impossible to turn a wide plain of asphalt into a place where the general public would gather, whereas a single tweak of the bylaws could reinvent Belmar's piazza as a town common. In ten years, or fifty, it could be a skate park or the terminus of a street market or a place where that nice gay couple from the Belmar farmers' market could distribute their pamphlets.

I thought of Dundas Square in Toronto, which had been built a few years before to turn the busiest pedestrian intersection in Canada into a more useful public space. Dundas Square was, in essence, just an open expanse of granite paving stone, tricked out with a few inconspicuous fountains, a rain shelter, a raised platform for public performances and some bench seating. It had been consciously modelled on the traditional European square, with ambitious dreams of becoming a place like Piazza San Marco, the broad plaza in front of Venice's grand cathedral, which has long been one of the most atmospheric (and most photographed) public spaces on the planet. The key lesson the designers of Dundas Square took from the tried-and-true European model was that the most successful public spaces often had no preordained purpose. They just *were*. I remember hearing quite a bit of griping about the austere, character-less nature of the square when it was first unveiled in the fall of 2002, but the first time I visited it for an event specifically planned to occur there the following March, I needed no further proof of its success. It had been designated as the starting point for the Toronto instalment of one of the largest anti-war protests in human history, and it proved perfectly suited to the task. It was exactly the kind of event, unfortunately, that would likely be prohibited from Belmar's piazza.

I later put this question to Steve Burkholder, asking him whether he saw any dissonance between the private piazza and the Jacobsian ideal of a successful urban space being one that encouraged spontaneity. "It's not gonna become Hyde Park by any means," he conceded. "But at the same time, Continuum wants that dynamic interplay of ideas and such, so you notice we do have bulletin boards over there. They're electronic, but at the same time, people can post certain things." Pending approval by the private landowner, presumably, though Burkholder didn't mention it.

Anyway, I didn't want to dwell too long on—or in—Belmar's carefully orchestrated piazza, and Hayner had more to show me, so off we marched. We headed east, down a laneway next to the movie theatre toward the well-hidden multistorey parking garage. New Urbanist ideals aside, suburban life is propelled by automobiles, so there was no getting around building the garage. Still, Continuum had done its best to gussy up the little walkway, putting in ivy-draped trellises and decorating the facing wall with pond-themed appliqués. The space rang with piped-in bird calls. "We call this Lilypad Lane," Hayner explained, "which is our attempt to make the walk between the parking garage and the theatre and main street, if you will, kind of an interesting and pleasant one."

We skirted the southern edge of the garage and emerged on a tidy residential street. On the near side stood a series of small storefronts built into the ground floor of the parking garage. The storefronts were spartan concrete cubicles rented out at around $100 a month or so as artists' studios. Hayner led me into one of the studios farther down the block and introduced me to its occupant—a thirty-something dude named Adam Lerner, Belmar's in-house curator of the fine arts. If you wanted to slap a face on the front of a brochure to convey in an instant the idea that this was not your father's suburban wasteland, Lerner's would surely do: his eyes were playful behind sleek square-framed glasses, his mouth encircled by a goatee and quick with a knowing grin. He was pure downtown cool, from the cuffs of his stylish jeans to the top of his shaven head. He had a laptop full of strange performance videos on his desk and Warhol and Pollock prints on the walls. Hayner confessed to being ill-equipped to properly introduce him. "Every time people ask me to explain what the Lab is," he said, "I can't do it justice." Hayner took his leave shortly thereafter, zooming off on a sleek silver Harley and leaving Lerner to explain the nature of his Lab.

"It's part museum, part think tank and part public forum," Lerner told me. "Holy mackerel," he finished, gently self-mocking. By which he meant the Lab was Belmar's contemporary art centre, the lead actor in its audacious effort to put the ex-mall on the national or even international map of the rarefied world of avant-garde art. The serendipitous route by which Lerner had come to pilot that plan marked a sharp turn back into the Jane Jacobs terrain of happy accidents and unexpected consequences.

Continuum's initial plan, Lerner explained, was to form a small-scale partnership with the esteemed downtown Denver Art Museum. To that end, Mark Falcone and the firm's director of marketing, Eliza Prall, paid a visit to the museum to suggest that a space be created at Belmar to house a rotating exhibit of a few of the museum's works, something modest like that. Instead, they got an earful from the developer of new programming at the museum. "The kind of programming that I specialized in as a curator," Lerner told me, "was programming that aimed to connect advanced practices in art—sort of international cutting-edge art exhibitions—to broad audiences." But since an ongoing architectural overhaul of the museum had proven far too all-encompassing to free up any resources for Lerner to work with, he leapt like a rabid bulldog at the tiny bone Continuum had thrown him. He put together a big presentation and went down to the Continuum office—while Falcone was away, alas—to explain why you just *couldn't* have a sustainable cultural institution in a forward-thinking New Urbanist showpiece without a much more ambitious contemporary art program of the sort that Lerner happened to specialize in.

Lerner's spiel went something like this: "If you attract national attention to what you're doing, then it's possible to have much more long-term stability. You're building greater intellectual equity with this institution. And when people around the nation believe in this centre, what it's doing, well then, that makes it more sustainable. Because people want to support it and want to believe in it and want to make it happen because there's all these people around who have an expectation of its continued existence. So that dovetails perfectly with the interests of Belmar, because Continuum's interests with Belmar are to create all the external context for the commercial entities to make sure they're sustainable over time. Right? So, as one commercial entity lives its lifespan, people will be encouraged to reinvest because there are all these external things: there's a really great streetscape, there's architecture, there's great parks, there's civic life, there's community. And part of that mix is having a public institution, having an art centre." His pitch proved sufficiently convincing that Prall and the other partners bought in despite Falcone's absence.

The Lab was established soon after—officially as the Laboratory of Art and Ideas—with Lerner as its director and curator. He hired a small staff, and plans were launched to locate a permanent exhibition space. In the meantime, Lerner assembled the funkiest, most playful, most *inviting* arts and culture program suburbia had ever seen. There was a lecture series called "Mixed Taste," in which two lecturers gave talks on utterly unrelated topics, first alone and then in tandem, at which point they were obliged to hunt for connections between, for example, cowboy yodelling and Michel Foucault, or Dada and monster movies. Another series, called "Art Fitness Training," was a four-part workshop that promised, on an oversized postcard done up like a breathless vaudeville poster, "to give all audiences the ability to appreciate even the MOST DIFFICULT *contemporary art!!*" Still another recurring event, this one music-themed, had brought to Belmar the music of Bjork as performed by a barbershop quartet and the selected works of Philip Glass performed by untrained amateurs clanging glassware. Discount admissions were offered not to students and seniors but "arbitrarily only on an ad hoc basis." At one event, Virgos and notaries public got in free. At another, anyone who could beat a bodybuilder in a thumb-wrestling match was admitted gratis. This, Lerner said, was the necessary "spoonful of sugar" to slide the unfamiliar fine-art medicine down suburbia's throat. "It's just a way of creating a moment of absurdity to deflate all the pretensions associated with high culture. I mean, we basically use humour, spectacle, arbitrariness and irony as techniques to just deflate the pretensions of culture. While still providing a really high level of cultural content."

If Belmar was a card game, I'm not sure if the Lab would trump the privatized piazza or if they'd just cancel each other out, but at any rate I left my meeting with Lerner with a much broader perspective on the potential for sustainable suburban living. A few months later, the Lab moved into its permanent space, somewhat ignominiously located across from a Dick's Sporting Goods outlet ("We're not Dick's," the directions on the Lab's website helpfully note). Its first exhibition was a multi-screen cinematic production called *Fantôme Afrique* by the British multimedia artist Isaac Julien. The Lab had co-commissioned the piece in partnership with Lisbon's Ellipse Foundation and the Centre Pompidou in Paris.

So then: on the site of a former shopping mall, across the street from a chain sporting goods emporium, deep in the suburbs of sprawling decentralized Denver, a co-production of Paris's most prestigious modern art museum had its North American debut. This is worth bearing in mind as you listen to Mark Falcone get all high-minded about what's being achieved in Belmar: "There's lots of choices and decisions that we make every day here that don't necessarily immediately translate into higher revenue or more profitability. And, in fact, it might be the other way around. But we know that they are all in pursuit of this bigger purpose, this bigger mission that we're trying to fulfill. I mean, we believe that there is a logical transformation that's gotta happen with the way we build the human habitat. And we believe that our role is to help accelerate that. And so we make choices all the time that don't necessarily contribute to any kind of an immediate increase in financial performance. Now, they're also not choices that put the project at risk unnecessarily. That's the key to the future. I think that the business enterprises that are going to allow the North American economy to be relevant, you know, fifteen years from now are going to be those business enterprises that have devoted themselves to providing services that enhance the quality of people's lives in a very holistic way."

Falcone also argues that there is greater value created, even from a corporate point of view, by taking this approach. Case in point: Continuum won the contract to redevelop Denver's landmark Union Station and environs—probably the most valuable patch of real estate in the city—on the strength of its track record. "We've earned a public trust in this part of the country that gives us access to enormously valuable pieces of land. And we have an enormous competitive advantage now as a consequence of that."

I feel obliged to mention here that New Urbanism has its critics, that they have legitimate points to make, that it is far from a done deal or a universal fix. It has produced some awkwardly theme-parkish developments. (Belmar's Lilypad Lane, with its stereo-amplified bird song, is a local case in point.) It came off in its early years as a little too pat, a bit on the one-size-fits-all side. To address this, Duany and Emily Talen issued a second iteration of the design philosophy called "transect planning," which conceives of the city as a continuum ranging from purely rural to purely urban in six "eco-zones" and acknowledges the different and sometimes divergent needs of each zone along that continuum. And New Urbanism has never directly confronted anthropogenic climate change. Though many of its precepts encourage energy-efficient design—transit instead of cars, walking over driving, smaller lots and smaller homes than the sprawling average, all the innate advantages of mixed use— New Urbanism doesn't specifically address, for example, how to light and heat those homes.

This duly noted, the movement's most dynamic role in the construction of sustainable societies might be simply that it inspired a former strip mall developer to say something like this: "Just because somebody wants a single-family detached home with a backyard and a place to store their two cars doesn't mean that they actually also want a soulless, homogeneous neighbourhood to live in that detaches them completely from all other aspects of their daily living needs. It doesn't mean that people, just because they want that single-family dwelling unit, also want thick traffic congestion and all of the other collateral consequences that came with providing that. And so our fundamental business proposition is that the more completely you solve a human need, the more richly you will be rewarded as a business enterprise."

Or let me put it this way: Belmar—flawed, over-privatized Belmar—changed the way I looked at suburbia. Once I'd seen it, every shopping centre and big-box plaza I saw looked like a city centre waiting to be born. I would notice the gaping holes between split-levels, the empty expanses between this subdivision and that one, and I would sort of daydream that all the missing elements of a sustainable community were growing there like weeds in a vacant lot. It was wish fulfillment, or fantasy, or maybe just the right kind of lens. The kind that lets you see all that hope lurking in the spaces in between.

Look long enough, and even the low, flat roof of a shopping mall starts to look like a garden waiting to bloom.

WAY DOWNTOWN, PURE GREEN

In one of the last essays she wrote before her death, Jane Jacobs—"Godmother of the American City," as one obituary headline put it—took to the pages of the *New York Times Magazine* to celebrate the arrival of a new kind of green space in the inner city. She observed the lovely new green roofs of Vancouver's courthouse and public library—carpets of vegetation in spaces heretofore bereft of life—and wondered if the salvation of the metropolis, or maybe even of humanity itself, might be found in their grasses and flowers. The essay's final paragraph read:

> In the age of the great plantation, it was widely supposed that cities and their people were unproductive parasites, idly battening on wealth created by rural and wild places. Many a smidgen of rural pasture, minus the grazing sheep, horses, mules, cattle or swine, has been inserted into cities with the deliberate intention of combating urban decadence. But this is a misunderstanding of social life and of nature alike. Indeed, in its need for variety and acceptance of randomness, a flourishing natural ecosystem is more like a city than like a plantation. Perhaps it will be the city that reawakens our

understanding and appreciation of nature, in all its teeming, unpredictable complexity.

The green roof, according to one version of its history, is a phenomenon as ancient and sacred as the Hanging Gardens of Babylon. The modern version, at any rate, first began to proliferate in Germany in the late 1980s. Fully 350 million square feet of German rooftop was crowned in green from 1989 to 1999 alone, and by one recent estimate, about 10 percent of all the roofs in Germany are now covered in vegetation. The plants on green roofs, like all photosynthesizing flora, inhale carbon dioxide and respire oxygen. They also reduce the amount of heat absorbed by the buildings below them on hot days and reduce the amount of heat lost on cold ones. They clean the water that falls on them and the air that surrounds them, provide habitat for birds and pleasant leisure environments for people.

There is probably no more universally applicable and easily installed feature yet devised for the many underused spaces in the modern metropolis. The green roof is a simple, elegant sustainable design strategy that brings useful life to formerly dead space with no real downside. Early versions might have been hard to keep alive and growing, but the kinks in the design have been all but completely sorted. So it's little wonder that the green roof has become one of the most widely adopted features in the burgeoning field of sustainable architecture. It's *de rigueur*, for example, in the work of cradle-to-cradle design guru William McDonough, who carpeted the roof of Ford's historic River Rouge factory in living green. The City of Chicago launched its multivalent effort to become America's greenest metropolis with a Green Roof Initiative that saw one installed on City Hall and another, purportedly the world's largest, atop the massive underground parking garage at Millennium Park. On my travels, I spied rooftop foliage atop apartment blocks in Freiburg, Germany, single-family houses in northern Scotland and office complexes in southern India. Robert Fox's LEED Platinum New York skyscraper will be green-roofed, and I just caught a PBS program the other night detailing the rapid spread of green roofs in urban China. The pollination, if you will, has been rapid, fertile and widespread.

For all their admirable aesthetic and ecological qualities, there is one thing that the vast majority of these green roofs are not: crops.

In very few cases is anything planted to be eaten. The roof of the historic Royal York Hotel in downtown Toronto is a notable exception: its green roof supplies fresh herbs to the hotel's luxurious restaurant. It has *yield.* In general, though, the idea that the modern metropolis could be a critical source of our daily bread isn't given much thought. Perhaps that's why a curious agricultural story from the heart of the most notorious slum in Los Angeles attracted so much attention. I mean, who would have imagined that you could plant a full-blown *farm* in South Central? And yet for fourteen years, starting in 1992, a 14-acre vacant lot in South Central L.A. provided the majority of the sustenance for about 350 impoverished families. Derelict land in the most neglected neighbourhood in one of America's least sustainable cities became *agriculture.*

For anyone who wasn't already a fan of hip-hop music, South Central L.A. first rose to global prominence as the epicentre of the 1992 riots that erupted in the wake of the Rodney King trial. Surprisingly, those same riots also gave birth to South Central Farm. In the aftermath of the devastation, the L.A. Regional Food Bank was granted permission by the city to open up a long-abandoned piece of municipally owned land in South Central to subsistence farming. It quickly became a verdant checkerboard of 20-by-30-foot plots. The farmers were primarily recent immigrants from Mexico and Guatemala who had grown up in agrarian communities. They cultivated lettuce, pumpkins and heirloom corn, planted trees that bore guava, tamarind, avocados and walnuts. "The things we grow here are the best things we eat," one twenty-year-old farmer told the *New York Times.*

Unfortunately, the land yielding this bounty had a checkered past that started to resurface shortly after the farm was founded. It had belonged to a developer named Ralph Horowitz, who passed it on to the city in the mid-1980s for $4.7 million in compensation after it was claimed under eminent domain. Horowitz, however, retained the right to purchase the land back should the city ever decide to sell it. He tried to do just that in 1995, and in 2002 he sued the city for failure to complete the sale. In August 2003, L.A. City Council approved the land's return to Horowitz for $5 million. He spent the next two years fighting in court to evict the farmers. In early 2006, with eviction imminent, the farmers and their supporters—including a handful of famous faces—undertook a constant occupation of the land in shifts.

The bodily removal of actress Daryl Hannah from one of its trees in June marked the peak of South Central Farm's short stint as a *cause célèbre* and sounded its death knell. By December 2006, the farms were ploughed under, and *L.A. City Beat* was reporting that the site had again "fallen into squalor."

There's a self-evident local tragedy in South Central Farm's short life, but it also revealed a latent potential in the modern metropolis, an inspirational force freighted with global import. It points the way forward, demonstrates the next step beyond the green roof: the city as farm, the spaces in between turned not just green but productive in the most basic sense. It might seem preposterous if it weren't already an everyday reality worldwide. For a short time, the South Central farmers joined ranks with the citizens of Addis Ababa, Ethiopia (who supply 79 percent of the city's milk), and Hanoi, Vietnam (who raise half its meat). There are an estimated 2.7 million urban farmers in Shanghai, 600,000 in Beijing. Indeed, the U.N. Food and Agriculture Organization estimates that two-thirds of the residents of the developing world's metropolises are engaged in some form of agriculture; so are the tenders of 8,000 small plots in Montreal and 80,000 in Berlin. I've seen artists' conceptions of high-rise greenhouses rising into the sky like office spires. The city, long maligned as the antithesis of environmental health, might prove Jane Jacobs right after all: it has ample room to birth an agrarian revolution.

It's an idea that arrives just in time. Because the modern business of agriculture, like the majority of economic activity as currently practised, is a rapidly unravelling, unsustainable disaster.

2

THE INFRASTRUCTURE OF HOPE

SEVEN

THE GREEN BOOM

[the economics of sustainability]

PRODUCE

I first heard about the South Central Farm from a farmer who tended land about as far away from South Central as you could get and still be in the continental United States. Geographically, the land was on the other side of the country, in the Blue Ridge Mountains of North Carolina. In terms of landscape, it was even farther away from derelict L.A.—a pastoral scene, a verdant patch of deep green tucked into the steep-sloped curves of a narrow valley. Despite this idyllic setting, Tom Philpott was a highly improbable agrarian. Until 2004, he had been a business journalist, the author of a column on high finance for Reuters, and a resident of New York City. He'd long been an avid gourmet, and he certainly knew quality produce once it hit a greengrocer's shelf or an elegant restaurant's artfully arranged plate. He'd also tended a community garden in Brooklyn and spent three months working on an organic farm in Italy. Still, chucking the young-urban-professional life in his mid-thirties to take up a farmer's hoe had entailed such an enormous leap into the unknown that it was easy to see it as a sort of bellwether of a much broader redirection of a society's priorities.

Here he was, for example, in the muted light of a cool morning in early spring, a pair of scissors in one hand and a plastic bowl in the other, leading me along a trickling Blue Ridge creek behind his cozy farmhouse toward a flat parcel of land carpeted in dark green. He bent and started snipping off leaves seemingly at random. Because Philpott and his fellow growers practise organic, no-till farming, many of their crops aren't arranged in ruler-straight rows separated by bare soil, so it took me a minute to realize he was harvesting tender baby spinach. He'd armed me with my own scissors, so I knelt down and did my best to find a leaf or two to add to his bowl. Philpott turned his attention to a plant with long, thin leaves in an adjacent plot. After a moment, I recognized it as arugula. There was a third spring green nearby, a fourth—exotic stuff was bursting from the fertile soil faster than Philpott could identify it all—and we clipped some of these as well and piled them into his bowl.

On the way back to the farmhouse, we stopped at a narrow plateau where the creek pooled slightly. Philpott reached in and plucked out a few of the weedy plants that protruded from the puddle. Watercress, he explained. Looking down at the delicate fronds, I realized that I'd been entirely ignorant until that moment of the ways and means of the cultivation of watercress, what it looked like as a living plant, why it was called, you know, *water*cress. It occurred to me that I was equally oblivious of the origins of maybe half of what I brought home from the grocery store on any given trip—I know what a banana tree looks like, but I'm pretty sure I couldn't readily identify a potato plant—and that I was no different from the overwhelming majority of the industrialized world's consumers in this regard. I asked Philpott what it took to grow watercress. Maybe the biggest no-brainer on the whole farm, he replied. Just scatter some seeds wherever the water pooled. Nothing to it.

I followed him back to his kitchen, where he set about making us lunch and explaining how he'd come to take up the farming life. Like much of the arable land in the area, Philpott explained, this small piece of property was once a tobacco plantation. The farm's mailing address placed it in a "rural historic district" called Valle Crucis, but a sign as you turned off the back highway onto the rutted country road identified it as Old Mans Hollow. This was just a bit farther up in the mountains from the stretch of Route 421 named for Junior Johnson, and it had probably been moonshine country once upon a time.

In the late 1960s, just as the tobacco industry was about to begin its long, steady decline, the land fell into the hands of a back-to-the-land hippie, who planted it with a wide range of exotic greens—New Age cash crops that he sold to the growing number of upscale restaurants that were popping up throughout the valleys and hollows of the Blue Ridge Mountains to cater to the burgeoning tourist trade. The back-to-the-lander was Bill Wilson, the father of Philpott's partner, Brooke, and he ran the place under the name of Springhouse Farm for the next thirty years. After the 2003 season, Bill decided to retire from professional farming and leave the valley, and before they'd had time to really think it through—"like an accident," Philpott told me, "it happened so fast"—he and Brooke and another New York couple decided to take over the farm.

This cosmopolitan crew moved to Old Mans Hollow in the spring of 2004. They were joined by Brooke's younger sister, Hillary, who'd worked on the farm with their father for a few years and was studying sustainable agriculture at nearby Appalachian State University and thus amounted to the resident expert. After a single-season apprenticeship in organic agriculture, the neophyte farmers rechristened the place Maverick Farms and prepared for its commercial rebirth.

By the time of my visit, matte-finish appliances of recent vintage adorned the Maverick kitchen, and modern art shared wall space with a pair of portraits of ancient agrarians in stoic repose in the living room. And in the middle of it, tying together this dichotomous *mise en scène,* stood Philpott: his fair hair shaved down to stubble, revealing the beginnings of a widow's peak, his angular face framed by boho sideburns, his voice still bearing traces of the staccato Manhattanite he recently had been and the drawling Texan he was born. He'd learned to call his new backwoods home a "holler," and he kept a sustainable-agriculture blog that was obsessed just then with the infiltration of the chemical giant Monsanto into the organic seed business. He was busy at the stove tossing together an *aglio e olio con verdura,* and then Hillary showed up with a parcel from a seed company, and he tore into that like a kid at a 4-H meeting. An urban hipster in rubber boots, a Blue Ridge gourmet pioneer, the mythic postmodern pastiche farmer of the Sustainable Republic (just maybe)—he tested the *al-dente-*tude of his pasta and then told me how Maverick Farms made its debut in the spring of 2005.

Back in New York, the Maverick farmers had participated in a somewhat newfangled small-farm enterprise called a CSA—community-supported agriculture. The CSA concept's origins are a little murky, but it appears to have emerged more or less simultaneously in Japan and western Europe in the 1960s. The Europeans, particularly Germans and Swiss, were inspired by the radical economic and agronomic theories of Rudolf Steiner (whose ideas also birthed the Waldorf school system). In Japan, CSA began with a grassroots movement of women concerned about pesticides. At any rate, this new agricultural system migrated to America in the mid-1980s, where it acquired the CSA designation and a mostly standardized structure, wherein a small farm sells a season's worth of produce in advance to a handful of customers (variously referred to as "subscribers" or "shareholders"). At regular (usually weekly) intervals, the CSA's subscribers either come to pick up or have delivered to them a box of whatever is ripe just then on the farm. By securing a guaranteed market in advance, the CSA farm can invest in the year's necessities without going into debt. The subscribers, for their part, get first-rate, organically grown produce at a reasonable price, while assuming a share of the farm's risk. (If a CSA's crop fails, there is no refund; it amounts to a kind of communal corporation.) The subscriber bases range in size from a couple of dozen to a mammoth 2,600-member CSA in New Jersey by the name of Watershed Organic Farm. At some CSAs, subscribers have the option of working a few hours a week on the farm to reduce the subscription cost; at others, the weekly pickups have turned into lively potluck parties.

The CSA movement is one of the few rays of hopeful light in the darkening sky of small farming in America, where an estimated 185,000 farms have gone out of business in the past thirty years. Since the emergence of the first "official" American CSA, circa 1985, the idea has spawned a widespread and fertile cottage industry. By the time of Maverick's debut, there were more than 1,200 CSAs nationwide, with 150 new ones opening each year.

Maverick Farms began with both modesty and overambition. They were cautious enough to sign up only eleven subscribers for their first season, but they also inaugurated a series of elaborate "farm dinners" to introduce themselves to the local community. Philpott, the former journalist, proved *too* good at crafting a press release—one local paper ran it verbatim, the other sent out a reporter to follow up—and the modest dinner party turned into five courses for several dozen paying customers. The neophytes displayed an urbane lack of reserve when it came to planting their first season's crops as well. "We were like, 'Let's do everything!'" Philpott told me. "And the feedback that we got from people was, 'Just give us more staple-ish kind of stuff.' So there's still some weird stuff in there, but mostly we're trying to do staples. But, you know, there's so many great varieties of stuff like chard."

We were tucking into our lunch by this point, and the first bite of his sublime pasta made most of the case for why a CSA was a better deal than a supermarket. Philpott had done little more than sauté the greens in olive oil and garlic, but they yielded a depth of flavour far beyond your usual polywrapped bag of spring mix. The arugula and the other arugula-like thing we'd picked lent an utterly distinctive nutty taste, and the spinach gave it a sweet balance. Had I been closer to home, I'd have driven off with a trunkful of Maverick's greens at whatever price they asked.

As it turned out, I was sampling the first delectable produce of a bumper micro-crop. Maverick's 2006 season—now with twenty-five subscribers, several farm dinners, a trio of interns from Appalachian State, a stall at the farmers' market in the nearest town, and partnerships with several other independent organic producers in the region—was a roaring success, a 10,000-pound harvest. And there are good reasons—far beyond matters of taste—to hope that the curious rebirth of a single Blue Ridge farm is the start of something much broader. Locally, Maverick represented the first new development anyone had seen in years up Old Mans Hollow way that didn't involve the ploughing under of mature soil to make way for vacation condos. But there is also a much deeper and multiheaded force to which Maverick provides one small counterweight, a great unsustainable beast hinted at in Philpott's blog postings about Monsanto and made much more explicit in a book he recommended to me as I was leaving: *The Omnivore's Dilemma* by Michael Pollan.

Pollan's subject is ostensibly the food Americans eat—the country's produce, which as Pollan notes is the very root of the word *production* and the most basic of market commodities—but his reporting calls into question the bedrock assumptions of our entire economic order. His revelation of the insanity driving America's industrial-scale agribusiness is particularly thorough and damning. This is ultimately the story of the triumph of a single crop: corn. Seen at the molecular level, where the kinds of food we eat leave their indelible signature, "North Americans"—as one biologist told Pollan—"look like corn chips with legs." Corn and its vast range of byproducts can be found in fully one-quarter of the foodstuffs on sale at the average supermarket. Meanwhile, 60 percent of the corn grown in the United States goes to feeding livestock, which in turn need to be pumped full of antibiotics to make it to slaughter weight on this alien diet. The corn-based food economy is underwritten by up to $5 billion per year in subsidies; the average bushel of Iowa-grown industrial corn costs $2.50 to produce but sells wholesale for only $1.45, with government handouts making up the difference in order to keep the price artificially low for the handful of megacorporations that manufacture most of America's processed food. And this twisted food chain is fuelled by a vast array of fossil fuel derivatives: petrochemical pesticides, gasoline in the engines of tractors and long-haul trucks, 50 gallons of crude oil consumed for every acre of corn produced. The result is a grotesque overabundance of cheap, overprocessed food, oversweetened with high-fructose corn syrup, that all but bankrupts its producers, ruins the landscapes in which it is produced and wrecks the health of its consumers.

In response to this lunacy, Pollan went looking for alternatives. One of the most compelling is Polyface Farm in Virginia, a small "beyond organic" operation that, in Pollan's telling, appears to be the most sustainable commercial farm in America. Polyface offers up gourmet-calibre meats and vegetables, and so deeply dedicated is its steadfast proprietor, Joel Salatin, to his principles that he won't ship his produce beyond a half-day's drive of the farm. Polyface certainly sounds like the ultimate goal, the model to which the business of food production should aspire. (In fact, it sounds like a near-perfect embodiment of William McDonough's cradle-to-cradle concept—the profit-making farm as *regenerative* enterprise, vastly improving the ecosystem in which it is located.) Alas, in the absence of a million clones of the indefatigable Salatin or a socioeconomic collapse so total it obliges us to farm that way, it's hard to imagine this goal being reached in a single step (or even a baker's dozen).

It was just such a wholesale economic failure that inspired the industrialized world's only major experiment to date with a radical revolution in sustainable agriculture. It happened in Cuba, during those chaotic years after the collapse of the Soviet Union that the Cuban government refers to as "the Special Period." In a 2005 report in *Harper's Magazine* on the aftermath of those tumultuous years, the environmental journalist Bill McKibben described it more evocatively as "the point in Cuban history where everything came undone." The Cuban economic system had been wholly dependent on the artificially high prices the Soviets paid for its export crops—sugar, in particular—the proceeds from which Cuba used to buy bargain-priced Soviet wheat, rice and machinery. With the Soviet Union's dissolution and the United States intensifying its trade embargo, the Cuban economy went into freefall. The agricultural sector, reliant on cheap Soviet fossil fuels for everything from the gas in its tractors to the pesticides coating its crops, was hit particularly hard; the United Nations estimated that the average Cuban's caloric intake fell from 3,000 per day in 1989 to 900 in 1993.

But Cuba, in part because it was a single-party police state, reorganized quickly, transforming its food production in just a decade into a world leader in organic, small-scale, post-carbon farming. Somewhere between half and two-thirds of Havana's food is now farmed inside its city limits, and 60 percent of the country's agricultural output, aside from sugar, is organically grown. As tractors were abandoned for oxen and ploughs, the ranks of Cuban blacksmiths swelled fivefold, and there were booms in veterinary medicine and yoke manufacture. Cuba's universities now buzz, McKibben reported, with the study of strange fungi and bacteria to combat pests and disease. Not only did Cuba survive the Special Period and learn anew how to feed itself, it now stands on better footing than almost any other nation to continue to do so in the oil-starved Anthropocene Era.

The Cuban revolutionary hero Che Guevara once called for "one, two, many Vietnams"—as many conflagrations as it took to bog down the machinery of industrial capitalism completely—but without the singular circumstances of embargoed post-Soviet Cuba, the prospects for one, two, many Special Periods seem slim. (And the citizens of functioning liberal democracies would quite rightly never willingly choose to endure such hardship.) Instead, we remain trapped in the jaws of Pollan's *Omnivore's Dilemma*—still free, that is, to eat whatever we like, giving not even a hiccup's worth of thought to how it's produced. The most immediately viable option Pollan uncovered to supplant the corn-fattened and oil-fuelled status quo was the one he dubbed "industrial organic." By this, he meant the single greatest success story in the contemporary grocery business, the buzzword-driven $11-billion boom that now amounts to "the fastest-growing sector of the food economy." Modern-day organic agriculture started from some of the same ecological principles Joel Salatin holds dear, and many of its pioneers were members of the same generation of back-to-the-land agrarians as the hippie farmer who first planted those excellent greens at Maverick Farms. But the rapid shift of organically grown food from counterculture fringe to supermarket mainstream has come only through significant compromise, creating a gap between the nature of officially "organic" and truly sustainable agriculture that now yawns so wide it verges on unbridgeable.

It's illustrated quite succinctly, actually, by the distance (literal and figurative) between the hand-picked spring greens that sent me swooning at Maverick Farms and the "spring mix" I can buy in the factory-sealed plastic tub with the Earthbound Farms logo printed on it at my local Safeway. Spring mix was one of the first and most successful mass-market organic products, and Earthbound was its commercial progenitor. Earthbound's origins hew extremely close to Maverick's: it started as a few rented acres in central California, cultivated by a Manhattan-raised couple gone back to the land in the early 1980s. They started selling their hearty lettuces to a local restaurant's gourmet chef, and when he moved away they bagged the stuff to sell to local grocery stores. Costco placed its first order for Earthbound Farms spring mix in 1993, and the rest is right out of a Horatio Alger plot: the Earthbound brand, which accounts for 80 percent of the organic lettuce sold in the United States, now draws its produce from 25,000 acres of industrially farmed California soil, and the spring mix product it more or less invented has become as much a staple of the modern supermarket as bland old iceberg lettuce and the flavourless winter tomato.

There remains much to be praised about Earthbound Farms and the industrial organic model it pioneered. Its crops are less vulnerable to pests and diseases than those grown by conventional industrial means, and its cultivation doesn't pollute the water table with toxic petrochemical pesticides. Earthbound even offers health and retirement benefits to its workers. Industrial organic producers have made huge compromises, but they aren't entirely *compromised*—they still represent the best industrial-scale agricultural option on the free market. Combine the increasingly well-stocked organic aisles of all those Wal-Marts and Safeways with the burgeoning brigades of CSAs, local farmers' markets and community gardens in a Western world increasingly anxious about its food supply, and it amounts to the vanguard, perhaps, of the kind of revolution in consumer consciousness necessary to start *seriously* rethinking the food we eat and the way it's grown.

There remain, however, some very tricky stats to wrestle with. Input-to-output ratios, for example. In Cuba after the Special Period, it takes 10 to 20 calories of mostly renewable energy to produce a calorie of food; a calorie of industrial organic lettuce, meanwhile, requires 60 calories of fossil fuels alone. As soon as it's snipped from the pesticide-free ground, that organic leafy green enters an industrial distribution system identical to the non-organic one. That is why I can buy a tub of Earthbound lettuce, more than 1,500 kilometres away from the soil in which it was farmed, on the frigid Canadian February day I write this, while Maverick's delectable arugula remains only a fond memory. Also, in a sense, why I'll always remember that Blue Ridge luncheon, whereas all I've ever remembered about out-of-season "spring" greens is the dressing they were tossed with. Food does not grow in 25,000-acre agglomerations or travel 1,500 kilometres to the dinner table without losing something of its essence. But as with so much of what makes a sustainable economy more robust, this ineffable gain can't be properly measured by existing tools. It describes something more rewarding to quality of life than to standard of living, a value added (or, rather, not subtracted) without regard to price or profit margin. Taste, vigour, indelible memory, joie de vivre—even great chunks of the carefully calibrated and minutely measured process by which light sweet crude becomes a cloud of smoke out a refrigerated transport truck's tailpipe—none of this is worth a thin penny to the gawdamighty GDP.

This is, in a sense, good news, because it means there are obvious ways to avoid catastrophic Special Periods of our own, though we need to rethink how we define economic health, and especially how we measure it. What we require, first of all, is a more sensitive gauge of what is valuable—and what isn't.

THE GDP FALLACY & THE AGE OF THE GIANTS

In the early morning of March 24, 1989, the oil tanker *Exxon Valdez* plowed into a reef in Prince William Sound off the coast of Alaska, resulting in the largest oil spill in American history and one of the worst and most widely publicized industrial disasters of its time. More than eleven million barrels of crude oil were sent splashing across the water. The vast oil slick killed marine mammals by the thousands, shorebirds by the hundreds of thousands, salmon roe by the billions. Images of doomed seabirds struggling vainly to free their wings from the thick black ooze blipped around the world and back again, becoming overnight a powerful symbol of the tragic downside of human industry; the very name of the ship became a shorthand for ecological catastrophe. The cleanup was extensive, public and costly, yet even today the sound's fragile ecosystem has not fully recovered. Oil remains trapped in the seabed's sediment, for example, where it is ingested by clams and mussels and then by the ducks and otters that feed on them, poisoning the entire food chain. By almost any measure, the *Valdez* spill was an unspeakable disaster.

By *almost* any measure. By the most widely used metric of a modern economy's health, however, the spill was a roaring success. According to one widely quoted estimate, it added at least $2 billion to the gross domestic product of the United States. It created jobs—more than ten thousand, it was said, at least in the short term—and it fed the cash registers of local businesses and employed the services of far-flung experts in the manufacture of oil dispersants, the operation of high-pressure hoses, the piloting of helicopters. Billion-dollar lawsuits were argued over by high-priced lawyers. Several years afterward, *The Economist* noted the fact of this "local boom," sagely explaining that it was "one of those instances where, because of the way countries measure GDP, a disaster appears to stimulate growth when all it really does is stimulate activity to limit the damage."

There is a name for the kind of lunatic accounting that assesses the *Valdez* disaster as a sign of success, and it is nearly as old as the dismal science itself. It's called the "Broken Window Fallacy," first delineated in an 1848 treatise by the French economist and essayist Frédéric Bastiat. In Bastiat's telling, there's this "solid citizen" named Jacques Bonhomme, a *francophonique* Joe Average whose "incorrigible son" smashes one of his windows. Some quick-witted passerby immediately notes that if it weren't for brats like Bonhomme's boy, there'd be no work for the glaziers, and doubtless the passing crowd murmurs its assent at this golden nugget of common sense.

Now, Bastiat was ready to concede to the pro-glazier lobby that the immediate benefit to the particular glazier who replaces Bonhomme's window is beyond debate. "*That,*" Bastiat emphatically declared, "*is what is seen.*" But what is seen, he expounded, is only half of the story: "if, by way of deduction, you conclude, as happens only too often, that it is good to break windows, that it helps to circulate money, that it results in encouraging industry in general, I am obliged to cry out: That will never do! Your theory stops at *what is seen.* It does not take account of *what is not seen.*" What is not seen, Bastiat argued, is that the six francs the honourable Bonhomme spends to replace the smashed window won't be spent to repair his shoes or buy another book or get a little smashed himself on the house plonk down at the *brasserie* that Friday night. Okay, so that last one is my example, but Bastiat's point is clear: "there is no benefit to *industry in general* or to *national employment* as a whole, whether windows are broken or not broken." There are ways to measure the impact of a broken window or an oil spill, in other words, but calculating the cost of fixing it and calling it a business opportunity isn't one of them.

Bastiat is hailed as one of the free market's most eloquent nineteenth-century champions, and his work influenced famed market economics guru Milton Friedman, among others. But somewhere along the way his condemnation of broken glass seems to have been swept under an overgrown rug. *Oh, baby, oh, how the world's business did grow,* to paraphrase another brilliant essayist by the name of Seuss. And so it came to pass, during those dark days of the Second World War, when Bastiat's native land was in fascist shackles, that the United States Bureau of Foreign and Domestic Commerce took to measuring its wartime industrial capacity by a simple, expedient linear arithmetic: the bean-counters tallied up all of America's income, no matter how it was made, factored in business taxes and capital depreciation, and called it Gross National Product (GNP). Fair enough,

I suppose: this was total war, and every bit of the nation's productive energy was surely aimed at the defeat of the Axis. If, say, you were spending a pile of dough to mend a bunch of ships shot up by a squadron of Japanese Zeroes, that was as useful to the war effort as building a whole new boat. After the war, GNP—or, more recently, its close relative GDP*—continued to be used as the ultimate economic bottom line, with nary a pause to consider whether a peacetime economy's progress might be better tracked by some measure other than the sheer volume of its cash transactions.

A half-century later, GDP growth has become the *sine qua non* of a healthy economy. Indeed, its calculation has become so closely linked to the measurement of progress that the two concepts are frequently treated as essentially synonymous. Hence the diligent tracking of GDP by such observers as, yes, *The Economist.* Sure, the magazine pointed out how, in that one case, the way countries measure GDP led to the obvious delusion of thinking a catastrophic oil spill was a useful thing, but in that same issue and every other, there are those couple of pages of charts and graphs at the back of the magazine where the important information is tabulated, and they inevitably begin with a list of GDP statistics for the world's primary economies. Because *that* is how we decide whether we're doing well or not—as economies, as nations, as a species.

It's the G that's the crux of the problem. G is for *gross,* which is not seen as an accurate measurement even of an individual business's health. No, to get to the real meat of even a purely money-making enterprise—its profit—you've got to calculate *net* revenue. You've got to subtract wrecked machinery and dumb investments and the compensation paid to the people whose livelihoods were ruined by your spilled oil, and only then do you know whether you've had a good year. And yet, at the macroeconomic level, the GDP fallacy persists in an endless rain of shattered glass, an ever-inflating sum of

---

* The main difference between the two measures is this: GNP measures all the revenue created by a nation's "factors of production" regardless of where that production occurs geographically, but doesn't count the revenue created by foreign-owned factors of production inside the nation in question; GDP does the opposite, counting all revenue within a country's borders regardless of who owns it but excluding all activity by its citizens outside those borders.

busted windows—*intentionally* busted windows, in some sense—that continue to be counted up as nothing but beneficial to the benevolent market economy.

So pervasive is the GDP fallacy, so central to the organization of the modern global economy, that its logic often drives the largest of its business entities as well. Energy companies, in particular. And, you know, 'twas ever thus, right? Actually, no. Walt Patterson, a fellow at Chatham House (an English think tank) and a prominent theorist and activist on energy issues since the dawn of the first OPEC crisis, told a curious story about the early days of electricity as part of a lecture he gave at the London Planetarium in June 2000. Thomas Edison's first electrical grid, Patterson explained, was a modest affair based entirely in lower Manhattan, a system that existed for the sole purpose of providing electric light, for which his customers paid a fixed rate per bulb. Edison owned and operated the power station, the wires, the fixtures—the works. But it wasn't long, Patterson continued, before there was "a critical change in the arrangements—the introduction of the electricity meter":

> From that time on, Edison, his contemporaries and their successors were no longer selling electric light; they were selling electricity, by the metered unit. The advent of the electricity meter had an additional consequence. If you are selling electric light, you want the whole system producing the light to be as efficient and cost-effective as possible. If, on the other hand, you are selling units of electricity as measured by an electricity meter, someone using less efficient lamps has to buy more electricity from you to get the same level of illumination. From the point of view of you, the seller, inefficiency on your customer's premises is good for your business. This perverse incentive has underpinned the electricity business for a century.

This is a textbook example of *what is not seen* and its destructive unintended consequences. A perverse incentive indeed: the standard electrical grid mired in perpetual inefficiency because its producers are *rewarded* for keeping it that way. It further benefits the producer—and *only* the producer—to centralize production and grow as huge as possible. It maximizes its efficiency (and only *its* efficiency) if it delivers coal or natural gas to one mammoth plant rather than a hundred small ones, if it builds one gargantuan dam instead of a thousand tiny ones. A full 25 percent of the price of electricity in the First World covers the cost of distribution over the vast snaking grids that spread out from these fat nodes, and more energy blows out the smokestacks of American power plants each year as waste heat than the sum total of Japan's annual energy demand in its entirety. And it all looks great to the mandarins counting the revenues, because all that extra cost and wasted power means that big inefficient electrical systems inflate GDP even better than a nightly window-smashing party.

Power generation is but one of the most glaring examples. The entire GDP-driven system has made a veritable religion out of growth for its own sake. There's no talk of human scale, only of scalability and "economies of scale" (a fancy way of saying *bigger is better, at least until we say otherwise*). "How my business did grow!" crows the Once-ler, nemesis of the Lorax and manufacturer of strange garments for fools in Dr. Seuss's whimsically tragic take on the unsustainability intrinsic to twentieth-century market capitalism. The Once-ler keeps biggering and biggering and biggering his Thneed business, ballooning his bottom line (and presumably fattening the GDP count at some Seussland general accounting office back in North Nitch). And what of the starved Bar-ba-loots with crummies in their tummies? The choking Swomee-Swans? The Humming-Fish with their gummed-up gills? Oh, baby, oh—what's that marvellous classical economist's catch-all? Ah yes: *externalities.*

Externalities: it's a punchline that David Suzuki has used a lot in his speeches and articles in recent years. Suzuki—a biologist by training and a TV star by trade—likes to tell the tale of how he'd found himself talking about economics so much in his work as Canada's most prominent environmental activist that he finally decided to go learn a bit about it. So he sat in on an introductory economics lecture at the University of British Columbia, where a professor expounded on the variables that had produced the overhead slide that charted GDP growth. Where on the list, Suzuki asked, were clean aquifers, healthy topsoil, the great living web of biodiversity that gives fishing boats something to catch and logging companies

something to cut down? The answer, of course: *externalities.*
"They've externalized the very sources that make economies possible," Suzuki inevitably concludes. Another of his standard lines goes like this: "Under our current economic system, you can never have enough and you can never have too much. In fact, our entire economy is predicated on continued, endless growth. Yet we live in a finite world, with finite resources and a limited amount of space to dump our wastes. Bit of a problem there."

But try telling that to the ever-biggering giants, the builders of global brands and long-tentacled electrical grids. Or to the technocrats overseeing the spectacular GDP growth of India, who persisted in the construction of the Sardar Sarovar Dam on the Narmada River in the northwestern state of Gujarat after years of protest and costly delays, even after $450 million in carefully counted World Bank loans was issued, gathered interest greater than that initial sum, and then was withdrawn. There they were in the first days of 2007, gleefully informing the press of the dam's impossibly biggered dimensions as the final buckets of concrete were poured to complete a wall 1,250 metres long and more than 100 metres high, a colossally scaled barrier bearing a price tag of $7.7 billion, the biggerest in a series of thirty dams that had been biggering India's GDP for thirty years and now majestically tied together 86,000 kilometres of canals, irrigated more than 4 million acres of farmland, would soon (it was alleged) churn out 1,450 megawatts of glorious electricity in a vastly biggered grid. (It was, to be sure, a stunning monument in its near-complete state: it appeared in press photos like a battlement built by a race of giants, the notched wall crowned by a vast assemblage of towering rebar pointed skyward like an overgrown army's spears.) And oh, baby, oh, how Gujarat's chief minister did crow. "India has taken a leap ahead," he declared. "The dam will change the future of the country."

That was beyond question. But not even the gloating chief minister deigned to speculate whether leaping ahead in such a fashion was good or bad for the people who had made their lives in the Narmada Valley, and there remained at least one sum that hadn't yet been calculated with any certainty. It was a particularly captivating externality, and its absence from all the ecstatic press releases sent Booker Prize–winning novelist Arundhati Roy first to her keyboard and later to the site of the dam itself to implore the state of Gujarat, the nation of her birth and the world in general to stop the completion of this gargantuan dam. "It's not hard to find out how many graduates India produced, or how many men had vasectomies in any given year," Roy wrote in a widely circulated, heartbreakingly futile 1999 essay. "But the Government of India does not have a figure for the number of people that have been displaced by dams or sacrificed in other ways at the altars of 'National Progress.' Isn't this *astounding?* How can you measure Progress if you don't know what it costs and who paid for it? How can the 'market' put a price on things—food, clothes, electricity, running water—when it doesn't take into account the real cost of production?" In 1979, when the dam's planning began, the Indian government estimated that the mammoth reservoir created by the Sardar Sarovar would displace 6,000 families. Its guess ticked steadily upward to 40,000 or so; Narmada Bachao Andolan, the most prominent of the activist groups opposed to the project, estimated at the time of the dam's inauguration that it would ultimately be more like 85,000, amounting to at least 320,000 people whose homes were destroyed by the project. They will all need new dwellings now, and every window on every new home will add a few rupees to India's upticking GDP.

In the meantime, Roy endorsed the limiting of damage, the tallying up of *what is not seen* and an attempt at compensation for the impact of *what is.* She figured it would be a struggle of a great many acts, none of them anywhere near the size of the magnificent Sardar Sarovar Dam. "We have to support our small heroes," she wrote. "We have to fight specific wars in specific ways. Who knows, perhaps that's what the twenty-first century has in store for us. The dismantling of the Big. Big bombs, big dams, big ideologies, big contradictions, big countries, big wars, big heroes, big mistakes. Perhaps it will be the Century of the Small."

THE WISDOM OF THE MIDDLE

It is often asked of a sustainable thing: Is it scalable? A wind farm or PV array, a vibrant neighbourhood or thriving farmers' market—is it scalable? It's comforting to a certain breed of contemporary mind, I guess, to think that it is somehow natural that all things expand to the inhuman scale of GDP-driven global capitalism, and that things that can't achieve such proportions are of no more worth than any other externality. What's being asked is whether a wind farm could be turned effectively into a coal-fired power plant or a farmers' market convinced to impersonate a chain of big-box grocery emporia. But the very problem sustainability presumes to address is a direct result of fossil-fuelled industrial society's unnatural scale. The better question would thus be: *Is it replicable?* The scalability question is irrelevant—it's not in the *nature* of many sustainable things to grow to that kind of size. Everything we've learned from a century's worth of the Big suggests that people's needs are often far better served by the Small.

This observation was eloquently translated into economic terms by E.F. Schumacher, whose 1973 book, *Small Is Beautiful: Economics as if People Mattered,* seemed for a time to provide a comprehensive solution to the wide array of ecological problems alluded to in Rachel Carson's *Silent Spring.* Schumacher's treatise sold in the millions, a great many of those books bought by the tuned-in, turned-on gang talking up radical change around then. It was an odd thing, really, this mild-mannered English economist becoming an intellectual hero to the counterculture. Schumacher was a statistician, a former chief adviser to Britain's National Coal Board, a half-lapsed Keynesian, and all of a sudden he was thrust into the role of international guru on the subject of Zen and the art of socioeconomic maintenance. It was tragic, too, because when the geodesic domes started springing leaks and the engines finally gave out on the VW microbuses, all those dog-eared copies of *Small Is Beautiful* were left behind to mould and rot, as though Schumacher was just too much of his time to keep on keepin' on. Which he wasn't. He was *ahead* of his time. The first great economic prophet, maybe, of the Anthropocene Era.

Decades before the full scope of the Anthropocene's problems was at all evident, Schumacher knew enough to recognize an unsustainable system when he saw it, and he reckoned that classical economics was a major source of its instability. "The modern industrial system," he wrote, "with all its intellectual sophistication, consumes the very basis on which it has been erected." The externalities, in other words, could not remain outside of our accounting forever without precipitating the collapse of the entire project. Moreover, the modern "economist-turned-econometrician," though he might be able to calculate GDP to the last penny, "would lose all his certainties if he even entertained such a question" as whether his calculations were "to be taken as a good thing or a bad thing. . . . The idea that there could be pathological growth, unhealthy growth, disruptive or destructive growth is to him a perverse idea which must not be allowed to surface." Which is why, I'd wager, we continue to hear from our most revered econometricians even today that the inescapable problems of anthropogenic climate change must somehow be "balanced" against growth, as if a healthy market economy were not wholly dependent, in anything but the immediate short term, on the health of the climate in which it functions. (Or, more perversely, as if the growth of an abstract measure were somehow more important than the survival of the people whose activity it enumerates.)

"Our most important task," Schumacher wrote, "is to get off our collision course." The first step in this process, he argued, was to "thoroughly understand the problem and begin to see the possibility of evolving a new life-style, with new methods of production and patterns of consumption: *a life-style designed for permanence.*" The emphasis is mine, added because it's the most succinct working definition of sustainability I've yet encountered.

The title of Schumacher's book only alluded to the nature of his solution. Schumacher was not a single-minded advocate of the Small, nor was he opposed to robust markets or international trade or any of the other unpalatable positions routinely ascribed to the heretics who dare to question the wisdom of growth at any cost. Schumacher *celebrated* the Small only to counter the out-of-control orgy of the Big he saw everywhere holding sway. And what he was *really* on about was the middle—or, more accurately, "the Middle Way," a concept he borrowed from the teachings of the Buddha.

Schumacher's survey of the topography of this middle ground is worth repeating in full:

> In the affairs of men there always appears to be a need for at
> least two things simultaneously, which, on the face of it, seem
> to be incompatible and to exclude one another. We always
> need both freedom and order. We need the freedom of lots
> and lots of small, autonomous units, and, at the same time,

the orderliness of large-scale, possibly global, unity and co-ordination. When it comes to action, we obviously need small units, because action is a highly personal affair, and one cannot be in touch with more than a very limited number of persons at any one time. But when it comes to the world of ideas, to principles or to ethics, to the indivisibility of peace and also of ecology, we need to recognize the unity of mankind and base our actions upon this recognition.

Schumacher imagined a "Buddhist economics" in which the "minimum means" possible—particularly those local means most readily available—would be employed toward any given end, with non-renewable ones used "only if they are indispensable, and then only with the greatest care." In his Buddhist-derived accounting, full employment would replace aimless growth as the baseline measure of success. He advocated "production by the masses" over mass production, with the provision of fulfilling work taking its place alongside the maximization of efficiency in the organizing principles of an individual economic unit.

If it all sounds overly optimistic—a little like the ramblings of a hippie, you might say—that's simply because Schumacher's clear-headed thinking has been badly mimicked by too many lesser minds who didn't quite grok the full import of his ideas. And also because his ideas swam so hard against the torrential current of their day. For some years after the publication of *Small Is Beautiful,* the wisdom of the Big seemed unassailable, and Schumacher came across in comparison like a well-meaning but ultimately unrealistic naïf. Even as copies of the book were flying off the shelves, industrial agriculture was inspiring revolutions in yield the world over, and massive multinational corporations were well on their way to acquiring the size and influence of nations. As the *Financial Times* columnist John W. Hunt wrote in 2002, the ideal economic unit was believed to be a huge company made up of "crystal clear and rational" components, the epitome of which was gargantuan IBM and its culture of "machine-like precision." But by 1993, Hunt further noted, IBM was posting annual losses in excess of $8 billion, and Schumacher's all-but-forgotten aphorisms finally found the beginnings of their moment. The corporate "downsizing" trend pioneered around then by IBM was much loathed for its ruthlessness by the sort of people who sympathized with Schumacher those many years before. Devastating as downsizing was, though, it was really just the beginning of the necessary return to human scale after so long spent in the thrall of the delusional cult of the Big.

Before long, conscious and unconscious Schumacher devotees began to pop up in the most surprising places. Richard Branson credits *Small Is Beautiful* for guiding the governance of his increasingly mammoth Virgin empire (he has always kept the individual business units small and distinct in deference to Schumacher, he explains); a 1995 *Times Literary Supplement* survey placed it alongside the works of Sartre and Jung in a ranking of the hundred most influential books since the Second World War; and a 2000 *Time* magazine list of the preceding century's heroes included Schumacher, noting that even the World Bank—the global figurehead of unbridled Bigness—had begun to see the wisdom of small-scale approaches. The emergence of the microcredit-peddling Grameen Bank as the new template for international development, and the subsequent awarding of the 2006 Nobel Peace Prize to its founder, Muhammad Yunus, provided further evidence of the proven economic wisdom of the Small.

All of this, however, was mere prologue. The main event—the earth-shaking demonstration of the revolutionary impact of the Schumacher model—is the coming of age of renewable energy, which is perfectly suited to his prescribed mix of small autonomous units overseen by large-scale organizational structures. There is room for industrial scale in the renewable-energy sector—the planet's windiest corridors, for example, places like the North Sea and the empty plains of west Texas, have already proven well-suited to giant-sized power plants. In general, however, renewable energy functions most effectively when the freedom of decentralized, small-scale power generation is coupled with global emissions agreements, forward-thinking national energy policy and internet-like webs of power distribution on whatever scale works best in each context. Small, big and mid-sized. The engine of a universal solution to climate change. It's been waiting in the pages of a dusty old bestseller for more than thirty years. And its time has arrived.

Almost anywhere I found sustainable life on my cartographic travels, I was looking at an homage to Schumacher. On a tiny island in a small country—Samsø in Denmark—I discovered a semi-autonomous small-scale post-carbon economy, partially tied to a national grid, aided and overseen by unobtrusive national and international policy. Samsø isn't scalable, but it *is* highly replicable. There is a Schumacher-like aspect to the hybrid car, and Germany's multitiered, overlapping transport system is a web woven from Middle Way threads. The homes built by Rolf Disch and Dr. Soontorn—any structure powered by renewable energy with a net-metering system in place that trades that power back and forth over a wider grid—are studies in the big / little balance Schumacher advocated. The Sustainable Age will be—dig it—*Schumacheresque.*

As far as economics is concerned, however, there's an even more powerfully disruptive concept hidden in the pages of *Small Is Beautiful:* nothing less than the first principle of a sustainable global market economy. "It is inherent in the methodology of economics," Schumacher wrote, "*to ignore man's dependence on the natural world.*" (Emphasis his this time.) For Schumacher, the problem begins on the first day of Economics 101. As every student dutifully learns, classical economics assigns an arbitrary value of zero to raw materials, labelling them "free goods." Only once a thing is put to productive use—mined, harvested, chopped down or burned, transformed from valueless nature into a commodity of some sort or other—does it enter into the purview of quantifiable economic activity. This, Schumacher argued, is lunacy, especially when the materials in question are ancient, formed over eons, non-renewable and thus irreplaceable. They should be understood instead as the very stuff of life, the only *truly* essential elements of economic activity. *Free* goods? Call them instead, he suggested, "natural capital."

Natural capital. Schumacher coined that particular phrase in 1973. There were a few—a very few—who thereafter dedicated their lives to it in one sense or another. Three of them conducted some experiments and tested some ideas, and then put it all together in a book called *Natural Capitalism,* published in 1999. And finally, in 2006, one of those three, Amory Lovins of the Rocky Mountain Institute, went to work for the largest purveyor of retail goods on the planet. Wal-Mart—the epitome of overgrown big-box Big business, China's eighth-largest trading partner all by itself—hired Lovins and his think tank to teach it how to make dozens of Schumacher-sized tweaks to its lighting and refrigeration, the trim of its trucks and the width of their tires. This was evidence, perhaps, of the dawn of the true Schumacheresque in the art of mainstream economics.

MAKING MONEY THE NATURAL CAPITALIST WAY

In recent years, physicist Amory B. Lovins has emerged as the figurehead, primary theorist and chief practitioner of natural capitalism. I've already discussed his work on several occasions, because there's really no talking about sustainability in our time without crossing his path again and again. It was pretty much inevitable that I would make a pilgrimage of my own to his Rocky Mountain Institute, and I did just that one sunny June morning, not long after it announced that it had taken on Wal-Mart as a client.

RMI's headquarters is half-embedded in the wall of a steep valley in Old Snowmass, a village just outside Aspen, Colorado. Built in the early 1980s, it's a low, elegant building with an undulating façade of glass and stone and a berm of piled earth covering its north-facing side. Lovins and his then-wife Hunter (RMI's co-founder) were intimately involved in every aspect of the design and construction. Its west wing was and remains Lovins's private residence, while the east wing houses the offices of part of the RMI staff, which has overgrown its original headquarters to occupy a larger office on the grounds of a nearby wildlife refuge formerly owned by John Denver. If the geography of hope is to some extent a map of the Schumacheresque, then RMI HQ is almost like its museum, a living diorama containing damn near every sustainable-living idea devised since the place first opened its doors twentysome years ago.

Lovins was away when I visited—off revolutionizing someone's energy efficiency, no doubt—so my tour guide was Cory Lowe, RMI's twentysomething outreach coordinator. Lowe's appearance and demeanour—of a college linebacker and the president of the campus entrepreneurs' club, respectively—were my first clues, if any were needed, that I'd arrived at a place as far from a handmade geodesic dome as you could get and still be on the front edge of eco-friendly design. Lovins, Lowe explained, likes to talk about "hot showers and cold beer." His philosophy is that sustainable living doesn't need to require any major material sacrifices (a *New Yorker* profile of Lovins bore the subtitle "Environmentalism's most optimistic guru"), and he has always eschewed lifestyle activism. Which, I suppose, is why the first feature Lowe pointed out was RMI's solar-heated hot tub.

We proceeded to the roof, where a head-spinning assortment of solar-energy technologies has been mounted, and then back down into the main building, where a head-spinning assortment of practically everything else under the sustainable sun resides. The front wall of the main office space consists primarily of a sloped bank of glazed double-paned windows with an ultra-sheer layer of polyester and a thin cloud of krypton gas between the glass, a hyper-efficient heat-trapping system that got its first commercial installation at RMI headquarters. Beneath the windows sits an expansive tropical garden and pond. The garden is embedded in thermally massive foundational materials; the whole set-up amounts to a less homespun version of the front façades of Mike Reynolds's Earthships, and serves many of the same purposes (particularly passive solar heating and cooling). The lights are fitted with several varieties of the most efficient bulbs in the free world and connected to a photo sensor that determines how much artificial light is needed and automatically dims the bulbs accordingly. The kitchen area that Lovins shares with his staff is tricked out with a refrigerator that uses 8 percent of the commercial norm and the world's most efficient model of dishwasher. It goes on and on like this, and there are no incidental details. The energy and water savings provided by the kitchen faucet apparatus warrant half a column in the visitors' guide.

It's to the credit of Lovins's showers-and-beer approach that RMI headquarters feels, for all of its exhaustive living-lab touches, both businesslike and homey. I don't know what your office is like, but RMI HQ beats the hell out of mine. And in its mix of old and new, homespun and next-generation high-tech and everything in between, it tells a semiotic version of Lovins's career, his steady arc from freaky fringe to Wal-Mart mainstream, tracing the same trajectory as the Schumacheresque sustainability concept itself.

At one point in the tour, Lowe and I were standing on the border between the greenhouse area and the main office space. Lowe was leaning on a filing cabinet, and he picked up an abstract sculpture lying there, an oblong, curving piece of some sort of black metal. This, it turned out, was neither metal nor really a sculpture: it was a sample piece of the carbon-fibre composite material developed at RMI, ultra-lightweight and super-strong. Lovins hoped to see it replacing the structural steel frames of automobiles one day, and a company called Fiberforge had been established to market the stuff. It was the kind of manufacturing material, I assume, that Lovins talks about when he meets with his clients at the Pentagon to discuss radically improving the efficiency of the U.S. military's immense fleet of motor vehicles. Lowe handed me the thing like it was about as remarkable as a stapler and turned his attention to the pond behind us, letting out a surprised grunt. He'd never seen both of the resident turtles out sunning at the same time before; in fact, he hadn't known there even *was* a second turtle.

There was a sort of utility room near the entrance wherein Lovins did his laundry and kept the wall-sized bank of nickel-iron batteries that stored the power from the solar panels on the roof. They were cumbersome old things, those batteries, and they were embossed with Chinese ideograms. Lovins had scavenged them from a decommissioned Chinese submarine back in RMI's early days. They stored the excess production of the three generations of rooftop PV panels, which themselves comprised a working exhibit on the evolution of solar power. And then, serving as a gentle, contrasting grace note, there was a pretty little stone fountain down in the garden. It had been included in the design as an "acoustical mask"—white noise to ensure that the office space didn't feel in any way eerily silent or tomblike. One day a good while after it was built, a Japanese visitor came through, and it just so happened that he was a professional waterfall tuner. He was aghast at the discordant notes being sounded by the falling water, and he rearranged the stones in the catchment area so that the fountain would sing its trickling song within the soothing alpha-wave frequency. The white-noise fountain now had perfect pitch. What had once been a place of jury-rigged, half-foraged, way-out solutions had become a place of ultimate creature-comfort refinement.

RMI's headquarters was neither a temple for the worship of technology nor a refuge from the scourges of modernity. It was neither an activist's hive nor a post-apocalyptic oasis. It wasn't an innovative recycling centre or a cottage industry craft shop, not a residence or an office or an R&D lab or a think tank. It was all of those things together. *Seamlessly.* The water sounded its ageless alpha-wave tune, the space-age carbon fibre awaited its chance to remake the science of transportation, the old Communist batteries held their charge, and the photo sensor stood on guard to tell the lights what to do. It was intoxicating, in its way, to try to absorb it all. Like stepping into a puddle to find yourself sunk up to your chin, totally immersed in a parallel sustainable universe. It was like Lovins had been through it all already, tried and failed and tried again until he got it right; like he'd thought of *everything.*

And when you read his writing, you realize he pretty much has.

Amory Lovins began almost exactly where E.F. Schumacher left off. Just three years after the debut of *Small Is Beautiful,* Lovins published a vehemently argued essay entitled "Energy Strategy: The Road Not Taken?" in the October 1976 issue of the influential policy journal *Foreign Affairs.* In the essay's opening passage, Lovins outlined two paths for America's energy policy. The first—the status quo—would be "a rapid expansion of centralized high technologies to increase supplies of energy." Lovins preferred a highly divergent alternative torn right out of Schumacher: "The second path combines a prompt and serious commitment to efficient use of energy, rapid development of renewable energy sources matched in scale and in energy quality to end-use needs, and special transitional fossil fuel technologies." Lovins was motivated at the time by grave concerns about nuclear proliferation, but the direction he advocated—the pursuit of which would occupy the whole of his professional and personal life thereafter— would in time prove to be just as relevant to the emerging calamity of climate change. And so even as most of the world pursued what he called the "hard path"—costly nukes, outsized power plants, a biggered, wasteful mess of a global energy regime—Lovins marched steadfastly down the "soft" one, founding a think tank in a sparsely populated valley near Aspen to work out the technical details and crunch the numbers of a sustainably powered future.

Writing about Lovins's work a quarter-century later, Walt Patterson remembered him as a figure whose ideas inspired two polar-opposite reactions: "Of course! Of course! It's obvious! Why didn't I think of that?" was the thinking on one side; "There goes Lovins again with his crackpot ideas, trying to undermine the fabric of right-thinking society" went the other. In the 1970s, the crackpot camp far outnumbered the genius camp, but Lovins—stubborn, obsessive and utterly unwavering in his commitment—soldiered on oblivious. By 1999, when he and Hunter joined the green entrepreneur Paul Hawken to publish *Natural Capitalism: Creating the Next Industrial Revolution,* Lovins was a fringe hero about to step confidently into the very centre of the most important discussion of our time.

If you imagine the geography of hope as a bridge between the Anthropocene Era and the Sustainable Age, then *Natural Capitalism* is an impressive first draft of the blueprints for that structure. It's the first systematic, scientific articulation of what a sustainable industrial society might look like. It is also something of an ersatz *Bildungsroman* for Schumacheresque green commerce, the synthesis of a thousand wild ideas into a set of sound, sober and universally applicable principles.

Lovins et al. introduced their natural capitalist system with a forcefully worded provocation:

> What would our economy look like if it fully valued *all* forms of capital, including human and natural capital? What if our economy were organized not around the lifeless abstractions of neoclassical economics and accountancy but around the biological realities of nature? What if Generally Accepted Accounting Practice booked natural and human capital not as a free amenity in putative inexhaustible supply but as a finite and integrally valuable factor of production? What if, in the absence of a rigorous way to practice such accounting, companies started to act *as if* such principles were in force? This choice is possible and such an economy would offer a stunning new set of opportunities for all of society, amounting to no less than the *next industrial revolution.*

The authors imagined a future economy still governed by "democratic, market-based systems," but those systems' inputs would now be properly valued—the ecological ones especially. To this end, they estimated the full value of "biological services flowing directly into society from the stock of natural capital"—water to drink, air to breathe, trees to form into lumber and energy-dense liquefied carbon to turn into gasoline—at a minimum of $36 *trillion* per annum, which was just shy of 1997's gross world product of $39 trillion.

In addition to the meticulously calculated stat, still quoted often by Lovins and RMI's staff, that the modern automobile was at best operating at 1 percent efficiency, *Natural Capitalism* detailed at length the "perverse subsidies" built into the current industrial order, from the billion-dollar giveaways granted to the German coal industry to the hundreds of millions the U.S. government was then handing to tobacco farmers to the effective "welfare" granted to the U.S. auto industry in the form of the hundreds of billions in "hidden costs" it wasn't asked to pay. The authors noted that America's nuclear power industry has received $1 trillion in public money over the years, while delivering to Americans in return less total energy than wood does. The natural capitalists explained how a typical can of cola—just the container—costs much more to produce than its fizzy contents and yet is essentially given away for free. And they noted that the routine corporate practice of buying equipment based on "lowest first cost" (the cheapest price tag, that is) has created an inefficiency epidemic. "Every first-year business student knows that the correct way to allocate capital is to compare investments' results over the long run," they wrote, "not choose the option that requires the least initial investment regardless of future return." They reckoned, for instance, that just the purchase of inefficient distribution transformers by American electric companies amounted to a $1-billion-per-year misallocation.

In place of this wasteful, misguided mess, *Natural Capitalism* presented a four-point plan, "four central strategies of natural capitalism that are a means to enable countries, companies, and communities to operate by behaving as if all forms of capital were valued":

1. "Radical Resource Productivity." This is the business-speak shorthand for Lovins's efficiency obsession. Use every kilowatt, get the most out of every pound of bauxite or board-foot of timber. Reduce and reduce, and then reduce some more. And reuse that minuscule amount, of course, and recycle it all at the end.
2. "Biomimicry." On this point the authors quoted directly from William McDonough, who placed biomimicry—the imitation of nature's total efficiencies and seamless symbioses—at the core of his cradle-to-cradle design theory. A sustainable world doesn't need to be constructed from scratch, Lovins et al.

observed; we merely need to imitate nature's success at building it. (Spider silk—several times stronger than bullet-stopping Kevlar—is a favourite example of a natural "product" crying out to be biomimicked.)

3. "Service and Flow Economy." This is the natural capitalist response to Walt Patterson's "perverse incentives." If energy companies were not selling you units of electricity and gas but leasing you light and heat and the rest, they'd be "incentivized" like nobody's business to make sure you were provided with those services at top efficiency; their profitability would indeed depend on it. Plus durable goods would no longer be designed with intentional obsolescence in mind, as most cars and appliances, for example, currently are.

4. "Investing in Natural Capital." An economic process that yields more than it takes. Industrial production as a regenerative activity. Sustainability's holy grail, basically.

Like most revolutionary manifestos, *Natural Capitalism* is an ambitious book, and it can seem, on its surface, far-fetched and impractical. It is thus worth noting that Lovins and Paul Hawken began their professional collaboration as founding members of the advisory team assembled by Ray Anderson of Interface to guide the transformation of his carpet business into the world's first sustainable multinational corporation. They were central figures on this "eco dream team," and indeed Ray's aforementioned epiphany struck him in 1994 while he was reading *The Ecology of Commerce,* the book Hawken wrote prior to co-authoring *Natural Capitalism.** The details of the first phase of Interface's metamorphosis appear frequently in the pages of *Natural Capitalism,* and the company was in many

---

* Anderson credits his consciousness-raising in part to Daniel Quinn's *Ishmael,* a powerfully evocative novel about the global environmental crisis, told from the point of view of a super-intelligent gorilla terrified for the earth's future, which has inspired a grassroots social movement dedicated to back-to-basics survivalism. The book is far less fanciful than it sounds, but the recommended course of action of many of Quinn's most fervent readers—a deliberate return to a pre-agrarian hunter-gatherer society—seems unlikely to gain widespread acceptance except in the event of the apocalypse it aims to forestall. Inasmuch as it's proving rather difficult in the meantime to convince people to voluntarily sacrifice their suvs, the idea of talking them into abandoning agriculture doesn't strike me as the first step down a hopeful path.

ways the proving ground for the ideas that later appeared in the book. Point being, there's probably no large-scale commercial enterprise on the planet that is as fully committed to natural capitalism as Interface is, and so a return to the industrial frontier of western Georgia seems in order.

By the time of my visit, Interface's LaGrange facilities overflowed with superficial details attesting to its natural capitalist bona fides. On our way into the R&D facility, for example, John Bradford stopped to point out the parking spots closest to the main entrance, which were reserved for carpoolers and hybrid drivers. But what was truly revolutionary about Interface was the thousand little things you couldn't see from the sidewalk, all the layered changes that occurred when natural capitalism's four tenets were pursued with the zeal most companies reserve only for growing their revenue. The resource productivity measures provided some of the flashiest stuff, from the vivid paint on the Cool Blue recycling system down to the multihued cones of yarn on the factory floor, the waste from which had been reduced by 92 percent at the LaGrange manufacturing plant. Companywide, Interface had shrunk its total landfill-bound waste by two-thirds as of 2004, saving the company an estimated $222 million in operating costs. (In this, as in all of Interface's sustainability measures, Ray's Epiphany dictated a 2020 deadline for the end of garbage entirely.) There was also a flashy new showroom up in Atlanta, which had been awarded a LEED Platinum rating for its myriad hyper-efficiency features, and Interface subsidiaries even farther afield were changing their ways as rapidly as the main office was. A furniture fabric subsidiary called Guilford of Maine, for example, whose feedstock had included all of 0.8 percent recycled material in 1996, was deriving 89 percent of its products from used plastic bottles as of 2002. It had also introduced a new fabric made from corn.

Interface's biomimicry measures were even harder to detect, because for starters a carpeted institutional hallway won't ever be a field of grass. Still, its Entropy line of carpet tiles had been decorated with abstract shapes inspired by the random patterns of fallen leaves on a forest floor, which meant the tiles were much more interchangeable than conventional patterns. This allowed for the replacement only of worn patches, reducing cost and waste in one stroke. And the company's quarterly "out-of-the-box meetings," Bradford argued, were also a kind of biomimicry, bringing together members of those disparate departments least likely to interact to work together on problems and develop symbiotic relationships. It sounded a bit like trying to introduce a variety of species of animals raised in captivity into the same patch of wilderness, a workplace aiming to become more ecosystem than zoo. "You want to see a good fight," Bradford said. "Put a bunch of biologists in a room with a bunch of engineers. It's nasty."

The emergence of a service-and-flow economy at Interface was a little easier to detect. It was embodied in a program called Evergreen, which the company called its "product of service" option (this was Hawken's original terminology). The program involved leasing carpet to customers instead of selling it outright, with servicing and replacement of worn-out patches included in the terms of the contract. First introduced in the late 1990s, Evergreen quickly revealed the limits of a single natural capitalist enterprise when its customer base remained mired in pre-Anthropocene thinking. Interface's big institutional clients, for example, often had internal cultures or accounting practices that either precluded the leasing of carpet entirely or divided up the cost of the lease across various departments in a way that obscured the long-term savings the program offered. It also confused the hell out of banks unaccustomed to the idea of a "perpetual lease."

These obstacles surely came as no surprise to the company, though, because, as Bradford explained to me, they'd had to overcome a whole pile of them internally. We were pacing the humming factory floor at the time, and Bradford was bellowing over the din about how they'd eliminated several steps from the production process by inventing a thing called a "portable creel," which had greatly reduced the amount of wasted yarn. (A creel is the cone the yarn is spooled on, for the record.) The old way of making Interface carpet tiles resulted in a lot more creels with just a little yarn left on them at the end of a production run, which meant a lot more nylon trucked to the landfill. And since yarn is the most expensive part of making carpet tile, it made intuitive sense that it was good for the company to reduce the amount it wasted. But for some Byzantine reason—something to do with when in the production process the volume of yarn was measured—it appeared to the accounting department as an increase in cost, and so the portable creel idea led to a year of internecine warfare.

Bradford: "The only way that you could get the real answer was by jumping completely off of that cliff—with no straddle, you know, keeping nothing on the rock, so to speak, and being in complete freefall, 100 percent there. So that you could change the measurement system and really know. But any time that you were half here and half there, you could never really know, because you had to employ both measurement systems, and then neither one was right. Okay? So finally we came down and basically said, 'I believe this, and we're going.' And sure enough, it was right."

In *Natural Capitalism,* Lovins et al. discussed pretty much the same phenomenon, referring to it as "tunneling through the cost barrier." "Economic dogma holds that the more of a resource you save, the more you will have to pay for each increment of saving," they wrote. "That may be true if each increment is achieved in the same way as the last. However, if done well, saving a large amount of energy or resources often costs *less* than saving a small amount. This assertion sounds impossible, and indeed, most economic theorists can 'prove' it won't work. Blissfully unaware of economic theory, however, intelligent engineers put it into practice every working day as part of an approach called *whole-system engineering.*" They cited the example of insulating a building, which will eventually yield diminishing returns, reaching a point where another layer of insulation reduces energy bills by only a tiny fraction, even though it costs as much to install as the first layer (which yielded savings large enough to justify its price tag). This is the cost barrier. If, however, the building is so well insulated that adding another couple of layers eliminates the need for an entire high-priced furnace, the savings become so great that they "tunnel" back through the cost barrier. (The accompanying graph looks like a decapitated bell curve, with a steep upward pitch above the cost-barrier line, followed by a basically flat plateau in the money-losing sector and then a cliff-like plunge back downward into profitability.)

In Interface's case, its accountants were measuring only part of the yarn savings, which didn't seem to be worth the cost, whereas its R&D people were looking at the huge savings yielded by reworking the entire production process—and *feeling,* in their no-bullshit engineers' guts, that it added up. This is yet another example of the importance of the company's *total* commitment to natural capitalism, its refusal to yield to even the most persuasive conventional wisdom. The existing economic order has its own self-fulfilling measurements, its own circular logic; it would be foolish to think that a complete realignment of the system would make economic sense by the same accounting measures that deem worthless the elaborate process by which crude oil is formed over millions of years, a geological miracle so rare that stored energy of this quality exists only in scattered precious pockets. This is a political economy as well that finds no fault with discarding the elaborately spun and virtually indestructible petrochemical silk derived from this amazing liquid after just a few years of use. That leap off Bradford's rhetorical cliff was, in fact, a leap back toward grounded reality.

In any case, the financial disasters anticipated for Interface on any number of fronts have never materialized. The carpet tile business as a whole weathered an intense recession in the late 1990s, which Interface navigated better than its competitors. Its revenues are now back on the rise, and it claims at least a one-third market share in the commercial carpet tile business, which Ray Anderson credits in no small measure to the enormous goodwill Interface earned by becoming the corporate face of natural capitalism. "Sustainability doesn't cost," he wrote in 2004, "it pays."

Which brings us to the system's final pillar—becoming a restorative enterprise—which is the only point that remains beyond Interface's immediately foreseeable grasp. After all, its chief product is a stew of potentially lethal petrochemicals, and it can't go and plant more nylon. Anderson has suggested, however, that the company's ability to lead other businesses down the path to sustainability might be its restorative enterprise, its reinvestment of natural capital. After all, Anderson has become the corporate face of natural capitalism, the first profit-mongering CEO to jump off that cliff. And Interface offers daily testament to the logic of natural capitalism as the price of "IFSIA" ticks by without preamble or asterisk on the scrolling stock-price banners. Natural capitalist business is still business. Sales were up 14.7 percent in 2006.

I was at my local mall the other day, hiking down the concourse on my way to a movie, and I felt a sharp twinge of familiarity, a déjà vu sort of thing. I couldn't place it for a long moment. And then it hit me:

the carpet. It was the same pattern I'd watched spooling off the creels back in LaGrange. It was from their Entropy line, one of the money-saving, waste-reducing, biomimicking forest floor patterns. It wasn't there because anyone in the mall's management company cared particularly about sustainability. It wasn't there because they needed an easy way to look like they were suitably concerned about climate change. It was there because it was quality institutional carpet from an industry leader. It had some nifty new features, too, that made it stand out from its competitors.

It was natural capitalism in its natural habitat. Which is—dig it—*everywhere.*

THE GREEN BOOM

In 2003, Amory Lovins and a handful of his colleagues at RMI published a sort of sequel to *Natural Capitalism* entitled *Small Is Profitable.* It's a veritable catalogue of the Schumacheresque, a compendium of "207 ways in which the size of 'electrical resources'—devices that make, save or store electricity—affects their economic value." It's as good an indication as any of the way times have changed for Lovins that the book is structured more as a technical study for business leaders than as a persuasive essay for a general audience. (It begins, for example, with an "Executive Summary.") The world has come spinning around to Lovins on a thirty year time delay, finally ready to join him at the foot of the trail he first suggested blazing back in that 1976 *Foreign Affairs* essay.

In a sense, *Small Is Profitable* is the business-school textbook version of the oft-reported experience of hanging out with Lovins on one of his efficiency benders. Here, he says, are two-hundred-odd ways of making money. There are more than enough to choose from, and surely a couple of them—a dozen, a hundred—are your size. You don't need a capital-E Epiphany to join in, is the subtext. You don't need to give a shit, really, about projected greenhouse gas concentrations for the year 2050. You just need to be interested in making more money.

Lovins would surely prefer more companies to go cliff-jumping through the cost barrier with Interface, but in the meantime he and his colleagues have embarked upon reducing the energy required by every one of Wal-Mart's stores by 30 percent and doubling the fuel efficiency of its trucking fleet. They've given up on trying to convince a major American automaker to build one of their super-efficient carbon-fibre Hypercars, instead consulting with the U.S. Department of Defence in the interest of seeing the vehicle get its first use in military green. The hot-showers-and-cold-beer philosophy means that Lovins will work with organizations that many old-guard environmental groups have dedicated themselves to opposing, because if the goal is an ecologically sustainable planet ASAP, then corporate behemoths and military-industrial complexes will have to be energy efficient too. And so when Lovins popped up in the pages of *Scientific American* in September 2005, he was only too happy to report that his approach had been adopted by everyone from BP (which had saved $650 million on the way to meeting its 2010 greenhouse gas–reduction goal by 2001) to DuPont (greenhouse emissions down 72 percent, $2 billion saved).

Even a casual perusal of any given newspaper's business section in recent years would quickly reveal further evidence of the emerging green boom, with a mix of big and small organizations the world over bragging about initiatives of all sizes to save energy and make money. The wind-power industry now employs 235,000 people worldwide, and the solar-power business has been expanding annually by at least 40 percent through the first five years of the new millennium, leading one analyst to dub this its "tornado phase." Another analyst, from the French bank Crédit Lyonnais, predicted that the solar industry would grow from its $7 billion in 2004 revenues to $40 billion by 2010. General Electric plans to draw 60 percent of its revenue growth from its Ecomagination line of hyper-efficient and renewable-energy technologies. And then there's that gigantic GDP-growth poster child China, whose government has employed William McDonough to plan some of its new green communities. "This is the largest economic opportunity in human history if we get it right," McDonough has said, speaking for China but also for anywhere energy is wantonly wasted and fossil fuels profligately burned.

A green boom, then, born of the historic convergence of three factors: a threat, a perversion and (most importantly) an opportunity. The threat, of course, is anthropogenic climate change. The cloistered world of big business has been slow to recognize how disruptive climate change will be to its bottom line, but in the past few years the global market system's self-appointed barometer of permissible risk—the reinsurance industry—has been sounding the alarm. Reinsurers are enormous financial bodies that insure the insurance companies themselves, so they absorb much of the economic damage created by large-scale disaster. The reinsurance business was hit hard by the most infamous calamities of recent years—the 9/11 terrorist attacks, Hurricane Katrina, the Asian tsunami—and it served as an early-warning system for the alarming growth in overall "catastrophe losses," which rose from about $1 billion per year in the United States in the 1970s to $71 billion in 2005 alone.

In response, Swiss Re (the world's largest reinsurer) co-commissioned a climate change impact study, committed itself to carbon neutrality by 2013 and created a $350-million "clean energy fund." At the same time, Munich Re (the second largest) has become a corporate leader in the call for action, publicly insisting that there is "no doubt" of a direct link between climate change and the increase in claims. Their clients, meanwhile, have begun to refuse policies to homes in low-lying coastal areas, which climatologists have long warned would be the first hit by the extreme weather patterns accompanying the first years of climate change. Taken together, the actions of the insurance business at all levels broadcast a clear warning, which was succinctly summarized by the subtitle of a 2006 report published by the insurance giant Lloyd's of London: *Adapt or Bust.*

The perversion at play in the green boom's first phase is that complex and tangled web of counterproductive structural features built into business as usual. It's best exemplified by the GDP fallacy, which simply underscores the urgency of the need for change and the benefits that will accrue from it. Walt Patterson offers a particularly concise refutation of the "logic" of the market economy in its present form:

> Commentators scrutinize the prices of fuels and electricity, and analyze their movements minutely. However, in our modern interconnected society the prices of fuels and electricity by the unit have long been essentially artificial, shaped by preferential tax regimes, subsidies and cross-subsidies, cartels and outright monopolies, as in the case of electricity networks. With this in mind the highly respected chairman of Ireland's Electricity Supply Board, Patrick Moriarty, once remarked succinctly, "The price of electricity is what the government wants it to be."

Much the same can be said of fuels. Except for short-term advantage, price is not a good enough criterion.

What's true for energy holds for business in general: a global market economy built by and for fossil-fuelled industry, measured by its internal yardsticks, has failed at the task of signalling its own impending collapse. Left to its own devices, it will implode, overwhelmed by the relentless force as all it has deemed external comes rushing back in.

The default reaction to this looming calamity has been panic and denial, both of which have been particularly acute among the keepers of the economic status quo. The panic manifests itself in the form of outrageous overestimates of the cost of action and unfounded underestimates of the efficacy of alternatives, the painting of apocalyptic portraits of impossibly deep depression, the insistence that it is those who call for change who are the short-sighted opportunists. The denial, meanwhile, is exemplified by that breed of blinkered thinking that persists even now that the facts of the Anthropocene's climate are widely accepted, its more pernicious manifestations ranging from dreams of an emissions-free energy regime still driven exclusively by the Big (next-generation nukes and clean coal and biofuels) to preposterous magic-bullet solutions (one of these involves enveloping the planet in a dust cloud to partially block out the sun, which is an idea stolen pretty much verbatim from the evil nuclear-power baron Monty Burns on *The Simpsons*).

Picture the natural capitalists skipping through this cartoon carnage with a carefree whistle. "America is confronted, as Winston Churchill said, by insurmountable opportunities." This was the big-picture analysis promulgated by Lovins et al. in *Natural Capitalism,* and although they spoke parochially to the United States alone, the message applies as widely as the transaction of business does. "Because there are practical ways to mitigate climate concerns and save more money than such measures cost, it almost doesn't matter whether you believe that climate change is a problem or not: These steps should be taken simply because they make money."

And that's without even mentioning the cost of *not* acting, which in the long term would be dire indeed.

EIGHT

THE NON-PARTISAN ENVIRONMENTALIST

[the ideology of sustainability]

BEYOND KYOTO (JUST A LITTLE POLICY)

In October 2006, Sir Nicholas Stern of Britain's Government Economic Service issued a policy document entitled *The Economics of Climate Change*. Stern was the former chief economist for the World Bank, and he'd initiated his study at the behest of the Chancellor of the Exchequer. So this was, to be sure, *top-level* policy wonkery, but it was policy wonkery nonetheless. Which made the reaction to it all the more surprising: the "Stern Review," as it quickly came to be known, made headlines the world over, and by early 2007 Stern was off on a speaking tour of North America, just like any newly minted bestselling author. It said quite a lot about the extent to which public priorities had shifted that a British government paper reviewing the economic implications of a complex scientific issue had made its author an ersatz international pop star.

"The evidence shows that ignoring climate change will eventually damage economic growth," Stern wrote. "Our actions over the coming few decades could create risks of major disruption to economic and social activity, later in this century and in the next, on a scale similar to those associated with the great wars and the economic depression of the first half of the 20th century. And it will be difficult or impossible to reverse these changes." Stripped of its wonky language, Stern meant that the shit had either hit the fan or was just about to.

There remained, however, well-founded hope that the most catastrophic dimensions of climate change could be avoided. Stern estimated that a 30 percent reduction in global greenhouse gases could be achieved by 2050 with a total cost amounting to only a 1 percent reduction in projected worldwide GDP—a heresy, no doubt, coming as it did from a former World Bank economist trained in the art of maximizing growth at all costs, but a minor one compared to the cost of *not* acting, which Stern estimated at somewhere between five and twenty times that price. At his sombre report's launch, Stern noted that the global economy had tripped hard on an "externality" of epic proportions. "This," he asserted, "is the greatest market failure the world has seen."

It followed, then, that the first response to the situation would have to be from *outside* the market; it would have to be public, not private. British Prime Minister Tony Blair rose to the challenge immediately, declaring the Stern Review "the final piece of the jigsaw"—the last jagged scrap of information required to make the case for the necessity of rapid and widespread action. To that end, Blair unveiled a policy framework that included new worldwide emissions targets, massive investment in new technologies and a global cap-and-trade scheme. It all sounded quite promising, maybe even Schumacheresque—a healthy dose of carefully orchestrated global order, enabling the right kind of regional-scale freedom to attack the problem. The only stumbling block was that the grave problem delineated in the Stern Review had resulted from the failure not just of markets but of worldwide political leadership, the overwhelming majority of which had to date proven maddeningly useless at figuring out how to even begin to tackle the problem. "The report is clear," Blair wrote in the British tabloid *The Sun* the same day the Stern Review was issued. "We are heading towards catastrophic tipping points in our climate unless we act." He was absolutely right; there was no time to waste. Probably no time, either, to wait for policy to take the lead.

It's no accident that I haven't mentioned the most famous name in the climate change game until now. The Kyoto Protocol: wildly idealistic from a political angle though only mildly ambitious from a practical one, widely ratified but only sporadically acted upon, loved by those who yearn for its ends and loathed by many of those who must contend with its means. Kyoto is both a monument to hope and a pretty lousy vehicle for leading the response to the great Anthropocene threat. Even in its current, semi-stalemated condition, it represents one of the broadest agreements on pretty much anything in human history—a pact between 169 nations at last count to reduce greenhouse gas emissions by 5 percent or more by 2012. Its great failure, though, is that it delves too far into specifics, becoming an econometric numbers game easily deflated (at least rhetorically) by the same short-sighted technocrats who enabled the climate change mess in the first place.

I have no interest in wading into the political and scientific morass surrounding Kyoto, except to note that it strikes me as the product of a pre-Anthropocene mindset. It apprehends a universal problem of unprecedented scope and outsized scale, and responds with a call for action of proportions just as monumentally Big—a nearly impossible dance of global socioeconomic synchronicity. Earlier, I mentioned the "stabilization wedges" proposed as tools for climate change mitigation by a pair of Princeton scientists, one of which was a PV array the size of Hawaii; Kyoto strikes me as analogous to offering the world a choice between literally carpeting Hawaii in solar panels or opting out entirely. That's not to say Kyoto should be abandoned necessarily. It's a powerful symbol of the general direction the world's activity must take, a permanent appeal to our better selves in the same vein as the Geneva Convention and the Universal Declaration of Human Rights, which continue to serve a purpose even when signatories ignore their obligations under them. It might turn out, in the long run, that Kyoto or a more finely tuned successor treaty becomes the enduring engine of a concerted global effort to return civilization to a sustainable footing. To suggest that it *must* be in place before decisive action can be taken, however, is some kind of folly.

There's not a single point on the map of this geography of hope—not the smallest atoll of the most remote archipelago—that owes its existence to the Kyoto Protocol. The digital revolution analogy is again revealing: as with the dotcom revolutionaries in their garages and converted warehouses, the pacesetters in the sustainability movement are far ahead of policy, particularly compared to Kyoto or any other multilateral arrangement. The problem might be global, but its best on-the-ground solutions to date have all been devised piecemeal, often at the local level of a municipality or a single community or organization, at most at the size of a single nation-state. Still, even if many of the solutions are not directly connected to policy—they are not overtly *government* projects—the best are propelled by smart, subtle legislation. Policy undoubtedly has a key role to play, but not the only one and not necessarily the lead.

A particularly dramatic case in point emerged recently in the United States, whose federal government has proven singularly resistant to action. So intransigent, indeed, that ten of its largest corporations—Fortune 500 companies all, from aluminum giant Alcoa and chemical behemoth DuPont to energy powerhouses like BP America, FPL Group and Duke Energy—chose to join four major environmental groups in January 2007 to form a coalition called the U.S. Climate Action Partnership, thus to lobby the feds for mandatory limits on greenhouse gas emissions. The absurdity is worth underscoring: big-time industrial polluters were advocating *for* regulation. Their goal was not at all altruistic—they simply wanted a role in crafting the policy that would govern their dirty businesses, and they were keen to join the cap-and-trade game, buying and selling the rights to release cubic tons of carbon dioxide on a robust and secure market. (Buying carbon credits from cleaner companies is presumed to be cheaper, in the short term, than abandoning lucrative but emissions-heavy business activities.) Tony Blair alluded to cap-and-trade as well in his call for a global carbon market, and Nicholas Stern has been optimistic about the idea in his post-report appearances, arguing with particular vehemence that "major gains" would be best achieved by an interconnected global network formed from the emerging national and regional carbon markets around the world.*

---

* The European Union's Emissions Trading Scheme (far and away the most ambitious cap-and-trade regime extant) has thus far demonstrated both the enormous potential and the serious challenges involved in international emissions trading. In 2006—only its second year of existence—the ETS generated $25 billion in revenue, accounting for more than 80 percent of the worldwide emissions credit market. Emissions limits were set so high, however, that nine thousand of the ten thousand polluting factories covered by the

Beyond establishing a vigorous trade in permissions to continue being part of the problem, though, what's a policymaker interested in becoming part of the solution to do, in the absence of a binding international agreement? Perhaps not surprisingly, Denmark—the home of the world's first post-carbon island—is also a pacesetter in terms of policy. In addition to introducing one of the world's first cap-and-trade programs in 2001 (which was folded into the broader EU scheme in 2005), the Danish government has been taxing CO_2 emissions by the tonne since 1991, and it has offered tax incentives to the wind industry since the 1970s. The results, as I've noted, range from Denmark's global leadership in renewable-power generation and wind turbine manufacturing to a majority of its chilly climate's heat being produced by hyper-efficient combined-heat-and-power schemes to substantial emissions reductions during a period of robust economic growth.

In the absence of thirty years of bureaucratic practice, however, there remain simple, powerful legislative tools available to any national government with sufficient daring and backbone to ignore the inertial weight of certain breeds of conventional wisdom. There is, for example, a device known as a feed-in tariff, which has almost single-handedly vaulted Germany to the global forefront in renewable energy. A nation neither exceptionally sun-kissed nor particularly windswept is a leader in the generation of power from both, and it's a thriving industrial powerhouse in the production of equipment to do more of the same. And all of this came largely thanks to the world's most ambitious feed-in tariff, best known by its German-language initials, EEG—short for *Erneubare-Energien-Gesetz,* usually called the Renewable Energy Sources Act in English.

Feed-in tariffs are a kind of price subsidy, first introduced in California in 1978 to spur the renewable-energy business in response to the last energy crisis. (Those first iconic California wind farms owed their existence in part to this pioneering feed-in tariff.) The idea was to

scheme generated less greenhouse gas than their allowances, which precipitated a steep decline in the market price per tonne and nearly unravelled the whole project. It also produced a net *increase* in total emissions of about 1 percent, which, although less than the total growth in emissions for 2005, was still troublingly contrary to the scheme's goal. As of April 2007, a number of EU countries were promising to bring in much more stringent caps in order to establish a more stable and robust market.

inflate the price of green energy to its "avoided cost" rate—the total cost to society if the same power had been produced by fossil fuels. This has long struck the purveyors of prevailing economic wisdom as the gross intrusion of socialistic central planning into what should be a robust free market, a strain of particularly bold heresy in certain obsessively rational econometric circles. Which is why it's a bit surprising to find such a measure doing so well in notoriously rational Germany.

The EEG is a remarkably straightforward piece of legislation: passed in 2000 and recalibrated in 2004, it obliges German power distributors to buy energy from renewable sources at fixed rates well above market prices. The subsidies vary in intensity depending on the power source, and they scale down over time (twenty to twenty-five years under the current version), at which point an open energy market is presumed to take over. The text of the legislation is Teutonically blunt as to its intent and unambiguous as to its necessity:

> The purpose of this Act is to facilitate a sustainable development of energy supply in the interest of managing global warming and protecting the environment and to achieve a substantial increase in the percentage contribution made by renewable energy sources to power supply in order at least to double the share of renewable energy sources in total energy consumption by the year 2010. . . .
>
> In some cases, the cost of the production of renewable energy sources is still much higher than the production cost of conventional energy sources. This is largely due to the fact that the overwhelming share of the external costs associated with the generation of electricity from conventional energy sources is not reflected in the price; instead, these costs are borne by the general public and by future generations.

The EEG, then, is a correction to the acute externality crisis detailed in the Stern Review, an attempt to bring *actual* rationality to the energy market, using the inflated price of renewables to compensate for the external costs of fossil fuels and thus hasten the growth of the domestic renewable-power industry. Its success on both counts is detailed in growth stats so staggering they seem like a kind of boasting. The boom in Germany's solar industry has become particularly renowned. At the end of 1999, shortly before the EEG was passed, Germany had a fledgling 58 megawatts of installed solar-energy capacity. By the end of 2003, the total was 408 megawatts, and when the solar-power subsidy was increased in a 2004 amendment, the country's solar regime *really* exploded, nearly quadrupling in less than two years. The three largest solar power plants in the world came online in Germany in 2006, and growth has been so intense that it has precipitated a global short-term shortage in the industrial-grade silicon needed to manufacture photovoltaic cells. The domestic manufacturing industry has boomed just as dramatically. Freiburg's Solar-Fabrik, to name just one German solar-power system manufacturer, grew by 75 percent in 2004 and continued to set quarterly sales records throughout 2005 and 2006. The EEG has also been a magnet for foreign firms. In the fall of 2005, for example, the U.S.-based PV manufacturer Evergreen, which was already making 70 percent of its sales in Germany, broke ground on a $79-million factory near Berlin.

In large part because feed-in tariffs mandate "artificially" high prices for renewable power, they've always been unpopular with the free market's appointed sages. The balance of evidence thus far, however, suggests that feed-in tariffs fare much better than more orthodox "market-driven" approaches. The United Kingdom, for example, introduced an avowedly market-based strategy to its energy policy in 1998—a device known as a Renewable Obligation Certificate (ROC). The ROC was a type of credit note issued to renewable-energy generators, one ROC for every megawatt of green power produced, with Britain's electricity suppliers then obliged to buy 3 percent of their total output in ROCs. The idea was based on rock-solid Economics 101 logic: the initially scarce ROCs would skyrocket in price as power companies scrambled to meet their quotas, enticing established businesses and entrepreneurs alike to get into the renewable-power game— "encouraging market entry," in the dry technocratic language of a 2004 Cambridge-MIT study that compared ROCs to the German feed-in tariff.

The study examined the two countries' renewable-energy policy regimes starting in the early 1990s. Both had set a goal of jump-starting their respective domestic wind-power businesses. In the decade that followed, the British approach failed to meet its stated targets, while Germany's feed-in tariff and its similarly configured predecessor not only achieved their goals but bested the U.K. version at encouraging competition and fostering a domestic wind turbine manufacturing industry. (Discouraging competition, the report noted, is a "frequent criticism"—unfounded, it turns out—of feed-in tariffs.) The only obvious superiority of the ROC strategy was that it drove down the cost per unit of wind energy more rapidly than the feed-in tariff. If, however, the price per unit in Germany was adjusted to account for the full lifetime of the power plant and for its demonstrably inferior resource base (that is, the fact that it's considerably less windy in Germany than in Britain), then even the *price* of German wind power was cheaper. It was no accident, the report concluded, that the global wind industry was dominated by Denmark, Spain and Germany—three of the first European countries to adopt feed-in tariffs. (The very first had been Portugal, in 1988.) If more renewable energy and a solid foothold in the global power business of the future were the goals, the feed-in tariff was the best tool yet devised.

No wonder, then, that when Astrid King, a senior official from Germany's environment ministry who had played a key role in the passage of the EEG, addressed a conference of the world's energy bureaucrats in Mexico City in early 2006, she used the time to indulge in a little gloating. As she noted, sixteen of twenty-five EU countries and at least forty more national governments worldwide had drafted feed-in tariffs of their own by that point. Back in Germany, meanwhile, the stats grew ever more encouraging. The initial goal had been 12.5 percent of the country's electricity from renewables by 2010 and 20 percent by 2020, but since it had already hit 10 percent under the turbocharged EEG, King had to wonder if 25 percent wasn't a more reasonable estimate for the later date. And it was all thanks to one ambitious legislative manoeuvre.*

Even in the absence of national initiatives—indeed, even in the face of an obstructionist federal administration—there remains plenty of room for sustainably oriented policy at lower levels of government. California Governor Arnold Schwarzenegger, for example,

---

* It warrants mention that a preparatory first step built into Germany's EEG mandates two-way access to the power grid. If a German homeowner chooses to put solar panels on the roof, the system will include a residential meter that measures both consumption *and* production. This practice is usually referred to as "net metering," and it's been introduced in more than thirty U.S. states, a handful of Canadian provinces and dozens more countries

broke ranks with his Republican allies (and amazed long-time critics of his Hummer-driving ways) by passing America's most ambitious emissions-reduction law in the fall of 2006. California was, in a sense, following the lead of the U.S. Mayors Climate Protection Agreement, a municipal-level commitment to meeting the targets prescribed in the Kyoto Protocol, in pointed defiance of the U.S. federal government's intransigence. That pledge was first drafted in early 2005 by the mayors of ten cities, primarily in the Pacific Northwest. It quickly gathered momentum and media attention, and at last count it had been signed by 407 municipalities representing sixty million Americans nationwide. Signatories ranged from the heads of tiny burgs (Bessemer, Alabama; Shepherdstown, West Virginia; North Pole, Alaska) to the mayors of the nation's most mammoth metropolises (New York, Boston, Chicago). The least surprising name on the roster had to be Tom Potter, the mayor of Portland, Oregon, who joined as one of the original ten with a sort of avuncular nod: "We are proud that the people of Seattle share our vision for turning the crisis of global warming into an opportunity to transform our economy and leave a healthier planet for our children and grandchildren." He was of course obliged to note that Portland had by that point been busy for over a decade implementing America's *first* municipal emissions-reduction plan. Portland was all by itself, way out in front. Again.

By the time the Mayors Climate Protection Agreement started making major headlines at the December 2005 Kyoto talks in Montreal, Portland's climate change strategy, introduced in 1993, had begun to yield some enviable data. Greenhouse gas emissions were down 13 percent per capita and had stayed essentially flat overall during a period when most of North America had seen double-digit emissions growth. All new municipal buildings in Portland were required to earn LEED Gold ratings, and the city had the most total LEED certifications of any municipality in the world (this in only the thirtieth-largest city in

---

around the world, many of which weren't ready to make the larger leap to feed-in tariffs but were at least willing to legislate the infrastructure for decentralized micropower. It's a vivid illustration of the degree to which most of the world's energy policy is tilted toward the carbon-burning Big that until recently most countries had done nothing to permit small renewable producers to even enter the market.

the United States). Portland residents were the highest per capita purchasers of hybrid vehicles in America, and emissions-free commuting by bicycle or on foot was up 10 percent in the last ten years of the twentieth century, putting the city's 700 miles of dedicated biking and walking paths to ample use. And it all started with a series of interconnected policies as audacious in their way as Germany's EEG.

As I noted earlier, Portland is home to a highly engaged progressive community, which first coalesced around strident opposition to a proposed downtown freeway in the early 1970s. The movement's champion at the state level was Tom McCall, who was elected governor in 1973 on a platform that was fervently anti-sprawl. Under McCall's storied leadership, Oregon's government passed the two key pieces of policy that have made Portland the model of urban planning it has become. The first of these, which united state senators representing left-leaning urbanites with those representing conservative farmers, was an unprecedented statewide land-use law that created a powerful oversight department to manage urban growth. A subsequent law, enacted in 1979, created "Metro" (the Metropolitan Service District, a regional government for metropolitan Portland) and gave it responsibility for enforcing the region's new Urban Growth Boundary, a firm line in the sand beyond which urban asphalt was forbidden to cross. Most of what has come to define modern Portland—the density sufficient to support top-notch mass transit and non-motorized commuting, the emissions reductions and LEED constructions, lavish praise from *Outside* magazine for its outdoorsy liveability and from the *Wall Street Journal* for its managerial success at controlling sprawl—have followed from these solid policy foundations.

Policy alone, though, tells only part of the story. Or, more accurately, policy tells no stories at all. It's a backdrop at best (and often a rather drab one). An urban growth boundary, even a more explosive device like the EEG—these are mere abstractions until they spark a populace to animated, excited action. It's the stories shared around the campfire that provide the real fuel of social change.

THE LORAX FALLACY (AS LITTLE POLITICS AS POSSIBLE)

"It is important to keep in mind that Portland's story about itself—or any community's story about itself—is more than a concatenation of events, outcomes, and key players." This is Bradshaw Hovey, an urban planning professor at Texas Southern University, writing about the evolution of a sustainable Portland in the journal *Utopian Studies* in 1998:

> In Portland's case, at least, it is also partly a myth or legend which carries a message about what kind of people Portlanders are, what the community values and what it opposes, about the right and the wrong way to do things in Portland, what it means to be a member of the community, and ultimately, what kind of a city they collectively wish to be. As such, the story is not just a tale to tell, but a powerful instrument with the capacity to celebrate past victories, to honor heroes, to warn future participants about right and wrong conduct, and to instruct outsiders about how things ought to be done.

The whole, in other words, is much greater than the sum of its parts. A stack of policies is not a society, and a group of politicians is not necessarily a movement, and none of it on its own would inspire Portland or any other community to greatness. Far from it: the very subject of politics—of preening politicians and their dreary policies—has come to be a widely recognized symbol of our age's civic malaise, the stalled engine responsible for its potentially fatal inertia. Who really expects anymore that dramatic, positive change will come to their lives from the current round of trade talks, the next stage of Kyoto negotiations, the coming election cycle or the one after that? Who's still holding out for a Churchillian fight-them-on-the-beaches battle cry or a Kennedyesque "Ask not what your country can do for you" or a reprise of Trudeaumania? And how dire must the situation become before we all agree that there's no one at the helm capable of leading us on this march?

This is the part of my journey where I'd hoped to insert a kind word about some sitting elected official of international stature—or even a promising candidate—who fully embraced the climate change challenge and embodied the hope of the Anthropocene Era. In good conscience, I can't think of one. (This is not to say there aren't leaders, only that they are not the sort of people who get invited to G8 summits.) The American government remains a global pariah on the issue, but the now-deposed Canadian government that ratified Kyoto can boast of a track record on emissions reductions no better than George W. Bush's. Even Denmark, global sustainability leader though it may be, is governed at present by reactionaries. Britain's Tony Blair often talked a great game, but that was always his speciality, and his soaring rhetoric's translation into ground-level action was mostly disappointing.*

In the vaunted free world in general, the alleged protectors of liberal democracy remain nearly everywhere trapped in an antiquated dichotomy of left and right that traces its origins and any number of its lingering divisions to the seating locations of representatives during the French Revolution. And nowhere has the disastrous stalemate created by this political divide been more apparent than on the subject of climate change, which finds itself subsumed in old debates about corporate tax rates, union jobs, farm subsidies, military misadventure and a thousand other luxuries that should be rendered irrelevant by the spectre of a volatile global climate hostile to human life as currently conceived.

What I mean is this: the environment, as an actual physical thing, is not a political issue. It is not open for debate, at least not in the same way that marginal tax rates or trade agreements with China are. It is not a human invention, nor a force capable of being bent entirely to human will. Quite the contrary, we are wholly dependent on its mercy for every single breath we take. The same delusion of externalities that permits economic growth to be balanced *against* maintaining a healthy planet also feeds the misconception that one can be, in any real sense, anti- (or for that matter pro-) environment. That it could be a political issue and not the sea in which all political issues swim. Sustainability should be built into enlightened constitutions alongside—*ahead of*—all other rights and freedoms, woven

---

* Case in point: Blair—apparently as much under the sway of centralized, externality-blind thinking as any current world leader—lurched eagerly for the putative magic bullet of nuclear power. He remains ignorant, it would appear, of the sage and as yet uncontested wisdom of *The Economist,* which has stated baldly of nuclear power plants that "not one, anywhere in the world, makes commercial sense." And this is without even somehow working into the price of atomic power the full cost of ten thousand years of hazardous-waste storage and the lunatic risk of widened traffic in fissionable material in an age of asymmetric warfare.

into the very fabric of political life the same way it needs to be folded back into the global economic system. The first unalienable right in America's Declaration of Independence is *life*, and it means nothing—no civil right does—without a sustainable climate in which to function. It *should* be that simple. But here comes a colossal understatement: It isn't.

So ridiculously and reflexively has the universal human problem of our age been cleaved into left and right that the two sides can't even agree on the terms of the discussion and what they mean. "Global warming" is addressed, and so contradictory data is produced attesting to record lows that January in Timbuktu. "Climate change"? Doesn't it always? Is this a question of public interest or private profit? Do we need better policy or greater public awareness, higher taxes or more efficient industry or a full-blown global revolution in consciousness? Think of it, ultimately, as a misconstrued and mostly artificial dichotomy between business as usual and personal virtue. A dichotomy maybe not quite wholly *false,* but certainly catastrophically mismatched and grossly overstated.

Think of it, let's say, as the Lorax Fallacy.

The Lorax, by Dr. Seuss, might be the first masterpiece of Anthropocene children's literature. Originally published in 1971, it's a Seussian take on *Silent Spring,* with echoes of the fall from grace in the book of Genesis. After a portentous preamble set in a bleak landscape verging on post-apocalyptic, the story opens with the arrival of a pilgrim named the Once-ler—by covered wagon, no less—to an Edenic glade. Primary-coloured Truffula Trees rain bountiful fruit upon playful bear-cub-like Bar-ba-loots, as carefree Swomee-Swans soar overhead and gleeful Humming-Fish splash in a nearby pond. The industrious Once-ler immediately realizes that the Truffula Trees' silken, perfumed tufts are a textile-manufacturing opportunity of the first order, and in no time at all he has a bustling factory up and running, churning out miracle garments he calls "Thneeds." (A Thneed, of course, is "a Fine-Something-That-All-People-Need," ready to serve as anything from a cozy sweater to a bicycle seat.)

The moment the Once-ler fells his first Truffula Tree, he's accosted by the Lorax—a cantankerous, elfish creature with a bushy muzzle—who claims to speak on behalf of those trees and the rest of the pristine wilderness besides. The Lorax demands an immediate and total logging ban, but the busy Once-ler pays him no mind. His business rapidly grows (*Oh! Baby! Oh!*), augmented by a factory staffed by his extended family and fed by an industrial clearcutting machine called the Super-Axe-Hacker. The Lorax brings sick, starving Bar-ba-loots and smog-choked Swomee-Swans to the factory to intensify his appeal, but still the Once-ler carries on biggering his Thneed business. Four great chimneys belch smoke into the sky as trainloads of Truffula tufts roll in one end of the factory and trucks adorned with the slick slogan YOU NEED A THNEED zoom out the other. Finally— inevitably—the Super-Axe-Hacker takes down the last Truffula Tree with "a sickening smack." The Once-ler's family, instantly redundant, hightails it back elsewhere, and the Lorax reappears just long enough to heave himself into the sky and vanish forever.

The Lorax closes where it began, with a wide-eyed boy's visit to the Once-ler's lonely tower on the far edge of town. The disgraced industrialist, stirred from his twisted, cynical solitude, tosses down the very last Truffula seed, urging the boy to plant it and nurture it, in the hope that just maybe the Lorax and the rest of the dead landscape's colourful creatures will return. The story ends, then, with little more than a grim hope, a singular *maybe* laden with qualifications and contingencies.

The Lorax is, on the surface, a pretty solid primer of first-wave environmentalism, and it has been widely interpreted as Seuss's statement of solidarity with the frontline soldiers of ecological defence. And yet when I recently made intimate reacquaintance with the book, I couldn't help but notice how fully it outlined the movement's tactical shortcomings and intellectual blind spots. How much it seemed like a warning about the fate not of Truffula groves but of effective political discourse. It occurred to me that this story might not be a cautionary tale about environmental devastation at all, but rather an allegorical warning about the tragic consequences of human miscommunication.

If the Lorax is meant to be the book's more sympathetic character, he is barely so. He first appears to the Once-ler bellowing orders in a voice "sharpish and bossy." He's openly contemptuous of the very idea of a Thneed, and he knows nothing and cares less about the Once-ler's intentions, his plans, his *needs*. "I meant no harm," the Once-ler insists. "I most truly did not." But still the Lorax barks out his gripes, dragging the "dirty old Once-ler man" along to lecture him about his factory's Gluppity-Glupp and Schloppity-Schlopp and the trouble it's causing. He pisses the Once-ler off royally, is what he does; the last overwrought bout of Thneed factory expansion occurs almost as a retort. The Once-ler may be dismissive of the Lorax, indifferent to his factory's toxic impact on Bar-ba-loots and ignorant of the looming threat of deforestation, but the Lorax *doesn't listen either.* He doesn't stop for even a moment to consider the possibility that the Once-ler might have reasons for his Truffula axe-hackery, that he might even have a *right* to make his own livelihood. Worst of all, he never tries to figure out *why* the Once-ler does what he does. He just scolds. He lectures. He hassles and pesters.

This is the essence of the Lorax Fallacy: the idea that there could be diametrical opposition on a question as basic to human survival as the fate of the planet. The Once-ler's obvious error is an all-too-familiar one of abysmal resource management, but the Lorax is also culpable, because he never acknowledges the Once-ler's essential right to a productive existence, dependent as he is on the planet's bounty for his survival just as fully as the most elegant, innocent Swomee-Swan or the lecturing Lorax himself. This is (intentionally?) underscored by the illustrations, in which the Once-ler appears only as a pair of green gesticulating arms. *The Lorax* is thus an escalating argument between an incorporeal, dehumanized businessman and an inhuman snorting animal. The only *people* in the book are the saps who buy up the Thneeds and the kid who shows up at the end to find out what the hell happened.

In *The Lorax*'s narrative arc, the dissolution of the ecological debate into two warring factions has been foretold, the environmental movement's own decline clearly etched. From the moment the first Truffula Tree is chopped down, the Lorax does little but hit back with slicing oratory, and the conflict soon becomes intractable. Even as total devastation approaches, there is no attempt at co-operation, no recognition of mutual self-interest. In the end, there's only the dimmest hope of redemption. This catastrophe is our own, and it's not strictly a product of the Once-ler's short-sightedness. He's not innately evil or insatiably rapacious; he's just a business-minded guy doing his biggering job the only way he knows how. The Lorax, like too many righteously indignant protectors of nature, eagerly reinforces the false notion that "nature" can be divorced from human existence and defended as if it were a separate and sacrosanct temple. He resists the encroachment of humanity with a single-minded zeal equal to the Once-ler's axe-swinging.

In the years since the environmental movement's first interventions on the earth's behalf, a common popular criticism has been that environmentalists care more about whales and condors than they do about people. It might be inaccurate, overstated, fed by the well-funded rumour-mongering of its opponents, but the prevalence of this sentiment says nothing very good about the movement's ability to transform itself from an activist counterculture into a mainstream voice of the universal public interest.

I'm reminded again of my own brief stint in the activist army, tromping door to door as a Greenpeace canvasser, begging for spare change to fund a battle that brought little but despair even to those of us who were deeply immersed in it. There was one evening in particular I spent door-knocking in an affluent suburb of Kingston. I'd raised a princely five bucks in the first two hours, and the get-the-fuck-off-my-porch vibe was as thick as the humid Ontario summer air. I walked away from one particularly hostile dismissal to find my partner, a veteran campaigner and one of the local office's stars, seated on the curb, smoking a cigarette. I lit one of my own and we fell into a familiar desultory dialogue laced with bile for all the ignorance in the world. He started talking about the horrors of the local DuPont chemical plant. About how, even if you decided in a Once-lerish bout of spite to become the worst consumer you possibly could, seeking out a Freon-filled refrigerator, aerosol sprays, gas-guzzling vehicles and triple-wrapped plastic everything, you'd still do no more harm to the planet's ecology in your lifetime than the DuPont plant did in a week. (Or maybe it was a month, or else a year. A short while, anyway.) The hypothetical damage seemed to hang there in the thick air, shrouded in the smoke from our cigarettes. I had to wonder what chance a brigade of glorified panhandlers armed with pamphlets and clipboards had against something as relentlessly powerful as that. And the money we raised? Destined, perhaps, to cover the operating costs of some daring stunt that might find barely 15 minutes of minor fame in a story tucked on a deep inside page next to the distant foreign news.

And yet this was and remains one of the core strategies of many environmental activist groups: grandstanding attempts at the public humiliation of their big-business foes. Admittedly, it was for a time an effective approach. When the enemies were still Once-lerishly wanton in their axe-hackery, it was sometimes enough to catch them in the act, put the crime on public display and wait for an outraged populace to demand redress from its elected officials.

In May 2006, I went to see David Suzuki speak at a Calgary church. He was on a book tour for his new autobiography, and his presentation consisted primarily of a slide show of his life and times. The pictures from the early days of his activist work were particularly moving. Here was a pristine beach, backing on a stand of impossibly ancient and monumentally tall trees. These were the Queen Charlotte Islands off the coast of British Columbia, and here were the Haida, their sovereign residents and reliable stewards of their unique ecology for thousands of years. Next came the activists in parkas and pony-tails, Suzuki among them, arriving to join the Haida in defence of their land against a criminally insane logging permit. A stand was made, a victory secured. The B.C. government soon announced a moratorium, and the island was declared a national park a few years after that. In the final slides from the sequence, hands were raised in triumph and bodies danced in ecstasy.

On this night, Suzuki was touting a policy document called "Sustainability within a Generation." He noted ruefully that when Calgary's own Stephen Harper, a staunch Conservative, had become prime minister the previous fall, Suzuki had requested a meeting to discuss the plan, which outlined a policy path to sustainability for Canada by 2030. Harper's office summarily refused. Suzuki, recently voted the nation's fifth-greatest citizen of all time by the CBC's view-ers, was unworthy of even a brief chat. There would be no victory dance any time soon. Times had emphatically changed.

It would require an acute strain of wilful delusion to maintain the belief, in today's political environment, that the solution to climate change will begin with policy or that it will be led by politicians of national or even international stature. The established pattern—a problem identified, awareness raised, the crisis addressed by the elected guardians of the public interest—has proven too narrow in its scope and too politically charged to deal with a crisis as universal as climate change. Too many of the veterans of those delirious conservation victories, however, seem stuck in their old habits. Just a couple of months after Suzuki's speech, for example, I was flipping through the local paper and found a wire-service item in its usual spot on an inside page. "Greenpeace Targets Crop," the headline read. The photo underneath showed a field of corn in France. Greenpeace activists had carved a huge encircled X into the field—"a contamination symbol," the caption noted. There was no accompanying story, and the two-line photo caption was a jumble of jargon about genetically modified crops and French court orders and something about a map pulled off a website. It was late July 2006. Europe was in the clutches of the worst heat wave since the deadly hot summer of 2003, and France was being hit particularly hard: about forty people had died from the heat, and Paris's water table had reached a twenty-year low. If the soaring temperatures were not a direct, scientifically incontrovertible result of climate change, they were certainly the exact sort of extreme weather phenomenon that had made people increasingly receptive to addressing the topic with the gravity it deserved. And Greenpeace had apparently decided that the best use of its time and resources in France was to cut a hieroglyphic into a field of sun-baked corn. The leadership vacuum evidently extended beyond the halls of government.

It was like Dylan put it: *Don't follow leaders, watch the parkin' meters.* Or was it this one: *You don't need a weatherman to know which way the wind blows*? Take your pick. You could shake those subterranean homesick blues either way.

THE VISION THING (A FEW BIG IDEAS)

In the absence of bold elected leadership, there has nevertheless been progress. Dylan, for his part, ditched the tarnished revolutionary warrens *like a bird that flew, tangled up in blue.* And following *his* lead, there have been some determined folks who just kept on keepin' on. One of them, a Bangladeshi banker named Muhammad Yunus, won the 2006 Nobel Peace Prize for his efforts. Yunus shared the award, actually, with the Grameen Bank, the pioneering financial institution he founded in the mid-1970s. He might've called it the Schumacher Bank: Grameen's approach to lending money was so consistent with the economic philosophy outlined in *Small Is Beautiful,* it could've been the book's epilogue.

In a former life, Yunus was a doctrinaire economics professor at Bangladesh's Chittagong University, dutifully instructing his students on the ways and means of GDP growth and externalities. But when the skeletal victims of the brutal famine that ravaged rural Bangladesh in 1974 began to turn up in the city streets, they disarmed Yunus completely. "Nothing in the economic theories I taught reflected the life around me," he told a PBS documentary crew years later. "How could I go on telling my students make-believe stories in the name of economics? I needed to run away from these theories and from my textbooks and discover the real-life economics of a poor person's existence." He began with personal loans that amounted to little more than pocket change. In 1976, he founded the organization that would become the Grameen Bank, and in 1983 it became a full-fledged financial institution under a special legislative act of Bangladesh's parliament.

Grameen's strategy—*microcredit,* in a word—is simple, effective and easily duplicated. The bank loans relatively small amounts of money to Bangladeshi villagers in groups of five, with no collateral aside from peer pressure. If any member of the group defaults on a loan, no one in the group can receive further credit. It's a revolutionary approach to both banking and international development, tinged with socialist heresy, but it has produced incontestable results: more than $6 billion in loans to date to about seven million clients, 97 percent of them women (even more heretical in the intensely patriarchal society of rural Bangladesh). The Grameen strategy has yielded a repayment rate in excess of 98 percent and an ever-expanding family of microcredit-financed rural improvement plans, including low-cost telephone services and the installation of more than seventy thousand small-scale "solar home systems" by Grameen Shakti, a non-profit renewable-energy spinoff company. Grameen Bank has also produced a model that has been mimicked by aid groups large and small the world over. In one of the poorest nations on earth, Yunus and his microcredit institution have single-handedly decentralized a pair of industries (banking and international development) formerly as monolithically Big as, for example, the energy business, and at the same time put money into the hands of millions of rural women— the poorest and most powerless members of Bangladeshi society. Grameen is the first major lending institution, it would seem, of the

Schumacheresque middle, balanced between the left-wing fervour for enlightened public institutions and the right-wing obsession with private capital.

Still, there were critics of the Nobel committee's choice, particularly among the more dogmatic quarters of the global anti-corporate left. In most cases, this was mere pedantry—*a banker? what did* banking *have to do with peace?*—but Yunus's work had also attracted more involved critiques. These focused primarily on Grameen's willingness to consider working with multinational corporations. Several years earlier, Yunus had agreed to co-operate in the launch of something called the Grameen Monsanto Centre for Environmentally Friendly Technologies, which would have served primarily as a means for the petrochemical giant Monsanto to loan poor Bangladeshi farmers money to buy its pesticides and genetically modified seeds.

The potentially exploitive aspects of the proposed Grameen-Monsanto partnership were enumerated for Muhammad Yunus in a cogent and sharply argued open letter sent to him by Vandana Shiva, one of India's most prominent and effective environmental activists. Monsanto, Shiva wrote, peddled technologies that "pose a threat to ecosystems and agriculture. . . . Grameen Monsanto Centre will become a partner in the destruction of biodiversity and farmers' livelihoods supported by free access to biodiversity. You will have contributed to the establishment of monopolies on seeds through patents . . . or through technologies like the 'Terminator' which are designed to prevent the germination of future generations of seed so that farmers are forced to buy seed every year. Your microcredit support to the spread of Terminator seeds or patented seeds will not liberate the poor; it will enslave them irreversibly."

Shiva knew this terrain intimately. Since the early 1980s, she had led a grassroots organic movement of Indian farmers through an organization that came to be known as Navdanya (Hindi for "nine seeds"). In 1994, an American agribusiness company called RiceTec attempted to obtain patents for a widely planted strain of basmati rice—the predominant Indian varietal and the staple food of hundreds of millions on the subcontinent—initiating a protracted battle that would bring Shiva and her organization to global prominence. Navdanya began a boisterous public protest campaign in 1998, and by 2001 RiceTec's most significant patent claims had been struck down in court. It was just as this battle was reaching its peak that Shiva wrote to Yunus, addressing him as a wayward comrade. "You have made a name for yourself in the annals of history through your innovation and commitment to the poor in setting up the Grameen Bank to serve rural women in Bangladesh. I am sure you will not want your efforts to be hijacked as a marketing strategy by Monsanto." Shiva's letter was dated July 4, 1998; just over three weeks later, Yunus dissolved the partnership with Monsanto.

Shiva's plea had been widely circulated in activist circles, however, and Yunus's achievements were subsequently flagged with a suspicious asterisk: *nearly worked with Monsanto.* In the wake of his Nobel moment, Shiva was soon called upon for her take on the authenticity of his virtue. "Microcredit: Solution to Poverty or False 'Compassionate Capitalism'?"—this was the slanted title of a debate between Shiva and the current Grameen chair, Susan Davis, on the syndicated progressive radio program *Democracy Now!* (There and elsewhere, Shiva duly noted that she admired Yunus's work and was relieved that he had broken his deal with Monsanto.) It was, alas, troubling testimony to the bunker mentality of the old-guard left. Muhammad Yunus, among *bankers* surely the planet's most ardent champion of sustainable solutions to rural poverty, was the peddler of "false" strategies only if the goal was no banks whatsoever, if loaning money even at relatively low interest, even for unimpeachable causes, was intrinsically impure. And he and Shiva were opponents only if there had been any number of enormous strategic miscalculations on the part of the broader progressive movement. What no one bothered to ask on *Democracy Now!* was to my mind the most obvious question: How was it that two committed crusaders for social justice and sustainability, working among essentially the same kinds of people facing nearly identical problems in bordering countries, weren't working *together?*

In the attempt to bait Shiva into a denouncement of Yunus, there were echoes of the countless internecine squabbles that have contributed to the political left's maddening ineffectiveness in its response to climate change. A persistent, dogmatic politics of personal virtue—insisting as it sometimes does that you are only as committed as the vehicle you used to get to the protest march, judging you readily on the content of your last meal—has created a "movement" so segmented and internally divisive that it confuses soft allegiance with strident opposition and qualified agreement with outright dissent, and it thereby refuses to fully recognize the rules of the larger life-and-death game it claims to be playing. If the fate of humanity itself is hanging in the balance of the climate change debate, is it prudent to demand complete ideological purity from some of your most prominent and successful would-be allies?

At the same time, factions of the movement have ignored the larger game entirely. Vandana Shiva's efforts on behalf of Indian farmers, for example, are certainly to be lauded. But demonizing Monsanto will accomplish little in the long run unless the impoverished people she works with gain access to tools like microcredit that will give them options other than the short-term salve of deep-discounted, genetically engineered seed. And, moreover, unless the climate their crops depend on returns to some sort of stability. At the hearts-and-minds level of public perception, such compartmentalized strategies have been disastrous. As more and more of the world awakens to the difficult facts of the Anthropocene Era, the people with the greatest depth of experience in addressing the issue seem, in the public eye, like some of the least credible people to speak on behalf of its interests. The movement doesn't lack for great big exciting ideas—Shiva's effective grassroots campaign to limit the power of corporate seed companies provides an example as laudable as Yunus's Nobel-winning microcredit revolution. What it lacks is the unifying vision that would put both of them on facing pages in the same sustainability playbook.

"The Death of Environmentalism," that incendiary 2004 essay by Michael Shellenberger and Ted Nordhaus, was in essence an attempt to knock progressive politics out of its familiar ruts and instigate a dialogue on the pressing need for the formulation and implementation of just such a playbook. The essay began with a brief, grateful acknowledgement of the many substantial achievements of the old guard, but it quickly pivoted to more pressing concerns: "At the same time, we believe that the best way to honor their achievements is to acknowledge that modern environmentalism is no longer capable of dealing with the world's most serious ecological crisis." The authors invoked the memory of Martin Luther King's legendary "I have a dream" speech, and wryly noted that the fate of the civil rights movement might have been far less impressive if King had attempted to inspire the masses gathered at the foot of the Lincoln Memorial by repeatedly invoking the slogan "I have a nightmare." Their conclusion pointed toward a new kind of vision: "Environmentalists need to tap into the creative worlds of myth-making, even religion, not to better sell narrow and technical policy proposals but rather to figure out who we are and who we need to be."

In the months before the essay's publication, Shellenberger and Nordhaus had been working with former Sierra Club president Adam Werbach and other like-minded reformers on the construction of a new political movement. Their efforts produced a broad coalition of American activists, labour leaders and lobby groups. In a deliberate break with the flatlined past, this new coalition chose to skip over the standard environmentalist metaphors of protection and defence when it went looking for a name, deciding instead to use the space race as its rhetorical touchstone. It introduced itself as the "New Apollo Project for Energy Independence and Good Jobs" (later shortened to "the Apollo Alliance"), and set as its goal the achievement of full energy independence for the United States within a generation, in the process renewing America's manufacturing base by building a robust domestic clean-tech industry. The sociopolitical model for the plan was John F. Kennedy's 1961 commitment—an outrageously expensive, borderline-preposterous notion at the time—to land a manned mission on the moon by the end of the 1960s.

One of the most startling passages in Adam Werbach's autopsy of the environmental movement—in the speech he delivered just a couple of months after the publication of "The Death of Environmentalism"— was his recollection of one of the Apollo Alliance's first initiatives. In 2003, Werbach and his colleagues trekked to a few down-at-heel Rust Belt burgs in Ohio and Pennsylvania to conduct focus group research among "undecided, working-class swing voters"—the ones who would decide the fate of America's presidential election a year later. Initially, the assembled subjects were simply asked how things were going. They responded with a litany of hardships: manufacturing plant closings, dead-end service-industry wage slavery, toiling at two jobs just to scrape by; environmental concerns were far down the list. Next, the same anxious people were presented with the Apollo Alliance's vision: a federally funded mission to create a clean, self-reliant energy regime, with people like them employed in its construction. The reaction, Werbach explained, was nothing short of revolutionary: "What had been a roomful of tired and semi-depressed working folks transformed itself into a roomful of excited, optimistic Americans in a period of just twenty minutes. The energy emanating from the room was palpable. And then something extraordinary happened. Nearly every single person in the room started to sound like Sierra Club members. I could hardly believe what I was hearing. They waxed poetic about solar panels. They spoke of their children's future—their future—and the planet's future."

The Apollo Alliance took its results to "anyone who would listen." It quickly convinced the Sierra Club, several prominent politicians and practically every major union in the country to sign on to its vision. Soon after, it was adopted by John Kerry as a key peg in his campaign to become the Democratic Party's presidential candidate. Once he had won the nomination, however, the broad, holistic version of the plan that'd so inspired those Rust Belt focus groups was dismantled by Kerry's campaign staff, who insisted on keeping "energy independence" separate from their other key talking points. The idea of federal investment in renewables was abandoned in favour of endorsing deficit reduction, and energy policy and job creation were treated as separate and unrelated issues. Kerry lost the election, and many pundits argued afterward that his defeat hinged on his failure to articulate an inspiring and holistic vision of America's future. Werbach's reaction: "I almost slugged a wall."

His frustration is perfectly understandable. I have to wonder, though, if part of his problem lay in hoping that the Democratic Party of 2004 could transform itself overnight into an engine of leadership and inspiration worthy of Kennedy's best and brightest. The green-jobs platform and the space-race metaphor were smart choices, clearly articulating a vision of a nation's renewal through the pursuit of a seemingly impossible goal at an extremely rapid rate. But the plan foundered, at least in its first flight, on the grim realities of contemporary politics, splitting apart into unrecognizable fragments in its collision with issue-obsessed pollsters and talking-pointed advisers.

A larger problem, though, may have been simple timing. This was one of the key lessons contained in Malcolm Gladwell's *The Tipping Point*, a mammoth bestseller about the nature of social epidemics—a book so successful that its own title was transformed into a contemporary proof of the phenomenon it detailed, becoming so ubiquitous that it was reduced almost overnight to cliché. A "tipping point," in Gladwell's definition, "is that magic moment when an idea, trend or social behavior crosses a threshold, tips and spreads like wildfire."

The public perception of anthropogenic climate change may have breached just such a threshold in the year after the Apollo Alliance's failed attempt to induce one—in August 2005, when a major American city, pretty much in its entirety, was reduced to ruins by a single storm. In the wake of Hurricane Katrina, as images of a devastated New Orleans made it all too gut-wrenchingly clear how fragile our existence was in the face of an agitated climate, it became much more difficult to claim that there were diametrically opposed "sides" to be taken in matters of ecology. In those first astonishing days after New Orleans was inundated, the only "side" was whichever one pointed to higher ground. There was humanity, and there was an abyss. And so when *Newsweek* spoke the following year about "a post-Katrina future" in which environmentalism was "hot" and sustainability an enticing new rallying "banner," it needed no further elaboration for many readers. Enough people—even in skeptical America—now *got it.*

The ferocity of the problem that came crashing through Louisiana's breached levees carried it as far and wide as live satellite feeds could reach. Maybe it was the disorienting televised spectacle of a whole city in the world's wealthiest and most powerful country reduced to rubble, the continuing story of a flailing salvage operation, the implicit notion that this could happen *anywhere*—but whatever the impetus, the runoff from the unprecedented storm circled the globe. A survey conducted in thirty countries in April 2006 found that 90 percent of the total respondents were ready to declare climate change a "serious" problem. A clear but smaller majority in twenty-three of those countries was willing to go so far as to say "very serious." The other seven, where only a minority saw the permanent manmade alteration of the world's climate as *very* serious, consisted of six developing nations—and the United States.

In an extraordinary case of accidentally flawless timing, the October 2005 issue of *Harper's Magazine,* which had gone to press just before Katrina howled ashore, contained an essay by the

American activist and writer Rebecca Solnit entitled "The Uses of Disaster." It touched upon previous calamities far removed in time and space, from San Francisco's devastating 1906 earthquake to the terrorist attacks of 9/11, from the recent Asian tsunami to the 2003 hurricane that battered Halifax. Solnit's subject was not the human devastation at the centre of these disasters (which she acknowledged was often incalculably large) but the enormous opportunities for renewal at the margins. "Around the periphery of many disasters," she wrote, "is a far larger population of people who are unhurt but deeply *disrupted*. Often enough, many of those people find the disruption deeply satisfying as well as unnerving." Disasters, she explained, often produce a temporary suspension of centralized authority, and the balance of evidence suggests that human populations react to those anarchic interludes not with panic and chaos and clawing scrambles to save themselves but with incredible selflessness and renewed purpose. Solnit: "Again and again, we see a latent civil society—a *community*—arising from the ruins of some disaster and becoming the grounds for connection and joy. Moreover, for those who are not overwhelmed, for those who improvise substitutes for the electricity or the heat or the house itself, disaster can give them a sense of potency and purpose that everyday life lacks. The problem comes from outside and is clearly identifiable, as is the necessary response—put out the fire, sandbag the river, rescue the trapped, restore the power."*

Anthropogenic climate change, many now agree, is a disaster of unprecedented magnitude, but it is unfolding at the geological pace of glaciers and ocean currents, and the extent of the damage from today's emissions won't be felt in full for half a century or more. There exists an outside chance of a Hollywood-scale catastrophe (the action thriller *The Day After Tomorrow* took a far-fetched and vastly overstated version of one of these as its premise), but its more likely impact will be a continuing accumulation of problems on smaller scales in seemingly isolated pockets over much longer time frames—here a drought, there a deluge, wildfires on the outskirts of Sydney

---

* In an online postscript, Solnit suggested that the chaos in New Orleans was caused not so much by authority's absence as by its ferocious and misdirected return—by the official blockade of the bridge that led to higher ground, for example.

and a pine beetle plague in the forests of western Canada. To address this amorphous and intermittently manifest disaster with the clarity Solnit described—a problem coming from outside, clearly identifiable, with a necessary response—might be the greatest challenge facing those who would take charge of the public discourse about climate change and guide us to the high ground of sustainability. The crux of this problem is ultimately *social:* our response will benefit from improvements in technology and more finely tuned policy, but the essential factor is the creation of the collective will to build anew.

Solnit, summing up: "Disaster makes it clear that our interdependence is not only an inescapable fact but a fact worth celebrating—that the production of civil society is a work of love, indeed the work that many of us desire most." There's that, as well: *a fact worth celebrating.* Maybe that most of all. We run from nightmares; we aspire to live in certain kinds of dream.

THE NEW GREEN DREAM (A MUCH BETTER VIEW THROUGH A NEW KIND OF FRAME)

The mechanics of rapid, widespread social change was the focus of *The Tipping Point,* and *stickiness* was another of the buzzwords widely disseminated in the aftermath of the book's own tipping point. "The Stickiness Factor," in Malcolm Gladwell's taxonomy, was a nebulous, almost mystical force, which made it all the more powerful. "The hard part of communication," Gladwell wrote, "is often figuring out how to make sure a message doesn't go in one ear and out the other. Stickiness means that a message makes an impact. You can't get it out of your head. It sticks in your memory." Stickiness plants jingles in your brain and renders slogans unforgettable. It's the glue of the information age.

A more recent book, *Made to Stick,* an acknowledged companion piece to Gladwell's book by the sibling social-behaviour researchers Chip and Dan Heath, expanded on this concept. Assembling a wide cross-section of the kinds of stories that "stick"—from proverbs and folklore to urban myths and clever public relations stunts—the Heaths found that sticky ideas are usually simple, unexpected and concrete in detail (ideally appealing directly to the senses). They appear credible and they appeal to their audience's emotions more than their intellect. (They are thus generally not laden with statistics.)

Finally—perhaps most importantly—they are *stories*. Not arguments, not policy briefs, certainly not scientific reports. Stories.

One example the Heaths cited prominently was a public health problem first identified in the early 1990s: the average bag of movie popcorn contained 37 grams of saturated fat, nearly twice the recommended daily maximum intake. The coconut oil many theatres used to pop their corn was, it turned out, a huge threat to public health. The stat, though, meant nothing to a general audience. (How much was 37 grams? How bad was saturated fat?) So the researchers who made the discovery chose to announce their findings at a press conference, standing at a table laid out with a full day's worth of unhealthy eating: greasy bacon and eggs, a McDonald's lunch, a steak dinner. Here was the movie popcorn's saturated fat load as a diorama, and it told a story of reckless gluttony instantly recognizable to anyone with a stomach. It hurt just to look at it. Shortly thereafter, responding to blanket mass-media coverage and constant customer inquiries, most of North America's major movie theatre chains phased out coconut oil.

The movie popcorn story was a rare example of maximum stickiness. At least as often, the Heaths warned, important information was lost to a pervasive "villain." They referred to it as the "Curse of Knowledge," which they explained like this: "Once we know something, we find it hard to imagine what it was like not to know it."

The Greenpeace crop-circle stunt I mentioned earlier was a textbook case of the Curse of Knowledge. To a Greenpeace campaigner, the pictogram carved into that farmer's field in France was instantly recognizable as a contamination symbol, and the only possible conclusion to be drawn from it—in an instant, surely—was that this was a field of genetically modified crops, which *as everyone knows* represent a tremendous threat to the health of consumers and the planet in general. To the overwhelming majority of average folks scanning it for a bleary moment in their morning paper, though, it might as well have been the group's logo or a DO NOT ENTER sign, a mathematical representation of the speed of light or the molecular weight of chlorophyll, and so anyway pass me the sports, I wonder if the Jays won last night. You gonna finish that bagel?

But the crop circle, despite the faulty assumptions on which the stunt was based, was at least an *attempt* to speak to the general public on the potentially universal plane of symbols and images. The climate change debate has been far more prone to complete incomprehensibility, a tale told by activists and scientists in a bewildering stream of obscure technical terms and decontextualized statistics, timelines that dwarf human understanding and weather forecasts so minutely tweaked as to seem inconsequential. *One degree warmer? I won't even have to change my shirt for that! And what's this about the last ice age?* How *many years ago? Parts per* what *now? Is that, like, a lot?*

Beyond this accursed flow of decontextualized knowledge from the purported experts and advocates, the mediascape has been awash in confusing and contradictory messages of other kinds: dire warnings about problems of impossible magnitude coupled with snappy lists of five or eight or ten ridiculously trivial "things *you* can do" to solve them; vivid portraits of future-tense catastrophe that verge on fetishistic, followed in the next breath by vague, almost offhand references to strategies for avoiding them. In hotels the world over, I regularly encountered the newly ubiquitous bathroom card urging guests to hang their towels back on the racks, thus avoiding unnecessary laundry loads, which would, I was assured, *save the planet!* And then I would crawl into bed with yet another thick volume on the imminent arrival of ecological doomsday, slogging though pages of tedious science, harrowing statistics and minutely detailed descriptions of bleached coral and polar bear corpses, to come eventually to a slim final chapter of bullet-pointed policy recommendations or half-hearted plans for a spontaneous revolution in human consciousness. Which seemed, as I reached wearily for the light, about as likely to bring salvation as my damp towels dutifully hanging from the bathroom rack. It was the vivid horror, not the dim hope, that stuck.

To its credit, a significant segment of the environmental movement has awakened in recent years to the fact that its messages are woefully deficient in glue. And so, alongside the Apollo Alliance's impassioned calls for political reform and the launching of new moonshot-scale campaigns, there also emerged a pair of high-profile studies—one in the United States, the other in the United Kingdom—on the effectiveness of the movement's "framing" of the climate change discussion. The American study, undertaken by a communications think tank called the FrameWorks Institute on behalf of a handful of prominent environmental groups, explained the term like this: "Framing refers to the way a story is told, its selective use of particular symbols, metaphors, and messages." It is through existing "frames"—deeply planted, long-established story structures flowing through the popular consciousness, built upon myth, cultural bias and (increasingly) the structural and ideological biases of the mass media—that people "assign meaning to unfolding events." These frames, and the way in which a new piece of information fits into them, determine whether we respond to a news report about the unprecedented melting of arctic ice, for example, by installing solar panels, stocking up on canned goods, drafting a stern letter of protest (or support) to our local government representative, or shrugging and changing the channel.

Neither the American nor the British study offered much in the way of praise for the environmental movement's framing skills. The U.K. study was the more recent, published in the summer of 2006 by the Institute for Public Policy Research (IPPR), a prominent British think tank. The IPPR's researchers had pored over hundreds of recent newspaper clippings and hundreds more broadcast news stories, advertisements and online documents, searching in vain for clarity. This was the study's opening summary: "The research found that the climate change discourse in the UK today looks confusing, contradictory and chaotic. . . . It seems likely that the overarching message for the lay public is that in fact, nobody knows." Still, the IPPR uncovered several dominant currents amid the static (which currents it calls "repertoires," essentially identical to the FrameWorks study's "frames"). The most common of these repertoires was an alarmism that sometimes came across as "a form of 'climate porn,'" followed closely by a "small actions" theme that often seemed like it was being presented as the antidote to the alarmist story. "Bringing together these two repertoires without reconciling them, juxtaposing the apocalyptic and the mundane, seems likely to feed an asymmetry in human agency with regards to climate change and highlight the unspoken but obvious question: how can small actions really make a difference to things happening on this epic scale?"

The dominant themes uncovered in the American media by the FrameWorks analysis spoke to a similar state of confusion. In the

United States, the report explained, climate change "tends to be framed in one of two ways—as scary weather, or as an economic issue." Neither version served the cause well. The weather story, appearing to discuss a force beyond human control, provoked "a kind of adaptive response," a "head-for-the-hills" self-preservation mindset. The economic story, meanwhile, made climate change seem like "a necessary evil, the inevitable byproduct of industrialization," and in this context, calls to change behaviour seemed "impractical" and the organizations calling for the changes appeared out of touch with reality.

Both studies described a dysfunctional communications strategy and a public debate pointed in two hopelessly counterproductive directions. Either the problem was so enormous and intractable that it lay well beyond our ability to address it in any meaningful way, or else the recommended solutions seemed absurdly trivial. Either way, there wasn't much to be done. This wasn't something that could be *engaged*.

To bridge the gap between the apocalyptic countenance of the problem and the workaday banality of some of the first steps toward a solution—to craft sticky messages, that is—the IPPR report recommended employing the devices of mythology. Specifically, the report suggested the celebration of "ordinary heroism," which it noted was a British cultural tradition dating back at least to the "Dunkirk spirit" of the Second World War. And now *there* was an astute observation—a powerful and malleable metaphor, and also a *precedent*. After all, some of the twentieth century's first successful environmental campaigns were austerity programs enacted throughout the free world during the war. Victory gardens and victory bonds, the careful accounting of every scrap of precious tin and rubber, even fuel conservation campaigns whose posters needed no updating whatsoever to be applicable to the Anthropocene.

The FrameWorks study, for its part, was a little more conceptual in its suggestions for improving the framing of the debate. And because it was anticipating an American audience still confused or in some cases openly hostile to the facts of the issue, its first priority was to make comprehensible the very facts of climate change. The key, the study argued, was a carefully orchestrated message that moved from the universal to the specific—an inversion of the norm. FrameWorks recommended beginning not with terrifying scenarios or confusing emissions stats but with universal values like responsibility and ingenuity. (*Is it* responsible *to rely on one energy source?*—this was an example of an effective framing question.) The next stage of the message would "bring global warming down to earth" and "make it manageable," explaining the problem in simple language with a shortened timeline, and replacing the plight of exotic animals with a human face. Finally, the message was to be hammered home with a "simplifying model"—a straightforward metaphor that painted a clear picture of the nature of the problem. This might involve describing the greenhouse effect, for example, as "a man-made blanket of carbon dioxide that traps heat." Beyond this, the report suggested a reasonable tone that put a high priority on solutions, and it recommended employing traditional authority figures in the delivery of the message—captains of industry, scientists, clergy, those sorts of people. The FrameWorks study did not specifically mention narrowly defeated presidential candidates who had lost the White House as a result of a Supreme Court ruling, but the rest of its structural notes might sound familiar nonetheless to anyone who saw the Al Gore documentary *An Inconvenient Truth.*

A documentary about Al Gore's PowerPoint presentation on the climate crisis—this could not possibly have struck many people at first as a film concept destined to become one of highest-grossing documentaries of all time and an Oscar winner that would turn Gore from punchline into elder statesman on the most pressing issue of the day. Not to mention doing more all by itself than any other half-dozen climate change campaigns to educate the public on that very urgency. *An Inconvenient Truth* was the FrameWorks study come to the multiplex: a well-known public figure, a clear, concise and carefully structured presentation, a reasonably toned delivery that was by turns passionate and self-effacing.

In one of the film's most effective scenes, Gore is on stage in a lecture hall, pacing in front of a screen as wide as the stage itself. Two near-identical spiking curves run the width of the screen, tracing 650,000 years of fluctuations in global CO_2 concentrations and average temperatures. Gore reaches the edge of the stage. He points from the top of the pictured range 5 feet above his head to the bottom at his feet, explaining that, for the densely populated northeastern United States, this gap means "the difference between a nice day and having a mile of ice over your head." He pauses just long enough for the graph's scale to sink in. "Keep that in mind," he continues casually, "when you look at this fact." Current CO_2 concentrations are then added to the graph, which veers sharply skyward. "Now if you'll bear with me," Gore continues, "I want to *really* emphasize this point." He steps onto a motorized platform at stage left, a contraption like a fire engine's cherrypicker, and ascends smoothly to a height a couple of storeys off the stage, where the graph of the projected CO_2 concentration for the middle of the twenty-first century finally ends. "You've heard of 'off the charts,'" he notes with gentle irony as he nears the apex. He notes that the *fact* of this projection is not in dispute, only its import. Some skeptics, he says mildly, think this would be just fine. The audience laughs. They *get it*. How could they *not?* The message is as sticky as a series of Burma-Shave billboards.

Notwithstanding Gore's stature as a deposed Democratic presidential candidate, the scene is reasonable, non-partisan, *universal*—a perfectly framed climate change message, a diorama every bit as powerful as a table piled high with three meals' worth of saturated fat. It was also well timed, the film's release coming less than a year after Katrina's wrath, before the storm's aftershocks had receded into the generalized white noise of the contemporary mediascape. There was a question being asked with renewed urgency—*How could this have possibly happened?*—and if *An Inconvenient Truth* didn't quite answer it directly, it spoke to the concern with greater compassion and clarity than the shrugs on offer from the authorities whose duty it was to address it. The film described a clearly identifiable problem, and if it didn't have a tremendous amount to say on the subject of necessary responses, it did demonstrate in no uncertain terms that responses *were* necessary. And fortunately, there was around then a nascent wave of next-generation environmentalism emerging to sketch the form those responses might take.

This New Green movement was a bit older than Gore's PowerPoint roadshow, actually, dating back at least as far as the last years of his service as vice-president of the United States. It traced its roots back through the surprisingly energetic presidential campaign of Howard Dean and the millennial series of riotous protests against World Trade Organization meetings and G8 summits to the first cultural and communal flowerings of the digital boom. It has emerged as a whip-smart and web-enabled movement, cautiously optimistic but rarely naive, ironic and sometimes cynical, but with far less of the old green despair. You can read a rough draft of its new take on the subject in the titles and taglines of the handful of online magazines and countless blogs where it's being hammered out at digital speed via multiple daily updates.

Among the most prominent names is *Grist,* which promises "doom and gloom with a sense of humor." *Grist* is an online magazine where you might find a thoughtful twelve-part analysis of the fallout from the Shellenberger/Nordhaus "Death of Environmentalism" essay or the profile of an activist skateboarder working to transform his sport's dominant image from a nihilistic "extreme" branding exercise into a holistic, green-minded individualism more consistent with skating's punk roots. "Another World Is Here," declares the self-confident tagline that greets readers of *WorldChanging,* while *Treehugger* inserts poised self-mockery right into its title. Both sites overflow with upbeat briefs, features and user comments on a whole other green world indeed. New items on these sites sometimes number in the dozens on a given day, testifying by their sheer volume to an inexhaustible plenitude of solutions simply waiting for the status quo to catch up to them. Through this New Green lens, it's finally possible—*easy,* almost—to detect a quality that had long been in scarce supply in environmentalist circles: hope. Posting by posting, a new set of frames is being assembled— in that post-Katrina *Newsweek* feature on "hot" environmentalism, *Grist* founder Chip Giller referred to it as a "rebranding of the environmental movement."

It's a revealing choice of phrase. *Branding* is an advertising term, reeking of mindless consumerism and capitalist hubris. It verges on antithetical to the movement's countercultural, anti-industrial roots, and it's *exactly* the right way to phrase the necessary change in tone, tactics, *intent.* Indeed it's nearly the same terminology that was employed in the concluding recommendations of the framing study by Britain's IPPR: "Ultimately, positive climate behaviours need to be approached in the same way as marketeers approach acts of buying and consuming. This is the relevant context for climate change communications in the UK today—not the increasingly residual models of public service or campaigning communications. It amounts to treating climate-friendly activity as a brand that can be sold. This is, we believe, the route to mass behaviour change."

THE END OF AWARENESS & THE REBIRTH OF MR. CLEAN (A LOT MORE MARKETING)

Bill McKibben's *The End of Nature,* first published in 1989, is widely regarded as one of the first great works of climate change journalism, the Anthropocene analogue to *Silent Spring.* Long before the climate crisis became daily news, McKibben anticipated its epochal import, describing it as "the end of nature." He meant that *everything* had been altered—that there was not a single place left on earth that could truthfully be declared untouched by human hands, pristine in the way the Romantic poets meant it. "A child born now will never know a natural summer, a natural autumn, winter or spring," he wrote. "Summer is going extinct, replaced by something else that will be called 'summer.'"

Though McKibben's subject was the Anthropocene Era's defining problem, his strategic thinking and rhetorical tone hewed much closer to the conservationists' laments of the previous era. He was stuck in the past he was laying to rest, attempting to rally troops to a cause by asserting that it was essentially lost. McKibben trafficked in consciousness-raising, working toward the activist's grail of public awareness. It was an approach that made tactical sense in Rachel Carson's day, when a heartrending description of those particular recently deceased eagles could precipitate the banning of certain toxic chemicals and thus the salvation of the bald eagle as a species. But what was a reader to do with the enlightened awareness that there was no more nature at all? McKibben gestured, almost flailing, toward a transformation far beyond raised consciousness, wondering what might still be salvaged "if we began to truly and viscerally think of ourselves as just one species among many." He pointed toward the "deep ecology" movement, which advocated an unprecedented revolution in consciousness far beyond anything found in the daydreams of even the most exuberant Marxist, after which humanity would understand that the rights and freedoms of the natural order in its totality were ultimately of greater value than those of any individual species (least of all a single arrogant member of the most dominant one).

The environmental movement's faith in the power of consciousness-raising has unfortunately persisted even after long years of gesticulating inertia and despite the recommendations of the blue-chip studies commissioned by and for its members. On a recent visit to the Natural Resource Defence Council's global warming website—this is just one incidental example—I was confronted with a banner ad that read: "Wear this T-Shirt, Hat and Bracelet and Help Stop Global Warming." It was a trivial detail, but appearing on the site of one of the lead funders of the FrameWorks study, it seemed particularly egregious in its disregard for everything from proportion to simple eloquence. If this was the state of the art in the creation of green consciousness, then someone ought to tell them about those T-shirt cannons used to distribute corporate freebies at sporting events.

The miscalculation in the latest awareness campaign from the prominent green organization Environmental Defense amounts to a more subtle but ultimately far graver error, because it demonstrates a nuanced understanding of the *style* of a well-framed message but none of the substance. The campaign goes by the slogan "Fight Global Warming," and its centrepiece is a pair of beautifully crafted commercials undeniably capable of holding their own on big-time broadcast TV. The first, entitled "Tick," begins with a series of tightly focused headshots of grave-faced children reciting a litany of climate-related tragedies at an accelerating pace that verges on overlap, while a clock ticks ominously as a soundtrack. "Our future . . . is up . . . to you," the kids warn, followed by a horror film's pregnant pause, that weighted silence before the slashing knife emerges. A voice-over urges a visit to the campaign's website—"while there's still time." In the second ad, a series of pretty shots of bucolic rural life is intercut with scenes of a man standing in the middle of a long stretch of train track, talking about "irreversible consequences" of global warming that might still be thirty years off. "Thirty years?" he blithely asserts. "That won't affect me." A train roars toward him at full speed. He steps out of the way with time to spare, revealing an angelic blond girl standing alone on the tracks. Cut to a tight shot of her face at the last moment before impact, her haunted eyes staring blankly into the camera. And cut to white text on a black screen: "There's still time."

These are dramatic ads, jarring and forceful. They demand to be heard, remembered, acted upon. But in what way? What are we, the viewers, being made aware of? Clearly, something terrible is happening—unforgivable abuse is being visited upon these children—and just as evidently it's our fault. It has something to do with the weather, or else some scientific discovery that's been in the news a lot lately, but how could either of those things be anybody's fault? These ads contravene the recommendations of the framing studies so thoroughly it seems almost intentional. They represent the best persuasion techniques the free world has to offer, being used to reinforce a crippling long-standing stereotype of environmentalism as a hectoring chorus of guilt, shame and self-righteous fury. *My* reaction to these ads is to wonder where the hell these guys get off coming into my living room and bombarding me with this shrill accusatory crap—and I'm clearly already on their side. The Environmental Defense campaign is of a piece with Greenpeace UK's super-slick ad in which an SUV driver is mercilessly ridiculed by his co-workers like a grade-school geek (right down to the KICK ME sign). Stripped of its hip cinematography, this stuff is right out of the bitter-pill school of environmental communications, hellbent not just on raising my awareness but on teaching me that *I am wrong*. (I want these kids dead, if you will, and only these "Fight Global Warming" folks can protect me from my sick, selfish nature.)

You might sell shoes with these tactics—the visceral imagery, the stark language and wrenching horror-flick pacing—but never with this kind of strategy. Effective advertising doesn't win an argument—it *seduces* you. It doesn't explain why you *should* want this thing, it just makes you want it. Nike never felt compelled to explain the rules of basketball, nor did it pester you with reasons why the Chicago Bulls were the team you needed to root for. It simply offered shots of Michael Jordan's wizardry so kinetic and poetic that even the most inert of couch potatoes would want those shoes at whatever price was asked.

Among environmentalists, however, consciousness-raising has persisted as a strategy well beyond its usefulness. In the aggregate, the movement continues to demonstrate a deep ambivalence about achieving the mainstream success required by its own stated goals, demanding the authority to reshape that mainstream without becoming fully part of it. If Nike were a green group, it would lament the fact that non-ballers were traipsing around in those special shoes, even though it was all but bribing them to buy a pair. Environmentalists have generally wanted not supporters but *converts:* true believers, cleansed of impurities, committed to the cause not for anything so venal as their own self-interest but because they want to be *holy.*

This, for example, was the message I found on nearly every shelf of an extraordinary grocery store in Taos, New Mexico. Cid's Food Market is housed in a nondescript warehouse structure out on Route 64, on the northern fringe of downtown Taos. It's big but not huge, and in a metropolitan setting it would seem like your typical post-hippie natural foods emporium. Taos, however, is a small mountain town of barely five thousand, and so Cid's exudes the same parallel-universe vibe that pervades the entire valley. It isn't just a niche alternative to the big supermarket south of town but a legitimate rival of pretty much equal stature. If those Environmental Defense ads represent fire and brimstone from the green pulpit, then Cid's is the consumer front for the cleansing ritual. And it was, at any rate, the most thoroughly environmentalist supermarket I've ever set foot in.

Wandering the aisles at Cid's told me a lot about the predominant approach to green marketing to date, and its limits. As near as I could tell, the produce section was *entirely* organic. All the coffee was organic, too, or else shade-grown or fair-trade or all of the above. The store wasn't purely vegetarian, but what meat there was had lived a life of relatively free mobility, had been fattened on a natural diet, killed humanely, netted sustainably. The deli meats—ham and sausage, aged and cured meats in a wide range of styles—all proudly proclaimed themselves nitrite-free, and it said something about Cid's, I guess, that none of them explained why that was important. (Perhaps because I'm overly lax in my faith, I don't know offhand the self-evident sins of nitrites.)

The sheen of virtuousness was even thicker in the aisles of packaged goods, where the dominant label motifs were either Eden-before-the-Fall or pre-industrial pasture, which at a walking pace blurred into a smear of essentially the same scene. The number of photo illustrations and artists' renderings of life-giving trees set on rolling hills against a divine sun significantly outnumbered the "suggested serving" pictures preferred by chain-store heathens. Westbrae Natural's canned beans and Woodstock Farms' peanut butter had essentially the same pastoral scene on their labels, although Woodstock Farms also had a few (much smaller) pictures of peanuts. One brand just came right out and called itself Garden of Eatin'.

I should mention that, for the most part, I liked shopping at Cid's. (I would trade ten of my hometown Safeways for the plentiful salsa aisle at Cid's.) Still, I started to realize nearly an hour into my visit that I felt a little . . . off. Was it the lighting? The thin mountain air? Then it dawned on me: it was from having to concentrate so hard. There wasn't a single label at Cid's that was instantly familiar, and almost none of them made any extra effort to advertise what they were. The pasta sauce section looked not like an Italian feast nor even an Italian garden but like the same damn pre-industrial pastoral idyll that was everywhere else. The canned vegetables were more likely to be wrapped in another Edenic scene than in a picture of anything as mundane as a chickpea or a green bean.

I kind of lost it, finally, in the household product aisle. Seventh Generation is far and away the dominant brand of organic, eco-friendly cleaning products in North America, and every product Seventh Generation makes has the same packaging. They're all in white plastic containers, and every one sports a label adorned with a big green primordial leaf. The *fonts* are the same. I had to lean in and squint to figure out which one was the dish detergent and which was the all-purpose cleaner. Seventh Generation wasn't selling me its products, it was selling me its ideology. It couldn't give a shit, evidently, whether I needed lemony-fresh clothes or a failsafe spot cleaner for my daughter's flung spaghetti sauce. It wanted me to be *aware,* to understand that buying its products was better for *everyone.* It was peddling a kind of repentance. If it took more effort to shop at Cid's, well, was that so much to ask for my sins? For all of ours?

Somebody should introduce Seventh Generation to Mr. Clean. Better yet, why not talk to the guy who used to give Mr. Clean his marching orders? His name's Marc Stoiber, and he's got a few ideas about how you make Seventh Generation as popular as the brawny bald dude. Or, more broadly speaking, how you take everything they sell at Cid's and all the stuff they're talking about at Environmental Defense's "Fight Global Warming" site, and you mix it up with Mr. Clean's might and some of that *Grist Magazine* moxie and every lurid lowest-common-denominator come-on in the professional hawking business, and that's how you *really* create a new paradigm for the movement. He summarizes his mission, tagline style, like this: "Fast-forwarding the future." Or like this: "Making sustainability sexy." He's got a million of 'em, I'm sure.

Now, Stoiber is, to say the least, an unlikely environmental hero. One of his most recent world-beating exploits, for example, was the rejuvenation of that aforementioned Mr. Clean brand for Procter & Gamble. Those non-biodegradable landfill-bound Mr. Clean AutoDry wipes for your car? That copolymer compound of formaldehyde, melamine and sodium bicarbonate calling itself a Mr. Clean Magic Eraser? All that petrochemical ultra-convenience stuff they sure as hell don't sell at Cid's? Stoiber was one of the guys who made it all ubiquitous. This was during his salad days as executive creative director for the global advertising agency Grey Worldwide in Toronto. Before that, he'd plied his trade at other mammoth agencies from Hong Kong to Dusseldorf. He'd won a Clio and a Lion d'Or at Cannes. He was a big-time Swingin' Dick Ad Guy. And in 2005, he chucked it all away to dedicate himself to the quixotic task of putting some of that swagger to work in the service of sustainability.

I met Stoiber on Granville Island in his hometown of Vancouver. It was fitting in its way: Granville Island had once been a filthy industrial dockyard and now it was an ultra-hip mixed-use district centred around a showpiece farmers' market. And here, seated by the window at a hotel café, looking out over the water, was a P&G pitchman who'd gone green. He looked and dressed early thirties, though he was probably a few years older than that. He talked in the good-natured, razor-sharp, wiseass tone endemic to adland, explaining how he'd gone from working with the planet's largest consumer-goods manufacturers to advising crazy geniuses who made compost from landfill.

The ad game, he readily admitted, had been all kinds of fun—providing the giddy thrill, for example, of watching the revamped Mr. Clean's sales grow by the millions, changing the stock of every grocery store in North America with a few solid brainstorming sessions. Stoiber was self-effacing enough, though, to know that if he wasn't giving Mr. Clean a makeover, some other Swingin' Dick would. "And I thought, Is this the way I want to live?" he told me. "You know, just being a cog in a big industrial wheel." He was starting a family, getting to the age when a cool job is no longer in and of itself fulfilling for a certain kind of person. He relocated from Grey's high-powered Toronto office to its quieter Vancouver outpost. Took it easy, cruised. Wondered what the point was.

One day, he met a woman who ran a lobby group that fought for "tax shifting"—nudging the tax burden to reward clean companies and punish dirty ones. A simple little policy wonk's game, but the bottom line was potentially huge. And *lasting*. Stoiber wanted to sign up, join the fight right there, but there was no place in policy wonkery, really, for a slick pitchman such as he. And so instead Stoiber quit the corporate advertising business to found a boutique ad agency he named—simply, boldly—Change Advertising. There was, after all, no shortage of nutty professor and crunchy granola clients in Vancouver, which was the birthplace of both Greenpeace and fuel-cell pioneers Ballard Power Systems. And as Stoiber quickly learned, these sustainability people were *desperate* for his kind of help. They just didn't necessarily know it yet.

One of Stoiber's first attempts to embrace his new clientele was a visit to the Social Venture Institute, a sustainability think tank on a bucolic isle at the north end of the Georgia Strait, the native habitat of the save-the-whales crowd. He met a handful of green entrepreneurs who immediately triggered his P&G-honed radar, both with their huge potential and with a key reason why it was still latent. Stoiber: "They tended to create what they're doing based upon a sense of mission. 'I'm gonna save the world by making this coffee; I'm gonna save the world by doing that.' And I came from the outside, and I looked at this and I went, 'Hmmm, I don't know if that's gonna work so good.' Because consumers don't go, 'Oh, dammit, I'm gonna buy this mission.' They go, 'I'm gonna buy this *coffee*, it tastes good.'"

He signed on a few clients—the aforementioned landfill-to-compost company, another business that was hauling old-growth deadfall from the bottom of reservoirs to produce luxury hardwood—but mainly he met a lot of polite smiles and stiffened backs. The sense of mission, he found, had a corollary: a hostility to smooth-talking outsiders telling them how to carry out the consciousness-raising crusade. "A lot of 'em were pretty resistant to real change," Stoiber told me. "Like focusing on the consumer and saying, 'What does the consumer want and how do I line up with that?' Which is the *first* thing that Procter would do. Procter would go out and research till they're blue in the face on what do consumers want. Then they'd invent it. These guys would invent it and say, 'Tah-daaahhh! It's a nose-hair replacer.' And you go, 'But I'm trying to *get rid* of nose hair.' 'Yeah, but this nose-hair replacer's good for the world!' 'Yeah, but I don't want it.' 'But it's good!' So you're just like"—he dropped his voice to a stage whisper—"You gotta change it."

To that end, Change Advertising created a couple of tools for sustainable start-ups, seminar-like sessions with slick smooshed-together names that serve as a P&G-style boot camp. ThinkChange is a brand-birthing lab, walking its recruits through everything from concept and name to logo design. The other tool, BrandImagine, is a storytelling workshop in which his clients learn to ditch pie charts and stats for the fine art Stoiber calls "painting the mystical web of bullshit." (Tellingly, Stoiber would eventually work as much with behomoths like Unilever as with mission-oriented start-ups on the process of making green funky.)

There's a significance to Stoiber's work that potentially extends well beyond the specifics of such incremental changes to a few small British Columbia companies, and it reverberates outward from the one Big Idea that drives him. He firmly believes we will save the world from anthropogenic climate change (*if* we save the world) not because we've been swayed by Al Gore's data or inspired by some legislator's impeccable logic or moved to altruism by just the right plea from an activist's pamphlet or a cereal box—but because, in the Ad Guy vernacular, we think it'll get us laid. "My thought," Stoiber told me, "is that capitalism got us here, and human nature and avarice and greed and all that stuff got us in this mess, and it'll get us out." It's a bold assertion. Also sort of glib, highly counterintuitive and possibly illogical. Not to mention borderline heretical to half a century of thinking on ecological issues, much of which has been predicated on the core principle, deeply rooted in self-evident fact, that runaway human consumption is a primary *cause* of the problem. That it's the Swingin' Dicks with their lurid come-ons for all those wildly unnecessary and grotesquely wasteful copolymer compounds that caused most of this mess, and that the only way out is to excise them and their whole avaricious system from the body politic like cancers. Which is, of course, why Stoiber's potential clients eye him warily.

Talking to Stoiber, though, I could find no obvious reason to be leery. I was completely under the spell of a sensation that had seemed in short supply in even the most hopeful spots on my map and was all but absent from the old guard of the environmental movement. It was a quality you sure didn't find on the packages at Cid's. It was that Ad Guy's infectious energy, that crazy-seductive hard-rockin' big laugh of a guy who knows how to *move product.* Stoiber exuded the same quality he was trying to sell his clients on: a sexy, head-bopping, the-world-is-ours optimism. It was all there in the spiel he'd done for a regional renewable-energy group, which he was now recounting for me. "I said, 'You know what we gotta do, we gotta stop thinking about ourselves as the alternative and start thinking about ourselves as what we are, which is the future. The future is young, it's six-pack abs, it's, you know, girls playing volleyball, it's havin' a good time, drivin' fast cars—*that's* the future. Everybody wants to be part of the future. Everybody wants to be younger, everybody wants to be cool and hip.'"

So here was a guy who had scaled to the pinnacle of a profession entirely dedicated to persuading people to do things they weren't sure they wanted to do, to buy (or buy into) things they hadn't known they needed. Which was exactly the task the environmental movement's fancy studies had been assigned. Wasn't a champion Ad Guy just what the New Green needed? Someone to teach it to exude self-confidence, allow it to become Deep Green, with the whole sustainability thing hard-wired into the system, sure, but buried beneath an enticing sheen of sheer *desirability?* Think of those matching Seventh Generation labels, and then go to your local supermarket and note the half-dozen separate, distinct, uniquely logoed P&G brands of laundry detergent alone, each with its own elaborate identity and target market. The sustainability movement could learn a *lot* from P&G. It could learn how to be Deep Green. How to sell an idea to people whether they think they're interested or not. How to move beyond awareness to real, billions-served *change.*

Stoiber is not quite a lone voice in the wilderness on the subject. It has been proven repeatedly in the marketplace that virtue alone reaches market saturation at a very small percentage. One British green-marketing study found that while 30 percent of consumers claimed to be concerned about the ecological soundness of the things they bought, only 3 percent actually changed their buying patterns in line with this concern. And so Toyota has sold most of its Priuses not on their piety but on their fuel economy, and the home-appliance giant Electrolux markets its ecologically friendly line not as green but as super-efficient. And I read in the *New York Times Magazine* a while back about this brilliant new diaper by the name of gDiaper, which I'd have bought for my daughter yesterday if it had made it to Canada yet. The *Times* piece noted that the name is intentionally vague: the diapers consist of a permanent pant with biodegradable, chemical-free, flushable liners, so it could be *g* for *green* if that's your thing, but the pants are the funkiest looking diapers you've ever seen, so the *g* might mean *groovy* or *gee-whiz.*

The thing is, when my daughter was born I did as much research on the subject as I could manage in my sleep-deprived delirium. I couldn't crunch the numbers completely, but it looked like a pretty close race between non-biodegradable disposables sent forever to the landfill and running our washing machine (fed by a coal-and-gas grid) almost constantly for two years or so to wash the cloth ones. And yes, there was a solid self-interested argument to be made in favour of the disposables (which were freighted with the promise of a tiny bit more sleep and were even recyclable in some jurisdictions, though not yet in ours), and so that's what we went with. I knew it might be seen as sacrilegious in some green quarters, but mostly what I thought was that it was *absurd* for each and every conscious consumer out there to be trying to fashion an instrument from old slide rules and divining rods in order to figure out which diapers were least damaging, like this was the best way for our creative energies to be spent. And *that* made me want Marc Stoiber's Deep Green revolution to just come and conquer my supermarket already, so I could go pick between six kinds of gDiaper based on my mood that day and not have to wonder whether I'd been sufficiently virtuous to be able to continue speaking with legitimacy on environmental issues.

Then, not long ago, I saw the "Proper Education" video, and in the first gleeful moments of its afterglow, I thought maybe victory had finally arrived. "Proper Education" was a remake of Pink Floyd's signature hit "Another Brick in the Wall, Part 2" by Eric Prydz, a Swedish club DJ of considerable renown. It was released as a single in early January 2007, along with the best three-minute sustainability commercial I've yet seen. The video, shot in atmospheric black-and-white, opens on a grim concrete English council estate (in overt reference to the Floyd version's original video). A knot of teenagers in school uniforms—mixed of gender and race, but not self-consciously so—has gathered in the estate's central courtyard. One dude starts handing out bricks to the others. Propelled by the marching beat of this clubbed-up nonconformist tune, the kids fan out across the estate's apartment towers on foot and on skateboards and BMX bikes, leaping and rail-sliding all over the place. They stage daring apartment break-ins, dropping their bricks in toilet cisterns and stuffing them in the backs of refrigerators, switching incandescent bulbs for compact fluorescents and shutting down the master power on all manner of electronic appliances idling on wasteful standby. At the video's close, one of the kids flips a hacked switch, and all the lights go off in the council flats and a second set comes back on to spell out SWITCH OFF in towering letters. Cut to a black screen. White text: YOU DON'T NEED AN EDUCATION TO SAVE THE PLANET.

The first time I saw "Proper Education"—as a YouTube clip on my laptop, directed there by *Grist*—I stared awestruck and goofily grinning. It was like an edgy indie hybrid of *Mission: Impossible* and an "extreme" sport-drink commercial. I knew I'd just seen first-rate agitprop, a prime specimen of a potent framing tool. This was a bandwagon people would jump on without knowing or caring where it was heading or who was driving, simply because they wanted to be part of it. Never mind policy and screw awareness: let's *rock,* dude.

This, it turned out, was the primary goal of the organization that had collaborated with Prydz on the video. Global Cool was a new climate change action group that had launched the previous fall, introducing itself in the person of heartthrob actor Orlando Bloom, who made the official announcement. The organization's primary goal out of the gate was to reduce global CO_2 emissions by a billion tonnes via the sort of incremental efficiency measures the hip kids demonstrated in the video. Peer-pressuring people into conserving energy is ultimately a kind of awareness campaign—Global Cool is not, that is, a *total* break with the old paradigm—but still there was something to the "Proper Education" video that seemed like a new and more infectious strain of hope. Something much more muscular and infinitely more persuasive. This was not a better way to solicit donations but a whole new way to make people want their very own piece of your scene. This was the fat, insatiable belly of the mass-communications beast, that billion-eyed monster with a million tentacles reaching into practically every dark crevice and flickeringly lit living room on the planet, and it could snake its way almost anywhere.

Here's a case in point: Huai Kra Thing. It's a place about as far from *everywhere*—everywhere I knew, anyway—as I'd ever been, and it was the first place I thought of when I heard of Marc Stoiber's sustainability campaign. I thought of it again watching "Proper Education." Huai Kra Thing is a tiny village tucked in a deep, lush valley in the hills of northwestern Thailand. It's an hour out of the regional capital of Mae Sot, the last fifteen minutes down a deeply rutted track navigable only by four-wheel-drive truck or on foot. I'd gone to Huai Kra Thing to see an innovative renewable-energy project: a small run-of-river hydroelectric plant being built on the fast-flowing creek up the valley from the village. It was an amazing project, and I'll come to it in a minute, but one of the most remarkable things about it was what happened at the end of the hard day's work building it.

The rank and file of the construction team consisted of young Karen men from the village itself—members of a hill-tribe minority for whom the Thai language and the bustle of Mae Sot were mostly foreign—and a group of students from an engineering school at a nearby Burmese refugee camp. In the early evening after the first day of construction, the workers returned to the village, soaked in sweat and covered in dust, and then they disappeared into their thatch huts. I found a seat on the covered patio of one of the huts, which was serving as the crew's mess hall, figuring they'd all be along shortly. Before long, I noticed the lads gathering in the clearing just up the hill from the patio. Almost all of them had changed into professional soccer jerseys and logoed T-shirts from one faraway league or another, and they soon had a pickup game going. The fact of the game itself was amazing enough—soccer was virtually unknown in Thailand until the advent of satellite TV in the early 1990s, and the first fantastically flickering screen had arrived in this village within the last three years—but my jaw dropped even lower as I gawked at the jerseys. The dusty clearing was a lurid blur of Manchester United red and Chelsea or maybe Italian blue and Brazilian national green and gold. One chest read VODAFONE and another said PARMALAT, and on nearly every breast was stitched a Nike swoosh or that ascending trio of Adidas bars. Electricity was wondrously new in Huai Kra Thing and an indoor toilet still unheard of, but the elongated tentacles of the global mass-marketing machine had already reached this Karen village at the end of several kilometres of deeply rutted trail.

This was the kind of jerry-built, just-in-time, exhaustively global consensus needed to avert catastrophic climate change and launch the Sustainable Age. And it had come here only because those Karen and Burmese boys just had to have some little piece of it. They understood that this was the future.

NINE

NGO 2.0

[the development of sustainability]

JUST DO IT

Here's another scene from the Thai village of Huai Kra Thing, this one an unprecedented and quietly exhilarating Anthropocene tableau. A young Karen man stands on the edge of a small clearing on the banks of the narrow river above the village. He's wearing an army-green field jacket and a floppy blue hat, and he's working at a length of newly felled bamboo with his well-worn machete. A long, thick, cigar-like cheroot hangs casually from his lips like a punctuation mark; he's hard at work but nonchalant, so skilled at the task it comes to him as easily as a drag on the smoke. The clearing is filled with others equally absorbed in their roles: a couple of foreign experts, a handful of students from America, a veteran logistics man from the nearest city, but mostly other young Karen like him. The guy chomping on the cheroot joins another guy now—this one in a camouflage jacket and a blue headscarf—and they begin to arrange their long lengths of split bamboo into a lattice. Surrounded by great stands of bamboo maybe 100 feet tall, the forest floor thick with 5-foot fronds of jungle underbrush, they toil at the project as if they built run-of-river hydroelectric plants all the time, as if Ph.D.-toting Americans with UN funding came through Huai Kra Thing with the predictable frequency of monsoon floods. As if it weren't the case that the village came to know its first electric light just three years before.

Felled bamboo poles lie in a pile alongside a stack of baby-blue PVC tubing. Sacks of cement have been stacked at the riverside next to a scattering of sack-sized boulders. Great rolls of black cable squat next to the path like overlong jungle snakes. The balance of forest primeval and state-of-the-art industrial manufacture is almost flawless. The guy in the camo jacket squats now to tweak the half-formed lattice, reaching behind himself in a practised motion to slide his machete into a bamboo scabbard strapped to the small of his back by a strip of leather. A belt, it turns out, black and worn, with an embossed inscription repeated at uniform intervals: JUST DO IT. Woven bamboo, tooled steel and Nike apparel: three disparate epochs in human industry, bound together in a harmony that amplifies the easy relationship between the river and the small hydro turbine. This is surely what is meant by the phrase *sustainable development*.

The concept of sustainability first gained widespread prominence via the field of international development, where it has been a much-discussed topic and a core goal since the mid-1980s. The path to that goal has remained an elusive one, spied in brief shining glimpses, like a clearing seen through the jungle's thick underbrush. The hydro project on the riverbank outside Huai Kra Thing was a particularly vivid snapshot of what sustainable development can look like, a place where the wide expanse between good intentions and everyday reality has been more or less closed, and I'll return to it shortly. First, though, a few words about where those intentions came from—and how they strayed so far from that reality.

HOPE'S WHOLESALERS (SINCE 1945!)

In Germany, the final moment of the Second World War—the Nazi capitulation at midnight on May 8, 1945—has been called *die Stunde Null.* "The Zero Hour": the time when the clock was reset. It was a term neither of deletion nor of absolution. *Die Stunde Null* was simply an exhausted acknowledgement that however this ruined society was to rebuild itself, it had to begin with a total, permanent, irreparable break with the past. "Beyond the zero"—this was Thomas Pynchon's phrase, from the opening salvo of his monumental novel

Gravity's Rainbow, describing in even more extreme terms the existential bomb crater humanity found itself trapped in at the end of the war. It was a place even farther afield than the German phrase let on, so Pynchon implied, a land of wakeful zombies in which everything was possible and nothing mattered and the best thing might be if nothing ever mattered again. Humanity had extinguished its soul and yet continued to function, walking dead through never-again-land.

Oh, but the busy minds who'd led the war effort would truck with no such nihilistic nonsense, and even before *die Stunde Null,* the still-idealistic American president, Franklin D. Roosevelt, had put in motion a process by which humanity's *next* last best hope would come into being. Beginning with the Bretton Woods conference in 1944, Roosevelt and the other Allied leaders undertook the planning of Europe's reconstruction and the founding of institutions to ensure—and this time, they meant it—that such cataclysms would be laid to rest in the fascist boneyard alongside the corpse of the demon Axis. From Bretton and other plenary sessions late in the war there came, in more or less direct lines, the United Nations, the World Bank and the International Monetary Fund, and in particular the massively ambitious European Recovery Program—the legendary "Marshall Plan"—out of which was born, before long, the Organization for Economic Co-operation and Development (OECD) and the entire ideology, infrastructure and apparatus of that great and good project variously known as "foreign aid" or "development aid" or "international development."

The Marshall Plan began with an act of U.S. Congress in April 1948. Its stated goal was to rebuild a ruined Europe (and later Japan), a $17-billion megaproject. It was by most reports a wild success—not just for western Europe, which got the kickstart it needed to move beyond *die Stunde Null,* but also for the booming American economy, whose factories and farmers' fields churned out shiny new products by the boatload to be bought with all that money their government had handed out. By the time the Marshall Plan was complete, the megaproject approach had proven so lucrative and gosh-darn peace-in-our-time *hopeful* that it continued rolling right along. The newborn United Nations had diagnosed most of the world with a potentially fatal disease called "underdevelopment," and the remedy was as much foreign aid as the rest of the world—particularly the industrial nations united under the OECD banner—could muster. For the first few years of the 1950s, this meant all the spare food the OECD had to give, but in short order it became a more codified and technocratic arrangement whose activity encompassed every aid-able aspect of modern life. In 1955, a wide swath of this underdeveloped world met for the landmark Bandung Conference, out of which eventually emerged the Non-Aligned Pact (wherein many such countries formally opted out of the Cold War) and an official acceptance by the participants of the UN's assessment of their socioeconomic ills. Thus was born the "developing world," and with it a vast apparatus of development ministries, charities and aid organizations to carry out the ridiculously ambitious, borderline-evangelical work of constructing a whole new world order.

Thereafter, international development became a fast-growing global business—one of the first truly globalized industries—doling out literally trillions of dollars over the past fifty years and spawning a prolific subspecies, the non-governmental organization (or NGO), which by one recent estimate counted as many as fifteen thousand separate bodies in its ranks. If there was a disease, international development was there fighting it; if there was a famine, international development was handing out gratis sacks of grain to end it. If water needed pumping or purifying or a field could do with more sophisticated ploughing—whatever the dust-caked villagers of the world required—international development was there. It was the wealthy world's preferred exporter of that most precious commodity: hope. And it did the job *wholesale.*

This was a permanent global extension of the Marshall Plan's historic precedent, wherein the United States (in some sense the only true victor of a terrible and decisive war) chose not to take its conquered territory as its own and snatch up the loot, but instead opted to rebuild. To offer ally and defeated foe alike the magnificent freedom that had fed its victory, and even to provide most of the tools to make that freedom last. It promised to be the beginning of an exciting new era—the *Pax Americana,* the golden age of liberal democracy—but also the end of another, the ignominious colonial period, whose legacy lay buried in the smouldering ashes of Europe's devastated imperial capitals. Or so it was hoped, though in practice the new tradition mirrored its predecessor in more ways than it intended (or at any rate let on). Consider, in particular, the accidental precedent established by one of the colonial era's final visitations of horror upon the soon-to-be-so-called developing world: the partition of India.

July 1947: the British Empire, rapidly dismantling, was preparing to bring its two centuries of divide-and-conquer reign over the Indian subcontinent to an end by handing over sovereignty to not one independent nation but two. Partition was a heart-wrenching, bloodletting cleavage, the jagged carving of an Islamic nation from the far eastern and western reaches of India that served no one but the politicians—particularly the British, who were eager to vacate the subcontinent as quickly as possible while avoiding a civil war. India, long the most precious jewel in Britain's imperial crown, was to be evacuated like a sinking ship. On July 8, there arrived in Delhi one Sir Cyril Radcliffe, a lawyer and wartime bureaucrat. It was the first time his feet had fallen on Indian soil, and he'd come to the subcontinent for his first and only major cartographic mission. Completely lacking in specialized knowledge of his task or even a *general* understanding of the place where it was to be carried out, he was given barely five weeks to draw the borders that would separate Pakistan from India. The result became known as the Radcliffe Line, and the complete ignorance of local geography, culture and history that informed it was a significant exacerbating factor in the grisly communal slaughter that erupted almost immediately after it became an official boundary on August 15, 1947.

For the next half-century, the Radcliffe innocent-abroad approach would stand as a sort of accidental model of international development: deputized Westerners with grandiose ideas formulated on the other side of the world and authority far beyond their experience would parachute into developing-nation backwaters the world over to quickly bring about great change. Few of these projects would turn out as lethally awful as the partition, and some would accomplish useful, even vital things, but the *logic* of the system—or lack thereof—would remain strikingly similar.

In recent years, an apostate by the name of William Easterly—formerly a World Bank economist, currently of New York University and the Center for Global Development—has been one of the most prominent and strident critics of the global aid trade's manifest illogic. It's a tricky role, because arguments for serious reform to the *practice* of development can easily wind up confused with an attack on its *intentions,* and it's hard to argue against such good intentions. Who, after all, is against feeding the hungry, curing the sick, bringing useful tools to people who need them? Still, this was a system with glaring flaws, wedded as it was to a centralized, fossil-fuelled econometric model that saw GDP growth as the first and best measure of successful development.

Over two books and a handful of essays, Easterly has assembled an exhaustive catalogue of the system's intrinsic structural weaknesses. In certain instances, the problem is a case of numbers literally not adding up. In a 2002 article in the influential journal *Foreign Policy,* for example, Easterly quickly dismantled a widely quoted World Bank stat claiming that a $1-billion increase in foreign aid could lift 284,000 people out of poverty. The World Bank's formula works out to $3,521 per person, even though poverty, in development terms, is defined as per capita income of less than US$365 per year. It costs substantially more to "develop" someone out of poverty, apparently, than it does to simply buy them out for ten years.

To explain this discrepancy, Easterly pointed to a range of systemic problems, most of which reveal a deleterious obsession with the Big: big projects, big gestures, big numbers with lots of zeroes after them. International development favours large capital projects with easily measured "outputs" (clinics and schools, machines and factories, *stuff* to cut ribbons on and tour visiting celebrities around) over less photogenic upkeep and infrastructure projects (doctors and teachers and the equipment to allow them to keep those facilities functional, for example). What's more, its primary measure of success comes not in the form of quantifiable results or glowing feedback but in the sheer volume of aid money it has dispersed. (This is an obvious analogue to the GDP Fallacy; Easterly likes to compare it to measuring the quality of a movie by the size of its budget.) Foreign aid, Easterly wrote, was so unwieldy in its proportions—dominated by mammoth organizations and development banks with billion-dollar budgets at one end of the process, attending to the world's poorest people living on pennies a day in tiny villages at the other—that the system amounted to a "well-intentioned cartel." To access its charitable largesse, a potential client was required to navigate a bureaucratic apparatus just as oversized, submitting reports hundreds of pages long and completing multi-point policy checklists—a process so arduous it essentially guaranteed that only similarly bloated government bureaucracies at the receiving end could qualify for aid.

In his most recent book, *The White Man's Burden,* Easterly illustrated the counterproductive priorities of the development game with a surprising case study of its failure. The project began, as so many fundamental development issues do, with a glaring problem and a simple solution. The problem is malaria, a mosquito-borne disease that infects up to half a billion people a year and kills about a million of those it infects; the largest share of the deaths occurs among very young and very poor African children. The solution, obviously enough, is to prevent infection, and the easiest way to accomplish this is to install mosquito nets impregnated with insecticide. The nets cost next to nothing, anyone can use one, and along with the distribution of dirt-cheap medicine for those few unfortunate souls who still wind up infected, they could easily reduce the malaria problem to almost nothing. The snag, Easterly explained, is that giving things away for free tends to lead people to assume they have no value. The nets often end up for sale on the black market, or employed as fishing nets or even wedding veils. Seventy percent of the nets given away in one distribution project in Zambia were never used as anti-malarial screens. This, to Easterly's mind, is as good an argument as any that the West, despite its best intentions, has met the tragedy of global poverty with its bureaucratic equal: "the tragedy in which the West spent $2.3 trillion on foreign aid over the last five decades and still had not managed to get 12-cent medicines to children to prevent half of all malaria deaths. The West spent $2.3 trillion and still had not managed to get $4 bed nets to poor families."

Escaping this tragedy, Easterly argued, will require some novel approaches and the abandonment of half a century of received wisdom. He cited the counterexample of a malaria project that worked. Recently, an American NGO called Population Services International started *selling* its mosquito nets in Malawi. New mothers at rural clinics were charged 50¢ (with the nurses pocketing a 9¢ sales commission), and the nets were also sold in the cities for $5 each. It was certainly counterintuitive—it might even seem callous—for an *aid* group to charge impoverished Malawian women for its wares. But it worked. Within four years, the proportion of the nation's children sleeping under mosquito nets rose from 8 percent to more than 50 percent.

Like a great many failed development projects, the initial mosquito-net mess was a case of the *process* of development overwhelming its goals: a solution was parachuted in from the faraway West, but no one asked the recipients what they needed, what they valued, how *their* systems worked. For a quarter-century, international development bodies had spent billions of dollars trying to improve the livelihoods of the world's poor *without their input.* In the guise of altruistic, ultra-rational development, the imperial mindset lived on. It took a quiet revolution, decades into the game, to encourage some of the more reform-minded aid organizations to give it a try.

Still, the revolution finally did come, in fits and starts, and bottom-up approaches to international development (or at least approaches other than *exclusively* top-down ones) have become increasingly common. The aforementioned Grameen Bank and the microcredit movement it helped inspire provide a stellar example, but even some of the members of Easterly's bureaucratic "cartel"— the UN and the World Bank, for instance—have added funding schemes that disperse middling amounts to many small projects in addition to their usual lump-sum awards to oversized government initiatives. Still, the top-down, expert-driven model is far from extinct. In fact, it has so deeply permeated the conventional wisdom that even as formerly underdeveloped nations come to stand on their own, they sometimes hobble themselves by inflicting the old illogic on their people.

Witness the rural electrification scheme recently implemented by the government of Thailand. By the first years of the new millennium, the former developing nation had become a sometime Asian tiger, a fast-growing Pacific Rim player—an "emerging market," in the argot of certain aid bureaucracies. Thailand even found itself in possession of sufficient revenue largesse and bureaucratic wherewithal to mount its own development projects. And if one of the most fundamental prerequisites for modern development was electricity, then bringing solar power to hundreds of thousands of

Thai villagers who'd never switched on a light or bathed in the bluish glow of a TV newscast seemed like a reasonably solid pillar on which to raise itself to the stature of its former donors.

The Thai approach appeared to overflow with progressive thinking and fringe benefits. It would see small, eco-friendly "Solar Home Systems" installed in 300,000 rural households. There would be no need for an expensive expansion of the national grid into remote, sparsely populated regions, and the project would give a huge boost to the domestic renewable-energy industry. Thailand would get its first national-scale taste of twenty-first-century sustainability even as the poorest of its people would finally discover the wonders of the twentieth-century mediascape. (In addition to two fluorescent light fixtures, each Solar Home System was to be equipped with an AC plug to provide juice to household appliances—TVs in particular. The gift of TV—and thereby, it was promised, valuable civic information—to the heretofore underinformed rural Thai masses was one of the most vaunted goals of the project, proudly championed by the country's prime minister, the former media baron Thaksin Shinawatra.)

The mixed blessings of the boob tube notwithstanding, it all looked like the best kind of sustainable development, a mass leapfrog from the pre-industrial to the Anthropocene that came off without any obvious hitches. Thailand's Ministry of the Interior summarily dispersed the necessary funds to the Provincial Electricity Authority, which took bids on the installations and eventually handed three-quarters of the contracts to a Thai company called Solartron. (The remaining contracts went to a competing company called Bangkok Solar.) In two short years, beginning in April 2003, about 190,000 Solar Home Systems were installed throughout rural Thailand: 190,000 single PV panels, 120 watts each, wired up to a battery, an inverter box with an AC plug, and two 10-watt high-efficiency fluorescent lamps. Thailand added almost 23 megawatts of solar power to its national energy mix, quintupling its overall capacity, and the project also spurred Solartron to 30 percent-plus annual revenue growth rates.

It was, it seemed, a bona fide emerging-market success story, green-tinged and gleaming, the sort of thing you found tucked into the feel-good slot in the international news. Villagers got a free source of clean power, Prime Minister Thaksin had an excuse to pose for the cameras (by all reports a much-loved pastime) in the guise of Southeast Asia's environmental champion, and I had good cause to book passage on an overnight bus to the newly electrified hills of northwestern Thailand.

I made plans to meet up with Chris Greacen, the head of a Bangkok-based NGO called Palang Thai. Greacen is an enthusiastic young American married to a Thai woman, and his group, near as I could figure ahead of time, had partnered with a handful of like-minded organizations to form the Border Green Energy Team (BGET), which had taken on the job of tidying up some of the oversights in the government project in a handful of villages outside the city of Mae Sot. They were also working with Burmese refugees in some capacity. It all sounded promising.

I arrived before dawn at the bus station on the fringe of Mae Sot, a regional capital long known as a gateway to Burma, now bustling with the manufacture of cheap textiles for export. The bus station was a dingy expanse of cracked concrete covered by a high roof of rusty tin. It was lit by sickly fluorescents, and hard-luck cases loitered next to the coffee stall. It was January 2006, and on the TV above, the disembodied heads of Steven Spielberg and George Clooney confirmed their Oscar nominations like breaking news from a distant and much more carefree universe. It all seemed to confirm the nasty picture of Mae Sot I'd had painted for me on the ride up from Bangkok by an American NGO worker. He was half-drunk and earnest nearly to the point of rage, and he talked of textile factories that were the grim, exploitative equal of any Third World hellhole. He snorted with skepticism at my mission, cynical in a manner I'd encountered before among fieldworkers in foreign aid. He'd seen enough to know he was not in the business of exporting hope but of staunching the bleeding on a badly wounded body that might or might not make it through this night, or the following year.

A group of fresh-faced American teenagers had been on the bus with me, and they were greeted at the station by another American, thin and hollow-eyed but still somehow boyish. I went over and introduced myself. This was Greacen, whose NGO had spearheaded the BGET project. The American teens were from a Pacific Northwestern college, passing through as part of an international development work-study tour. We piled into the flatbed of a Toyota pickup and bounced our way to a small compound on the fringe of downtown Mae Sot—the headquarters of a Taiwanese NGO that was one of Palang Thai's partners in BGET. Greacen was busy seeing to the final preparations for the couple of weeks he would be spending in the hill village that was our destination, but still, by the time the sun had burned off the dawn's mist, I'd managed to gather enough background to learn that the Thai government's solar program was riddled with potentially fatal flaws. By the searing light of this subtropical day, the program barely seemed worth a second glance, let alone an all-night bus ride.

The government and its subcontractors, as a BGET field report on the rural electrification scheme explained, had done nothing to ensure that the solar panels would continue to function properly after they were installed. In the manner of any old input-driven development body, they'd focused entirely on driving up the six-digit figure recording total installations. After all, that was the number that earned Thaksin his bragging rights and fed Solartron's revenues, and the wire services didn't blip feel-good stories about routine maintenance training around the world. There were no local PV-panel repairmen in rural Thailand, and no readily available replacement parts. The Solar Home Systems came with two-year warranties—extended to five years for the panel itself—but what of it? "The key problem with the warranty system," BGET's report noted dryly, "is that villagers do not know it exists." Warranty claim forms appeared to be non-existent, so BGET created one of its own and appended it to its report.

It all made for an especially pointed example of the mismatch between overgrown bureaucracies and village-scale projects: the Thai government was being outperformed, at least in one province, by an ad hoc coalition with a full-time staff you could count on one hand and no permanent operational funding. BGET was a loose partnership among several NGOs active in renewable energy in the Mae Sot area: Greacen's Palang Thai, which had formed primarily to help draft renewable-energy policy in Bangkok; the Taiwanese aid group TOPS (Taiwan Overseas Peace Service); a regional charity called the Karen Network for Culture and Environment; and a U.S.-based funding body called Green Empowerment. BGET had formed a couple of years before the electrification program to provide solar power for mobile medical clinics in Burma, and shortly thereafter it branched out into building small-scale hydro power in remote Thai villages. Around the same time, government-sponsored PV installers started showing up in the countryside, so BGET launched a series of weekend seminars on the proper operation, routine maintenance and basic repair of the Solar Home Systems—a project that was at its halfway mark by the time of my arrival. In less than a year, they would train more than two hundred technicians, enough to look after about half the installations in remote, mountainous Tak province. And along the way, they would launch the project I had unknowingly come to see.

Drawn by one of those feel-good wire-service clippings, I'd made my way to northwestern Thailand thinking I was there to see the uplifting spectacle of solar panels in Burmese refugee camps, the extension of forward-thinking Thai government policy into one of the most desperate places on earth. Proof, perhaps, that renewable energy was truly useful *everywhere* and that sustainable development was far from an oxymoron. What I was really looking for, though, was an antidote to the withering bloodshot-eyed realism of the foreign aid worker on the bus and a rebuttal to the catalogue of failure in the BGET report. The evidence of a broken development model was all too easy to find, but what of a new way forward?

THE DANCE OF THE MACHETES

To get to the village of Huai Kra Thing, we piled into the back of a pair of Toyota four-by-fours—there was me, the American college kids, several permanent BGET members and a half-dozen engineering students from a nearby Burmese refugee camp—and we drove an hour out of Mae Sot into another world. We started on the flat national highway out of the city, then travelled up a winding secondary highway into hills covered in thick green jungle, then followed a rutted country road and finally descended into a lush valley along a half-overgrown track pitched as steep as a flight of cellar stairs. We crossed an invisible border, as well, passing from modern Thailand into the homeland of the Karen people, a mountainous region that straddles the official border with Burma. (The vast majority of the 6.4 million Karen live on the Burmese side, in a state of deep misery and ongoing guerrilla war with the brutal totalitarian government of so-called Myanmar.)

The village we reached at the end of the steep track was set in a wide clearing in the valley. There were about forty households, all living in traditional Karen dwellings: bamboo-walled, thatch roofed, perched on stilts against the monsoon floods. Outside many of these, a single PV panel had been erected on a steel pole as tall as the house's stilts. Shower stalls and outhouses stood behind many of the houses, and some villagers kept pigs and chickens in pens underneath. The narrow river that had carved the valley emerged from the dense forest just above the school to trickle through the village and down the terraced, irrigated slope into the lowlands below. There was a community centre, a small clinic and a missionary church—none of them permanently staffed—and very little else. Until the rural electrification program had shown up, there had been no electricity. But once BGET completed the construction project it was starting that day, there would be a small, run-of-river hydroelectric power plant in the forest above the village to supply the community centre, clinic and school with electricity for the first time ever. And something more: the head of a trail that would lead me to the new model of international development I'd been seeking, one that just might be the start of a truly sustainable export trade in Western hope.

Huai Kra Thing's hydro plant was the fourth to be built by BGET, but it was the first of its kind in a number of ways. It was the first to receive UN funding, through an unconventional Small Grants Programme run through the United Nations Development Programme (UNDP), a strategy perched halfway between business as usual and Grameen-style grassroots lending that had been born in the wake of the 1992 Earth Summit. As an outgrowth of BGET's tireless efforts to work with readily available technology, the plant's turbine was being jury-rigged from an off-the-shelf centrifugal pump run backward. (Instead of using power to pump water, it would in effect use water to pump electricity.) As well, it was to be BGET's first hands-on training session for Burmese refugees learning about civil engineering, and for American coeds learning what a truly grassroots, thoroughly sustainable development project looked like.

The workings of the project possessed an elegant, uncomplicated seamlessness. It was green-powered. The technology was simple, mechanical and readily available throughout Thailand, and the twenty-odd villagers who assisted in its construction each day would not only be deeply, personally invested in it—through buckets of what the old dotcom boosters used to call "sweat equity"—but also well-versed in how to maintain it. Furthermore, the Karen of Tak province were desperate for electricity; they *wanted* the project.* The hydro plant was thus a welcome addition to village life, a project everyone was happy to work on, which lent a certain seamlessness to the work crew, as well. A couple of the experts overseeing the project had arrived from as far away as North America, to be sure, and the village kids eyed our pale faces curiously. (When I took out my camera to snap a couple of shots on the way past the school, the entire student body assembled in front of me in barely a minute to pose for an impromptu class picture.) But a number of the project's other overseers came from Karen villages in the same province, and anyone who wanted to hike up to the site was welcome to lend a hand. The project was so fluidly integrated with its environment that you could barely tell where the NGO ended and the developing country began.

At the same time, this was uncharted territory, and it was stalked by disarray at every turn. Greacen was confident that an inverted centrifugal pump *would* do the same job as a hydroelectric turbine, but he'd never actually, you know, *built* one. The little retaining wall that was erected to dam enough water to cover the mouth of the intake pipe came together through a process of trial and error that would be instantly understood by anyone who had tried to block the flow of the local creek as a kid. And credentialed expertise was in sufficiently short supply that *I* was recruited to squint through the little surveyor's device to confirm that said intake pipe was being mounted on the right grade. There were probably a hundred things that would've disqualified the Huai Kra Thing hydro plant from traditional development funding, but each one only made it that much more ingenious, unprecedented, *electric*. Consultations on the subject of local conditions and priorities were happening minute to

---

* Chris Greacen told me a story about the nearby village where BGET had built its previous microhydro plant. Prior to its arrival, many villagers ran lights off freestanding car batteries; when they were drained, the villagers would haul their batteries out to the main road and hitchhike 20 kilometres to get them recharged. The village temple, meanwhile, had been lit by a diesel generator.

minute, in a half-dozen muttered conversations—in English and then in Karen, in pidgin Thai mixed with broken English—as well as in universal gestures by the dozens. And quietly orchestrating it all, even as he insisted he was just another worker in the crew, was a trim, elfish Burmese refugee named Polchai, a kinetic mass of contradictions in constant motion, indefatigable and inspiring, a living, breathing embodiment of the project's surprising juxtapositions. And an authentic avatar, it seemed, of the most hard-earned kind of hope—the kind that mixes steely-eyed realism with delirious promise so seamlessly you come to think they're the same thing.

Anyway, here came Polchai, a cheroot hanging from the side of his mouth, hopping from rock to rock in flip-flops as he crossed the roaring stream to the flat part of the riverside path where the BGET braintrust had decided to locate the powerhouse. He'd been coming and going with some regularity all morning, skipping down from the clearing another few hundred metres up the path, where he was overseeing the construction of the intake pipe, to consult with the lanky American lad he called "Dr. Chris" about yet another on-the-fly adjustment to the project plan.

If you asked him, Polchai would tell you he was twenty-five years old, because that was when he first crossed over from Burma into Thailand, but he was at least in his fifties. He moved, however, with the light and careful step of someone half his age who'd perhaps been trained in the martial arts. Nothing in his fluid movements hinted at the shards of shrapnel he still carried in his body. He arrived for these impromptu conferences like a soldier reporting for duty, standing at attention in a pink golf shirt and black denim, a little handwoven tote bag of the sort tourists like to buy strung across his chest bandolier-style, waiting for marching orders. Polchai was maybe 5 feet tall, and "Dr. Chris" towered more than a foot above him. He would ask Polchai a question, and Polchai would roll his cheroot from one side of his mouth to the other and puff on it thoughtfully. Then they would exchange a few more words, a raised eyebrow or two, and Polchai would turn to the crew hauling stones out of the river and say a few quiet, firm words in Karen, and three or four of them would dash off up the steep, heavily treed slope above to hack down another few lengths of bamboo or down the path to fetch a length of PVC tubing.

The hydro plant was, for the most part, a dead simple design: water entered a PVC tube in the intake pond above, gained speed and force as it roared downhill, and came rushing through the power-house to set the turbine spinning before exiting through an outflow pipe to rejoin the stream. The turbine, meanwhile, turned those gyrations into electric current, and a series of brackets hung from trees all along the path back to the village, from which, soon enough, heavy-duty electric cable would be strung. Still, there were many fine details to be discussed, everything from where to place the power-house to keep its base from being chipped away by the swelled stream in monsoon season to how steep the pipe needed to be to churn enough RPM out of the turbine. Most of all, there was concern about a great fallen log just above the powerhouse site. The log looked immobile now, older than god and heavier than stone, but in five years, or ten, during a particularly fierce monsoon, might it be jostled loose to crush the hydro plant to splinters?

We returned to the village for lunch with the felled-log issue still unsettled. The village women had laid out a simple meal of rice and a variety of stewed vegetables in richly flavoured gravies. We ate communally on a covered patio in the village, and afterward I found a quiet spot at the edge of the patio to make some notes. That's when I noticed Polchai, half-hidden behind a pile of the American students' backpacks, hunched over a book. I wondered for a moment if he was chewing over the engineering details of the project, consulting some obscure textbook or other, but his manner was distant and serene. He was reading the Bible. Polchai, along with everything else, was a Christian convert.

We hiked back up the hill to the worksite in the steamy heat of early afternoon. I would have mustered a moment's complaint if not for the eight villagers trudging along behind us, managing somehow not to collapse under the 100-plus kilograms of dead weight they were hauling up the steep path. The turbine was mostly a great hunk of forged metal, and they'd raised it up on a bamboo stretcher apparatus like a colonial potentate. They lurched along in a semi-military near unison, each step ending with a buckling pause just long enough that I would start to wonder if that step was the last. Then shoulders would heave and knees thrust forward, and in that way—somehow, barely, impossibly—they got the miserable thing up to the powerhouse site. I continued up the hill to see how work was coming along on the intake.

Beneath a steep stretch of creek that was almost a waterfall, a pond was beginning to form behind the half-finished dam. A handful of young village girls were wading through the water, reaching down to haul up mud to dump into the plastic sandbags the BGET crew had brought. One of them wore a T-shirt that said ROCK NEVER DIE ART PROJECT. For all I knew, the Huai Kra Thing hydro plant was all that as well.

A while later, I hiked back down to check on the progress of the powerhouse, and that's when I encountered the dance of the machetes. All along the path around the gravel bed where the powerhouse was to be erected, Karen men were hacking at lengths of bamboo. Their well-worn knives had vicious blades a foot and a half long, the tips overwide like scimitars. Someone arrived with another 20-foot length of bamboo from the hillside above, and a couple of the men leapt on it with casual efficiency, cutting it into shorter lengths with a few ferocious chops. One of the workers picked up a 6-foot tube of bamboo and buried his blade a quarter of the way down its length with a single swing, and then he pounded it against the hard earth like a sledgehammer on an anvil until the pole split in two along a clean, straight line. Then he split it again in half, and again. In this way, each piece of wood was reduced to long, thin strips, the machete blades now tracing delicate little whittling chops instead of wide arcs, the drone of the jungle drowned out for a time by the groaning sound of splitting bamboo.

There were seemingly limitless uses for the stuff. A short piece of bamboo could be made to lie flat but still intact by hacking a dozen surgical incisions at either end, and this was how the Karen got their floor mats and fashioned the side panels of their homes. Or it could be split into thin strands, then tied tight around joints or woven into a rope or a basket, and this was how the Karen got a great many other things. Or—as in the task at hand—it could be cut into inch-wide strips and piled into a stack of pliable 6-foot lengths that could be woven into a lattice the exact size of the powerhouse's foundation. When the time came, this would provide the mould and the reinforcement for the concrete the BGET folks had hauled in from Mae Sot. Karen boys were scattered along both banks of the river, blades dancing, sending little slivers of bamboo flying off in all directions, reducing the wood to those near-identical strips. Here was the project's precarious, awe-inspiring balance in a single detail: the Karen were fashioning bamboo trees into rebar.

By late afternoon, the tree-mounted brackets were ready for the cable. We finished the day's work spread out in a long line down the path toward the village—the Thai villagers and Burmese refugees, Polchai and Dr. Chris, the college kids from America and the writer from Canada—all of us working together now, passing electric cable hand to hand, keeping it free of kinks and tangles. One day very soon, that cable would deliver electricity as sustainable as any on the planet to a village that had had none at all just three years before.

THE KAREN FANTA WISDOM RUNNING HIGH

Evening in Huai Kra Thing. A few of us had quick, cooling bucket showers, and the Karen boys came out to play their evening soccer game before dinner. I watched for a while and then headed down to the dining hall. It was empty except for the family who staffed the kitchen and a pair of BGET strategists reviewing the long day's progress. By which I mean Polchai was sitting there with his colleague Watit Hathaipassorn, who was sort of seconded to BGET from the Karen Network for Culture and the Environment. They were smoking cheroots and passing a 1.5-litre plastic bottle with a Fanta label on it back and forth. Watit waved for me to join them.

"You try some Karen Fanta?" Watit said with a sly grin, proffering the bottle and a small teacup. The bottle was half-full of a hazy whitish liquid that was clearly not orange pop. He filled the cup, and I knocked it back in two quick gulps. It was starchy and only mildly searing—some sort of home-brewed rice wine—and in almost an instant it gave the warm colours of the tropical sunset a smeary impressionistic vividness. It had occurred to me—after my shower, walking back through soft evening light to the dining hall with a mild honest ache in my joints—that the one thing Huai Kra Thing most notably lacked was cold beer. After a couple of cups of Karen Fanta, I realized that cold beer, like steel rebar, had its perfectly sound local analogues.

I talked to Watit for a bit about how the project had come together. Watit seemed to be around Polchai's age, and they interacted like peers and old pals, but as a Karen with the good fortune to be born Thai, Watit had had the less traumatic life. He was, by the sound of it, the NGO equivalent of the regional fixer. He knew how to charm village elders, how to make microhydro sound just right to skeptical locals, how to fill out UNDP grant applications and entice aid organizations from Taipei to Amsterdam into lending a hand. Watit filled a dozen roles in the BGET schema, and one of them was to find welcoming valleys for its projects and ensure that all the logistics were sorted. Dr. Chris knew his voltage ratings and circuit schematics backward and forward, and Polchai—a civil engineer in Burma once upon a time—knew how to build waterworks, but when you wanted a ride back into Mae Sot, for example, you went to Watit.

Before long, Greacen and the American students joined us, and we sat in a wide circle, passing the Fanta bottle with winking ritual import. Dinner passed in a pointillist blur of fellowship and hearty Karen country cooking, and then I cornered the esteemed Dr. Chris to talk about the fate of the world.

Though Greacen had looked a little worn out back at the Mae Sot bus station at five in the morning, his general vibe—particularly when he was knee-deep in a jungle stream in his hiking shorts, gnawing on a juicy engineering problem—was that of an aw-shucks Eagle Scout ecstatic to be in the great outdoors doing something useful. He'd get so excited talking about it that his voice sometimes squawked and broke like an adolescent's. "I do this stuff 'cause it's fun," he told me with a chuckle. "It's fun to muck around in streams and build stuff and hang out with these people that are really friendly and get out in the woods. So that's a real selfish reason. But at least it keeps me coming back." It was work he'd been returning to again and again since elementary school. He had been one of those gearhead kids who like to tinker with gadgets, build circuits, read techie magazines. His undergraduate degree was in physics and he'd built a solar cell as his thesis project, but it wasn't until after graduation that his natural inclination met its higher purpose. Diploma in hand, Greacen shuffled off to India and spent six months in the remote Buddhist kingdom of Ladakh in the high Himalayas, and nothing was the same after that. There he saw ageless sustainability in its natural habitat, and it left him sufficiently inspired to set off on the mission that brought him, these twenty years later, to the Thai jungle to attempt to duplicate its incomparable harmony.

Ladakh is a rugged high-altitude desert along the banks of the Indus River. It's nominally part of the Indian state of Kashmir, but Ladakh was a traditional, communal agrarian society with a culture and language so closely linked to the famous Buddhist kingdom over the high passes to the northeast that the first Western visitors, trekking along the ancient Silk Road between China and central Asia, dubbed it "Little Tibet." By the time Greacen arrived in the mid-1980s, however, roads had been laid over some of the highest navigable mountain passes on the planet to bring Indian army detachments in—there was a stretch of disputed Chinese border in one direction and divided Kashmir in the other—and that cleared the way for the whole wide world of development. A process that had taken many decades or even centuries elsewhere was washing over parched Ladakh in just a few short years.

"The collision between the two cultures has been particularly dramatic, providing stark and vivid contrasts"—so began Helena Norberg-Hodge's revelatory analysis of that clash, *Ancient Futures: Learning from Ladakh.* Norberg-Hodge was a British linguist who came to the valley shortly after the road from Kashmir was completed, eventually becoming one of the first English-speaking people to master modern Ladakhi. She also became a vocal proponent of sustainable development before the term had even been coined, founding the Ladakh Ecological Development Group (LEDeG) in 1983 to advocate on behalf of small-scale, grassroots-driven development aimed at preserving and enhancing a fragile, magnificent culture that she'd come to see as a shining example of true sustainability. In *Ancient Futures,* Norberg-Hodge detailed the extraordinary social and ecological order extant in pre-development Ladakh, a communal way of life that had allowed thousands of people to live healthy, stable, fulfilling lives for centuries in one of the harshest climates in the world. "The Ladakhis belong to their place on earth," she wrote. "They are bonded to that place through intimate daily contact, through a knowledge about their immediate environment with its changing seasons, needs, and limitations."

Norberg-Hodge was sure we had much to learn about sustainable living from the joyful, frugal Ladakhi people, and she was even more convinced that the standard-issue development model being trucked in by Indian technocrats from the plains below and by foreign experts from farther afield was fundamentally unsound. She outlined the "one-dimensional view of progress" being visited upon the Ladakhis, in which GNP became the "prime indicator" of success and a nonsensical economic order thus emerged in which wheat flour from Punjab was cheaper than traditional Ladakhi barley and cement from even farther away was a more "economical" building material than the mud that had sheltered Ladakhis against the vicious Himalayan winter for countless generations. Norberg-Hodge: "It was like starting from zero, as if there had been no infrastructure in Ladakh before development. . . . The intricate web of roads, paths, and trade routes, the vast and sophisticated network of irrigation canals maintained over centuries: all these signs of a living, functioning culture and economic system were treated as though they simply did not exist. Ladakh was being rebuilt according to Western guidelines—in tarmac, concrete, and steel." It was like another volume in *The Adventures of Tintin: Le Corbusier au Petit Tibet.*

In response to business-as-usual modernist development, Norberg-Hodge and her LEDeG colleagues—Western and Ladakhi both—pioneered an approach to sustainable development at the scale of a small Buddhist kingdom, seeking out appropriate technologies and durable compromises between ancient and modern. One of their first and most successful initiatives was the Trombe wall, a passive solar heating system in which a south-facing wall is painted black and outfitted with two layers of glass, trapping the sun's warmth during the day and radiating it into the house at night.* Ladakh, as Norberg-Hodge noted, was blessed with more than three hundred sunny days each year, and the cost of a Trombe wall was about the same as one *dzo* (a local hybrid of yak and cow). LEDeG also introduced solar ovens and solar thermal water heaters, greenhouses and gravity-fed water pumps, microhydro and the odd PV cell

* The skyscrapers of Sir Norman Foster—New York's Hearst Tower and Calgary's forthcoming Bow Building, for example—owe most of their vaunted energy efficiency to essentially the same technique. The Trombe wall itself was a century-old patent by the time it found its way to Ladakh.

or two to power a few lights. Early in her treatise, Norberg-Hodge noted that the "largest expense" the Indian development commissioner had to contend with was the outsized 4-megawatt hydro plant on the Indus, which had cost millions of dollars and taken two decades to build. LEDeG was accomplishing similar ends with meagre but much more finely tuned means in a few short years.

This was the Ladakh Chris Greacen arrived to discover in the mid-1980s—a magnificent traditional society that had just been shoved forward into the overlit modern age and was still blinking at the bright lights and trying to find its footing. For Greacen, it was pure revelation. It was, he said, "the first real incidence I saw where human beings actually seemed to contribute to the greenness of a place. The valleys humans inhabited were, like, *green* because of the agricultural systems these guys had built."

I knew *exactly* the scene he was describing. I'd first set eyes on Ladakh in the summer of 1999, and I remember staring out the airplane window agog at the landscape below. The valley was a study in lifeless greys and browns, a wide stretch of dust and boulders, and then at the village's edge, just over a ruler-straight line, a verdant field of primary-green barley began. Buddhist scholars often talk about the Void—that empty nowhere of total consciousness, the place of ultimate peace where meditation, in its most advanced state, can take you. The Ladakhis, keen followers themselves of the Buddha's Eightfold Path, needed only to walk to the edge of their gardens to contemplate it in the flesh, to understand how arbitrary and precious life was. (I've only ever seen this perfect division between irrigated green and desert brown in one other place: on the fringes of Las Vegas golf courses and subdivisions.)

Awakened by Ladakh's endangered ecological balance to the potential uses of his education, Greacen—newly minted physicist, designer of a homespun solar cell—soon fell in with Norberg-Hodge and her fledgling development projects. Greacen: "LEDeG at that time was building microhydro projects and solar ovens, and messing around with solar energy and stuff like that. So seeing these types of technologies at a village scale was also pretty inspiring."

After his Ladakhi epiphany, Greacen worked for a while on a handful of counterculturally bent green-tech initiatives. In 1995, he returned to school at UC Berkeley to become Dr. Chris. He thought he might go to Nepal after graduation to work on renewable-energy projects there, but he met a Thai woman working on her Ph.D. at Berkeley. He followed her to Bangkok, got married and started his little NGO to work on policy stuff and build the occasional solar module for Burmese medics.

And that brought us back to this fated night in Huai Kra Thing. Greacen, sitting cross-legged, his limbs a bit gangly, marvelled at how quickly his pet obsession had gone from "this realm of wackos and hippies and dope-smokers" to a place where the solar industry was growing at 40 percent per annum and he was using UN money to bring microhydro to rural Thailand. He made some back-of-a-banana-leaf calculations and guessed that if you excluded labour (which here in Huai Kra Thing was mostly gratis), then the project would cost about $4,000 to produce 2 kilowatts of electrical capacity. That was two bucks a watt, about double the price of a giant dam being built just then over in Laos. "We're in the ballpark," he said. "Even doing these types of technologies." By which he meant the patchwork pump and the on-the-fly conferences with Polchai and everything else about the scale of the thing—so small and labour-intensive, he noted, that it couldn't make a large enough blip at a quick enough pace to meet a World Bank installations quota.

I wondered if it deserved more credit than a World Bank spreadsheet knew how to measure, and I almost talked Greacen into grandiloquence. "You know," he said, "the dam might well wash out during the rainy season. But in some ways that's not that important. Because they know how to fix it. And they have the incentive to fix it. And so we're building a technology that we're trying to build as well as we can. But more important, we're building the capacity and the interest to fix it if things do break. And try to keep things as simple as possible. And that's real essential for these things. And I think that highlights the difference between this type of project and, say, the Solar Home System project. Where they're kind of, the Solar Home Systems are parachuted in, in a sense, and the installation company spends, you know, three hours installing the system and then they're gone, and nobody ever sees them again. Whereas we spend weeks engaging the community, building these systems with the community, and then we'll be in touch with them over the long term."

We walked across the village clearing a little while later under a sky so dense with stars it looked fake to urban eyes. We bunked down on bamboo floors, Dr. Chris and I and three other BGET members, an American named Andrew trading yuks with a Karen technician named Yo Ten like Eagle Scouts on a camping trip. It was sweet and silly and—Greacen was right—it was *fun*. It was like life, not like a spreadsheet at all. And that *had* to be worth something.

SHRAPNEL

As we strolled through the village on our way back up to the construction site on the morning of the second day, I saw kids rolling tires with sticks like in a movie about the 1920s, a grandmother walking a baby along the path, another kid chasing a puppy, giggling. They wouldn't be able to see the power plant from here. They wouldn't hear it or *breathe* it. That had to count for something, too, didn't it?

Up at the powerhouse site, Polchai and Dr. Chris batted around the question of the fallen log again, and it was decided that it had to come down. Several villagers set dutifully to work, climbing on top of it and hacking deep cuts into the great log, first with their machetes and then with a two-person crosscut saw. It seemed impossible that they would ever make it through all 8 feet of its diameter, but eventually they did.

Later in the day, I sat for a while with Polchai near the intake pool to ask him a little more about the hard journey that had brought him to Huai Kra Thing. He was courteous and honest to a fault, but he wasn't much for yarns and clearly didn't want to talk too much about it. Between drags on one of his omnipresent cheroots, he acquiesced to telling me a skeletal version of the story. He'd been a civil engineer in Burma, where he worked on waterworks. He'd first come to Thailand in 1979, settling in a refugee camp, and then in 1995 he started working for NGOs. I asked him what he had done from 1979 to 1995. He chuckled—not a particularly mirthful laugh, mostly just resigned to a certain kind of thorny fate—and puffed his cheroot. "If we lie," he said, "we must lie forever, you know? If we say the truth, only one time. You're honest, and everything is good." He paused. "But at the time I was KNLA."

The KNLA—the Karen National Liberation Army—had been fighting a protracted guerrilla war against the Burmese military junta since it came to power in 1949. Polchai organized and trained soldiers and conducted raids over the border. In 1983, he was wounded in action, and he fled to Thailand for good in 1985, carrying a few scraps of the junta's shrapnel with him. He continued to work as an organizer in the refugee camps, and then he must've decided the camps had become more of a home than that perversion called Myanmar ever would, because he married, fathered five kids—four boys and a girl—and set to work building water-supply systems for the camps themselves. He was convinced, he told me, that he would never return to Burma. If there was sadness in that declaration, it was the barest tinge; Polchai didn't waste time on nostalgia. From the mid-1990s on, he had worked as a technician for a range of NGOs: Médecins sans Frontières, a Taiwanese NGO and now a Dutch refugee group, which was sponsoring his participation in the Huai Kra Thing project. "Which one I work for, I don't know," he told me. "I know I work for poor people."

We talked about family after that—mine and his, all the things your children teach you about what life is about and what it's for—and then he apologized if any of his answers were not helpful, excused himself and bounded off to get back to work on the hydro plant, half-jogging, eager and tireless. Polchai was a refugee from a war nobody cared about, a member of an ethnic group few have even heard of, marginalized in two countries and truly at home in neither at present, maybe forever. And from what I saw at Huai Kra Thing, he brought to his work more spring in his stride, more integrity in his labour and more spirit in his disposition than pretty much anyone I've ever met. I thought of the shrapnel in his body—now and forever—and what it meant that he soldiered on, humble and dignified, expecting nothing but what was presented for him to do. And he knew that the only thing to do in the face of seemingly insurmountable odds and unimaginable strife was to carry on, every day, making the world around him as good as it could be.

Think of Polchai—I do—any time you hear about what kind of sacrifice is too great in the fight to build a sustainable world. Think of him—I do—when emissions reductions are declared too steep or the task at hand beyond human ingenuity or village-scale renewable energy too small for the task. Tell Polchai he's being unrealistic. Tell him he doesn't understand the costs. Ask to see the scars from his wounds, ask how his kids are doing in their school at the refugee camp where they've lived their whole lives. And then try to tell him anything you think he doesn't already know about how hard it is to keep moving forward.

· I returned to Bangkok by overnight bus that night, so I only learned how the project turned out a couple of months later, when I read Greacen's post-mortem report. The turbine was moved a bit to dodge the potential flight path of the last, immovable piece of the giant log. It was cemented in place, and a bamboo-walled hut was erected to house it. They'd botched a glue joint in the incoming pipe at first, and it had burst and flooded the powerhouse, but thankfully nobody was hurt and none of the major equipment damaged. (And it was to BGET's credit that this hitch was duly noted, with photos, in the final report, even though it caused no permanent damage.) By mid-February 2006, the turbine was generating a steady stream of 1.6 kilowatts of power, and the lights went on in the Huai Kra Thing community centre for the first time ever. The new power plant could be revved up to 3 kilowatts, but that required diverting an awful lot of the river's flow. Besides, no one in the village reckoned they needed that much power. And they ought to know.

TOXIC SLUDGE, BAD APPLES & DEVELOPMENT'S REDEMPTION

Here's a little more Karen Fanta wisdom I forgot to mention. Toward the end of my conversation with Chris Greacen, he got to talking about the potential for a village-sized electric company. He was imagining a place like Huai Kra Thing outfitted with a hydro plant that not only lit the village but sold power back to a grid. We speculated on the feasibility, wondered whether something like that might be able to reduce the number of poor rural Thais pouring into places like Mae Sot to work in textile-factory squalor. Greacen mused on the idea of quitting the NGO game completely, starting up a little entrepreneurial venture of some sort. I thought of the dynamic team of inventive misfits he'd assembled in BGET, the nimble way it dealt with problems it hadn't anticipated and claimed the *terra incognita* of pristine jungle and new-fangled renewable energy as its natural habitat. I told him it sounded kind of like an internet start-up already.

Now, that *really* got Greacen going, and pretty soon he was telling me about this company he'd heard of right there in Thailand, and how what they'd done was so goddamn clever and smack-your-forehead obvious and especially all kinds of *profitable* that it made him think he should be writing a business plan of his own. Greacen chuckled all through the tale, an ever-widening grin on his face. This was some kind of yarn. It started with cassava, a gnarly root vegetable that requires an intensive processing regime to render it into something people want to eat in any quantity. Thailand is the world's second-largest producer of processed cassava—much of it converted into tapioca starch—and its countryside is littered with processing plants.

Greacen: "To make it into tapioca, they have to cook this cassava thing, and they peel it in some factory, and all of the peel sludges then go into this wastewater stream. And the factories have in the past had a bunch of holding ponds where this stuff slowly rots anaerobically, in terms of the methane, really bad for the atmosphere. So this company says"—he clapped his hands with go-get-'em enthusiasm—"'Hey, we've got a deal for ya. We'll take all of your wastewater, sign a contract for all your wastewater. Which means you don't have to have all these holding ponds, which means you all of a sudden have land that's useful for something else. And give us a piece of land that's about the size of a football field, and we're gonna build a biogas digester on it. And then we're gonna take the gas that we produce from this thing, and we're gonna sell that back to you at 80 percent of the cost of fuel oil'—which is what they use to fire their boilers for cooking all this stuff. 'And we're gonna generate electricity with the excess gas that we have, and we're gonna sell that to you at 80 percent of the retail cost of electricity that you now buy from the utility. *And* we're gonna take excess gas from those two things, because we have even more gas that we can produce, and we're gonna back-feed the grid and sell it to the utilities, and you can have 20 percent of all of those revenues, and we'll keep 80 percent. *And* after ten years we'll give the plant to you for free.'" He closed with a mighty exclamation point of a laugh.

"Who's doing this?" I asked.

"This is a company called CleanTHAI. And it turns out that these things make so much biogas that even under those terms, these guys make really good money. So . . ." He paused to let another intense wave of laughter roll through. "It's an impressive model. And they actually make good money just on the basis of the gas sales and the electricity sales—if you throw in the carbon credits you get for the avoided methane emissions, it's about double. So things like that, where people look at stuff from just a completely different angle . . ." He didn't have to finish: he wondered about getting into things like that. Who wouldn't?

Greacen's CleanTHAI tale had all the too-good-to-be-true trappings of an urban legend—not to mention that licence-to-print-money exuberance of the kinds of stories that fuel speculative investment bubbles. He'd heard it from some other international development field operative, by the sound of it, which only added to my suspicion that it might be one of those tall tales told around the campfire to warm the hearts of hope's tired soldiers. Still, I made a note to check it out.

Months later, I reached one of CleanTHAI's first investors by phone in a hotel room in Beijing. Jeffery Dickinson was the Asian regional manager of a New Jersey firm called E+Co, and he quickly confirmed the core details of Greacen's story. (He was, it turned out, the fellow field op who had supplied it.) CleanTHAI, Dickinson explained, had spun out of a company called PhilBio, which had set up a chain of biogas digesters at methane-rich pig farms across the Philippines. An American entrepreneur had seized on the idea of bringing the same concept to Thailand's cassava processing industry, but there was some skepticism about the viability of biogas floating through Thai industrialist circles, which Dickinson attributed to a couple of poorly conceived earlier efforts by domestic firms. The entrepreneur, for his part, had a deal with a highly reputable New Zealand company called Waste Solutions, which boasted state-of-the-art biogas technology. What he didn't have was the capital to make it all happen. E+Co specialized in providing financing and business development support for the renewable-energy business in just these kinds of situations, so Dickinson and his team kicked in a couple hundred thousand dollars in seed capital and some battle-tested advice on developing a business plan, and with that package they coaxed Thailand's largest cassava processor to let them set up shop on its premises in the industrial town of Korat, northeast of Bangkok.

CleanTHAI's biogas plant, Dickinson explained, was called a covered in-ground anaerobic reactor—a CIGAR—and it consisted primarily of a single pit, 100 metres square and maybe a dozen metres deep, covered in plastic tarp. It was fed the cassava plant's wastewater through one series of pipes, and in an organic process the CIGAR converted that waste to methane gas and non-toxic waste. The gas exited through a second set of pipes, some of it destined for the cassava factory's boilers, the rest burned to generate 3 megawatts of electricity. Both the gas and the power were sold back to the cassava plant at 20 to 25 percent below market rates. If it wasn't quite the licence to print money Greacen had described, it *was* a tidy little commercial enterprise. In what's known as a BOT arrangement— short for "build-operate-transfer"— CleanTHAI's plant is expected to run for ten years as an independent company, at which point its ownership will devolve automatically to the cassava processor. By that time, it will have generated a comfortable profit for CleanTHAI.

More important, the plant was turning ecologically hostile wastewater into non-toxic effluent and reducing the potency of its emissions by a factor of more than twenty. (Combusted biogas is a much less intense greenhouse gas than the raw methane formerly respired by the untreated wastewater.) It had also reduced the enormous field of seventy-five settling ponds formerly required to turn that water into a soup clean enough to be discharged down to the equivalent of about four, freeing up an enormous patch of real estate. "It's been up and running without any shutdowns to the factory since we started it," said Dickinson. "I think almost every cassava owner in the country has been there now to see it." The concept thus proven, Thai cassava processors were now setting up their own biogas digesters, and owners of other types of processing plants throughout East Asia—potatoes, sugar cane, beer, pigs—were keen to get into the biogas business.

When I got off the phone with Dickinson, I was unclear as to whether this E+Co was a sustainable development NGO, a renewable-energy advocacy group or a venture capital firm. Understandable, I guess, because it turns out E+Co is a wicked-clever hybrid of all three, a next-generation development boutique that fills the gaps between direct aid and economic development, trims the unnecessary bureaucracy and top-down inefficiencies of business-as-usual international development, and so seamlessly straddles the rift between public and private enterprise that it makes you wonder what kind of delusional thinking produced such a chasm. Until you talk to its founder,

. Dickinson's boss Phil LaRocco, who'll tell you exactly where that chasm came from. He also just might have worked out the formula for building a great many sturdy bridges across it.

"The root of it makes it easy to understand." This was LaRocco, on the phone from his office in New Jersey, explaining where E+Co came from and why it didn't fit into any of the status quo's tidy slots. His no-bullshit Brooklyn accent blasting through the development game's save-the-world pieties and academic pedantries like a Big Apple cabbie through heavy traffic, LaRocco explained that he'd spent most of his career as an official at the Port Authority of New York and New Jersey, the quasi-public body that manages everything from JFK Airport to the World Trade Center. By the end of his tenure, he'd risen to the position of Director of World Trade and Economic Development, a job that required a rare mastery of the fine art of balancing private demands with the public interest—a commercial airline looking for a new terminal, for example, and the airport where it's to be located. It blurred LaRocco's point of view permanently. "Nothing in my mind," he told me, "is purely public or purely private."

In the early 1990s, after two decades of service, LaRocco left the Port Authority to oversee a portfolio of charitable investments for the Rockefeller Foundation. He came to the job—and the international development field in which it was immersed—a disruptive mutant. "The thing that happened during that twenty years," LaRocco said, "was my DNA had been altered slightly." He didn't get why you'd go with a "pure command-and-control" scheme emanating from Washington or London via some developing world's capital-city bureaucracy on one project, and then turn *just* to the local private sector for something else. He couldn't understand why the development of energy infrastructure was treated as a separate thing from the alleviation of abject poverty. And this idea that you'd "develop" a country first and only *then* think about its ecology? "We'll get rich first, then we'll clean up"—this is how he put it. "Well, that's just stupid."

More than anything, though, he'd never been fully converted to the received wisdom of conventional international development. "People will say the goddamnedest things," he said, "because they think they're true." Ask them for evidence, though, and marvel at the silence. Were small farmers and modest entrepreneurs in developing countries *really* bigger credit risks than incompetent bankers and labyrinthine, kleptocratic government bureaucracies? "Only the rich can afford not to pay," as Muhammad Yunus of Grameen Bank once put it. Was 30 percent *really* the only acceptable rate of return on such risks? And finally—maybe most of all—if you were trying to figure out what kind of "development" people needed in rural Thailand or downtown Timbuktu, would it help to *ask* the people who lived there? "Yuh *think?*" LaRocco wondered. "Which, if I ever write a book, that's gonna be the title. Pure Brooklynese: *Yuh Think?*"

Understand: like many critics of development-as-usual, LaRocco wasn't against aid per se. Shelter for refugees, medicine for those suffering from curable diseases, sacks of grain for the victims of famine—these were worthwhile projects for the rich world's tax dollars and its aid bureaucracies, no matter how inefficiently or intermittently the jobs were done. Sure, there was that old adage about the limited efficacy of giving a man a fish, but if the guy was on the verge of death and you were sitting there with a crate of salmon, then by all means let him have some. What's more, Big Fish Inc. likely wasn't going to be able to reconcile a sufficient volume of free handouts with its sacrosanct bottom line, so it probably made sense to set up some kind of public-sector international network to take on the task of distributing free fillets where they were needed.

LaRocco, though, was working in the teach-a-man-to-fish sector, and that's where it paid to be much more studious, more flexible and responsive. Was giving a guy a rod and reel, baiting it up real nice, and then jetting back to Paris or New York the best way to help him catch his own food? Did he have a boat? And if not, who should build it and who should drive it? What if he was more of a net mender or market-stall hawker at heart? What if he didn't *like* fish? Or there weren't any to catch, or no one to buy the surplus once he did?

If these sound like thuddingly obvious questions, I should point out that they are forgotten frequently enough to give rise to a whole subgenre of folklore, widely and enthusiastically traded in development circles, about how often no one thinks to ask them. E+Co's Jeffery Dickinson, for example, told me about a big project a while back in impoverished Nepal—"which," he noted, "was absolutely spoiled with development money in the '80s and '90s." (If Western-style liberal-democratic prosperity was purely a function of aid spending per capita, rural Nepal would surely be the Beverly Hills of Asia by now. Instead, it's home to the world's most active and influential Maoist insurgency. You do the math.) Dickinson's story, at any rate, was about apples, and how America's largest development bureaucracy, the United States Agency for International Development (USAID), decided that apples would be the key to orderly economic progress in rural Nepal. So these latter-day Johnny Appleseeds littered the Nepali countryside with apple trees. Soon there were bountiful harvests, and salvation was clearly at hand. Except that the USAID experts had recommended varieties that sold well in Western supermarkets but weren't particularly noted for their ease of transport or storage. And even the most durable varieties of apples are still a more fragile commodity than eggs. And they're fairly bulky besides. Plus rural Nepal has precious few smooth roads. Actually, rural Nepal has almost no roads at all. Dickinson: "It was a complete mismatch. Now you go across the hills of Nepal and there's apples everywhere, and people are feeding 'em to their pigs and they're making 'em into fertilizer. And, you know, it's a burden, basically."

Yuh think?

In answer to his own question, Phil LaRocco moved on from the Rockefeller Foundation in 1994 to found E+Co. It was intended to be a sharp deviation from the status quo, but at the same time it maintained many of the superficial trappings of any development body and swam in some of the same pools; in time, it took to calling itself "a public purpose investment company" in its brochures. E+Co was established as a non-profit corporation with a tight focus on broadening the use of renewable-energy technologies in the developing world. It got most of its money at first from institutional donors, but it managed its clients like any other investment firm: performing due-diligence checks, drafting formal business plans and signing binding agreements, sitting on their boards with spurs at the ready, guiding these green start-ups from their big ideas to the point where any old investor would be happy to back them. It worked a bit like one of those high-tech business incubators that were all the rage during the dotcom boom, providing relatively small amounts of start-up capital and more liberal doses of mentoring and expertise.

E+Co's most dramatic break with standard development agency practice was probably its unrelentingly businesslike nature. It didn't fund projects; it grew companies. It didn't give grants; it provided loans. It had institutional donors to cover its operating costs, but its investors received returns on their investments. The rate (about 6 to 8 percent nowadays) might not have been anything to turn heads in Silicon Valley, but it was a far cry from apples rotting by the bushel on a Nepali hillside. Finally, although E+Co backed techie companies and liked to invoke the metaphor of "disruptive technology" so celebrated in said Valley, it wasn't technology-driven. His clients, LaRocco said, innovated not in terms of gizmos themselves but in terms of their application. "We think of ourselves not so much as a disruptive technology but as a disruptive *technique*," he told me.

Just look at CleanTHAI. Nothing about its biogas digester was technologically innovative, and E+Co's backing was pretty minuscule and had nothing to do with R&D. LaRocco: "We put in $197,500 of what today is probably, I don't know, close to a $10-million project. But what we did that was hugely important was that, of that $197,500, the last $47,500 was devoted specifically to creating the feasibility study so that they could present this project to the cassava plant owner. And the service we provided there wasn't to tell people, you know, about anaerobic digestion—because what I know about anaerobic digestion you can put in a thimble and still have room for your finger." No, what E+Co did that was so critical was to piece the deal together. The international development field could be a forbidding landscape pockmarked with wide craters—between donor and recipient, between good intention and effective action, between a bright idea and its implementation—and E+Co specialized in navigating that terrain. In addition to selling the cassava plant on the concept, its officials found a keen third-party investor with much more money than they had: Moulay Hassan, the crown prince of Morocco, whose Al Tayyar Energy company became CleanTHAI's first major partner. Al Tayyar's involvement led to a follow-on investment from the International Finance Corporation (the World Bank's private investment arm), and just like that biogas was a going concern in the Thai cassava industry, and CleanTHAI was debt-free and soon to be profitable. E+Co replaced aid recipients with entrepreneurs and developed small businesses instead of projects. LaRocco called it "mezzo-finance": not the village-scale loans of Yunus's Grameen Bank, but not some World Bank–financed dam that took twenty years to build, either.

Mezzo-finance—it was a precise echo of E.F. Schumacher's call for a new model of international development built on "intermediate technology." And it reverberated right through Schumacher's own extension of the give-a-man-a-fish platitude, which went like this: "On a higher level: supply him with fishing tackle; this will cost you a good deal of money, and the result remains doubtful; but even if fruitful, the man's continuing livelihood will still be dependent upon you for replacements. But teach him to make his own fishing tackle and you have helped him to become not only self-supporting, but also self-reliant and independent." And now came the E+Co post-script: give him the tools and the capital to become not just a subsistence fisherman but a seafood-industry entrepreneur.

I'll let LaRocco expound: "What E+Co says is, we have this wonderful asset out there. They're called people. And most of this asset has really not been used. One of the most powerful resources that anybody's research will turn up is the power of a man or a woman to make a living providing goods or services to his or her neighbours." Internally, E+Co referred to their work as a hunt for "champions"—eager entrepreneurs with powerful ideas and significant local knowledge who simply needed a few tools, a bit of money and some guidance.

Now at this point, we're starting to verge on the generic platitudes of any given development agency's mission statement—or any old corporation's, for that matter. Sure, dude: It's all about *empowering* the individual. People are our greatest natural resource. We are family. *Yuh think?*

On the other hand, there is, for example, an E+Co champion by the name of Harish Hande, who figured out, for instance, that the difference between good development and bad development might come down to a simple equation: $10 \times 30 \neq 300$. This was the case, at least, when you were counting in a villager's hard-earned rupees.

FUZZY MATH, OR CHANGING THE WORLD ON 10 RUPEES A DAY

I landed in South India just a few days after my visit to northwestern Thailand. I was hot on the trail of E+Co, though I didn't know it yet: it was months before I would figure out that all these nifty innovations I kept stumbling upon had a common backer. What I found, instead, was a surprisingly robust solar-energy industry. Solar water heaters, as I mentioned earlier, were all the rage. There were all those ads on the backs of rickshaws in Bangalore, of course, but I also spied fully operational systems on the roofs of low-rise office complexes in the techie suburbs of Hyderabad and atop government buildings in Chennai. I spent a pleasant evening at my hotel on the outskirts of Mysore watching macaques wrestle and slide across the building's smooth solar thermal panels. I also had occasion to meet a handful of people working in India's fledgling renewable-energy industry, and when I mentioned the water heaters, they all had the same reply: SELCO.

The Solar Electric Light Company was American in origin and had moribund subsidiaries up and running in a couple of other developing countries, but its heart and soul was Indian. SELCO India was based in Bangalore and overseen by another ambitious Ph.D., Dr. Harish Hande. Hande and his company had not built or installed a single one of the solar water heaters I'd seen—his business was focused on small-scale Solar Home Systems in the villages—but in some sense they all owed their existence to his work, at least any of them that had been put in place using borrowed money. In true E+Co fashion, Hande had pioneered not a new technology but a powerfully disruptive technique: he'd sold rural banks on the idea that solar power was a good investment. Also, as I said, that a loan payment of 10 rupees a day was not the same as 300 rupees a month (i.e., $10 \times 30 \neq 300$). He'd changed the way banks did their math.

Harish Hande was certainly no stranger to cold, hard data: his undergraduate degree was from the prestigious Indian Institute of Technology, and he had earned his Ph.D. in engineering at the University of Massachusetts at Lowell. But he'd graduated uncommonly keen to test his doctoral dissertation under real-world conditions, so he co-founded SELCO India in 1995 (later partnering with an American named Neville Williams to found the greater SELCO network). Hande then returned to India to learn that it took a different kind of calculation to make his lab results add up out in the sun-baked villages of Karnataka. Hande: "SELCO basically started with three myths. The three myths being that poor people cannot afford technology, poor people cannot maintain technology, and you cannot run a social venture commercially."

SELCO's founding mission was to bring small-scale solar power to those villages—not as a gift of foreign aid but as a capital loan. And so Hande's first task was not to apply for grants or solicit donations but to convince the small village banks of rural Karnataka to finance his

Solar Home Systems installation by installation. For months he went village to village and bank to bank. He pitched and argued, and when that didn't work he pestered and cajoled. He camped out on front stoops. *Literally.*

Picture it: the self-satisfied manager of a tidy little bank branch out in some dusty Indian backwater arriving at work one morning to find this obsessed academic sprawled across the threshold, all wrapped up in a sleeping bag, with his head on his backpack, babbling on and on—again—about solar power for the villages. One of them finally caved, and Hande bugged him further to get a letter of intent, and then he took *that* to the bank in the next village and the one after that to shame them into signing their own. And that's how it went for SELCO's first couple of years, with E+Co chipping in a bit of capital ($107,500, to be exact) to expand SELCO's range and help it set up a headquarters in Bangalore. Once Hande had finally exasperated enough bank managers to get the business up and running, scattered dots of electric evening light began to pierce the dark of the villages of South India. Kids continued their education into the night, and cottage businesses sprang up around solar-powered sewing machines. And the key points of Hande's doctoral thesis—that poor people *could* afford technology and social ventures *could* function as commercial enterprises with third-party financing—were pretty much proven.

In one sense, however, the hardest battle remained to be fought: he had to change the way banks counted. SELCO's fuzzy math started with a woman who wanted to replace the kerosene lamps in her vegetable stall with solar-powered electric bulbs. The trouble was, she explained to Hande, that she couldn't afford the monthly payment, which was 300 rupees. She *could,* however, manage 10 rupees a day. This was because she had no savings—no way to sock away the capital to make that first monthly payment—but she was already spending 15 rupees a day on kerosene. If the instalments were daily, she could have a Solar Home System. And so it was back to the banks for Hande, this time to argue that 300 rupees a month wasn't the same as 10 a day.

SELCO wasn't done with its unconventional mathematics curriculum, either. It had started working with a Grameen-style microfinance institution in the state of Gujarat, an outfit called the Self-Employed Women's Association (SEWA) Bank. SEWA had pioneered a "moratorium" system in which not only could you repay daily, but you also got 365 days over the term of your three-year loan when you could default without penalty. (In essence, you had a two-year loan, but it could be paid back over three years if you needed the extra time.) The system provided a bit of breathing room for the hut-scale entrepreneurs SEWA lent to, and it was just as helpful to SELCO's clients. A certain number of them, for example, had turned themselves into some of the world's tiniest electric companies. They would buy a SELCO solar system, set it up on their little street stall, and then sell their excess power to a handful of adjacent stalls. But what if there was a flood at some point and no produce made it to market for a few days? Or vegetable prices skyrocketed one day, and no one could afford to buy anything, and so the entrepreneur's customers couldn't pay their power bill that day? These were the dimensions in which small-scale solar could have its most dramatic impact, but it needed financing to match. It needed the fuzzy new SELCO math.

It was hard to argue with SELCO's sums: at last count, the company had twenty-five branch offices and about 170 employees throughout India. SELCO had sold around seventy-five thousand Solar Home Systems—*sold* them—thereby enabling a couple hundred thousand poor Indians to study in the evening, start up home businesses, join the modern world on village-sized terms. What's more, every one of them had executed a textbook leapfrog: rather than graduating first to India's absurdly unreliable grid, they'd vaulted directly to decentralized renewable energy. They'd found a path to modernity that *didn't* require coal-blackened skies and toxic-soup rivers. Clean tech, Hande had proved, could be the new status quo for the hundreds of millions of people around the world who had never lived in a house with a light switch.

Beyond all this, SELCO's technique was infectious. The company had won over countless bank managers across the subcontinent to the idea that solar energy was a sound investment for their banks' money. So in the late 1990s, when the Indian government decided to encourage the installation of solar water heaters, the minister in charge—well-briefed by Dr. Hande on the verities of his field-tested hypothesis—chose to subsidize the interest rate on small loans instead of giving the money directly to manufacturers as a per-unit capital subsidy. This made the solar heaters much more attractive investments for the banks, and in turn led more or less directly to the booming industry I saw pitching its wares from every other rickshaw in Bangalore. A few years after the Indian government's subsidy was in place, along came the UN Environmental Programme (UNEP). In response to a proposal submitted by none other than Dr. Hande, UNEP partnered with two Indian banking chains to set up the Indian Solar Loan Programme, which used interest-rate subsidies to spur the installation of sixteen thousand more Solar Home Systems.

None of this had dulled Hande's tenacity, as far as I could tell. I talked to him in the fall of 2006, not long after he'd been showered with awards (including the prestigious Ashden Award for Sustainable Energy, a British laurel sometimes referred to as a "green Oscar"), and he was keen to twist his math further and debunk even more myths. SELCO had been rocked that year, along with everyone else in the industry, by the worldwide PV panel shortage, but Hande saw it as the spur he needed to become "a one-stop energy solution." He was looking into high-efficiency cookers and biogas. He told me that he asked his sales teams to meet targets not just in rupees but also in number of households, lest someone score one big contract and not work hard enough to get a 10-rupee-a-day lady in the next village on board. He detailed the arguments he still sometimes had with his investors because SELCO took the time not only to bring solar electricity to some rural woman's home but also to help her find a market for the linens her sewing machine could now produce. "We have to look at the holistic approach," he said. "Technology is just a part of it. We have to spend equal amount of time in creating those other linkages. Else poverty cannot be solved, else technology will not get into the rural areas, else technology makes no sense."

When he wasn't taking flack for paying too little attention to his bottom line, Hande ran into trouble for even having one. He was making the rounds of investors interested in funding "social enterprises," he said, but many of them had to pass because SELCO was a "for-profit," and they invested only in NGOs. But grants, as far as Hande was concerned, were a form of institutionalized hypocrisy. How could he ask the villagers of Karnataka to be self-reliant if he was dependent on handouts himself? "The whole concept of *project* has to be abolished, actually," was his irritated summation.

You could almost hear Phil LaRocco's Brooklyn drawl over his shoulder: *Yuh think?*

SCALE & SCALABILITY

The offices of E+Co's first major spinoff venture—E+Co Capital–Latin America, a fund management company and a for-profit through and through—are located, as if for symbolic convenience, behind the gleaming office tower of ICE, Costa Rica's state-owned electricity monopoly, in an upscale suburb of San José. E+Co Capital works out of a modest office in a squat complex on a quiet residential street, either hiding in ICE's shadow or else lying in wait to trip it up. At any rate, its mission is sharply at odds with state-owned power monopolies, and because of the long shadow ICE casts across Costa Rica, much of E+Co Capital's investing—exclusively in small-scale renewable energy, in keeping with the interests of its parent—occurs elsewhere in Central America. Its origins may seem counterintuitive as well: the proximate cause was a standard-issue large-scale relief effort, but the company's higher purpose is all about moving beyond the development model embodied by such grand relief efforts.

First, though, to that proximate cause, which was explained to me in meticulous detail by Fernando Alvarado, the studious CEO of E+Co Capital. I met him at his San José office on a Thursday afternoon so languid it seemed like I'd interrupted the complex's security guard from a siesta on arrival. Alvarado ran through his company's short history in fluent, Spanish-accented English and an understated boardroom tone. It began, he said, with Hurricane Mitch, which raged ashore in 2000 and devastated vast swaths of the Central American coast. In its aftermath, USAID launched a broad, multipronged reconstruction initiative that included a well-financed program to involve renewable-energy projects in the rebuilding. E+Co, which already had several clients producing green power in the region, won a contract to conduct seminars for potential USAID partners—entrepreneurs, investors, NGOs—on how to improve their proposals. As was so often the case, there were artificial limitations to what kinds of enterprises got funding, and it struck Alvarado and his colleagues that a lot of the greatest potential for renewables in Central America was in the hands of small, underfunded businesses, many of them family-owned, that would never qualify for a development bank's money.

These were not quite the same breed as the usual E+Co client. They weren't bright ideas in need of a business plan; they were going concerns, often already profitable, in need of a financial boost.

One example Alvarado noted was a small-scale hydroelectric plant in Guatemala that had been feasibility-studied and business-planned and all that jazz and just needed a couple million in investment capital to actually get built and start churning out megawatts and turning a profit. And so E+Co investors were solicited far and wide for their interest in putting money into a straight-up private equity fund to capitalize on the increasingly robust renewables market in Central America. In due course, a $20-million fund was raised, and a small company called E+Co Capital–Latin America was incorporated in 2005 to manage it.

So went the yawning, quiet-day-in-suburban-San-Jose version of the story. Up in New Jersey, however, Phil LaRocco had a much more ambitious idea in mind. In *his* version of the story, E+Co Capital was the second prong in a three-part response to that inevitable global economy question—*Does it scale?*—which in LaRocco's case came to him in the form of a cut-to-the-chase challenge from one of E+Co's most prominent private investors. This was a philanthropist named Alan Parker, who had spun a small fortune in duty-free shops into a pretty damn vast one in global finance by handing it to George Soros to invest at just the right time. In LaRocco's recollection, here's how the query was phrased: "Okay, I love the work you're doing. But please stop telling me about it. Tell me how you're going to get it to scale." It surely appealed to all that was pure Brooklynese in LaRocco, all that *yuh-think* bluster. It said: *All right, bub, if you're so goddamn clever, if you've fig-ured out why the UN and USAID and that righteous dude from U2 in the bug-eyed shades are ass-backwards about how best to spend our chari-table millions and spread our best intentions—well, then, how are you gonna take your scheme to the next level? Whaddaya need to get beyond a vegetable-stew factory in Thailand and a few mud huts in Hindustan? Whaddaya need for a worldwide launch of NGO 2.0?* LaRocco: "From a person like him, that's not the kind of question you glibly just answer. You go away and you think about it."

So he did, and so did the rest of his organization. They chewed on it for about six months, and they decided a few things. One was that E+Co, as currently conceived, ought to mostly stick to its strengths. Contrary to the conventional wisdom that any successful enterprise should grow to unsustainable girth, E+Co chose to remain at the scale where it could continue to do its best work. It was skilled and knowledgeable in the development of small renewable-energy enterprises, so it would just keep on keepin' on. The second conclusion, though, was the one that gave rise to E+Co Capital. It involved identifying regions and industries where the potential for growth was beyond the scope of even a tireless champion of Harish Hande's calibre. Central America—the first case in point—was laced with rushing rivers, and several of the region's governments were uniquely keen on small-scale renewables of all stripes, so why not become its first serious venture capital firm for mezzo-financed green energy? "That," LaRocco told me, "was our first answer to Alan Parker's question about how you get to scale, because that can actually double our impact by only adding about 5 percent to our infrastructure."

There remained a final tactic, the hardest one with the highest stakes, the one about how to take over the (developing) world. How to create two, three, many E+Cos? It was a tricky question, which LaRocco breached with uncharacteristic ambiguity. "Now, we dabbled with partnerships," was how he put it, "and we've learned a lot." These were hard lessons, though it was Alvarado who told me that part of it.

A couple of years back, Alvarado explained, E+Co had partnered with the UN on a big multinational initiative called REED (Rural Energy Enterprise Development). The idea was to go off on a world tour—to Africa and Brazil and China—and train local entrepreneurs and NGOs in the construction of sustainable renewable-energy businesses. Who knows how the UN conceived of the thing, but from E+Co's point of view it looked like a golden opportunity to evangelize. Alvarado: "We wanted to sort of clone the E+Co model to certain local NGOs, so that they would continue working in a similar way to ours, and then we wouldn't be needed anymore in those countries."

So how did that go? Two, three, many E+Cos?

"I would say that in general the experience was very, very bad," Alvarado said. And then he did something entirely at odds with his polished boardroom style: he sighed. Everywhere they went, he explained, they ran into NGOs fiercely resistant to their ideas. They didn't like how E+Co complicated things for the recipients of their aid. They didn't see the point of due-diligence checks and formal signed agreements. They saw no compelling reason to seriously reform the top-down, project-oriented development model, let alone abolish it. A couple of NGOs out of the dozens they worked with seemed ready to try a trick or two from E+Co's public/private hybrid approach, but those were notable exceptions. "The conclusion," Alvarado said, "was that maybe our model is so particular that, number one, it is not necessarily so easy to understand, and, number two, that often we are maybe a little bit naive to think that NGOs, who have specialized, always, on a certain type of model, would easily evolve or embrace new models that maybe meant much more work than what they had been used to."

So much for converting NGOs to the E+Co way. Back to LaRocco in New Jersey, a good while after the hard lesson was learned for the organization's next gambit: "Now we're serious about partnerships. We're looking to work with powerful entities in markets where we're not represented." After the REED mess, E+Co switched its focus to lending bodies like Grameen Bank that were more readily adaptable to its model. That collaboration led to a bit of friendly intellectual piracy—a new way of conceiving of E+Co's larger purpose—because in working with Grameen, LaRocco learned that the total number of transactions conducted by microfinance institutions was by even the most liberal estimates somewhere around 100 million. "We originally thought you had to get to 800 million people served in order to really effect a change. We changed our minds. I believe, based on what we've learned from microfinance, that if we can get our model to 100 million people by the year 2020 we'll have changed business-as-usual permanently. And the importance of that shift was, that places more emphasis on our being self-reliant as an organization. We could never have reached 800 million. But you know, we're just weird enough to think that we could get to 100 million."

It is, to be sure, a big number, and E+Co does not take its numbers lightly. It is keeping a careful count: as of January 2006, it stood at 2,836,588. Just under three million people with access to green electricity because of E+Co's work. That represented 567,071 households around the world getting their power from 120 clean-energy businesses. Direct investment of $16,707,243, paired with third-party investments of $111,304,741. One model, and who knew how many would-be champions out there in the wide world ready to give it a try.

A hundred million served: that's some kind of ambitious. Crazily idealistic for a bunch of business-minded folks who work at village scale. It seems almost like a utopian fantasy. Unless you'd spent any time around *actual* utopians lately. Their fantasies are generally not that practical. Which isn't to say they haven't got a disruptive technique or two of their own to share.

TEN

THE DALAI LAMA & THE DUDE

[sustainable community]

PRAYER FLAGS & USEFUL MYTHS

Contrary to its eventual lexical legacy, Sir Thomas More's *Utopia* was not a book about a perfect society. The name itself is cunningly, punningly ambiguous: it translates literally from the Greek as "no place," but it plays on a homonym meaning "good place." Published at the dawn of the English Renaissance in 1516, *Utopia* appeared to be a subtle provocation to the European intelligentsia of its day, a playful portrait of an idealized land across the sea held up as a mirror to some of the more extreme rhetoric then in fashion on the Continent. There was a satirical bent to the book, an overstatement of the benefits *and* the drawbacks of a society built on humanistic reason alone. It was to some degree an allegorical attempt to demonstrate the *folly* of attempting to create perfection with nothing but eternally fallible human hands. A warning, in a sense, not to dismiss long-standing traditions and deeply held faiths completely.

Utopia was one of the Renaissance's first great secular parables, a useful myth about the limitless potential for progress and renewal just across the sea. It was also a sort of prophecy, foretelling the unprecedented flowering of utopian community-building soon to emerge in the New World. In America—named for Utopia's first

European visitor, Amerigo Vespucci—the myth found its first, best home in a place that would before long declare itself to be humanity's last, best hope.

There was utopian talk among America's Puritan founders even before they left England for the New World in 1629. As they awaited departure aboard the *Arbella* at Southampton, the fiery preacher John Cotton addressed them as agents of God's "special appointment" on a mission of enormous responsibility and global import. The society they were leaving was fallen, beyond salvation, and it was only by God's grace that they were to be conducted across the ocean to begin anew the project of redemption. They landed in Massachusetts firm in the conviction (at least as far as their preachers were concerned) that they had arrived in New Canaan, the Promised Land, the sacred ground to be prepared for Christ's return. And even when the Second Coming proved less forthcoming than they'd hoped, the tone of their rhetoric rarely faltered, and it set the stage for a young America teeming with utopian experiments.

As the historian Sacvan Bercovitch explains in *The American Jeremiad,* the lofty sermons about New England's divine mission intoned by those first Puritan preachers soon spread far beyond the Massachusetts Bay colony's backwoods religious communities. The Puritan jeremiad—that call to Christian duty for a task of apocalyptic scale—became the rhetorical core of mainstream American political life and the ideological engine for the most elaborate nation-building project in modern history. Transferred from the religious realm to secular public discourse, Bercovitch writes, the jeremiad created "a country that, despite its arbitrary territorial limits, could read its destiny in its landscape, and a population that, despite its bewildering mixture of race and creed, could believe in something called an American mission, and could invest that patent fiction with all the emotional, spiritual, and intellectual appeal of a religious quest."

Bercovitch traces the jeremiad's fingerprints from the deck of the *Arbella* through Henry David Thoreau's call for a revival of the American pioneer spirit to Martin Luther King's insistence that the American Dream could be redeemed by the addition of black faces to its epic mythological landscape. "Where much is given . . . much is demanded" was Bercovitch's shorthand version of John Cotton's message to the Puritan founders as they prepared to depart for the

New World, and do note how closely this matches with Spider-Man's present-day pop creed: "With great power comes great responsibility." Over the intervening centuries of tumult and transformation, during which Bible-thumping sermon slowly morphed into comic-book slogan, puritanical America became a freewheeling model for the whole world, the energetic and prosperous embodiment of that greatest of Enlightenment ideals: democracy. Wherever were found "huddled masses yearning to breathe free"—so declares the inscription at the base of the statue erected at the entrance to this Promised Land—they could look West to see a bustlingly animated diorama of Thomas More's long-ago prophecy, and they would know which direction to head in search of a better future.

It's worth noting, as well, that the twentieth century's greatest wave of utopian experimentation coincided with the unravelling of America's useful myth, amid the disillusioning chaos of the Vietnam War. Within America and without, the young and progressively minded turned away from the established order, rejected (at least rhetorically) the increasingly dubious benefits of modernity, decamped (often rashly) for a thousand new utopian islands. In downtown flophouses and rural idylls alike, the West's privileged youth established communes and back-to-the-land agrarian ventures, set up model farms and free schools, distributed cheap drugs and esoteric philosophy and free love. A great many of the key features of the nascent Sustainable Age whose contours I've charted—renewable energy and organic agriculture, the revitalization of derelict cities and the decentralization of social control—trace their origins at least in part to the haphazard utopian projects of the 1960s. In a sense, the social experiments of that era served as a sort of R&D lab for today's broader sustainability movement.

Utopia has become an imperative. I uncovered this phrase in the library of one of those 1960s-era communities, and it speaks to the urgent necessity of the sustainability project in the Anthropocene Era. Sustainability must replace democracy as the beacon held aloft to the fragile planet's huddled masses, and to do so will require more than energy technologies and policy tools. Sustainability needs to become a unifying story of hope, a useful myth foretelling the arrival of a new kind of human community. After all, the high-minded talk of Europe's Renaissance philosophers, the breakthroughs in shipbuilding and navigation—this kind of stuff *enabled* the discovery of the New World and the birth of the modern age, but it didn't supply anywhere near all the energy for that extraordinary social upheaval. The formidable motive power of hope—embedded in useful myths of Utopia and New Canaan and America, of a new kind of *community*—provided perhaps the most essential fuel.

> Causes and effects assume history marches forward, but history is not an army. It is a crab scuttling sideways, a drip of soft water wearing away stone, an earthquake breaking centuries of tension. Sometimes one person inspires a movement, or her words do decades later; sometimes a few passionate people change the world; sometimes they start a mass movement and millions do; sometimes those millions are stirred by the same outrage or the same ideal and change comes upon us like a change of weather. All that these transformations have in common is that they begin in the imagination, in hope.

This is from Rebecca Solnit's *Hope in the Dark*. The book is ostensibly a long-time political activist's memoir, but Solnit's subject is universal, because hope is the infinitely renewable fuel of all great and lasting social change. "To hope is to give yourself to the future," she writes, "and that commitment to the future makes the present inhabitable. Anything could happen, and whether we act or not has everything to do with it."

Out of action are movements born—also communities and even nations. The United States was, at its best, a collection of activist movements—of minds set afire by the dreams of liberty and salvation contained both in Gutenberg's mass-produced Bibles and in the writings of the Enlightenment's secular visionaries—and, for a long time after its birth in revolution, America remained a diverse and impossibly grand utopian community. Now sustainability's moment has come, and thankfully it is predisposed to the idea of community. The two concepts are indeed practically inseparable, because the very idea of "a lifestyle designed for permanence" (to reiterate E.F. Schumacher's precise phrasing) implies the existence of a sustainable community in which it can function. In the places where I found the most fully formed examples of sustainable society, I invariably discovered vibrant communities that predated the wind turbines and solar panels (sometimes by many centuries).

Nearly as often, I found symbolic evidence of a single, unifying myth: a tale told in the semaphore of prayer flags. Long strings of little handkerchief banners in red, gold and blue, inscribed with Buddhist prayers in intricate black Tibetan script, the wind flapping them skyward for the karmic benefit of whoever had hung them and anyone who gazed upon them. They were like hope's national flag, the optimistic primary-coloured banner under which it marched. I saw Tibetan prayer flags on the mesa outside Taos and in the cobblestone lanes of Danish cities. They waved in breezes from northern Scotland to southern Germany. And in due course I went to a Tibetan village and got some of my own, and they blow in the steady wind of a prairie spring as I write.

It seemed inevitable somehow: this geography of hope would have been incomplete without a Tibetan place name.

UTOPIA IN EXILE

On March 10, 1959, after nine years of tense coexistence following the incursion of the Chinese military, the Tibetan people took to the streets in the capital city of Lhasa to oppose the occupation. The insurrection was easily crushed, and a week later the fourteenth Dalai Lama—the country's secular leader and spiritual figurehead—fled to India, arriving in the old British hill station of Dharamsala by the end of March. In time, a refugee population numbering more than 100,000 would pour over the mountains into India and Nepal. Although much of Tibet's body, still six million strong, remains in its ancestral lands, its head and heart now reside in a patchwork exile nation of refugee settlements scattered across the Indian subcontinent. For the exiles, the physical land of Tibet has become little more than a vision on the distant horizon, a memory, a dream pursued with desperate resolve.

This is how it looked, for example, in a series of paintings my host showed me when I visited the Bylakuppe Tibetan settlement in the Coorg Hills of Karnataka. He was an affable, generous young man named Dorjee Tsering, and he lived with his extended family in a complex of interconnected courtyards and bungalows in the countryside, where he helped manage the family farm and dreamed of bringing modern aesthetic techniques to traditional Tibetan art. His paintings were stacked against the wall of his living quarters and makeshift studio, a small space the size of a motel room, and he rifled through them with the naked frankness I've often encountered in Tibetans. He had painted portraits of Gandhi and famous Tibetan lamas, the Potala Palace in Lhasa, the emaciated Buddha (this from the period of the Buddha's life in which he lived in extreme asceticism in pursuit of enlightenment). He'd also done a number of Tibetan landscapes in an almost photorealist style—these, like the Potala, he'd copied out of magazines. Dorjee sometimes painted under the pseudonym "Chidor K."—almost like something out of Kafka—and it struck me that there was an accidentally postmodern character to his work, in that his paintings were of places he was from but had never been, copied from photos of the home he'd never lived in. Because of this, they were also ineffably sad.

I'd come to Bylakuppe, a rural township of rolling hills and farmland about 100 kilometres west of Mysore, ostensibly to survey the progress of the Tibetan community's organic farming movement. I gathered it had been gaining momentum since the new Kashag, the exile government's cabinet, introduced organic agriculture as a strategic goal back in 2001, and it struck me as a particularly hopeful story: state-of-the-art sustainable farming by indefatigable refugees. Really, though, I'd come to see the homeland of hope's common flag, to see why sustainability's front ranks, dedicated as they were to lifestyles built for permanence, had united under a banner representing such a seemingly perilous existence.

It is ultimately the Tibetan nation-in-exile being honoured by the prayer flags: its durability, its resourcefulness, its tireless spirit. This is not just because the "Free Tibet" movement exists almost exclusively in the Tibetan diaspora, but also because it has given rise, ironically, to communities by all reports healthier, more vibrant and infinitely more sustainable than the ones being ground down under the Chinese. Beyond the organic agriculture, *this* was why I'd felt compelled to come to the byways of exiled Tibet: because underneath the inescapable tragedy that had made these communities necessary, the so-called refugee camps of Tibetan India were simply overwhelming in their hopeful energy and enduring strength. I hope it doesn't diminish their loss—nor discount the palpable rage, particularly among younger Tibetans, at the injustice visited daily upon their homeland—to note that they've built exile communities that are much closer to sustainability than most of the untrammelled communities we inhabit in the free and wealthy West.

Although the home of the Dalai Lama and the Tibetan government-in-exile in Dharamsala is the most famous of the Tibetan settlements, several of the largest are actually in India's far south. About fifty thousand Tibetans—half the exile population—live in a handful of sprawling farming communities scattered around rural Karnataka, and it's here that you'll find several of the most significant monasteries and colleges. The settlements date to the mid-1960s, when the Indian government, faced with the problem of a village atop a Himalayan ridge filled to capacity with refugees, bequeathed to the Tibetans several swaths of marginal land to settle the overflow. The land grant comprised extensive tracts of dense jungle and scrub wilderness, some of it populated by wild elephants, tigers and poisonous snakes. The Tibetan refugees, battling tuberculosis and typhoid as well as fierce, unfamiliar fauna, set about the arduous work of clearing the land, thus to take up the equally exotic practice of monoculture farming. Some of them had been nomadic herders or subsistence farmers before they'd fled their homes, but the Indian countryside was being turned upside down just then by the Green Revolution, and the Tibetans soon joined its ranks.

Although the Green Revolution sounds like an offshoot of the environmental movement, it was actually a top-down global transformation from subsistence to industrial farming. It began with Mexican wheat production in the 1940s and, through the co-operation of several large-scale philanthropic organizations (especially the Rockefeller and Ford foundations) and a rotating cast of national governments, it spread throughout the developing world. By switching from preindustrial agricultural techniques to petrochemical fertilizers and pesticides, high-yield hybrid seeds and industrial irrigation, farmers around the world saw exponential growth in their yields in the revolution's first wave, which enabled great chunks of the developing world to produce enough food to feed themselves for the first time in generations. The Green Revolution was predicated, however, on intensive monocropping, which in the long term exhausts the nutrients in the soil, demanding more and more "external inputs" of artificial fertilizers and pesticides to keep the land producing at profitable rates.

The Tibetan farms in India, which had been established on poor soil to begin with, were in a sense the bellwether of the revolution's approaching crisis on the subcontinent: farmers in the Tibetan settlements began to report dramatically declining yields by the late 1990s. Building on a directive from the Dalai Lama that called for the development of the infrastructure of a future Tibet guided by the core Buddhist principle of non-violence, the newly elected cabinet of the Central Tibetan Administration (or CTA, the government-in-exile) decided in 2001 to begin actively encouraging a move to organic agriculture in all the settlements. Studies commissioned by the CTA shortly thereafter found "no vestige of micro-organism left" in the soil being farmed by most Tibetans; the soil, in other words, was essentially dead, surviving only on petrochemical life support. In the fall of 2002 and into 2003, the CTA launched an organic-agriculture training program to create "agricultural extension officers" for each settlement and to launch test farms. The newly deputized officers trained under Vandana Shiva and her Navdanya organization, on the organic farms in the New Age settlement of Auroville, and with Masanobu Fukuoka, a Japanese "natural farming" guru who has developed a beyond-organic agricultural technique that requires no tilling, no plowing, no weeding and not even *organic* pesticides. Using CTA money and provisions, a 100-acre demonstration farm was set up at Kollegal, a Tibetan settlement south of Mysore. It reported a 35 percent increase in yield in 2004, and more farms have joined the organic movement with each new planting season since. A second test farm was established at Bylakuppe, and it was this new institution I'd come to the Coorg Hills to see.

Dorjee Tsering drove me to the test farm on his motorbike, roaring down country roads that curved and dove through rolling pasture dotted with coconut palms. Eagles circled low over vast golden fields of Green Revolution corn as we motored through. We came upon a handful of young monks in burgundy robes lazing on a bridge over an irrigation canal like Mark Twain characters. They waved and smiled as we passed. At the crest of the next hill, we arrived at a sandy driveway marked by a handpainted sign reading TIBETAN FARM PROJECT/TIBETAN CENTER FOR ORGANIC AND NATURAL FARMING.

The project complex was a handful of low bungalows arranged around a shaded courtyard that backed on 86 acres of experimental fields planted with millet, sorghum and sunflowers. We were greeted by a stout man with a wide, deeply lined face and greying scruff, who introduced himself as Dorjee, the project director. He led me to a small table in the shade while Dorjee the painter jogged off behind one of the nearby buildings, returning a moment later with three young coconuts. He hacked their tops off with a machete and we sat together and slurped back the sweetest coconut juice I've ever tasted as Dorjee the farmer explained what organic agriculture meant to exiled Tibet.

"We came to India to preserve our culture, identity, all these things," he told me. The key to reaching those goals, he said, was to build cohesive communities. They had to be more than temporary camps—they had to embody the future Tibet to which their inhabitants hoped to one day return. The Dalai Lama envisioned free Tibet as a "peace zone," a model for the world, and that had to be built on a foundation of food production that did no harm to the earth. The farmers were naturally skeptical of such big and sudden changes, and it was more expensive in the short term to fertilize fields with cow manure, but Dorjee was convinced they would eventually come to see the wisdom of a more self-sufficient existence, something closer to the lightfooted pastoral tradition that had been taken from them by the Chinese invasion. "This is our culture," he said. "We need to live according to our culture."

When we were finished our chat, Dorjee the painter took me farther up the road and then down into a wide valley, where the Bylakuppe settlement's main monastery was located. The campus was dominated by a towering new temple—barely a year old as of my visit—whose swooping, multitiered pagoda roof gleamed brilliant gold in the afternoon sun. It didn't look in any way temporary—not like the makeshift prayer hall of an exiled people but like the proud new cathedral of successful immigrant settlers. The main meditation chamber was an airy auditorium with three-storey vaulted ceilings and a polished wood floor. A trio of immense golden Buddhas kept stoic watch from the rear of the chamber, and the walls were covered in riotous, intricately detailed murals depicting the vast pantheon of Tibetan demigods and demons, dancing skeletons and multi-armed monsters, delicate lotus blossoms and skulls with eyes that protruded on stalks. It was the same stuff seen on display in Tibetan monasteries everywhere, fascinating but formal, and I thought then of how Dorjee talked about making Tibetan art that was more reflective of his time and place. He didn't want his culture to be strictly a museum housing old ways or a shrine to a happier past; he wanted it to be a living, evolving, dynamic force, the beacon of a brighter future.

It struck me that it was already a sort of beacon. That was why I saw prayer flags in so many of the other places I'd been. There was something in the Tibetan people's steadfast resolve to remain true to their principles and maintain their dignity even amid the hardship of half a century of exile that spoke to the better part of the human spirit in a way few other things could. If a refugee camp could strive to become a sustainable community—could begin to achieve it, could inspire like-minded souls around the world to do the same—well, then, couldn't *any* place?

I haven't yet mentioned how I met Dorjee Tsering. I'd arrived in the late morning on a bus from Mysore, deposited at the roadside in the old Karnatakan village of Bylakuppe. I'd walked along the roadside strip of concrete bungalows and market stalls, asking for directions, eventually making my way to an intersection half a kilometre up the highway. A couple hundred metres down a side road, a broad arch welcomed visitors to the Tibetan settlement. I was just coming up to the arch when I heard a voice call out to me from a chai stall at the roadside. It was Dorjee, sitting over a plate of idlis, his goateed face and smiling eyes half-hidden beneath a Boston Red Sox baseball cap. He waved me over and I took a seat next to him at the stall's only table and explained why I was there. He immediately announced that he would take me wherever I needed to go. First, though, why not have a cup of tea, a bite to eat? When we were finished—he insisted on paying—I told him he could just take me as far as the settlement office if he wanted, but he waved it off. "If someone comes and they don't know how to find what they need," he said, "I have a responsibility to assist." He said it just like that, in the same matter-of-fact way that he later told me about his paintings, about the monastery, about his cousin away at school up north. And the thing was, I had *known* something like this would happen. I'd come, after all, without permits or even a contact name, because it was safe to assume, at a Tibetan settlement, that *someone* would help you out. It was just one of those things people did when they lived in a real community.

On our way back to the main road, I asked Dorjee to stop at a small bazaar just before the settlement gate so I could buy some prayer flags. He agreed, but only on the condition that I wait to hang them until he found out what the most auspicious days were. He worried for my karmic health—he was more anxious about this, actually, than about anything else we'd discussed all day. Amid talk of the distant hopes for Tibetan freedom and the collapse of the Green Revolution and the problems his family was having remitting money to his cousin, it was the *only* thing he fretted over.

I like to think Dorjee's concern was in some small way a manifestation of the structural strength of the community I'd just seen. There may have been deep loss in the subtext of his paintings—in their subject matter—but there was headstrong optimism in his *painting.* Dorjee did his Buddhist best to live in the here and now, to make the most of Bylakuppe—to make it an *enviable* place to live. Think of the kind of dedication that takes—amid a stateless existence, amid systemic poverty and abiding grief—and the kind of cohesion it creates. As a free and living and distinct culture, Tibet is only as strong as these hardscrabble refugee communities. That might be the bedrock of sustainable community right there: the recognition that any society's elements—its energy regimes or planning schemes, its green businesses or climate change policies—are only as enduring as the community in which they operate. Fly a line of prayer flags, then, in recognition of exiled Tibet's courage in the face of tragedy, but also—*especially*—in thanks for its extraordinary example, and for its indomitable will to create a durable way of life. To teach us all how to rebuild it anew.

THE SUSTAINABILITY LABORATORY

I arrived at the Findhorn Foundation in northeastern Scotland the week after it had been chosen as a training centre by the United Nations. It was soon to become a place the UN sent people to learn to build the kinds of communities that the Tibetans had constructed from scrap materials in exile. In the alphabet soup of UN bureaucratic jargon, Findhorn had been named a CIFAL centre for UNITAR's Decentralized Cooperation Programme; decoded, this meant it was now the primary sustainability school for students at the UN's autonomous in-house training and research institute (UNITAR, that is). Further decoded, the UN designation was pretty much the highest-profile recognition yet of Findhorn's native gifts for cultivating and imparting wisdom, particularly on the subject of building sustainable communities.

I spent a good deal of time on my travels immersed in utopian experiments. I visited an American shopping mall reconfigured as an old-school downtown, a German film studio reborn as a community centre and a Danish naval installation turned into a full-blown commune. I spent a week in Auroville, in southern India, where the devotees of the yogic philosophy of a long-deceased guru have built a self-proclaimed "City of Dawn." But nowhere else did I find a sustainable community as carefully constructed as Findhorn.

The UN's recognition, then, was in many respects perfectly understandable. Findhorn—a cozy New Age enclave of about four hundred on the shores of Moray Firth, near Inverness, officially dubbed "the Findhorn Foundation" to distinguish it from the old village of Findhorn a couple of miles up the road—was a shining example of sustainable living on a number of fronts. It had been an agricultural pioneer since its founding in the early 1960s and a trailblazing research and training institute in such fields as community building and conflict resolution for nearly as long. It was home to dwellings with grass-carpeted roofs and others made from straw bales or recycled whiskey barrels. The entire community's waste was treated at one of the world's largest Living Machines (an innovative organic waste-treatment system). And it was the site of a full-blown "ecovillage" of wind-powered, hyper-efficient green homes, which was just the most obvious reason why it had served as the birthplace of the Global Ecovillage Network (GEN), a constantly expanding virtual community of sustainable-living experiments the world over. Auroville was a member of GEN, and so were hundreds of other "intentional communities," from Ecovilla Navarro in Buenos Aires to Kibbutz Lotan in Israel to Crystal Waters in northeastern Australia. And their hub—the aggregator of their best practices and an elite laboratory in the concoction of new ones—was Findhorn.

There were other reasons, however, why the addition of Findhorn to UNITAR's training-centre ranks was a bit unusual. It was the only UNITAR centre in northern Europe, for example, and the only rural one—there were now twelve in all, and the rest were in big cities like Shanghai and Atlanta and Curitiba, Brazil. More than that, though, Findhorn was the only one that had begun its life as a trailer park on a decommissioned Royal Air Force runway, not to mention the only one whose sandy soil had been coaxed to yield 40-pound cabbages by a founding trio whose horticultural strategy was drawn from direct conversation with God and an angelic choir of sprites, elves and plant *devas.*

The day after I arrived, I went to see Mari Hollander, the current co-chair of the Findhorn Foundation, to learn a bit more about the journey from talking to God in plain English to teaching policy implementation skills to UN contractors. I was a little wary, as I'd heard more about the mystic side than the workshopping. But Hollander—like almost anyone you might meet at Findhorn, from the English psychologists there for a weekend seminar to the friendly old Scottish caretaker planting seedlings up on the ridge above the village—was no less down-to-earth than any randomly selected committee co-chair. (I suppose it *does* warrant mention that she was unfailingly gregarious and open in her demeanour, which qualified, in my experience with civic officials, as a marked eccentricity.) Here's Hollander, at any rate, cutting down-to-earthily to the chase on the subject of what Findhorn was all about: "If we were to offer anything to people as they pass through or hear about us, we would say, you know, whether you come here or not: Pause where you are, reflect on what you've got, be grateful for what you have, tune into what you need to do next, build support around yourself to enable you to do that. This will make your life a happier life and probably the world a better place. That's really the core message."

That message isn't far from the revelation that started it all: *Be still and know that I am God.* This was what a voice told a studious woman named Eileen Caddy as she sat meditating in a small sanctuary in Glastonbury, England. It was 1953, and she was recently separated from her first husband and visiting Glastonbury with her soon-to-be-second one, Peter. Though they had both been pursuing various courses of spiritual training, nothing to that point in her life had prepared Eileen for the voice of God Himself. "Following the experience," she later wrote, "I went through a painful period of conflict and tension when I kept hearing many different voices battling to be the first. I just kept listening and listening until I heard one clear voice again, and then all the others disappeared." From then on, this was the voice that guided the Caddys, first to a hotel in Forres, Scotland, which they managed with their like-minded Canadian friend Dorothy Maclean, and then to the Findhorn Bay Caravan Park up the road from Forres, where in 1962 the Caddys, their three school-age sons and their constant companion, Dorothy, set up house in a tiny English caravan and waited for the next set of divine instructions.

Peter, a former RAF officer and a practical man in many respects, spent that first winter in the windswept caravan park studying gardening books, and come spring he started to plant a few humble crops in the gravel next to the caravan. And then the necessary tools started simply to show up, as they always had for the Caddys since they began listening to the voice that spoke to Eileen. A straw bale fell off a truck, a young fellow up the road had some spare horse manure, and Dorothy discovered, to her surprise and delight, that with a little concentration she could converse directly with the *devas* that inhabited the plants. (*Deva* is a Sanskrit word meaning "shining one," and in Hindu theology it is used to describe any being possessing divine grace; *angel* is its closest Christian analogue.) Following Dorothy's instructions, Peter figured out how to stop his bean plants from flopping over and his cabbage leaves from wilting. Later that summer, he paid a visit to nearby Cawdor Castle, and he couldn't help but notice that his crops were far more robust than the ones in its garden, which had been cultivated for hundreds of years. The following year, Peter planted by his own count more than a hundred varieties of vegetables, fruits and herbs, and pretty much all of them thrived in the caravan park's denuded soil. The cabbages, in particular, grew to miraculously huge proportions—Peter weighed one at 42 pounds. Word soon spread of the Findhorn garden and its helpful *devas,* and its notoriety exploded when the Caddys and their horticultural exploits were featured on a BBC TV show in 1969.

"There is an intelligence in nature that can be contacted, and that really likes to be included." This was Mari Hollander's take on the *deva* concept as she talked me through a slide show of the amazing growth of the community at Findhorn. I watched as its eventful forty-odd years of history unfolded in snapshots. Here was a close-up photo of a giant cabbage, and then a long shot from above of the Caddys and Dorothy seated primly on a park bench in the small side-yard of their caravan, looking like a retired couple and their niece taking a rest on a visit to Kew Gardens or something. Their plants towered higher than the caravan's roof in the background. In the far distance were brown and grey wastes.

A couple of slides later, many more caravans appeared in a crowded shot: in 1970, an American New Age guru named David Spangler came to see the Caddys, and that, along with the BBC publicity, swelled Findhorn's population from a dozen or so to 150 over the next eighteen months. Other slides followed: landscaped lanes leading to smart trailer homes (these in the more semi-permanent North American style), a great industrial loom turning out rainbow-coloured cloth, a bearded gent in a busy pottery gallery, a postcard snapshot of the fortress-like Cluny Hill Hotel up in Forres (which the Findhorn Foundation, incorporated in 1972, bought and turned into a college in 1975). A slide a little later read ARIEL VIEW MID 1970's above a photo of at least a hundred white trailers in tidy rows along the old airplane runway, which now functioned as a busy pedestrian thoroughfare. Next there was a whiskey-barrel house in mid-construction, a wind turbine being erected, a signboard announcing the ecovillage project. Then the interior of the Living Machine: two tidy rows of industrial-sized plastic barrels filled with bacteria-rich water and overgrown with plants. Finally, bins of luscious produce from a bustling CSA operation (the first of its kind in Scotland, which Findhorn has been partnered in for a while now) and the crowded aisles of the well-stocked village general store.

A community: vibrant, welcoming and functional, though not like any other, because few modern communities are as deeply cherished or as carefully nurtured, and almost none are as close to truly sustainable. (A recent assessment sized Findhorn's ecological footprint at half the national average for the United Kingdom, translating to the smallest per capita environmental impact ever recorded for any community in the industrialized world.)

When the slide show was finished, I stood up to leave, and Hollander rose to give me a hug. "As we do," she said as we embraced—not embarrassed for herself but simply inviting me not to be, either. I stepped outside into a grey mist and went for a hike. I started along the paved runway spur that ran along the edge of the ecovillage—the most recent of three distinctive neighbourhoods in Findhorn (not counting a patch of the original caravan park site, which still hosts trailers and tents). There were solar water heaters on the roof and a surfeit of skylights, but in most respects it looked like any other new housing development. I continued past a row of low, tidy cottages being used as art studios and through the more whimsically designed Pineridge neighbourhood (here were the handful of converted whiskey barrels, among other dwellings), coming finally to a dirt walking path that led farther up the peninsula. There was shadowed forest to my left, a wide empty field to my right, the low utilitarian structures of the RAF Kinloss air base beyond that, and a cluster of four towering wind turbines up ahead.

It occurred to me to listen for the welcoming voices of forest *devas*, but the most distinctive sound was the occasional distant rumble of a reconnaissance jet taking off or landing at Kinloss. I'd spent the majority of my childhood living on air bases, so it was a familiar sound, even soothing, reminiscent of home. It was one of those funny things about community: you assumed that whatever kind you knew best, however strange, was the only suitable kind there was, at least for yourself, unless you somehow stumbled upon something entirely different. It struck me as well that I was less than 100 miles from the highland pasture my ancestors had been cleared off before their emigration to Canada in the late 1700s. I was, in a sense, as close to home as I'd ever been, and I was communing with the engine roar of military aircraft.

This was how I spent much of my time at Findhorn: on long walks, wondering what made a community and whether I'd ever really known one. I was there only a few days, but they were eventful ones, and there's a lot I could tell you about them. I could provide all the details of the Living Machine, a big greenhouse-like shed that smelled exactly like the marshes alongside the golf course in northern Alberta where I learned to play the Scottish national game. It was surely the only sewage treatment plant in the free world that could possibly be described as bucolic. (There's a resident carp in the pond just before the facility's outflow pipe, and there were Findhorn visitors literally camped in the building's shadow.) I could mention the speed-limit signs along the ecovillage's main drag that said GIVE WAY TO PEOPLE, PRAMS & PUSHCHAIRS, or the popular local bumper sticker that read DON'T DRIVE FASTER THAN YOUR ANGELS CAN FLY. I could tell you about a guy named Alex I shared a pint or two with one night down the pub, a quiet lapsed Quaker coming up on middle age who talked in his gentle Yorkshire lilt about the orientation weekend he'd just come through, like someone who had just emerged from a utopian dream, fully awake to the world for the first time in his life.

More than any of this, though, it was my meal at the Findhorn Community Centre that nailed the unique Findhorn vibe and brought the potential embedded in the idea of an ecovillage to electric life. I was having lunch with May East, a compact, animated Brazilian woman who described herself as a career "social change activist" and who had been instrumental in setting up the Global Ecovillage Network and the UN training program. She told me what Findhorn was for—beyond living in—in her estimation: "I think what we need today most of all is to have places where we can learn to do the transition. Because sustainability is such an important concept for our generation, as it was democracy for the generation that was creating revolution. But it can be a grail—like whenever you think you reach it, we don't know what it is. And it's like what we need is places where—without knowing where is it, how to define it—we have places where you can see that, you know, you have still rotten caravans and you have all the stages, how you can really do the transfiguration, the transformation, the transition. So living in a place like that—this is a laboratory. In a laboratory, you're not forming anything, you're really doing experiments all the time. And some things do work, some of them don't work. What does work, you then replicate for the world."

A great many Findhorn residents take their meals communally in the community centre cafeteria, and I had to strain to hear her over the buzz of conversation in the crowded room. East pointed to a nearby table and told me that was the "working group" overseeing the construction of Findhorn's new wind farm. Then she pointed to another table and another, her dark hair swaying and her turquoise jewellery clinking as she swivelled. Almost every one, she said, was hosting a lively meeting among a handful of Foundation members busy figuring out something or other about how to further Findhorn's progress. I was duly awed—the place positively *thrummed* with life. It was what every community centre in the world pretended to be: the pounding heart of the neighbourhood. Whatever was going on in Findhorn, whatever worked or didn't, nearly everyone was deeply engaged in the process.

Some months after I left Findhorn, I spoke by phone with Jonathan Dawson, the executive secretary of GEN Europe, who teaches sustainability techniques alongside May East at Findhorn. I still couldn't shake the electric charge I'd drawn from the simple act of eating lunch in the cafeteria, and Dawson told me something that seemed to explain it. One of Findhorn's core lessons, he said, was one we'd all known instinctively for the overwhelming majority of human history, which was that we thrived as people when we lived together in small, closely knit communities where we felt like we belonged, that our contribution mattered in ways we could touch. Dawson: "The ecovillage story is, we can have an ecological footprint half the national average, and come to the community—you will not see people suffering and sacrificing. Quite the opposite." There was a powerful, intangible added value to living in a sustainable community, a compound interest accrued by weaving together so many different accounts so tightly. "It not only saves resources to grow food, cook food, eat food together, but it actually makes you happier. Yeah." There was a long pause on the line.

"Maybe it's just that simple," I said.

"Maybe it *is* just that simple," he agreed.

LIVING DELIBERATELY

In the years since the Global Ecovillage Network first formed at a conference in Findhorn in 1995, there had been, in Jonathan Dawson's estimation, one big surprise: that the ecovillage concept hadn't proliferated all that quickly. Rather than spawning a thousand progeny each, the ecovillages in the network tended to become free-standing immersive learning centres, places to visit for a short time to experience the totality of sustainable life before returning to a less idealistic community with a few new tools to share. Dawson saw this partially as a function of three trends external to the ecovillages: the skyrocketing cost of land worldwide, increasingly restrictive land-use policies nearly as widespread, and a growing emphasis on individualism. Beyond this, there was at least one internal factor. "I notice," Dawson told me, "that ecovillages tend to be created by profoundly unreasonable, difficult people." He meant it as a compliment, even as he acknowledged that it pretty much guaranteed that his social movement would always be a minority one. There just weren't that many people in the world with the arrogance to decide that their whole society as currently configured was a write-off and the tenacity to go through with the mind-melting labour of building a new one from scratch. "I think that almost all ecovillages demand an investment in social process that most people don't want," he conceded. He remained enthusiastic, however, about at least one less arduous approach, an off-the-shelf model that met many of the criteria of an ecovillage. "I'm very impressed by New Urbanism and other schools of architecture that are seeking to encourage deeper community, simply through the architectural design. I think that there's much benefit to be had from doing that."

My own experience at Seaside on the Gulf Coast of Florida was mostly consistent with Dawson's optimistic assessment. There was much on Seaside's surface to invite scorn—much indeed to suggest something close to the inverse of Findhorn-style sustainability. Although Seaside is the birthplace of New Urbanism, which has since become the organizing principle for scores of more pragmatic communities, it is at heart a resort town, a place custom-built for naked conspicuous consumption. Seaside is often derided as a theme-park version of a functional community, and my first impression seemed to confirm that assessment: when I checked in at the town's rental office, I was handed a bundle of passes and maps tucked into a pamphlet overflowing with artful photos of old-fashioned holiday fun, some of them literally sepia-toned.

The next day, I went on a walking tour with Seaside's town architect, Leo Casas. As we walked its shrub-lined back lanes and colonial-revival boulevards, he addressed the argument that Seaside peddles "false history": "It's interesting, you know, that notion of nostalgia. It's what leads us naturally—we have that propensity as humans to want to seek those things that make us feel comfortable, that make us feel close to one another. That don't alienate us. And it just so happens that old towns do that. And so to imitate an idea in terms of its principles and its typologies and architectural language—you know, I'm not bothered by that at all. In fact, I like trying to recreate something that I loved experiencing. It's what we do with relationships with one another, it's what we do with food. It's what we do in life, to be honest."

If Seaside looked, on its surface, like a stage set, it *functioned* like a place much more akin to Findhorn than to any given suburb or Florida resort community. Seaside's back lanes had been carefully designed to remain a sort of undefined quasi-public space of sandy paths and beach-oak canopy, and people really did meet and chat with uncommon frequency as they strolled along them. The designated bicycle paths? On several occasions, I had to hop out of the way as parades of kids on bikes went giggling past. I saw whole families playing touch football on the narrow, brick-paved streets. Everything about the design of those streets—the width, the road surface, the lack of clearly demarcated lanes—obliged you to drive at a crawl on those rare occasions when you did need to drive. They didn't even need to post a speed limit. The general store kind of *felt* the same as Findhorn's village store, or at the very least it bore a closer resemblance to the Findhorn model than to a suburban strip-mall supermarket.

Life really was sepia-toned in Seaside. I found myself invited into the community *every night:* asked to join the table of three next to mine at the Italian place one evening, kept out at the local bar way beyond my intent by a gregarious local contractor the next. And one fine morning I was heading down one of the town's grand boulevards, and there it was: a lemonade stand. Two girls, maybe eight or ten, calling out eagerly to passersby from behind a little table with a pitcher and cups and a sign that said LEMONADE. But for the absence of a backward N and someone saying "Aw, shucks, mister," it could've been a Norman Rockwell painting. I stopped, of course. Bought a glass. Bought all of it. No wonder imitations were being built up and down the coast—and no wonder the sunny local paper ("Weather: Lustrous," read the banner) reported that $895,000 was the going rate for even the smallest and simplest of Seaside's homes. This was the asking price for a condo above a shop on the main square, a place that was originally intended as inexpensive lodging for the town's staff; freestanding cottages—built in the same styles and with the same inexpensive local materials as the shotgun shacks of the region's "Redneck Riviera" past—started at $1.6 million.

"The small-town life that Americans long for when they are depressed by their city apartments or their suburban bunkers is really a conceptual substitute for the idea of community." This is James Howard Kunstler in *The Geography of Nowhere,* and the implication of his argument is that people—the ones who have the means, that is—are buying up New Urbanist shotgun shacks at $1.6 million a pop mainly in an attempt to secure even an occasional short-term stay in the kind of welcoming environment that used to be the baseline in the construction of human habitat. The premium on a Seaside bungalow is, to his mind, a function of the depth of the erosion of community in the rest of America.

Earlier in the same book, Kunstler ruminated on what was missing from the places those people spent the other eleven months of the year: "Americans have been living car-centered lives for so long that the collective memory of what used to make a landscape or a townscape or even a suburb humanly rewarding has nearly been erased. The culture of good place-making, like the culture of farming, or agriculture, is a body of knowledge and acquired skills. It is not bred in the bone, and if it is not transmitted from one generation to the next, it is lost." In this light, utopian experiments like Findhorn and Seaside reveal their larger purpose for the rest of the world: they are postmodern nature preserves, laboratories where those invaluable place-making skills are being maintained and refined to await a climate catastrophe of sufficient scope—or, more optimistically, an epidemic of rational exuberance of sufficient momentum—to send the rest of us to their doorsteps to learn from their experience and borrow from their toolboxes.

Even stripped of Kunstler's abiding pessimism, the fact remains that these Anthropocene Utopias are sanctuaries for certain endangered ways of living. The same ways, indeed, that Henry David Thoreau trudged out into the wilderness to find for himself. Thoreau: "I went to the woods because I wished to live deliberately, to front only the essential facts of life, and see if I could not learn what it had to teach, and not, when I came to die, discover that I had not lived." This is perhaps *Walden*'s most famous passage, and with good cause: it's a bold and powerful statement of purpose, and followed as it is by a sort of declaration of independence ("Simplicity, simplicity, simplicity!") it has long been taken as the marching order for a certain kind of Romantic back-to-the-land philosophy, an ideological justification for the reflexive preference for pristine ponds over teeming cityscapes.

Utopia, though, is not a wilderness, and neither is a sustainable community. Thoreau's deliberate living, whether he knew it or not, was destined to bring him back to civilization. "I have always been regretting," Thoreau wrote shortly after his statement of intent, "that I was not as wise as the day I was born." And the first lesson of that day, of course, is that none of us can survive on our own. Still, Thoreau had a point—an essential one—and it echoed down to Bob Dylan a hundred years later in "My Back Pages": "Ah, but I was so much older then / I'm younger than that now." There is indeed much to be forgotten about what we think we know, much to be learned by stripping away the trivial complexities of life to find the simple core of what is necessary. Thoreau—again, whether he knew it or not— was an advocate not of pristine nature but of a more pristine mind, a less cluttered point of view. We will only return to life in isolated shacks, all of us, if the crisis of anthropogenic climate change completely undoes all that it means to live in a civilization and a lot of what it means to be human. To avoid that grim fate, we would all do well to live much more deliberately.

Living deliberately: this, in the end, is the common ideological thread linking an ecovillage in rural Scotland and a resort development in Florida vacationland. And tying those places to Danish Renewable Energy Islands, New Mexican survivalist communities, solar-powered townhouses in southern Germany and hydro-powered villages in the hills of northwestern Thailand. To live deliberately: this is the life's blood of these communities, of any sustainable community. It's a sort of social mortar, filling the spaces between renewable-energy projects and local inns and community-centre cafeterias and making these places whole. If these communities seem more vital than a great many others, if they have lessons to teach about how the rest of us could bring such vitality to our own communities, they begin, all of them, with the simple art of living deliberately. It is, in a sense, the opposite of a fantastical, far-off Utopia: it starts with here and now, with whichever *here* and *now* you happen to find yourself in.

Alas, there is a way-of-life corollary to Kunstler's lamented loss of a culture of good place-making: an atrophied culture of good *life-making*. Too few of us live deliberately because we've forgotten how. We make do with unsustainable communities because we don't know how to find our way to the kind of lives that would not only insist on something better but maybe even provide us with the skills to achieve it. I could point to drug-use rates or depression surveys or statistics tracking the amount of time we spend eating alone (or eating alone *in cars*) to illustrate the problem, but it might do to simply note that a 2006 research study estimated the "self-improvement" industry to be a $9.6-billion annual boon to the GDP of the United States alone. All that money spent, in essence, because we *want* more than this. We know we can do better. We're just not sure how to start.

But never mind the self-help racket. I should explain how it came to pass that I met up with a couple of thousand people in a city far from home. Said *fuck it, Dude.* Went bowling. Decided, at least for a night or two, to live deliberately.

SOME KINDA EASTERN THING

Here's what I did: in March 2007, I went to a kind of revival meeting in Seattle. I thought it might even be the nucleus of a newfangled sort of community, but it turned out to be more like a holy rite followed by a church social, a gathering of members of the same strange faith who would probably never know each other intimately. Still, it was quite the, uh, what-have-you. It was Lebowski Fest.

Like a great many attendees, I'd been wanting to go to Lebowski Fest since I first learned of its existence, because until then I thought mine was a private and highly anachronistic faith, shared only with a few friends. Our devotion consisted primarily of watching the 1998 film *The Big Lebowski* with compulsive frequency and talking about its meaning and quoting from its script(ure) with even greater regularity. Now this here story I'm about to unfold (and the faithful will recognize that I've already begun to lapse into said scripture) took place, or started to, back in the early oughts, just about the time of America's second conflict with Sad'm and the Eye-rackies. It started with a couple of fellas from Louisville, Kentucky—fellas by the name of Will Russell and Scott Shuffitt—who sold T-shirts at all manner of concerts and subcultural confabs in the region. And on this one occasion, at a tattoo festival, they were trading favourite *Lebowski* lines, and someone at another booth joined in, and it occurred to them that if tattoos were worthy of a festival, so was The Dude.

Now The Dude is the film's accidental hero (much as I don't *want* to say a *hee*-ro, 'cause what's a *hee*-ro?). But anyway, as the introductory voice-over I've been quoting heavily from explains, The Dude is "the right man for his time and place," and in *The Big Lebowski,* that's Los Angeles (pronounced roughly *Los Aing-uhl-uss* by the narrator, a drawling cowpoke known as The Stranger) at the start of the *first* Iraq War. The timing is just one of the dense assortment of American historical touchstones stuffed pretty much at random into *The Big Lebowski,* and since its creators, the sibling writer-director duo of Joel and Ethan Coen, are legendary lovers of the red herring and noted cinephiles to boot, it's safe to assume that any deep meaning or recurring allusion you find in the film is at least partially accidental and yet potentially meaningful. The legacy of the Vietnam War flows through the film, and so does the intellectual bankruptcy of gimmicky postmodern fine art and the moral bankruptcy of Reagan-era capitalism. Pastiche is sometimes talked about as one of pop culture's signature artistic techniques—perhaps its most potent one—and *Lebowski* is, among other things, a giddy riot of pastiche.

I'll be honest: like a lot of people, I had no idea what to make of it when I first saw it in the theatre. (It was a critical and box-office letdown in theatrical release.) *The Big Lebowski* is a wilfully convoluted tale about a half-stuck-in-the-sixties former radical—and I'm talking about The Dude here, who's played as a stammering, slouching antihero with masterful shambolic charm by Jeff Bridges—who spends most of his time smoking pot and bowling with his two pals, the gunnut Vietnam vet Walter (a gleefully unhinged John Goodman) and the quiet former surfer Donny (the ubiquitous indie-film character actor Steve Buscemi). In a partial homage to the Raymond Chandler classic *The Big Sleep, Lebowski*'s thin plot centres on a kidnapping: Bunny, the young trophy wife of a pillar of the local business community named Jeffrey Lebowski, which is also The Dude's legal name, is being held for ransom. Said trophy wife is a sometime porn actor, and her former boss sends a few thugs to The Dude's divey bungalow by mistake, looking for some money she owes. One of them pees on The Dude's favourite rug during the shakedown. At Walter's outraged urging, The Dude pays a visit to the millionaire Jeffrey Lebowski to ask for compensation for the soiling of his carpet, which encounter leads to him being sort of deputized to hand off the blackmail money to get the trophy wife back, dragging him into a half-assedly seedy L.A. underworld of porn producers, German nihilist bikers and avant-garde artists.

If you haven't seen the film three or four times minimum, you're likely *plenty* bewildered by now. I surely was during that first viewing, because I'd made the mistake of thinking I was watching a sort of detective story—as opposed to inhabiting an absurd and oddly cozy universe for a couple of hours. I only hit upon that key insight during my third viewing of *Lebowski,* and it then followed, by the fifth viewing at the latest, that it had become not only the funniest goddamn movie I've ever seen but also among the half-dozen best films in the history of motion pictures. It contains, for example, not a single throwaway line or incidental detail—not *one,* even the food the characters order at restaurants and how they order it has been carefully scripted to add to the lushness of the skewed universe—which is what makes it so durned interesting and so much fun on repeated viewing.

It's this density of detail that imbues *The Big Lebowski* with its potential for cult status, because it guarantees that new shit will come to light with each viewing, and that there's enough of it to build a sermon (or at least a half-baked pop philosophy) around. Pop obsessiveness has taken on a particular intensity in the Anthropocene Era, becoming a surrogate for the kind of deliberate living too often absent elsewhere in the social order. Maybe it's the pace of technological advancement and social change or the degree of media saturation or the failure of so many traditional institutions to keep up—or all of the above—but many of us Anthropocene kids have had only the movies and TV and pop music and a handful of other strands of ephemera to sate the universal ceaseless yearning for inclusion in something, *anything,* greater than ourselves. This stuff has filled the Common Book of Prayer in a multifaceted, constantly mutating quasi-religion. Jam-rock bands like the Grateful Dead and Phish formed one subgenre, sci-fi epics like *Star Trek* and *Star Wars* another. *The*

Simpsons was a religious rite for a time. And just recently I saw that someone had organized a festival around the beloved iconoclastic British comedy series *Father Ted.* Which brings us back to The Dude, and Louisville, and Lebowski Fest.

It started, like I said, with a couple of friends named Russell and Shuffitt in that unassuming Kentucky burg in 2002. They rented a local alley, invited their friends, planned a night of White Russians (The Dude's preferred cocktail) and bowling. They expected an intimate crowd of maybe 35 friends and acquaintances; close to 150 people showed up. The next year, attendance was more like *3,000,* and it included one Jeff Dowd, a former activist who had been jailed as one of the "Seattle Seven"* back in the early 1970s and had gone on to become a player in the nascent independent film scene in 1980s Hollywood. Dowd had arranged the distribution of the Coen Brothers' first film, *Blood Simple,* and his laconic mannerisms and alternate-reality lifestyle had provided the Coens with the model for the cinematic Dude. As of the second Lebowski Fest, The Dude himself had joined the faithful.

The Fest became an annual fixture of international renown from then on, and Russell and Shuffitt started taking their revival to a couple of new destinations each year: first New York and Las Vegas, then Los Angeles and Austin, Texas. Wherever they went, they attracted *Lebowski* devotees by the thousands—"Achievers," they called them, after the "Little Lebowski Urban Achievers," a charity for inner-city kids run by Jeffrey Lebowski in the film. Along the way, the Fest resolved into a standard format: a night of live music as prelude to a screening of the film, and then a second night of bowling, with the constant leavening presence of Jeff "The Dude" Dowd throughout. This was what awaited me in Seattle.

The first night of the inaugural Seattle Lebowski Fest (official T-shirt tagline: ENJOYIN' MY COFFEE) took place at a spacious downtown ballroom called the Showbox. It began with a pair of live

---

* In connection with a protest action in 1970, seven members of an anti-war group called the Seattle Liberation Front (The Dude and six other guys) were charged with "conspiracy to incite a riot." They became known as the Seattle Seven during the ensuing court case, which ended in a mistrial.

musical acts: first a local band called the Fucking Eagles (named for The Dude's peeved dismissal of the kings of seventies country rock), then a solo showman called Har Mar Superstar (a portly, balding dude who sang along to a sexed-up soundtrack of funk and R&B hits, karaoke-style, while copping mock-heroic poses). The joint was packed—the overall attendance was later estimated at just shy of two thousand, which was pretty good for an inaugural—and the vibe was of course convivial. The congregation skewed twenty-something and male, though there were folks of all ages in ample numbers and a third of the attendees at minimum were female. One of the most common configurations in the audience was the yin-yang duo or trio composed of one obviously hardcore Achiever and his friend or spouse or what-have-you. The Achiever—sometimes dressed as Walter or The Dude, or at least wearing a brand-new ENJOYIN' MY COFFEE T-shirt—would be scanning the place with a wide, ecstatic grin, while his companion(s) stood next to him looking bemused and/or good-naturedly exasperated, and in any case relieved that it *wasn't* just him after all. Meanwhile, The Dude himself worked the room with the ubiquity and panache of a veteran politician, play-ing a hybrid role that vacillated at random between M.C., guest of honour and official mascot.

After the musical program was finished, The Dude stepped up to the microphone to introduce the movie, shuffling across the Showbox stage like a cross between Keith Richards and a political firebrand as he delivered a monologue about his long, strange trip to silver-screen immortality that cycled in and out of coherence. He talked about receiving his first Lebowski Fest invitation by phone from Russell and Shuffitt, which had immediately put him in mind of a legendary *Saturday Night Live* sketch in which William Shatner berates a convention crowd of Trekkies, ordering them to "get a life." The Fest organizers assured him it wouldn't be that kind of thing, and his continued presence at Fest after Fest was evidence that he agreed. "It's like participatory art," The Dude announced.

The film started shortly thereafter, and as if to validate The Dude's story—parts, anyway—the crowd chanted along in near-unison to practically the whole thing. The crowd delivered Walter's bellowed assessment of the skill level of Bunny's inept nihilist kidnappers—*bunch of FUCKIN' amateurs*—in a syncopated howl, as if to dismiss anyone so ignorant as to challenge the righteousness of *Lebowski* writ. The nearest experience I'd ever had to this was mouthing the Nicene Creed along with the rest of the congregation at Mass as a kid. The key distinction being that I understood what I was reciting at Lebowski Fest, and I more wholly embraced its revealed truths. It occurred to me that this was what church was like when its stories spoke directly to the faithful. This was the power of a useful myth.

This was also about as much collaborative fun as you could have at a movie screening. The *real* participatory art was the next night at the bowling alley. Kenmore Lanes was a cavernous fifty-lane bowling centre on a desolate stretch of suburban boulevard north of the city, a generic strip-mall space across a wide asphalt savanna from a discount department store and a Starbucks with a drive-thru lane. On this Saturday night, however, Kenmore Lanes was thoroughly transformed, transported to The Dude's *Los Aing-uhl-uss*. Maybe a third of the crowd came in *Lebowski*-inspired costume, although the outfits were *so* inspired it seemed like almost everyone was. At one end of the mezzanine there was a small installation of *Lebowski*-derived art,* and there were two specially appointed satellite bars that served only White Russians. It was a masquerade ball, an art gallery, a performance-art venue—a happening, man.

It was also still a bowling alley, and so we rolled. We got ourselves shoes, bellied up to one bar or another to order up some Caucasians, stumbled down to the lanes with our drinks. We thought to ourselves, *Fuck it, Dude.* And we went bowling.

There were several dozen Dudes in attendance—many dressed in bathrobes or tattered cardigans, some in sunglasses, one carrying a big old eighties-style cellular phone—and they all rolled. There were probably an equal number of Walters, all of them in his signature hunting vest and shorts, and they sure as shit rolled. One lane was occupied by a handful of guys dressed as the defunct German

---

* Among the more accomplished pieces: a detailed diorama of the elaborate Busby Berkeley sequence precipitated by the dark sleep The Dude falls into when porn producer Jackie Treehorn drugs his White Russian; and *The Shroud of Turturro,* a skilful hooked-rug portrait of the actor John Turturro, who plays a purple-jumpsuited rival bowler and convicted pederast named Jesus in the movie.

techno-pop band Autobahn, the former project of several members of the nihilist kidnapping cadre. A group dressed in plastic pig masks and big shaggy brown capes (pigs-in-a-blanket, the meal one of the nihilists orders in an interstitial scene at a diner) filled another lane. One young woman wore a crown and a flowing purple robe over a simple bra and panties; it wasn't until I heard someone say *There goes the Queen in her damned undies* that I realized she'd come dressed as a spoken allusion made in the narrator's opening monologue. From then on, she was my pick for best costume. She lost to a beer-gutted guy dressed in a blond wig and Bunny Lebowski's bikini. But nevertheless all of them rolled.

It could be hard to concentrate on the pins amid the revelry. In particular, one Walter or another would, with jarring frequency, come stomping down from the mezzanine to the lanes and summarily holler, "Over the line!" or "All right, Donny!" These were guys who, you could tell, had been waiting for the chance to really let loose a Walter-sized bellow for a very long time. Still, with holy fervour, we rolled.

As I waited for a cab in the perpetual Seattle drizzle afterward, I got to talking to a guy from L.A. who said he'd now been to eight Lebowski Fests. This elicited a response from a couple of others standing next to us who had come up from Oregon. They had the delirious afterglow of people who still couldn't believe they'd attended their first, and one of them wanted us to know about the miraculous revelation that had brought them here. The guy explained that he'd been driving down the highway back home not so long ago when he spied a bumper sticker on the highway that said ENJOYIN' MY COFFEE, and he'd tailgated that car for a couple of miles like his salvation depended on it until he could make out the small print reading LEBOWSKIFEST.COM at the bottom, and that's how he found out about it. "I was a member of the fan club," he said, "before I knew there was one." And that about wrapped her all up, and I had to admit it was a purtie good story, which did indeed make me laugh to beat the band.

What in God's name are you blathering about? This is what Jeffrey Lebowski asks The Dude in a scene midway through the film, as our *hee*-ro stumbles his way through a stoned ramble about how he messed up handing off the ransom money to the nihilists. It's an apt question right about now: What's the *point* of *Lebowski* and its Fests? Now, finally, we're getting down to the fate of the whole durned human comedy, a topic addressed directly in *The Big Lebowski*'s final scene, as The Stranger and The Dude cross paths at the bowling alley's bar.

"How things been goin'?" asks The Stranger.

"Ah, you know," says The Dude. "Strikes and gutters, ups and downs."

The Stranger nods his agreement, and The Dude excuses himself to bring the beers back to his lane. "Take it easy, Dude," The Stranger says in parting. "I know that you will."

"Yeah, man. Well, you know, The Dude abides." And that's the last we see of him.

"*The Dude abides*," The Stranger echoes, savouring it like a prayer—or a mantra. "I don't know about you, but I take comfort in that. It's good knowin' he's out there—The Dude—takin' 'er easy for all us sinners."

The Dude abides: if you took a random survey at Lebowski Fest, the majority of those present would probably eventually ramble their way to some version of this as the explanation for why they'd come. Because something about the movie spoke to that part of themselves that just wanted their beloved rug back, the one that really tied the room together. The one, if you will, that gave life a sense of orderly purpose, that you could come home and step across and know from its familiar pattern and the way it tickled your feet that your troubles were over and you had nothing more arduous to wrestle with than whether or not your bowling team would make the semis. *Abiding,* you'll have to admit, is damn near synonymous with *sustaining,* and the desire to find that equilibrium—that state of grace—is pretty near universal. The Anthropocene Era is surely some kind of mess of a pee-stained rug, and it's hard for people to find their way to a place where they can just abide again. And that, maybe, is why a couple thousand people in seemingly any good-sized city in North America will happily spend a weekend pretending to live The Dude's life.

Rewind to the first night of Seattle Lebowski Fest. The Dude was up on stage doing his pre-movie monologue, and he told a story about a guy he met at a New York Fest a while back, a firefighter who had lost friends and colleagues in the chaos of the World Trade Center's collapse. The guy told The Dude he spent months afterward in a bottomless funk of post-traumatic stress, and pills and therapy couldn't touch it. About seven months on, he said, he watched *The Big Lebowski*—and laughed, really *laughed,* for the first time since 9/11. And that, said The Dude, was what Lebowski Fest was all about.

I'll admit it: I teared up. I stood half-drunk on the dance floor of the Showbox in Seattle, a city I'd first set foot in that morning, and I cried tears of hard-won joy. For that firefighter, yes, but mostly for myself, because I *belonged* there. I was among members of the same faith or tribe or cult or what-have-you, and there *was* comfort in that. I had come with my own patchwork quilt of a pastiche religion, and I'm sure everyone around me had their own, and *this* was the thing missing from the rest of our lives. The place in us where hope resided, the useful myth from which we drew the will and the wisdom to build real communities and live more deliberate lives.

This, ultimately, is the point of a belief system or faith or useful mythology, whatever name you give it and whether or not you think of it as divine: it allows you to abide the routine stuff of life with grace, clarity, even joy. To see how it's all connected, how it *all* matters—and to see, now, why the routine must change if we intend to carry on.

The eternal significance of learning to abide was the subject of a subtle, magnificent commencement speech delivered to the graduates of Kenyon College in Ohio by the American writer David Foster Wallace in May 2005. Wallace opened with a gag-like parable: "There are these two young fish swimming along and they happen to meet an older fish swimming the other way, who nods at them and says, 'Morning, boys. How's the water?' And the two young fish swim on for a bit, and then eventually one of them looks over at the other and goes, 'What the hell is water?'" The balance of Wallace's address consisted of the argument that the true gift of a liberal education (and here you can sub in reading a lot or travelling extensively or simply learning to live deliberately) is that it gives you the tools to see, understand, maybe even embrace and learn to love the omnipresent daily fact of the water.

Wallace chose as his water sample the everyday hell of a rush-hour commute followed by a stop at a crowded supermarket. He recapped the internal monologue all of us know, the one where everything's a hassle and everyone's in your way, the light's too bright and the lines too long, the muzak as plastic and nauseating as the cashier's *Have a nice day.*

Wallace:

> If you're automatically sure that you know what reality is, and you are operating on your default setting, then you, like me, probably won't consider possibilities that aren't annoying and miserable. But if you really learn how to pay attention, then you will know there are other options. It will actually be within your power to experience a crowded, hot, slow, consumer-hell type situation as not only meaningful, but sacred, on fire with the same force that made the stars: love, fellowship, the mystical oneness of all things deep down.
>
> Not that that mystical stuff is necessarily true. The only thing that's capital-T True is that you get to decide how you're gonna try to see it. . . . You get to decide what to worship.
>
> Because here's something else that's weird but true: in the day-to-day trenches of adult life, there is actually no such thing as atheism. There is no such thing as not worshipping. Everybody worships. The only choice we get is what to worship. And the compelling reason for maybe choosing some sort of god or spiritual-type thing to worship—be it JC or Allah, be it YHWH or the Wiccan Mother Goddess, or the Four Noble Truths, or some inviolable set of ethical principles—is that pretty much anything else you worship will eat you alive. If you worship money and things, if they are where you tap real meaning in life, then you will never have enough, never feel you have enough. It's the truth. Worship your body and beauty and sexual allure and you will always feel ugly. And when time and age start showing, you will die a million deaths before they finally grieve you. On one level, we all know this stuff already. It's been codified as myths, proverbs, clichés, epigrams, parables; the skeleton of every great story. The whole trick is keeping the truth up front in daily consciousness.

The trick, in other words, is to abide the strikes and the gutters and count on plenty of both. Or, as Wallace put it, to remind ourselves constantly, mantra-like, that this is water, *this is water,* and that's all there is. And it's from this commonplace stream that all hope flows: the certainty that *now,* no matter how troublesome, is transient. And the only thing certain about *later* is that it will be determined by the direction we all choose to swim.

One last thing: if there's a problem with the water, there are no higher priorities. Can't be. Ever.

EPILOGUE
A SUSTAINABLE CITY ON A HILL

April again.

Late morning on a chilly Thursday, and big, gentle flakes of snow drift and dance over the crest of Scotsman's Hill. There will be a spring, another new start, not far off, but it's not here yet. The city stretching to the horizon from below the cliff on which I stand is still a vision of fossil-fuelled wealth, laced with expressways and encrusted with single-purpose suburban tracts. It has been two years, nearly to the day, since I first gazed out and saw dusk on this horizon and then went away to hunt among windmills and solar panels for a new dawn. I thought I would find our sustainable future far from Calgary, but I've come back here now, after a year of living optimistically and another long while trying to figure out what it meant, because possibly the most important lesson I've learned is that if I can't find hope on the horizon I see every day from my own backyard, I won't find it anywhere. I've learned not to look for a clean slate or an empty prairie; there is no starting again from zero. The more useful skill, by far, is to learn to examine the same old vista with new eyes.

I thought often in my travels of the Puritans aboard their pilgrim vessel, adrift on the frigid Atlantic, as their shepherd sequestered himself in his cabin to scrawl out the blueprints of a new world order. John Winthrop's "A Modell of Christian Charity," written on the *Arbella* in mid-voyage in 1630, was not a policy document or a set of building plans; it was a call to a certain kind of resolve. The Puritans, Winthrop wrote, were sailing across the sea to confront a choice that was the same one facing all of humanity: grace or damnation. He reckoned their social project would be carefully watched— "as a citty upon a hill"—because the whole world was waiting to see which direction to move in. The project's failure would become a warning to all never to imitate such folly, and its success would usher in God's kingdom on earth. Astoundingly, Winthrop's self-important rhetoric was validated, in a sense, by the next three and a half centuries of history. The American republic built on those Puritan foundations, and the useful myths and ground-level realities of freedom and opportunity it inspired, *did* assemble themselves into a symbolic city on a hill: a beacon of democracy, a shining embodiment of the Enlightenment's most powerful and widely desired ideal.

Sustainability must now be conceived as democracy was for the past two hundred years: as a city upon a hill. It's not a single place but a point of view, a variably tinted lens for shifting the default perspective on climate change from despair to hope, and a set of tools for building durable societies anywhere they're needed. Right here, for example, in the city of my daughter's birth.

I look out now from Scotsman's Hill, and I see hope. It surprises me just how much. It's not obvious or easy and it's far from certain, but it's there nonetheless. I see the city with new eyes, through new lenses. This will have to be my sustainable city on a hill, because the piecemeal map I've assembled must in time become a map of the whole world. And even here in an oil capital we won't start from zero, not only because we can't but because we don't need to. Some of the pieces are already in place. There is a wooden staircase right in front of me that leads from the crest of the hill to the banks of the Elbow River below. There it meets an extensive paved network of paths that snakes through the entire city. You can bike or hike from the base of this hill to the heart of high-rise downtown or to the distant southeastern suburbs. When the weather permits, I strap my daughter into her caboose and bike her along these paths to daycare or the grocery store or the riverside park where the swings are.

And if I watch the near side of the commuter boulevard, I'll see an LRT train whooshing by before long, speeding around a system fed exclusively by those wind farms to the south of the city. The nucleus of a fully functional, state-of-the-art, emissions-free commuter network lies within a short amble of where I stand.

I look to the towering skyline, but I don't dwell for long on the plumes of heating exhaust billowing from the roofs. I recall instead the announcement not even a month ago that most of those buildings will before long draw their heat and air conditioning from a high-efficiency district energy system, and not long after that the city will be building its first combined heat-and-power plant to serve those high-rises. I note as well the gap in the jagged landscape between the Petro-Canada towers and the Hyatt Hotel—soon to be filled by the nation's most eco-friendly skyscraper, designed by Buckminster Fuller's old collaborator Norman Foster. In an oil baron's city, the most prominent landmark on the skyline will be a curving glass monument to sustainable architecture.

This is what I can see with no effort at all. If I look closer, with more care, hidden vistas of hopeful possibility emerge. I never noticed until now, for instance, that the Saddledome's bowed roof rises into a southwest-facing concrete embankment that cries out for retiling in PV panels. The north rim of the arena is hemmed in by a wide apron of multitiered parking lot, and through the most optimistic lens it's possible to imagine it replaced with a replica of Belmar—a vibrant downtown neighbourhood to weave the Dome more tightly into the city's fabric. Even through a more realistic squint, a lush carpet of parkland (or even farmland) replaces the grey concrete roofs of the parking lot with little effort at all. In the derelict, half-gutted old residential neighbourhood immediately north of the Saddledome, there's ample room for a couple of Rolf Disch's Solarsiedlung townhouse clusters, a handful of the sturdy single-family houses that populate the Findhorn ecovillage, a solar district heating installation like the ones I found on those Danish isles or indeed like the one recently completed on the outskirts of the commuter town immediately south of here. Already the hippest residential communities in the city are the handful of New Urbanist redevelopments on the downtown fringe; here in plain sight lies sufficient land for a couple more.

The Calgary Stampede—the city's signature summer party—controls significant swaths of the empty land I can see in the foreground, and they've already started on the construction of some kind of hotel-casino complex in one vacant section. When the Stampede braintrust announced the project, they felt obliged to at least pay lip service to sustainability, touting the way the complex closed the gap between the residential neighbourhood and the rodeo grounds and brought life and commerce to a desolate block. So would it be too fanciful to imagine a day not far off when they launch plans to build a new conference centre and trade hall that looks just like the Godrej Green Business Centre, LEED Platinum rating and all?

In the meantime, a single twentysome-storey condo spire has been rising in the middle of this urban desert for the past year or so. And though it might be enough simply to appreciate the way it will increase the neighbourhood's population density to a sustainable level, it's not hard, either, to imagine it as the last condo tower built without recourse to LEED certification, as the docket of the city planning committee fills up by the month with yet more proposals boasting LEED ambitions. And not hard to look just a little deeper and imagine a cluster of towers around that first one, each wrapped in a tight blanket of thin-film solar cells to take advantage of Calgary's three hundred days of sunshine per annum.

The wind often howls ferociously across the south rim of downtown Calgary. The torch-shaped Calgary Tower sways in it so regularly that the kitchen workers in the rotating restaurant at the top have learned to correct for it in their chopping, and it's rare that you can stand atop Scotsman's Hill without bracing yourself against it. How many wind turbines could fit along this crest, or along the roofline of the Stampede grandstand across the way? How long before every home standing on this hill has retrofitted its roof with a microturbine or two?

If I turn around, the bustling cityscape is replaced with a view of the low bungalows and old warehouses of my neighbourhood and a wide, sparsely populated industrial zone beyond that, which was centred on a thick backbone of train tracks. Calgary's intercity passenger rail service ceased under a ferocious cost-cutting wave in 1990, but a high-speed train through the heavily populated corridor north of the city has remained on the wish list ever since. I gaze out over the tracks and think of southern Germany, wondering how long it might be before I can start a trip to Edmonton or even to the resort towns in the mountains at a local train station instead of behind the wheel of my car. "(The provincial government has already launched a feasibility study.) The new LRT line that will run past the old chicken plant over yonder has already been planned; the only remaining quibble is the date of its inauguration.

On the far side of the tracks lies an old aluminum-sided warehouse that houses an extensive farmers' market, and I buy most of my produce there. At the peak of the harvest, the place is a riot of Hutterite and Punjabi farmers jousting for my business, creating one of my most treasured snapshots of the haphazard model of sustainable multicultural society that is perhaps Canada's greatest lesson for the world. The farmers' market is nestled amid a handful of low hillocks that line either side of a busy commuter highway. They're desolate little patches of vestigial prairie at the moment, but if I cock an optimistic eye at their gentle south-facing slopes, a dozen pioneering Earthships appear. I can cast the same gaze over the looming towers of the distillery and yeast factory and gravel quarry beyond, and imagine big pipes tying them together in an efficient web of industrial symbiosis.

I can stand here on Scotsman's Hill and assemble a map of limitless possibility, and that is practically the definition of a geography of hope. The most delirious fun is in conjuring up some of the fantastical future-tense ideas. What if, next to the condo tower, there was a ten-storey greenhouse like the prototype dreamed up by Dickson Despommier at Columbia University? What was the phrase William McDonough used in his lecture at the Calgary Hyatt just last month? "Think about Paris with farms on the roof." And then he paused, and he tapped the laptop in front of him, and on the giant screen above him there appeared a photorealistic artist's rendering of a Chinese agrarian landscape. A green checkerboard of rice paddies and fruit trees stretched to the horizon, and in the foreground a peasant farmer in a conical bamboo hat hiked across a paddy with two buckets of rice seedlings dangling on a yoke from his shoulders. It took a second to notice that the field he was walking across ended in a precipitous drop-off, separated from the next field by a ten-storey canyon. The entire scene was *on top* of a densely packed collection of apartment buildings. "And there's the new city," said McDonough, deadpan, and if that didn't get your pulse racing with excitement for our sustainable future, nothing would.

I remember the people I found already hard at work building that sustainable world, and I'm filled with an exuberance that's almost gleeful. This was the most reassuring aspect of my map-making expedition: the best and brightest are already on the job. And this, more than any of the gadgetry, is what really fills me with hope when I imagine it waiting for me down the hill: a sort of reunion. There's a hotel a little way past the Stampede grounds, a funky upscale joint called the Hotel Arts, which took over the premises of a dowdy old Holiday Inn on a lifeless block and turned it into one of the most desirable places to stay in the whole city, and I know they've got meeting space. It's not quite state of the sustainable art, but it would do for now. I can only imagine what kind of community-building strategies might emerge from a brainstorming session with Samsø's Søren Hermansen and Belmar's Mark Falcone and the fear-less May East of Findhorn. I'd love to hear what Jørgen Bjørgren's work as a farmer-activist in Aerø could do to improve the yields at Maverick Farms in North Carolina, and I'm sure Dr. Soontorn has learned a disruptive technique or two that would be useful to E+Co's Phil LaRocco. And both of them would love to meet Chris Greacen, not to mention Watit and Polchai. Imagine a mixed-use urban neigh-bourhood co-designed by Rolf Disch, Mike Reynolds and Duany Plater-Zyberk & Co. of Seaside fame. If I could put together an advi-sory board that included William McDonough and Amory Lovins, Interface's Ray Anderson and the Apollo Project's Adam Werbach, Jonathan Dawson of the Global Ecovillage Network and Kirsten Jacobsen of Earthship Biotecture, the Dalai Lama and The Dude, I don't know whether I'd start up the next Microsoft or start a revolu-tion, but either way I'd get Marc Stoiber to handle the marketing and I'm sure I'd be sitting pretty.

In the meantime, I stand here on Scotsman's Hill and I know the limits of what is possible, and I know we haven't even begun to explore them. I stand here alone, because I don't need to bring my daughter up here to see a sustainable city on a hill. She's already seen it. Parts, anyway.

My greatest hope, the one I'd set out on this journey to find, is that all of this represents the first faint glimmering of a sustainable dawn.

That the people who built it and the places where they began will populate my daughter's first memories, or at least that we can tell her years from now, as she prepares to inherit it, that she was there at the start. I hope she finds what we tell her about those days preposterous, not because they sound like postcards from some far-out fantasyland we once visited but because the details have become so commonplace. (*Once upon a time, dear, no one generated their own power, can you believe it?*)

I know that my daughter's first fuzzy understanding of the size and colour of life was formed in this geography of hope. If it has a first-born child, she might well be it, as she was there with me for long stretches of these travels. She learned to walk in a beachside restaurant on an island off the coast of Phuket in Thailand, stepping proud and confident across a wooden patio, clutching a menu for balance, more at risk of wandering too close to the monitor lizards next to the entrance than of stumbling into motorized traffic on that car-free isle. At the Phoenix Earthship construction site, she scooped up an old pickle jar and paced around the dusty clearing with a foreman's purpose, though we never did find out where she thought it belonged. She crawled, giggling, under the office coffee table of the New Urbanist mayor of Lakewood, Colorado, and she greeted Dr. Soontorn with a big grin at the Chulalongkorn University cafeteria.

She learned to talk on this journey as well. Her first word—the first completely coherent one, anyway—was actually a contracted phrase, an intrepid geographer's interrogation: *What is that?* At first, she would just point eagerly and demand to know: *Wuzzat?*

Wuzzat?

A bamboo tree.

Wuzzat?

The SkyTrain coming.

Wuzzat?

That's a wind turbine.

In time, her repertoire expanded. *Wuzzat?* she would ask. And then she'd consider, and often as not she'd be in a backpack carrier or hip-mounted sling or just in my arms or my wife's, and she'd lean toward the thing and say, *Oh go see.*

Wuzzat? That's a cactus, dear. *Oh go see.*

Wuzzat? An alpaca. *Wuzzat?* A tire wall. *Wuzzat?* Those are solar panels. *Oh go see.*

Wuzzat? A self-sufficient home. *Wuzzat?* The place where natural capitalism was born. *Wuzzat?* A sustainable community, and a group of dedicated, passionate souls committed to building it. A solution to the scourge of the twenty-first century, a future worth fighting for, the world we need.

Wuzzat?

Hope, baby girl. That's hope.

Oh go see.

[acknowledgements]

The production of this book involved a year and a half of frenetic travel followed by eight months of frantic and obsessive writing, during which time I amassed debts of gratitude far greater than I'll ever be able to repay in this lifetime. Hope's backbone, I've learned, is composed entirely of the kindness of family, friends and colleagues.

My greatest debt is to my wife, Ashley Bristowe, whose contributions to this book are too great to be properly enumerated here. Travelling companion, counsellor, business manager, photographer and webmaster, editor and researcher, pillar of support and wellspring of enduring hope—for these roles and a million others (from procuring baby medicine in Tamil Nadu to finding perfect accomodations in New Mexico to patiently talking me down from a thousand hopeless precipices)—I extend my most wholehearted thanks, and wish there was a better word for how much.

A simple thanks will have to suffice as well to convey my gratitude to my editors at Random House Canada: Anne Collins, whose faith in this project was immediate, immense and unwavering, and who went far beyond the call of duty to make it a reality; and Craig Pyette, who chipped away at the manuscript with a sculptor's precision until something coherent emerged. Thanks also to Matthew

Sibiga at Random House Canada for his enthusiastic support for the book, to Sue Sumeraj for cleaning up the messy copy, to Gillian Watts for proofreading it and to Kelly Hill for transforming it into an elegant text with a striking cover. And thanks as well to my agent, Emma Parry, who believed in it long before anything like coherence arrived on the scene, and to Neil Morton, my editor at the deceased *Shift Magazine,* who took a chance on the essay that birthed this project five years before that, when it was still mostly a barroom rant.

I would like to acknowledge the generous financial support of the Alberta Foundation for the Arts and the Canada Council for the Arts.

I would like to further acknowledge the life-saving generosity of the J.R.B. Bristowe Emergency Cashflow Crisis Relief Fund for Flailing Writers and the John & Margo Turner Emergency Laptop Replacement Grant—vital unregistered charities with a client list of one.

I am deeply indebted as well to Lutz Kleveman and the Drager Foundation for providing vital travel support and the most engaging and illuminating weekend of professional development I've ever had the good fortune to experience. Further thanks to *Alberta Venture, Azure, Canadian Geographic, enRoute,* the *Globe and Mail, Maisonneuve, Swerve* and *The Walrus,* all of which sponsored parts of the research and published the results (albeit generally in much different form).

In addition to the key sources of both information and inspiration cited directly in the text, my mapmaking journey was aided and abetted by more helpful, patient and giving souls than I could ever have hoped to find. My deepest thanks to Ian Connacher, whose passion for the task of building a better world has long been an inspiration and whose carefully curated library of books on that subject was invaluable to my research; to Thaba Niedzwiecki, Phet Sayo and Ji Hong Sayo, who provided a home base for my family in Bangkok for longer than I could have asked with more good humour and grace than I could have imagined; to John Johnston, who repeatedly provided shelter and proper English hospitality in lovely Shepherd's Bush, London; and to Carla Bellamy, who brought a holiday vibe and a thoughtful eye to my research in New Mexico and Colorado (and whose gift of *The Lorax* to my daughter informed this book in so many ways). And thanks as always to my generous and supportive parents, John and Margo Turner, and to my extended family

(Turners, McConnells, Bristowes and Horbows), who lent tolerance, levity and vital assistance of a thousand different kinds through the many months of this book's production.

I would also like to thank Sunil Abraham, Lee Schnaiberg, Bill Irwin, Gian-Carlo Carra, Richard Schindler, Nick Springer and Springer Cartographics, Turid "Guf" Hanevold Nielsen and her helpful staff at Brundby Rock Hotel in Samsø, Jesper Kjems (Energitjenesten Samsø), Rune Schmidt (Energitjenesten Aerø), Stephan Ghisler (Danish Wind Industry Association), Hanna Lehmann (Architekturbüro Rolf Disch, Freiburg), Thomas Dresel (SolarRegion Freiburg), Catherine McAlinden and Andy Hammerton (Co-operative Financial Services, Manchester), Victoria Bailey (South Bank Centre, London), Sharon Lee and Joyce Yao (Conrad Centennial Singapore), Lynda Goh and Muhammad Samad (BP Singapore), Peter Kong (Singapore Oxygen Air Liquide), Salinee Tavaranan and Andrew Pascale (Palang Thai), Walt Ratterman (Green Empowerment), Jos van den Akker (Auroville Renewable Energy), Chimey Rigzen (Department of Home of the Central Tibetan Administration, Bylakuppe), Randy Udall (Community Office for Resource Efficiency, Aspen, Colorado), John Anderson (Rocky Mountain Institute, Boulder), Gina Rodolico (E+Co), Eben Burnham-Snyder and Susanne King (Natural Resources Defence Council), Simon Retallack (Institute for Public Policy Research) and Lisa Hymas (grist.org).

[source notes]

The Geography of Hope is intended not as a policy blueprint or scientific paper but as an inspiring narrative, so I chose not to bog down the text with too much in the way of technical detail, statistics or footnotes. Furthermore, the parameters of some of the technological and social phenomena I discuss are shifting extremely rapidly, so I felt it best to avoid number-crunching as much as possible. (Fortunately, much of that arduous labour was accomplished by the British government's *Stern Review of the Economics of Climate Change* and George Monbiot's book *Heat,* both of which were published toward the end of my research. Tim Flannery's excellent climate change primer, *The Weather Makers,* also provided a detailed overview of the scientific story to date. I refer readers to those texts for more detailed analysis of the raw economic and scientific data of anthropogenic climate change.)

Despite the urgency of the topic and the intensity of the travel required by the reporting, I've done my very best to retrace the tracks of my research and verify every detail gathered on the fly; if I've failed anywhere, I hope the subjects and readers alike will forgive me and know that such minor errors as may have survived cast no doubt whatsoever on the main thrust of the book, that these things, and others like them, constitute the world we need.

I have detailed below only those key statistics, details and passages whose sources are not explicitly noted in the text itself.

My benchmark estimates of past, present and future carbon dioxide concentrations are drawn from widely quoted and uncontroversial sources. The pre-industrial CO_2 concentration of 280 ppm is taken from the Intergovernmental Panel on Climate Change's *Summary for Policymakers to Climate Change 2001: Synthesis Report of the IPCC Third Assessement Report* (2001). The current CO_2 level of about 380 ppm (as of 2006) is the estimate reported in George Monbiot's *Heat* (Doubleday Canada, 2006); it has also been quoted by David King, the British government's chief science adviser (see, for example, a BBC Online report of March 14, 2006, entitled "Sharp Rise in CO_2 Levels Recorded") and in sworn testimony made in a Vermont court in August 2006 by James E. Hansen of NASA's Goddard Institute for Space Studies. In "Stabilization Wedges: Solving the Climate Problem for the Next 50 Years with Current Technologies" in the August 13, 2004, issue of the journal *Science,* Scott Pacala and Robert Socolow of Princeton University's Carbon Mitigation Initiative assert that stabilizing atmospheric CO_2 at 500 ppm "would prevent most damaging climate change." In "A Plan to Keep Carbon in Check" in the September 2006 issue of *Scientific American,* Pacala and Socolow write that "at the present rate of growth emissions of carbon dioxide will double by 2056," to 560 ppm.

My data for the McBride Lake wind farm comes primarily from TransAlta, the parent company of the installation's developer, Vision Quest Windelectric. The estimated number of Alberta households that could be powered by the farm's output ("enough energy to power more than 32,500 homes annually") was found on TransAlta's website (www.transalta.com); by comparison, the metrics for estimating the average Western Canadian household's energy needs in terms of a power plant's capacity, devised by B.C. Hydro in its 2001 "Conservation Potential Review," yield a figure of 690 households per megawatt of capacity, which would put the McBride Lake total at closer to 52,000 homes. I went with the more conservative estimate.

I used the most conservative and straightforward calculation tool for my estimate of the amount of carbon dioxide emissions avoided by the use of McBride Lake's renewable energy. In April 2007, Bullfrog Power (a Toronto-based "green electricity retailer") released its "Emissions Calculation Methodology" for its customers, which estimated the average MWh (megawatt hours)of green electricity to reduce carbon dioxide emissions by 0.648 tonnes. As Ontario uses far less coal-fired power per capita than Alberta, I'm fairly sure the actual total for Alberta is higher, but Bullfrog's was the closest to a local and unbureaucratically obscured measurement I could find. (The IPCC maintains an "Emission Factor Database" for such calculations, but the current version—revised in 2006—is subscriber-only; the "default emission factor" for coal-fired power in the 1996 IPCC accounting was 0.77 tonnes per MWh, but I had more confidence in the Bullfrog calculator.) I also used the Bullfrog emission factor for my global calculation, which I'm sure yields a rough estimate at best, but since the point of including the figure was not to authoritatively calculate global emissions for Kyoto compliance accounting but to underscore a rhetorical point, I hope and trust readers will forgive my imprecision.

CHAPTER ONE: THE REBIRTH OF HOPE

The use of the term "Anthropocene" to describe the current geologic era was first proposed by Paul J. Crutzen and Eugene F. Stormer in a short article entitled "The Anthropocene," which was first published in 2000 in *IGBP Newsletter* No. 41 (the official news organ of the International Geosphere-Biosphere Programme in Stockholm, Sweden). For the era's start point, they propose "the latter part of the eighteenth century," because it marks "the beginning of a growth in the atmospheric concentrations of several 'greenhouse gases'" in ice core samples. "Such a starting date," they note, "also coincides with James Watt's invention of the steam engine in 1784."

My brief summary of the dire state of the climate crisis is based upon data and sources that have been widely reported and nowhere convincingly contested. The 650,000-year high in atmospheric carbon dioxide concentrations forms the centrepiece of Al Gore's PowerPoint presentation, made internationally famous by the 2006 film *An Inconvenient Truth;* the data were first reported in late 2005 in several peer-reviewed papers based on a five-year study of ancient ice core samples by the European Project for Ice Coring in Antarctica (see Siegenthaler et al. and Spahni et al. in the November 25, 2005, issue of *Science*). The scientific possibility of the melting of the Greenland ice sheet was outlined in *Avoiding Dangerous Climate Change*, a 2006 book collating the reports made at the U.K. Meteorological Office's 2005 conference of the same name; the threshold beyond which such a scenario became plausible was a 2.7°C increase in regional average temperature. The record level of melting in Arctic ice in the summer of 2005 was recorded by the University of Colorado's National Snow and Ice Data Center and widely reported (see, for example, *The Independent,* September 16, 2005). Jared Diamond noted the vanishing glaciers of Montana's Glacier National Park in his 2005 book *Collapse.* "At present rates of melting," he wrote, "Glacier National Park will have no glaciers at all by the year 2030." The emergence of "extensive meadows" on the northern tip of Antarctica beginning in 2004 was reported in Tim Flannery's *The Weather Makers* (HarperCollins, 2005). James Lovelock's prediction of inevitable apocalypse was first published in *The Independent* (UK) on January 16, 2006, and expanded upon in his subsequent book *The Revenge of Gaia* (Allen Lane, 2006).

My understanding of Joseph Campbell's ideas about the nature of myth is based primarily on his seminal 1949 study *The Hero with a Thousand Faces* (Princeton University Press). Adam Werbach's speech "Is Environmentalism Dead?" was delivered to the Commonwealth Club of San Francisco on December 8, 2004; my quotes are taken from a transcript of the speech published by the online magazine *Grist* on January 13, 2005. *Grist* republished Michael Shellenberger and Ted Nordhaus's essay "The Death of Environmentalism" (originally distributed at an October 2004 meeting of the Environmental Grantmakers Association) on the same date.

My figure for the amount of the industrial world's anthropogenic carbon dioxide emissions ("more than 75 percent") is extrapolated from several sources. The U.S. Department of Energy has reported that 75 percent of CO_2 emissions in the United States came from the burning of fossil fuels as of 2001, the European Environmental

Agency stated in April 2007 that 80 percent of the emissions in European Union countries result from energy production, and Statistics Canada announced in 2003 that 81 percent of Canadian CO_2 emissions were derived from energy production and consumption.

The section on Samsø's Renewable Energy Island project and Denmark's energy regime is based primarily on information provided by Søren Hermansen and the Samsø Energy Office. I also mined the office's files for further background information; a project overview prepared as part of the funding process for the Samsø Energy Academy was particularly useful for benchmark statistics and data. I also drew some background detail from reporting in the *Financial Times* (October 15, 2005) and *Discover* magazine (June 2004). The history of the Danish government's energy policy and Denmark's renewable energy industry (here and in chapter two) was drawn primarily from documents published online by the Danish government (both at their official website, http://www.denmark.dk, and at the Danish Energy Authority site, http://www.ens.dk) and two third-party studies: *Energy Policies of IEA Countries: Denmark 2002 Review* (published by the OECD and IEA in 2002) and *OECD Environmental Performance Reviews: Denmark* (published by the OECD in 1999).

CHAPTER TWO: THE RENEWABLE ENERGY ARCHIPELAGO

My description of the collapse of the Larsen B ice shelf is drawn primarily from a press release issued by the United States National Snow and Ice Data Center on March 18, 2002. Pacala and Socolow outlined their "stabilization wedge" concept in the *Science* and *Scientific American* articles cited in the "Prologue" note above.

My figures for the comparative sizes of Pacala and Socolow's solar-power wedge, the world's and Hawaii's total land mass, and America's total paved area are extrapolated from several sources: Pacala and Socolow's *Science* article, the 2003 book *Plan B: Rescuing a Planet under Stress and a Civilization in Trouble* by Lester Brown of the Earth Policy Institute, and the Information Please Database (http://www.infoplease.com) for general geographic statistics. Pacala and Socolow estimate that a PV array covering 2 million hectares—about 7,722 square miles—would generate sufficient energy to displace 2,000 gigawatts of coal-fired power (thus removing one billion tons of CO_2 from global emissions); if the array were evenly distributed worldwide by land area, the American share would be about 480 square miles. Brown estimates in *Plan B* that about 16 million hectares (61,776 square miles) of the total land area of the United States is covered by roads and parking lots.

E.O. Wilson's essay "Is Humanity Suicidal?" was first published in the *New York Times Magazine* in 1993; I quote from the version that appeared in his 1996 collection *In Search of Nature* (Island Press). My description of Poul la Cour's work is taken primarily from a series of short articles published on the website of the Poul la Cour Museum in Askov, Denmark (http://www.poullacour.dk). The details of the birth and evolution of the Rochdale Pioneers come mainly from the BBC, the Rochdale Pioneers Museum and the Rochdale Metropolitan Borough (all accessed online); the quote ("a self-supporting home colony") is taken directly from the founding document, *Laws and Objects of the Rochdale Society of Equitable Pioneers* (1844). The later history of the CIS/CFS and the Solar Tower is based on information (press releases, promotional materials, financial reports, etc.) provided by CIS itself, with the exception of the tower's own history, which includes some details from a case study published by the Twentieth Century Society on their website (http://www.c20society.org.uk).

The figure for money spent by Openwave Systems in the past five years was tabulated by adding together the company's total operating expenses as reported in its annual reports for 2003 through 2006.

The historic background and present-day realities of the renewable energy business on Aerø were drawn primarily from a brief issued by VE-Organisation Aerø (the present-day Aerø renewable energy association) and from the first-hand recollections of Jørgen Bjørgren.

Because I neglected to make a recording of Jeremy Rifkin's keynote lecture at the 2006 Ankelohe Conversations conference, the direct quotes attributed to him in this chapter are drawn from the transcript of an essentially identical presentation he made to an "Energy Smart" conference in Arlington, Virigina, the week before (May 22, 2006; the transcript was published by the Federal News Service). The details of the technology park in Aragon and Rifkin's assessment of its potential ("I saw the future") are from my notes on his Ankelohe lecture, augmented by a backgrounder published by the Foundation for New Hydrogen Technologies in Aragon.

CHAPTER THREE: OUT OF GAS

The Rebecca Solnit quote in the opening passage of this chapter appeared in *Hope in the Dark: Untold Histories, Wild Possibilities* (Nation Books, 2004).

My description of the final voyage of James Cook comes from two main sources: Richard A. Hough's *The Murder of Captain James Cook* (Macmillan, 1979) and especially "The Death of Captain Cook," a vivid narrative of that fatal voyage written in 1999 by Richard P. Aulie of the Captain Cook Study Unit (later the Captain Cook Society) and published online at the society's website (http://www.captaincooksociety.com). The quotes from the diaries of Cook and his lieutenant were taken from Aulie's account.

My figure for the share of greenhouse gas emissions created globally by transportation was provided by the 2002 report "Air Pollution from Ground Transportation: An Assessment of Causes, Strategies and Tactics, and Proposed Actions for the International Community," prepared by Roger Gorman for the Global Initiative on Transport Emissions (a joint body of the United Nations and the World Bank). The figure for the European Union alone comes from a 2006 study by the European Federation for Transport and the Environment entitled "Greenhouse Gas Emissions from Transport in the EU25."

Details on the life and career of Junior Johnson and the bootlegging tradition in North Carolina are taken from Tom Wolfe's "The Last American Hero Is Junior Johnson. Yes!"—originally published in the March 1965 issue of *Esquire*.

The investigative series "A Tank of Gas, a World of Trouble," by Paul Salopek, appeared in the *Chicago Tribune* on July 29, 2006. It provided me with the details of the oil business in Nigeria, as well as the figure for the number of barrels of oil pumped from the Niger Delta each day and the amount of gasoline burned by idling cars in the United States each year. The connection between the two—that 2.3 million barrels of crude yield 45 million gallons of gasoline (according to a ratio published by the Texas Oil & Gas Association of 19 gallons of gas per barrel), and that this figure is just a little more than the 44.1-million-gallon-per-day rate indicated by Salopek's idling-cars stat—is easily calculated from his data, but it's not mentioned in his report. (Salopek instead notes that 2.3 billion gallons per year is the anticipated yield from the proven oil reserves of Equatorial Guinea, "Africa's most promising new petro-state.")

My information on the history of Singapore's transportation policy is drawn from several sources. Among the most prominent were a 1997 report by Murray Hiebert in the *Far Eastern Economic Review* (reprinted in the *Vancouver Sun* on March 6, 1997); "Solving Urban Traffic Congestion: Singapore Shows the Way," by Govindan Sridharan in *Transactions of AACE International* (1993); *The Singapore Green Plan 2012*, published by Singapore's Ministry of the Environment in 2002; and *Natural Capitalism: Creating the Next Industrial Revolution*, by Paul Hawken, Amory Lovins and L. Hunter Lovins (Little, Brown, 1999). The details of the origins and growth of Portland's transit system are drawn from a range of sources as well, particularly, *The Geography of Nowhere: The Rise and Decline of America's Man-Made Landscape* (Simon & Schuster, 1993); "A Vision of Green: Lewis Mumford's Legacy in Portland, Oregon" and "The Connection Between Transit and Employment: The Cases of Portland and Atlanta," by Thomas W. Sanchez (both in *Journal of the American Planning Association* 65:3, 1999); "Urban Mecca" by Bob Ortega in the *Wall Street Journal* (December 26, 2005); and "Building the City, Structuring Change: Portland's Implicit Utopian Project," by Bradshaw Hovey in the journal *Utopian Studies* (9:1, 1998).

CHAPTER FOUR: HOME, GREEN HOME

Most of the story of the energy-producing homes designed by Rolf Disch in Freiburg and Dr. Soontorn Boonyatikarn in Bangkok is based on first-hand reporting and observation, but both architects also provided me with official documentation they had prepared by themselves. Additional background information on Disch's projects came from his firm's website (http://www.rolfdisch.de); the fine details of Dr. Soontorn's innovative design are detailed in *Bio-Solar Home Powered by the Sun*, written by the architect and published in a bilingual English-Thai edition by Chulalongkorn University Press in 2004.

The recent history and current status of the Vauban redevelopment project discussed in this chapter are derived from a variety of documents available at the Forum Vauban E.V. website (http://www.forum-vauban.de). The project's official submission for the 2002 Dubai International Award for Best Practices to Improve the Living Environment was particularly helpful. Additional background came from "Powerful

Change," by P. Curry, in the January 2006 issue of the journal *Builder,* from a feature report in the *Christian Science Monitor* ("New German Community Models Car-Free Living," by Isabelle de Pommereau, December 20, 2006) and from an interview with Thomas Dresel, director of SolarRegion Freiburg.

My summary of the "Sustainable Okotoks" initiative and the Drake Landing solar thermal heating project is drawn from my own reporting for *Alberta Venture* magazine ("Not Your Average Bedroom Community," September 2005), which included interviews with all of the key officials involved, among them the Town of Okotoks municipal manager and project managers at Natural Resources Canada, ATCO Gas, property developer United Communities and homebuilder Sterling Homes.

For my brief overview of the life and work of Buckminster Fuller, I am particularly indebted to an excellent feature story in the Winter 1988 issue of *American Heritage* magazine: "Who Was Buckminster Fuller, Anyway?" by Amy C. Edmondson. Further detail was provided by a variety of reports and documents at the Buckminster Fuller Institute website (http://www.bfi.org), "Bucky's World," by Drake Bennett (*Boston Globe,* October 23, 2005) and *The Dymaxion World of Buckminster Fuller,* by Robert Marks and R. Buckminster Fuller (Anchor Books, 1973).

The sections of this and later chapters on the broad strokes of modernism as a design and urban planning philosophy relied heavily on the analyses by Tom Wolfe in *From Bauhaus to Our House* (Farrar, Straus and Giroux, 1981) and James Howard Kunstler's books *The Geography of Nowhere* (Simon & Schuster, 1993) and *The Long Emergency* (Grove Press, 2005). The specific details of Le Corbusier's Pavillion de l'Esprit nouveau at the 1925 Paris Exposition were found in Robert Furneaux Jordan's *Le Corbusier* (Lawrence Hill, 1972) and a retrospective article on the Exposition in a 1988 issue of *World's Fair* magazine (reproduced online at http://www.retropolis.net/exposition/index.html). The details of Corbu's subsequent "Radiant City" plan come from his own 1933 treatise *Radiant City* (Faber & Faber). I based my description of GM's "Futurama" exhibit at the 1939 World's Fair primarily on images from the Bel Geddes Collection at the University of Texas and a *Life* magazine pictoral from June 1939.

The details of Nek Chand's life and work were drawn mainly from the files of the Nek Chand Foundation of Radlett, U.K. (available online at http://www.nekchand.com) and from "Nek Chand's Story," by Anton Rajer, in the Winter/Spring 2000 issue of *Folk Art Messenger* magazine. General background details on the origins and development of the city of Chandigarh came from *Chandigarh: The Making of an Indian City*, by Ravi Kalia (Oxford University Press, 1999), and *Chandigarh's Le Corbusier: The Struggle for Modernity in Postcolonial India*, by Vikramaditya Prakash (University of Washington Press, 2002).

For the history of the Taos Valley, the Taoseño counterculture and the modernist tradition in Taoseño art, I used the following main sources: *A Brief History of Taos*, by F.R. Bob Romero and Neil Poese (Kit Carson Historical Museum, 1992); *Utopian Vistas: The Mabel Dodge Luhan House and the American Counterculture*, by Lois Palken Rudnick (University of New Mexico Press, 1996); *Modernists in Taos*, by David

L. Witt (Red Crane Books, 2002); and *The Legendary Artists of Taos*, by Mary Carroll Nelson (Watson-Guptill, 1980).

Finally, my understanding of the science of thermal mass comes mainly from Michael Reynolds's lectures of the Earthship Biotecture seminar and from "Thermal Mass in Passive Solar and Energy-Conserving Buildings," a study by Bruce Haglund and Kurt Rathmann for the Vital Signs Curriculum Project (coordinated by the Center for Environmental Design Research at the University of California Berkeley).

CHAPTER FIVE: TAJ MAHAL 2.0

The capsule history of the U.S. Green Building Council and its LEED certification is based primarily on "The Path to Platinum," by Ken Shulman (a feature in the December 2006 issue of *Metropolis Magazine*), and on a joint interview with Chesapeake Bay Foundation President William Baker and Chief of Staff Chuck Foster in the January 2001 issue of the *AIA Journal of Architecture*. The specifications, technical details and LEED ratings of the first wave of buildings constructed under the regime were taken from LEED case studies posted at the U.S. Green Building Council website (http://www.usgbc.org). I found the backstory of the building of the Alberici headquarters in "Going Green," by Linda F. Jarret, in *St. Louis Commerce Magazine* (May 2005). The details of Robert Fox's green Manhattan skyscrapers came from a case study at the International Energy Agency's Photovoltaic Power Systems Programme website (http://www.iea-pvps.org/index.html), a news report from GreenBizNews.com ("Builders Break Ground on 'World's Most Environmentally Responsible High-Rise Office Building'," August 4, 2004), and a report in the *Washington Post* ("As Power Bills Soar, Companies Embrace 'Green' Buildings," by Steven Mufson, August 5, 2006).

The history and design details of the CII-Godrej Green Building Centre in Hyderabad were drawn mostly from the facility's own weath of brochures, backgrounders, monthly bulletins and other documents, as well as interviews with several CII-Godrej GBC officials. (The most important source not quoted directly in the text was S. Srinivas, Senior Counsellor.) Certain precise details of Bill Clinton's Hyderabad visit in 2000 came from a compendium of media reports at the Indian news portal Rediff.com (http://www.rediff.com/news/clinton.htm).

Silver Donald Cameron reported on Nova Scotia's trailblazing recycling program in the May/June 2001 issue of *Canadian Geographic* ("Recycling by the Sea"). The chemical compostion of Swiffer disposable duster sheets was taken from Procter & Gamble's own Material Safety Data Sheet for the product.

My description of the evolution and technical aspects of the CFL bulb is drawn from several sources: "Lighting a Revolution," a companion guide to an exhibit of the same name at the Smithsonian National Museum of American History (published online at http://americanhistory.si.edu/lighting/index.htm); "Lighting: An Energy Efficient Future," by James Cavallo, at *Home Energy Magazine Online* (http://www.homeenergy.org); several fact sheets at the official website of the Lamp Section of the National Electrical Manufacturers Association (http://www.lamprecycle.org); and "How Many Lightbulbs Does It Take to Change the World?" by Charles Fishman (*Fast Company*, September 2006). The statistics quoted on CFL recycling are taken from a NEMA fact sheet, "Lamp Industry Product Stewardship," a fact sheet from the Association of Lighting and Mercury Recyclers (U.S.), and a background study on CFL recycling produced by Pollution Probe for Natural Resources Canada. My brief overview of EPR is drawn from my own research and reporting for *Canadian Geographic* ("Waste Generation," May/June 2006) and from European Union directives published online at the European Union website (http://europa.eu).

CHAPTER 6: GREEN SPRAWL

My primary source for information on the Kalundborg Centre for Industrial Symbiosis was Noel Brings Jacobsen of Øresund Science Region and Roskilde University, but additional background detail was drawn from the following sources: case studies of the Kalundborg model produced by the United Nations Environmental Programme and Indigo Development (a California-based consulting company) and "The Case for Private Planning," by Pierre Desroches, in the Winter 2001 issue of *Independent Review*.

The overview of Yorkville's origins and transformation is based largely on *Before the Gold Rush* by Nicholas Jennings (Penguin, 1998). The section on Copenhagen's Free City of Christiania was based on first hand reporting; I'm especially indebted to Christiania residents Johannes Brandt, Belder Willejus and Peter Plett, Lulla Forchhammer (a lawyer representing the Christiania collective) and Rikke Reiter of the Danish Ministry of Palaces and Properties for their time and expertise. Some key statistical and historical details were drawn from *Christianias Guide* (the Free City's official guide, fourth edition, 2004) and from press releases and other documents at the Danish government website (http://www.denmark.dk). The description of the ufaFabrik development in Berlin is also drawn from first hand reporting, as well as brochures published by the ufaFabrik International Cultural Center. The Distillery District project details were found at the development's official website (http://www.thedistillerydistrict.com). The overview of the city of Malmö and the redevelopment of its harbour district is derived from documentation produced by the municipal government (much of it gathered at the "Eco-City" website, http://www.ekostaden.com); the collapse of Malmö's shipbuilding industry and the civic response to same is based on reporting found in "Powerful Change," by P. Curry (*Builder*, January 2006).

My synopsis of the rise and fall of the brutalist aesthetic and the history of the South Bank Centre cobbles together information from a variety of sources: "South Bank Embraces Skateboard Culture," by Samantha Ellis (*The Guardian*, August 5, 2004); "Who Will Save the South Bank?" by Deyan Sudjic (*The Observer*, September 24, 2000); "I Love Carbuncles" (the online companion to the Channel 4 documentary of the same title); and "From Here to Modernity" (an essay at the BBC/Open University website, http://www.open2.net).

Most of the detail about the decline of Santa Monica's Pacific Ocean Park and the rise of modern skateboard culture is found in the 2001 Stacy Peralta film *Dogtown and Z-Boys* and in a series of articles that film's co-writer, Craig Stecyk, wrote under various pseudonyms in the 1970s for *Skateboarder* magazine (particularly "Aspects of the Downhill Slide," written as Carlos Izan, which appeared in the Fall 1975 issue). I also relied upon Jeffery Stanton's excellent website chronicling the history of Venice, California (http://www.westland.net/venicehistory/index.html), for a handful of details; his reproductions of a wide range of period photographs and postcards depicting Pacific Ocean Park in its heyday were particularly useful.

In addition to materials found at the Aurora History Museum and provided to me by the City of Lakewood, my knowledge of suburban Denver's history was greatly aided by *Twentieth-Century Sprawl: Highways and the Reshaping of the American Landscape*, by Owen D. Gutfreund (Oxford University Press, 2004). James Howard Kunstler's recounting of the suburbanization of Saratoga Springs, New York, in *The Geography of Nowhere* also lent some key detail to the backstory of Mark Falcone and Continuum Partners. I found the full text of the Charter of the New Urbanism and other background information on the organization and its goals at the Congress for the New Urbanism website (http://www.cnu.org).

My brief synopsis of the origins and purpose of Toronto's Yonge-Dundas Square relied primarily on a series of articles on its construction by Christopher Hume that appeared in 2003 in the *Toronto Star* (particularly "A European Space," January 18, 2003).

The short history of green roofs in this chapter is drawn from the following sources: "Green Roofs in Urban Landcapes," by Eva Worden et al. (Document ENH 984 from the Environmental Horticulture Department of the University of Florida, 2004); a fact sheet produced by the Penn State Center for Green Roof Research; and the "Green Roof Timeline" that appeared in the September 2006 issue of *Metropolis Magazine.* My recounting of the short life and premature death of the South Central Farm in Los Angeles was based on a handful of contemporary reports, especially "Growing Food for Your 'Hood" and "Trouble in the Garden," by Dean Kuipers (*L.A. CityBeat,* January 28 and December 28, 2006) and "Antidevelopment Protesters Are Arrested at Farm Site in Los Angeles," by Cindy Chang (*New York Times,* June 14, 2006). The statistics cited on the size and scope of contemporary agriculture were found in "Growing Opportunity," by Don Butler (*Ottawa Citizen,* June 18, 2006).

CHAPTER SEVEN: THE GREEN BOOM

Lovins, Lovins and Hawken's *Natural Capitalism* (for full citation, see source notes on chapter three) provided the intellectual and analytical foundations for this chapter in its entirety.

As noted in the text, my critique of contemporary agribusiness and my understanding of the origins of industrial organic agriculture are drawn from *The Omnivore's Dilemma: A Natural History of Four Meals*, by Michael Pollan (Penguin, 2006). The overview of Cuba's Special Period and the resulting organic revolution is based mainly on Bill McKibben's "The Cuba Diet" (*Harper's Magazine,* April 2005); "The Power of Community: How Cuba Survived Peak Oil," by Megan Quinn (*Permaculture Activist,* Spring 2006); and "Has Cuba Shown the Way?" by Paul Phillips (*Canadian Dimension,* September/October 2006).

The basic facts of the *Exxon Valdez* oil spill were found in a case study published by the U.S. Environmental Protection Agency's Oil Program (posted at its website, http://www.epa.gov). Additional detail was drawn from *Cradle to Cradle: Remaking the Way We Make Things*, by William McDonough and Michael Braungart (Farrar, Straus and Giroux, 2002) and a BBC News report on the spill's legacy ("Exxon Valdez Spill Still a Danger," December 19, 2003). The *Economist* quote that acknowledges the mistake of equating disaster relief with economic growth was found in "The Millennium Bug: Millennial Economics," by Frances Cairncross, in the September 19, 1998, issue of the magazine.

Frédéric Bastiat's explanation of the broken window fallacy is found in *Selected Essays on Political Economy* (Foundation for Economic Education, 1995; also published online at the Library of Economics and Liberty, http://www.econlib.org). My wider discussion of the GDP fallacy drew statistical data and other information from the following: the Digital Library of the U.S. Department of Commerce's Bureau of Economic Analysis (http://library.bea.gov) for the history of economic growth measurement; "Energy 21: Making the World Work," by Walt Patterson (Institute of Energy Melchett Medal Lecture, London Planetarium, June 22, 2000), for details of Edison's original Manhattan light company and the inefficiencies of modern energy distribution; and *Power to the People*, by Vijay V. Vaitheeswaran (Farrar, Straus and Giroux, 2003), for the systemic problems of large-scale energy production.

I have combined direct quotes from two sources to assemble David Suzuki's critique of externalities: the first is the Cranbrook, B.C., *Daily Townsman* (May 2, 2003); the second is a short essay posted at the David Suzuki Foundation website ("Economy Needs a Better Goal Than 'More,'" February 2, 2006). Together, these closely approximate the version of this riff I heard Suzuki deliver in person at Knox United Church in Calgary, Alberta, on May 8, 2006.

My analysis of the Sardar Sarovar Dam project in India's Narmada Valley relied on a number of documents available at the Friends of River Narmada website (http://www.narmada.org), particularly Arundhati Roy's essay "The Greater Common Good" (originally published in a number of Indian newsmagazines in 1999). I also drew data and detail from a Reuters report and photos published on January 1, 2007.

In addition to information provided by John Bradford of Interface Inc., my snapshot of the company's sustainability program relied heavily upon company documents published at the Interface Sustainability website (http://www.interface-sustainability.com), as well as a handful of news reports and feastures on Ray Anderson's work, particularly an article on Guildford of Maine's transformation in the *Portland* (Maine) *Press Herald* (September 15, 2002) and a profile of Anderson in *Fortune* (May 24, 1999). Data and analysis for the section on the reinsurance industry was drawn from *Newsweek* (January 29, 2007), *The Economist* (September 9, 2006), *Fortune* (January 23, 2006) and the *Globe and Mail* (October 11, 2005).

CHAPTER EIGHT: THE NON-PARTISAN ENVIRONMENTALIST

"The Stern Review"—*The Economics of Climate Change*, by Nicholas Stern—was prepared for the British Treasury and published by Cambridge University Press in 2006. The full text of Stern's remarks at its release on October 30, 2006, are available at the website of HM Treasury (http://www.hm-treasury.gov.uk). Prime Minister Tony Blair's article responding to the report was published the same day by *The Sun* and is archived at the 10 Downing Street website (http://www.number-10.gov.uk).

The brief synopsis of Denmark's environmental policy in this chapter draws on the same sources listed in my note for chapter one. The English translation of Germany's Renewable Energy Sources Act from which I quote was found at the Forum for Solar Energy website (http://www.solarserver.de). The English-language full text of German Parliamentary State Secretary Astrid Krug's remarks to the International Grid-Connected Renewable Energy Forum in Mexico City (February 1, 2006) was found at the German Environmental Ministry website (http://www.-erneuerbare-energien.de/inhalt/). My analysis of the success of the German policy regime drew heavily on "Comparison of Feed in Tariff, Quota and Auction Mechanisms to Support Wind Power Development," by Lucy Butler and Karsten Neuhoff (Cambridge-MIT Institute Working Paper 70; quoted with permission).

My overview of environmental policy in Portland, Oregon, is based on the same sources as listed in chapter three.

The Economist's assessment of the commercial failure of nuclear power can be found in its March 24, 1998, issue ("Power to the People").

The short history of Grameen Bank and the professional life of its founder were assembled from a variety of sources, most prominently "Nobel Winner Yunus: Microcredit Missionary," by Jeffery Gangemi (*Business Week,* December 26, 2005); *The New Heroes*, a four-part documentary series first broadcast on PBS in 2005, from which Yunus's quote, published at the series' companion website (http://www.pbs.org/opb/thenewheroes/), was taken, and the Grameen Bank website (http://www.grameen-info.org).

This chapter's analysis of the merits of framing and stickiness in the creation of powerful media campaigns drew on the following sources: *The Tipping Point*, by Malcolm Gladwell; *Made to Stick: Why Some Ideas Survive and Others Die*, by Chip Heath and Dan Heath (Random House, 2007); *The End of Nature*, by Bill McKibben (Doubleday, 1989); "Warm Words: How Are We Telling the Climate Story and Can We Tell It Better?" by Gill Ereaut and Nat Segnit (Institute for Public Policy Research, U.K., July 2006); and "Talking Global Warming" (prepared by the FrameWorks Institute for the Climate Message Project, courtesy of the Natural Resources Defense Council, Washington).

CHAPTER NINE: NGO 2.0

The short history of international development that opens this chapter draws on a wide range of sources, including interviews and informal discussions with United Nations field and office workers and independent contractors working with the UN in Thailand, India and Nepal in 1999–2000 and 2006; interviews with officials from the development organizations E+Co, Palang Thai, the Border Green Energy Team and Green Empowerment in 2005 and 2006; and the following key background sources: *Freedom from Debt: The Reappropriation of Development Through Financial Self-Reliance*, by Jacques B. Gélinas (Zed Books, 1998); *Evidence for Hope: The Search for Sustainable Development*, edited by Nigel Cross (Earthscan Publications, 2003); "The Cartel of Good Intentions" (*Foreign Policy,* July/August 2002) and "The Utopian Nightmare" (*Foreign Policy,* September/October 2005), by William Easterly; "Aid: Can It Work?" by Nicholas D. Kristof (*New York Review of Books,* October 5, 2006); *Small Is Beautiful,* by E.F. Schumacher; *Ancient Futures: Learning from Ladakh,* by Helena Norberg-Hodge (Sierra Club Books, 1991); and official histories published at the USAID and Oxfam websites.

My brief overview of the partition of India and the Radcliffe Line is based primarily on "Splitting the Difference," by Amitava Kumar (*Transition,* no. 89, 2001); "The 1947 Partition: Drawing the Indo-Pakistani Boundary," by Lucy Chester (*American Diplomacy,* February 2002); and *Freedom at Midnight,* by Larry Collins and Dominique Lapierre (HarperCollins, 1997).

My chief source for the background information on Thailand's Solar Home System program was a handful of studies produced by Palang Thai and/or the Border Green Energy Team, particularly "Threatened Sustainability: The Uncertain Future of Thailand's Solar Home Systems," by Andrew Lynch et al. (June 2006) and "Sustainability and Thailand's Solar Home System: Is It Still Achievable?—Observations from Tak Province by Border Green Energy Team," by Fredrik Bjarnegard (prepared for the BITEC Renewable Energy Conference, July 2006). A number of key details were also drawn from a handful of reports in the *Bangkok Post* (June 2003–May 2005).

In addition to extensive documentation and case studies provided by E+Co and its clients, my portrait of the organization and its work in Thailand and India drew on the following sources: "He's a Light to the World's Poor," by Michael Laser (*New York Times,* May 8, 2005); "Indian Banks Find Interest in UNEP Solar Loan Approach," by Jyoti Prasad Painuly and Eric Usher (*UN Chronicle,* no. 2, 2006); and a SELCO case study at the Ashden Awards for Sustainable Energy website (http://www.ashdenawards.org).

Jeffery Dickinson's anecdote about the troubled history of apple farming in Nepal was confirmed in its basic detail by two studies: "Problems of Apple Production in Jinabang (Rolpa) and Mustang, Nepal, and Strategies for Sustainable Production" (USAID, 1996) and "Development Strategies for a New Nepal: A National Debate," a report based on the proceedings of a national conference in Kathmandu in December 2006 (published by Rural Reconstruction Nepal and the Centre for International Studies and Cooperation Nepal, March 2007).

CHAPTER TEN: THE DALAI LAMA & THE DUDE

In addition to Thomas More's *Utopia,* the short discussion of the origins and evolution of the concept of utopia in this chapter relied on a handful of documents and a historical timeline posted at the Oregon State University website and several summary reviews of Peter Ackroyd's 1998 biography, *The Life of Thomas*

More (particularly John J. Reilly's 1999 review, which is available at his website, http://www.johnreilly.info).

The historical detail on the first Puritan settlements in America comes primarily from *The American Jeremiad*, by Sacvan Bercovitch (University of Wisconsin Press, 1978).

My recounting of the historical origins of the Tibetan exile settlements in India and the organic farming movement in those settlements was informed by numerous press releases and project reports published by the Central Tibetan Administration, the Office of Tibet, New York, and the Canada Tibet Committee (most of these can be found via the CTA's official website, http://www.tibet.net). A short history of the Indian settlements posted on the website of Dzogchen Monastery (http://www.dzogchen.org.in) also provided some detail.

The section on the Findhorn Foundation's origins and growth is based on the founders' personal accounts of the community's early days, which appeared in *The Findhorn Garden* (Findhorn Press, 1975). Some background detail was also found in *The Findhorn Foundation and Community Visitor Guide* (Findhorn Foundation Communications, March 2006), as well as in several newspaper features, particularly an overview of the ecovillage in the *Financial Times* (January 18, 2003), a profile of Dorothy Maclean in the *Toronto Star* (May 6, 1990), and *The Guardian*'s obituary of Eileen Caddy (January 8, 2007). In addition to background information and documentation provided by the Global Ecovillage Network (much of it posted at the organization's website, http://gen.ecovillage.org), the birth of the ecovillage movement is well documented in "The Village Can Save the City," by Richard Register (*Communities*, no. 129, Winter 2005). The assertion that the Findhorn ecovillage has an ecological footprint half the size of the British average (and the smallest ever recorded in the industrial world) is based on a formal assessment conducted by the Stockholm Environment Institute at the University of York and announced in a press release dated April 18, 2007.

Finally, the quotations and paraphrasing from David Foster Wallace's Kenyon College commencement speech (May 21, 2005) are taken from a transcript of the address published online at http://www.marginalia.org and widely cited elsewhere.

EPILOGUE: A SUSTAINABLE CITY ON A HILL

The full text of John Winthrop's "A Modell of Christian Charity" (1630), from which the idea of America as a city on a hill originates, is available online via the Hanover Historical Texts Project at the Hanover College (Indiana) website (http://history.hanover.edu/project.html).

The quotation and paraphrasing from William McDonough's lecture on sustainable cities are based on a transcription of my own recording of the address, which was delivered in Calgary, Alberta, on March 15, 2007.

[index]

arbitrary statistics of, 36
building wind turbines, 32
in energy production, 281–82
fuel-efficient cars, 105, 112
for heating, 140
versus hidden cost of gasoline, 114–16
for households, 35
in housing, 136, 144–45, 147
hydrogen fuel-cell systems, 103
of industrial disasters, 278–80
in industrial symbiosis, 221
and jobs from recycling, 206–7
and organic agriculture, 276–77
per kilowatt hour, 51, 375
profitability of, 77–80, 304, 381, 385
savings for industry in, 189–90, 301–2
and solar energy as a capital loan,
   387–89
and subsidies in current system, 295
in urban redesign, 231
in utopian communities, 414–15
Cradle to Cradle. See McDonough,
   William
Crutzen, Paul, 16. *See also* Anthropocene
   Era
Cuba, 275, 277
Cyberabad (Hyberabad), 73, 193–201.
   See also India

Daimler-Benz, 98
DaimlerChrysler, 103
dairy farming, 31
Daley, Richard, 98
Danish Energy Agency, 67
David, Larry, 106
Davis, Robert, 247
Davis, Susan, 325
Dawson, Jonathan, 412–13, 434
Day After Tomorrow, The (film), 36
DDT, 15, 20, 223. *See also* Carson, Rachel
decentralized energy regime, 65
Deep Lake Water Cooling System
   (Ontario), 53–54
Deffeyes, Kenneth, 84
Democracy Now! (radio program), 325
Democratic Party (U.S.), 328

Denmark. *See also* Aerø; Renewable
   Energy Island contest; Samsø
Christiania, 225–27, 230
Copenhagen's public transit, 131
decentralized energy regime of, 65
Kalundborg, 28, 220–22
living deliberately, 416
policy in CO_2 emissions control, 309
renewable energy pioneers, 63–65, 312
response to opec crisis, 33–34
wind power, 34, 50, 52, 63, 75–77
Denver, Colorado, 249–50, 261. *See also*
   Belmar/Lakewood, Colorado
derelict chic, 225–29
Despommier, Dickson, 433
de Zengotita, Thomas: *Mediated,* 20–21
diapers, 348
Diaz, Cameron, 106
DiCaprio, Leonardo, 106
Dickinson, Jeffery, 380–84
disasters, 278–80, 303, 329–31, 337–38,
   425
Disch, Rolf, 136–38, 148, 161, 213, 289,
   431, 434
Distillery District, Toronto, 228–29
Dogtown and Z-Boys (film), 235
downcycling, 212, 220. *See also* recycling
Duany, Andres, 247–48, 261, 434. *See
   also* New Urbanism
Dubai, 190, 201
Duke Energy, 308
Dundas Square, Toronto, 256–57
DuPont, 302, 308, 320
Dwell magazine, 150–51, 170
Dylan, Bob, 15, 25, 66–67, 322, 416

Earthbound Farms, 276–77
Earth Institute, Columbia University, 17
Earthships. *See also* housing as
   sustainable
as adaptable, 174–75
building material for, 170–71
as built to last, 173–74
and bureaucratic difficulties, 175–76
communities of, 164
name and appearance of, 177–83

CHRIS TURNER is the author of the international bestseller *Planet Simpson: How a Cartoon Masterpiece Documented an Era and Defined a Generation*. He writes a monthly feature series on sustainability for the *Globe and Mail*. His magazine features have earned him four National Magazine Awards, including the 2001 President's Medal for General Excellence, the highest honour in Canadian magazine writing. His reporting on culture, technology and the environment has also appeared in the *Independent*, *Maclean's*, *Time*, *The Walrus*, *Canadian Geographic*, *Azure* and *Utne Reader*. He lives in Calgary with his wife, the photographer Ashley Bristowe, and their daughter, Sloane.